I0823753

Lee and His Generals

Lee and His Generals

Essays in Honor of T. Harry Williams

Edited by Lawrence Lee Hewitt
and Thomas E. Schott

The University of Tennessee Press / Knoxville

Frontispiece: T. Harry Williams. Courtesy of LSU University Relations.

Dedication Page Photo: Arthur W. Bergeron Jr. Courtesy of the U.S. Army Military History Institute, Carlisle, Pennsylvania.

First Edition.

The paper in this book meets the requirements of American National Standards Institute / National Information Standards Organization specification Z39.48–1992 (Permanence of Paper). It contains 30 percent post-consumer waste and is certified by the Forest Stewardship Council.

Library of Congress Cataloging-in-Publication Data

Lee and his generals: essays in honor of T. Harry Williams / edited by Lawrence Lee Hewitt and Thomas E. Schott. — 1st ed.
p. cm.
Includes bibliographical references and index.
ISBN-13: 978-1-57233-850-0 (hardcover: alk. paper)
ISBN-10: 1-57233-850-4 (hardcover: alk. paper)
1. United States—History—Civil War, 1861–1865—Campaigns.
2. United States—History—Civil War, 1861–1865—Biography.
3. Generals—Confederate States of America—Biography.
4. Confederate States of America. Army—Biography.
I. Hewitt, Lawrence L.
II. Schott, Thomas Edwin, 1943–
III. Williams, T. Harry (Thomas Harry), 1909–1979.

E470.L524 2012
355.0092—dc23
[B]
2011041681

In Memory of
Arthur W. Bergeron Jr.
1947–2010

Contents

Illustrations

Figures

Maps

Preface

Professor T. Harry Williams never got to enjoy retirement from his long teaching career at Louisiana State University. In fact, he had been hospitalized for over two months when he was officially retired on the last day of June 1979; he lived only seven more days before succumbing to a respiratory ailment, with half a dozen Ph.D. candidates still in his stable. An appropriate remembrance for the "Old Man," as he was affectionately known among his students, is long overdue. This volume grew out of discussions among former Williams students at Louisville, Kentucky, during the annual meeting of the Southern Historical Association in 2009. A goodly number of Harry's former students were contacted for this project. Some were deceased, others in poor health or overcommitted. Art Bergeron was eager to contribute an article on Harry Heth at Petersburg, but sadly, he died before completing it. This book is dedicated to him.

T. Harry Williams was a prince among scholars to study with: a great writer, an incisive reader, a gifted model of a great teacher, and wonderful, warm man. He always had time for his students. Although Harry's former students have followed disparate academic trails and have at least one unique tale to tell about him, they all share common memories of his verve, his often rollicking sense of humor, his playful verbal cut-and-thrust, and, most of all, his kindness and generosity. His beloved wife Estelle rivaled him in kindness. Their annual Christmas season get-togethers at their home near the LSU campus are legendary. Many a penurious graduate student became acquainted with the Baton Rouge Civil War Round Table, oft times more than once as his guest at their dinner meetings and at his home for pre-meeting libations, often with the guest speaker for the evening also present. Williams was also known to have silently supplied financial assistance to several students in special circumstances.

Harry's students have pursued studies in all of the areas of their mentor's expertise: American military history, the Civil War and Reconstruction, biography, and twentieth-century politics. So providing a suitable organizing schema for this collection of essays presented a challenge. Eventually we agreed to use Robert E. Lee and his generals as our focal point—a subject that the contributors found congenial and one that dovetailed nicely with almost all the areas that Williams explored. The only guideline for the essayists was that the articles focus on Lee or one of his generals.

Thus the focus of the essays in this collection, with but a couple of exceptions, is on discrete individuals. Certainly T. Harry Williams, as one of the last notable proponents of the "great man" theory in history—he would have put Abraham Lincoln, Huey P. Long, and Lyndon B. Johnson, the subject he was researching at the time of his death, in this category—would have found this fitting. For most of his career, T. Harry Williams was concerned with the Civil War, and though he started out as a political historian, he quickly mastered the military aspects of the conflict. Oddly enough, he never wrote so much as an article on Robert E. Lee, although he did take Lee's preeminent biographer Douglas Southall Freeman to task in an article for his depiction of the Virginian in *R. E. Lee: A Biography* (1934) and *Lee's Lieutenants: A Study in Command* (1942–44).[1]

Back when Civil War history focused mainly on the battlefields, it was common for writers to claim this general or that one as among the greatest commanders of all time. Harry was no exception. He named two generals as members of this elite category: Ulysses S. Grant was the first. But even the Williams students who contributed to this book cannot agree whether the second was William T. Sherman or Lee. T. Harry Williams, unlike some scholars, could not only revise his opinion about a topic but also acknowledge it in print. His revision of a previously lukewarm opinion of Winfield Scott in *The History of American Wars* (1981)[2] is a good example. Although Williams always placed Grant foremost among Civil War generals, as he delved more into the military aspects of the conflict, it appears that his opinion of Sherman diminished while his view of Lee ascended as he refined his own definition of what makes a "great general."

Williams first addressed comparative generalship in *Lincoln and His Generals* (1952):

> Lee is usually ranked as the greatest Civil War general, but this evaluation has been made without placing Lee and Grant in the perspective of military developments since the war. . . . Fundamentally Grant was superior to Lee because in a modern total war he had a modern mind, and Lee did not. Lee looked to the past in war as the Confederacy did in spirit. . . . The modernity of Grant's mind was most apparent in his grasp of the concept that war was becoming total and that the destruction of the enemy's economic resources was as effective and legitimate a form of warfare as the destruction of his armies. What was realism for Grant was barbarism to Lee. Lee

> thought of war in the old way as a conflict between armies and refused to view it for what it had become—a struggle between societies. To him, economic war was needless cruelty to civilians. Lee was the last of the great old-fashioned generals, Grant the first of the great moderns.[3]

In 1955, when he took issue with Freeman's interpretation, Williams wrote that the great biographer "does not place Lee, a great general, in the nexus of American military history" and concluded, "In the end, all the brilliance and fortitude of the greatest Confederate general availed little to save his country." In his article "The Military Leadership of North and South," published in 1960, Williams wrote: "The question of where to rank Sherman among Civil War generals has always troubled military writers. He is obviously not a Jominian, and just as obviously he is not a great battle captain like Grant or Lee."[4]

Williams came to realize that for a general to have achieved greatness in the American Civil War, be he modern or traditional, he had to be focused on the destruction of his opponent's army. Williams adjudged Sherman a Clausewitzian thinker, "a modern-minded general but [one who] didn't have it as a battle captain—good subordinate under Grant, but not good under independent command." A great general had to be a doer in combat. No matter how prescient his theories, a thinker had to excel on the battlefield to be great. The struggle between Grant and Lee was, he stated, "a clash of two great wills. . . . Grant would not allow Lee to establish a psychological ascendancy. . . . His will was equal to Lee's, . . . whereas Lee had imposed his will on every Northern general" except Grant.[5]

* * *

The essays herein fall roughly into three categories: fittingly, the book opens and closes with two essays about Williams himself. The book's lead essay is Frank Wetta's biographical sketch of T. Harry Williams, "pragmatic historian," a fulsome recounting of Williams's life, career, writings, and influence. A scholar from Wisconsin who spent almost forty years in the Deep South, Williams brought a Midwesterner's sensibilities and outlook to his work, though he easily adapted to what was for him a semiexotic environment in the steamy South. Having begun his writing career with a book about politics, *Lincoln and the Radicals* (1941),[6] Williams after many years as a teacher, writer, and lecturer achieved his greatest portion of fame with his Pulitzer Prize–winning biography *Huey Long* (1969),[7] a subject who, like Lincoln, was a pragmatic leader, fixed upon his goals and doing what was necessary to reach them.

The other essay about Williams is Roger Spiller's, the final one in this book; it serves to place Williams in larger historical perspective among writers on Civil War generalship. Spiller reminds us right at the start that Harry was "a Union man, through and through," and it was from that perspective that his writing and teaching has to be viewed. Williams deplored rigidity of thinking, a quality he found prominent in West Point officers, including Jefferson Davis and Beauregard. The great divide Williams drew among Civil War leaders was between modern men who understood the near totality of the Civil War and those who did not. Lee was in the latter category, unable to grasp the larger strategic implications of the conflict or learn as the war progressed. In the end, only character—"mental strength and moral power"—made for a great military leader. No Confederate general met these standards.

A second group of five essays in the front part of the volume addresses the military exploits of Lee himself and three of his battle captains. Most of the contributors to this volume are Williams students who began their studies with him in the late 1960s and 1970s. The sole exceptions are the writers of the next two essays. Charles P. Roland is T. Harry Williams's first "official" Ph.D.[8] He received his degree from LSU in 1951 and began his distinguished career as a historian at Tulane University the following year. He later spent many years at the University of Kentucky. Roland's essay on the generalship of Lee, a logical starting point, is the only one in the book that has been published previously—it has been lightly edited for its appearance here. It has rightfully earned its place as a seminal work of scholarship which has fertilized the ensuing discussion about Lee among legions of historians. Roland offers a stout but not uncritical defense of the Confederate chieftain. Originally an address given at a Civil War Centennial Symposium at Northwestern University in 1961 and first published in 1964, it has been reprinted many times, most recently in 2007 in Roland's *History Teaches Us to Hope: Reflections on the Civil War and Southern History.*[9] Roland argues for Lee's skills not only as a superb battlefield commander but also as a strategist who was constantly confronted by an enemy superior in manpower and material. While not overlooking Lee's limitations, Roland offers a cogent interpretation for the Virginian's greatness as a complete soldier.

Taking Roland's essay as his focal point, Brian Holden Reid of the United Kingdom conducts a masterful survey of Lee's historiographical reputation, beginning with the Lost Cause interpretation of Douglas Southall Freeman and Clifford Dowdey and ending in the present time. (We have unhesitatingly bestowed on Holden Reid the status of honorary T. Harry Williams student; he passionately aspired in the mid-1970s to study with Harry but was thwarted by unforgiving financial realities in Britain.) Holden Reid concludes that the basics of Roland's assessment of Lee, though altered and refined by such events as the Vietnam War, still hold sway against a revisionist school represented by such writers as Thomas L. Connelly and Alan T. Nolan.

Lawrence Lee Hewitt's essay on the Confederate career of Lieutenant General Richard H. Anderson seeks to redress what the author sees as a pervasive underestimation of this general's abilities and value to Lee and the Army of Northern Virginia. From his sterling performance at Williamsburg, Anderson went on to perform either superbly or far better than just competently in a host of engagements from Seven Pines to Chancellorsville, the Wilderness to Petersburg. Lee continuously recognized Anderson's abilities by bestowing more responsibilities on him, including eventually corps command. Which general on either side, Hewitt inquires, could claim to be as aggressive and successful as Richard Anderson?

The performance of the Confederate cavalry during the Gettysburg Campaign has rightfully earned the censure of historians of that famous battle. According to Joseph G. Dawson, General J. E. B. Stuart's round-the-Union-army raid did far more harm than good. Stuart was simply out of touch with the army for way too long. What's more, two much-needed cavalry brigades under Brigadier General John D. Imboden and Brigadier General Albert G. Jenkins committed the opposite sin by remaining in place far to the south of Lee's invasion force. The cavalry campaign was further distinguished by the excellent performance of the Union cavalry, which more than held its own with Stuart's seasoned troopers. Indeed, they helped establish a "new pattern" for the Union which lasted until the end of the war.

The forgotten man of the Petersburg Campaign, writes A. Wilson Greene, was General P. G. T. Beauregard, then commander of the Department of North Carolina and Southern Virginia, who was involved in operations south of Richmond from May 1864 until September. Justly renowned for his heroic and skillful defense of the city of Petersburg from June 15 to 18 against several attacks by a vastly more numerous enemy, Beauregard's achievement should not be overstated. According to Greene, despite the contentions of many writers about this phase of the war, Beauregard knew little more about Grant's intentions than did Lee, as his confusing and contradictory messages to Lee's headquarters attest. In fact, the near-fatal delay in the Confederates' deciphering of Grant's whereabouts and true intentions is more Beauregard's fault than Lee's.

The next section of the book explores the lives of four of Lee's generals away from the battlefield. Three essays concentrate on postwar careers, and George C. Rable's piece, the first of this group, shines a light on Stonewall Jackson's celebrated religiosity. Jackson's military campaigns and skills have elicited an outpouring of historical analysis and controversy. Jackson's devout if not fanatical Presbyterian faith, though always acknowledged, has not been subjected to as much scrutiny. Rable has done so, however, in an essay that traces Jackson's religious and spiritual development from an early piety and fascination with Scripture to the Christian icon he became. Recognized as such, his stern, unflinching reliance on Providence resonated powerfully in the evangelical South. Jackson's death at Chancellorsville, however, called such faith into question. Actually, though, upon reflection, it ironically helped illuminate heaven's divine decree that the Confederacy be defeated.

William L. Richter discusses the postwar career of Lee's "Old War Horse," James Longstreet. A man genuinely well intentioned and arguably the finest corps commander in the Confederacy, Longstreet became the bugbear and whipping boy of the Lost Cause brigades through a combination of his own ineptness, on and off the battlefield, and the "suspicions, confusions, and deceptions" of the postwar South. A prophet without honor in his own country, Longstreet nevertheless always had the best interests of white Southerners in mind. His reputation for anything less, Richter argues, is undeserved.

Thomas E. Schott's essay evaluates the postwar career of Jubal A. Early, Longstreet's number one nemesis. Though not an insignificant Confederate general, Early did more for the Confederate cause after the war than during it. He more than any other ex-Confederate was responsible for the construction of the Lost Cause myth, which explained away Confederate defeat on the battlefield and glorified Robert E. Lee beyond all reason. Although traces of the Lost Cause yet remain, Schott argues that it largely has become the purview of historians and neo-Confederates and is either unknown or ignored by the general population. By these lights, Early's former luster, if it can be called that, is considerably diminished.

Ralph L. Eckert also focuses on the postwar career of a top commander in Lee's army, Major General John B. Gordon of Georgia, in an essay that explains how and why Gordon came be known as "an apostle of peace and good will" in the turbulent decades after the war. A firm adherent to the "gospel of reconciliation," Gordon, though intensely loyal to his section, was also a loyal and proud American. Despite the charges of Gordon's critics that his embrace of national reconciliation and sectional peace was calculated and self-serving, Eckert maintains that from the beginning the Georgian was sincere and his praise of courage and sacrifice on both sides was heartfelt and genuine.

Though loosely organized around the character of Robert E. Lee, each of the essays here stands alone as a contribution to several different fields of Civil War scholarship. The subjects are as varied as the Williams students who have written them: military history, religion, the Lost Cause, biography, historiography, Lee himself. Few of the authors here have written previously on their subjects. And while it would be presumptuous to claim more for these essays than whatever merit a perceptive reader accords them, a goodly measure of originality and fresh thinking can be presumed in the majority of these pieces. All of them raise engaging questions about how we are to understand the seminal American conflict in our own time, as T. Harry Williams did in his. If nothing else, these essays demonstrate once again that the American Civil War remains a fertile field—like the rich, fertile black soil of the Mississippi Delta yielding to the plow generation after generation.

Ultimately, what each of the authors did was write a bit of history to honor the man who taught us how to do it and showed us over and over how it was done. T. Harry Williams's commitment to sound, imaginative scholarship and his spirit of broad historical inquiry are the sturdy unifying skeins that tie all these essays together. That and our affection for the Old Man and the debt each of the authors owes him. Our only regret is that this tribute to our mentor was so long in coming.

Lawrence Lee Hewitt
Thomas E. Schott

Notes

1. T. Harry Williams, "Freeman, Historian of the Civil War: An Appraisal," *Journal of Southern History* 21 (Feb. 1955): 91–100.
2. T. Harry Williams, *The History of American Wars: From Colonial Times to World War I* (New York, 1981).
3. T. Harry Williams, *Lincoln and His Generals* (New York, 1952), 313–14.
4. T. Harry Williams, "The Military Leadership of North and South," in *Why the North Won the Civil War*, ed. David Donald (Baton Rouge, 1960), 44.
5. Frank Wetta to Larry Hewitt, "Re: From the fountain of knowledge," Oct. 21, 2010, email; class notes, T. Harry Williams Civil War lecture, fall 1967, in possession of Frank J. Wetta.
6. T. Harry Williams, *Lincoln and the Radicals* (Madison, WI, 1941).
7. T. Harry Williams, *Huey Long* (New York, 1969).
8. Charles P. Roland began his graduate studies under Bell I. Wiley at LSU. Following Wiley's departure to Emory in 1948, Roland studied under Francis Butler Simkins. Though Roland never had a class with Williams and Simkins directed his dissertation, when Simkins left LSU in 1951 it was Williams who was given the honor of signing as Roland's major professor. Despite a friendship with Williams that spanned decades, Roland is still quick to say he was a Simkins student.
9. John David Smith, ed., *History Gives Us Hope: Reflections on the Civil War and Southern History* (Lexington, KY, 1970).

Acknowledgments

We extend our thanks to Scot Danforth and the entire staff at the University of Tennessee Press who, with unfailing expertise and good humor, assisted us in so many ways during the production of this book.

Our gratitude and thanks go as well to all the others who helped us: to our insightful readers whose suggestions materially improved the volume in several ways; to Peter Raccuglia on behalf of the Northwestern University Press for his gracious permission to use a revised version of Charles P. Roland's essay on Lee; to Judy Bolton, head of Public Services, Special Collections, Louisiana State University Libraries, who tracked down the wonderful photo of T. Harry Williams smoking his pipe in his Lincolnand office, and who, along with Jim Zietz, assistant director of Public Affairs, Louisiana State University Office of Communications and University Relations, enabled us to include the images of Professor Williams in this book; to Stuart Stalling, who created two original maps for this volume; to Ted Savas for allowing us to reproduce a map from *The Maps of Gettysburg: An Atlas of the Gettysburg Campaign, June 3–July 13, 1863;* to Simon Blundell for assisting us in the final production; and to the late Arthur W. Bergeron Jr., our friend and colleague, who secured reproducible copies of the images herein from the U.S. Army Military History Institute.

And finally we thank T. Harry Williams, our teacher and guide, who, out of often rough material, fashioned us into historians. Our debt to him cannot really be measured.

T. Harry Williams in his office at Lincolnand. Courtesy LSU University Relations.

T. Harry Williams: Pragmatic Historian

Frank J. Wetta

A Scholar's Life

T. Harry Williams was a Midwesterner by birth and education, a Southerner by choice and adoption. Born in the hamlet of Vinegar Hill, Illinois, on May 19, 1909, he grew up in Hazel Green, Wisconsin, where his father moved to raise sheep following the death of his wife. A precocious child, young Harry had read deeply in the classics, biography, history, and historical fiction by the age of fourteen. He received his undergraduate education at Platteville State Teachers College (1927–31), where he concentrated in history; however, the Great Depression killed off the high school teaching positions for which he had been trained. Following his father's advice, he enrolled in the University of Wisconsin to pursue an advanced degree. Unsure of what field to study, he contacted Carl Russell Fish, a Civil War scholar. Fish supervised Williams's master's thesis, completed in 1932, an analysis of the role of Radical Republican leader "Bluff Ben" Wade of Ohio. Williams continued at Wisconsin, this time under a young professor, William Best Hesseltine. While working on his dissertation, "The Committee on the Conduct of the War: A Study in Civil War Politics," completed in 1937, Williams taught in the extension division of the University of Wisconsin (1936–37).

In 1936, Williams gave an Armistice Day address to a group of Wausau high school seniors. The speech caused an uproar, and the superintendent of schools who administered the extension division removed him from his position. In 1968, in a conversation with one of his graduate students, Williams would recount the episode with no little amusement. But it was serious at the time. According to Williams, he had used the occasion to talk about Lincoln the crafty political artist, a theme he was just developing and one that became a staple of his Civil War lectures. The faculty and adolescent audience did not understand the nuances of his talk, and when the local American Legion raised a stink, the national press picked up the story. An editorial in the *Washington* (DC) *Herald* quoted him as saying that "Lincoln plunged the nation into war to save a tottering Republican Party" and that the Gettysburg Address was "the finest example of propaganda ever expressed in America." The editorialist encouraged the university to remove "the young Wisconsin extension teacher" from the classroom.[1] His family was anxious, and it looked as if a promising career had come to a sudden end. His father wrote to express his anxiety.[2] Williams, however, was not left twisting in the wind. Local 253 of the American Federation of Teachers sent a letter of protest to the University of Wisconsin.[3] Friends and fellow scholars from across the country sent messages of encouragement. Williams stated that S. I. Hayakawa, then at the University of Wisconsin, Madison, also intervened on his behalf.

In addition, Williams received several letters from Southerners who, like the high school audience and the American Legion, did not get the point either. The former secretary of the Arkansas Division of the United Daughters of the Confederacy was especially pleased, she informed Williams, "when you assailed the character of Abraham Lincoln."[4] From Florida, another neo-Confederate confirmed to Williams that his "attitude re Lincoln was correct—and you have nothing to recant."[5] In any event, the storm passed and Williams later accepted a new position at the Municipal University of Omaha, Nebraska (1938–41).

In 1941, Williams joined the history faculty at Louisiana State University in Baton Rouge and remained there until he retired in 1979. Because of his dramatic teaching and prolific writing, popularity and honors followed him all the days of his career. He served as editor of the Southern Biography Series published by the LSU Press as well as editor of the *Southern Review*. These recognitions included an appointment in 1953 to a Boyd Professorship at LSU and the Harmsworth Professorship in American History at Queen's College, Oxford University (1966–67). His colleagues elected him president of both the Southern Historical Association (1958–59) and the Organization of American Historians (1972–73).

During his years at LSU, Williams became a member of the Baton Rouge establishment. He developed a special relationship with the conservative society of Southern lawyers, politicians, and businessmen—the society of the country club and the Civil War Round Table. But it took time to adjust. "I much prefer the Middle West to the South," he wrote to Hesseltine, his mentor.[6] He later complained of the oppressive Louisiana heat: "This goddamn summer is killing me."[7] In time, however, he grew to love this South and its ways, and the South in turn adopted "T. Harry" as one of its own. (A governor of Louisiana once sat in the first row during a Williams lecture.) "I guess people down here would admit if pressed," his wife and research assistant Estelle ("a belle of de South," he called her)[8] reflected, "that Harry came from Up North somewhere, but they never mention it out loud. They've just taken him over as a native."[9] Williams was also attracted to the South's "sense of manners and its civility."[10]

This romantic view of Louisiana society forced Williams to defend his decision to stay teaching and writing at LSU during the turbulent years of the integration struggles. According to Estelle Williams, "His answer was always that he liked the South. He became a part of it, even at times speaking for the South; and the South, particularly Louisiana, rewarded him."[11] Nevertheless, he never turned his historical vision away from the failures of Southern history. On the issue of segregation, he explained, "I could understand their viewpoint without agreeing with it. What did bother me though was the shutting off of discussion of the question."[12] He hoped the South would find a practical solution to the problem of social and economic justice. Astute political leaders, he believed, offered the answers. His scholarship reflected this personal concern and hopeful estimation.

Catholic in his interests, his academic and popular writings covered a wide spectrum: congressional politics during the Civil War and Reconstruction, the development of the American military command system, Northern and Southern generalship and strategy, Abraham Lincoln as politician and commander in chief, Southern biography and politics, even journalism. (From 1956 until 1966, he wrote a column in the *Baton Rouge Morning Advocate* in which he critiqued history books and novels.)

The high point of his career came in 1969, when he won the National Book Award and the Pulitzer Prize for his biography of Louisiana governor Huey P. Long. But Williams never slowed down; devoted to his craft, he continued with new projects in his detached, book-lined study behind his house known as "Lincolnand." (His office at LSU was bare—a few files, a crudely retouched photograph on the wall showing Williams with a comical Lincolnesque beard, not much else.) Just beginning his study of Lyndon Johnson and, concurrently, completing a survey of American wars, T. Harry Williams died unexpectedly on July 6, 1979, from a respiratory illness.

Rising above Principle

The works of T. Harry Williams can be divided into two related categories—politics and generalship. Both categories share an appreciation for irony in history, a keen sense of humor, and a focus on the element of pragmatism in decision making. The genesis of his interest in the virtues of pragmatism can be seen in two early essays written in 1945 and 1946. In the first article, he traced the history of a little-known event in Reconstruction history, the attempt by certain whites in New Orleans, including the former Confederate general P. G. T. Beauregard, to end Reconstruction and carpetbag rule through the creation of a new political party based on an alliance of white businessmen and the elite of New Orleans black society. These white Reformers offered an end to racial discrimination in public conveyances, as well as in schools, employment, and business corporations. They even promised a significant share, perhaps control, of political offices. The "Creole Negro" leaders in turn would deliver the black vote on election day. The result would be political peace and economic prosperity in a new South. Tired of high taxes, the chaos of carpetbag government, and the constant race baiting of the Democratic opposition, the businessman accepted, though reluctantly, black political and civil equality if it meant bringing the situation under control; but the alliance died aborning. Unable to convince black leaders to leave their entrenched positions within the Republican party, unable to overcome the racial antipathies of the common white people of the rural parishes of Louisiana, and unable to see the need for professional political expertise, the white businessmen failed to achieve their goals. Although their objectives were essentially pragmatic, their methods were decidedly amateurish. They purposely excluded professional politicians, so fixed were they on the need for honesty and the need to keep the movement on a high moral plane. This fatal flaw doomed their enterprise. By eschewing the professionals, Williams argued, they left out one critical element in the equation. As he put it, "Unification was a reform movement run by amateurs. Its leaders made the mistakes that amateurs often make. The unifiers boasted that they had barred professional politicians from their organization, yet the hand of a professional would have saved the movement from some of its blunders."[13]

Williams contended that this was the case in general throughout the South. Unlike Northern businessmen, who had harnessed politics to economic ends, the good, the wise, and the wealthy of Southern society had allowed racial politics and its collateral issues to stymie progress. "The planter-capitalist class of the South thought and acted in terms of economic self-interest in a fashion similar to the industrial magnates of the North. The important difference," he concluded, "was that the businessmen carried the Northern people with them while the planters were unable to convince the white masses in the South that economics transcended racial supremacy."[14] The planter leadership, limited both in vision and in political talent, simply could not solve the vexing problems of Southern poverty and racism. It would take political operators of unique perception and rare ability to find solutions.

Williams explored these issues further in a series of four lectures delivered at Mercer University, published as *Romance and Realism in Southern Politics* (1961), in which he surveyed the course of political history from the antebellum period to the 1930s. The Old South, he noted, had developed a defensive mentality as it sought to hold off Northern attacks on its social system: "Under almost constant assault after the 1830s, in its response the South committed almost every political error in the book." For Williams those errors were mortal sins. "First," he charged, "it permitted the opposition to define the issue, slavery, thus putting itself at an immediate disadvantage. Second, it identified every other issue and, indeed, its whole way of life with the defense of slavery."[15] Last, the South shut off discussion of the topic: It would allow no dissent. The result was an abnormal political situation born of defiance and defeat, romanticism, conformity, and individualism. This was the litany of Southern failure that distorted the proper bargain and compromise that lie at the heart of a healthy political system. The South became a closed society devoted to a mystic vision—the moonlight and magnolias of the plantation ideal of both the ruling elite and the lesser white men. Indeed, Williams argued that the desire to preserve the old ways and fear of the future were the reasons for Southern secession—the fear that someday, maybe soon, maybe later, the North would touch the system of race relations in the South. The Lost Cause, enshrined in the hearts and minds of white Southerners, deformed the political system.

Williams identified alternative voices. Some, like the voices of the Louisiana Unification movement, were too weak or too hesitant to really change the system. The populists and the progressives also called for a newer South—one of honesty, stability, and economic advancement. But there was more agitation than action, and things never went much beyond symbolism and high-minded proposals. Again, Williams pointed out, the leaders lacked real political skill. They could win elections all right, but they never changed the system. It was true enough that the populist leaders, Tom Watson and others, had first appealed to economic and class interests. They argued that economics should transcend race, but nothing substantial came of it. Frustrated by their failures, they reverted to the ancient and reliable doctrine of race.

White supremacy continued to haunt the South; like Banquo's ghost, it kept showing up. Neither the populist nor the progressive were able to exorcise the specter. And when they discovered they could not get rid of it, they embraced it with open arms. At first it appeared that the progressives could make a realistic connection between political and economic issues. But in the end, things turned out pretty much the way they always had. With the failure of the populists and progressives, a new type of Southern leader emerged—Cole Blease of South Carolina and Theodore Bilbo of Mississippi, among others. These were the demagogues. "They made the masses feel important," Williams wrote. "They stroked the ego of democracy, they voiced the frustrations and the resentments of the submerged classes that had been stirred but not satisfied by Populism and Progressivism. They denounced in savage diatribes those whom they assured the people were their enemies—the Yankees, the Negroes, the patricians."[16] They seduced the common white folk and offered illusion in place of accomplishment.

Finally, after years of frustration and false hope, a voice of reality sounded. A leader emerged who made things happen. Huey Pierce Long, governor of Louisiana, made possible what others could only promise: good roads, medical care, and education. Most important, Williams asserted, he changed the political agenda to include black people in a realistic way. A pragmatic democrat, Huey proved to be a leader of real talent and radical vision. "He had a program," Williams wrote with approval. "He promised something and he delivered it. Long was the first southern mass leader to leave aside race baiting and appeals to southern tradition and the southern past and address himself to the social and economic problems of the present."[17] Here was the answer to the problems of the South; and in answer to commentators, journalists, and historians who charged that Long was a Southern demagogue or the dictator of some curious banana republic, Williams replied that Long was no more a demagogue or fascist than Boss Tweed of New York or Mayor Richard Daley of Chicago. Long was a unique leader who offered a counternarrative—an alternative agenda for Southern politics.

Huey Long became the subject of Williams's magnum opus—a nine-hundred-page biography. "I started with a predilection for Huey, as a realistic operator who got things done that needed doing in a Southern state with blind resistance to change," he admitted to a writer for the *New York Times*. "I believe a politician in America has an obligation," he emphasized, "to give people a better life; and I believe too, in a version of the great man theory, that certain men of power can change the course of history. I think Huey Long did that."[18] Here was no clumsy yokel come to high station. Long was an articulate, well-read, gifted politician, the kind of leader the South had needed for two generations. He was no charlatan, no race baiter, no timid reformer seeking progress without change. That is what explained Huey Long's remarkable appeal to the people. Williams quoted Huey's response to a group of reporters debating among themselves the nature of his power. "Oh, hell," Huey interjected, "say that I'm *sui generis* and let it go at that."[19] Huey was right—and wrong. He was truly unique in Southern history, but he could be classified by another standard.

Drawing upon the theories of philosopher Eric Hoffer, Williams saw Huey Long as a *mass leader*. The mass leader, he explained, "is a man who sets a popular movement in motion." This kind of leader exhibits "audacity, an iron will, faith in himself and his cause and his destiny."[20] He was a remarkable politician whose sometimes vulgar, sometimes ruthless methods were carefully calculated to achieve certain goals. He was a politician but one of extraordinary imagination, unbound by the traditions of the past or limitations of the present. Like other mass leaders, including Franklin Roosevelt, Abraham Lincoln, Mohandas Gandhi, and even Adolf Hitler and Benito Mussolini, he was a charismatic leader. Some of these were good men; others were evil or abused their power. But Huey was no fascist dictator. Historians and political commentators who leveled this charge simply misread Huey Long. He was a politician, but an unusual one in the context of Southern history.

Williams put it succinctly in an essay titled "Trends in Southern Politics." He contrasted the politico with the amateur, the ideologue, the romantic, and the do-gooder in public life. He regretted that the term *politician* had been discounted in the public's estimation and in academic circles. For Williams, the skillful politician got things done. His methods might be unorthodox and his political style offensive to those of refined taste, but he accomplished much where others proved unwilling or inept.

Williams believed that intellectuals misunderstood the nature of a true politician. Academic historians in particular and the intelligentsia in general, he asserted, denigrated the politician as a schemer, spoilsman, party hack, or political jobber. The *statesman,* on the other hand, in the professors' view, demonstrated foresight, high purpose, and unselfish devotion to an ideal. "The professors," Williams wrote, "have thought that the politicians should act much like themselves: debating issues with calm, balance, and scholarly restraint; presenting plans of doctrine, detail, and logic; acting, in short, like sweet philosophers."[21] Huey was no sweet philosopher; he was a tough, pragmatic politician. "Sometimes you have to rise above principle," Williams once remarked half seriously.[22]

Huey's position on race illustrates the point. No other issue in Southern life was so complex. Some Southern leaders had tried to transcend it and failed; others had used race to achieve power. Huey Long was different. True, in public statements he supported white supremacy and segregation; no politician in Louisiana could win an election unless he endorsed the prevailing system of race relations. As governor he did not support blacks voting, and as United States senator he opposed enactment of a federal antilynching law. In this Huey was no different than his fellow Southern politicians. Williams offered an interpretation: "His extreme talk, indeed, his whole racial stance, was a strategy. By seeming to be a complete segregationist, he reserved for himself a freedom of action on racial matters—he could then do some things that breached the pattern of segregation; he could give the Negroes certain rights that he believed they should have. The rights that he would extend were economic ones."[23] Here was the politics of pragmatism at its best (or most devious). A skilled politician—a cool operator—could change things.

At the time of his death, Williams was working on a biography of another Southern politician and power artist—Lyndon Baines Johnson. It was to be another study in the politics of pragmatism. In his presidential address to the Organization of American Historians in 1973, Williams drew connections between the political style and objectives of the two men. He outlined as well the fundamental differences. Whereas Huey was a genuine home-grown radical, Johnson was essentially a reformer. But they both sought change that would break the mold of Southern political tradition. Later, in "Lyndon Johnson and the Art of Biography," Williams summarized it this way:

> I have some tentative or preliminary thoughts or ideas about this man Lyndon Johnson. As I see him now, he was a liberal with a real compassion for poor people and a great believer in using the power of government to solve problems. But he was not, in my opinion, a radical, as Huey Long was. I see Huey Long as a radical. Huey Long, I think, would have subverted the system if he had to. Lyndon Johnson never questioned the capitalist system, never questioned the basis of capitalism.[24]

It is interesting to speculate how Williams would have interpreted Lyndon Johnson. If Johnson fits the mold of the shrewd political creature in the tradition of Lincoln and Long, how would he have explained Johnson's utter failure as a war president?

Public and Academic Reception

Historians can be inclined to be suspicious of a colleague whose books are appreciated by the layman. T. Harry Williams, however, was a professional historian who could claim a popular audience as well as maintain the respect of the academic community. His emphasis on narrative history and biography connected with informed readers. His study of Long, a masterpiece of political biography which he began researching in 1955, is the prime example. A selection of both the Book of the Month Club and the History Book Club, *Huey Long* (1969) went through six printings by March 1970; approximately two hundred thousand copies were sold. The National Book Award and the Pulitzer Prize recognized its merit. "Mr. Williams's book persuades me," Tom Wicker wrote for the *New York Times Magazine,* "that this was the voice of an authentic American radicalism, perhaps the most genuine we have seen: and so perhaps Huey Long came to believe . . . that in the end the great things he would do would have to justify the means by which he saw that he would have to do them."[25]

Hugh Davis Graham in the *Journal of Southern History* called the biography "methodologically pathbreaking." (Williams employed the oral history techniques pioneered at Columbia University in the 1950s and interviewed almost three hundred people for his research.) "A massive and sobering study in power, Cashian hell-of-a-fellow politics, and southern hair-trigger violence, it is also frequently hilarious," Graham judged.[26]

Not all have agreed with the positive reviews. Historian Alan Brinkley, for example, in his study of Huey Long and Father Charles Coughlin, the radio priest, held that Williams was wrong about Huey. True, he was not a fascist or racist demagogue, but neither was he truly radical or truly unique. Leaders such as these had been seen before; rather, Long represented "the urge to defend the autonomy of the individual and the independence of the community against the encroachments of the modern industrial state."[27] This was not unique in American history.

An Air of Romance

In addition to his interest in political history, Williams pursued parallel research into American military command, strategy, and generalship. The two interests defined his approach to history—a symbiotic relationship. Fascinated with the element of pragmatism in both political and military affairs, Williams had two careers as both a political historian and as a military historian. The virtues and talents of a successful politician illuminated in his studies of Lincoln and Long were similar to those of a successful general—a Grant or Sherman. On the other hand, failures of imagination and an impractical approach to the practical issues of politics and war can account for failure on the battlefield as they can on the home front—as in the case of Davis and Lee. For over a century, until the emergence of Huey Long, for example, Southern political development had been retarded (haunted) by the politics of romanticism and unreality. Likewise, the failures of the Confederacy during the Civil War, he argued, could also be traced to the "imperatives of southern culture" and Southern romanticism.[28] All recognized the élan often demonstrated by Southern commanders, but this was not enough to overcome the practical flaws in Confederate military planning and, ultimately, the practical application of Northern military power.

Williams identified this theme in his analysis of the reasons why the South lost the Civil War. A primary reason was Southern political and military leadership. Jefferson Davis, he stated directly, was a failure as commander in chief. He adopted a defensive strategy designed to hold the whole of Southern territory, but this only exaggerated the weakness of Southern manpower and turned the initiative over to the Union. Davis saw himself as an expert in military matters, but his constant interference in the War Department only served to make a weak strategy even weaker. He acted as if his country was an established fact, and he ignored the revolutionary nature of events. Abraham Lincoln, unlike Davis, was an astute political operator (a political artist) who understood the nature of events unfolding around him—both politically and militarily. Thus, Williams concluded, Abraham Lincoln, the pragmatic president, was superior to Jefferson Davis; U.S. Grant, the pragmatic general, was superior to Robert E. Lee. Lincoln was to Davis as Grant was to Lee.

For Williams the key to understanding the generalship of Grant and Lee lay in the vital characteristics of each man. Grant became the manager of a war that foreshadowed the shape of things to come in military affairs. In strategy, staff organization, and understanding of the basic nature of the conflict, Grant proved the better commander. Grant understood, as Lee did not, that this was a total war—or, Williams hedged, very near a total war. (Williams was influenced by the writings of British military theorist J. F. C. Fuller).[29] Total war aimed not only at the destruction of the armed forces of the enemy but also at the very foundations of their social and economic system. Failure to understand this characteristic of the Civil War reflected the burden of Southern history that Davis and Lee bore. For all their courage and their willingness to face the battlefield, they could not realize that the Civil War was different in kind from the warfare that had preceded it. Williams held that Lee was a great battle captain—the last of the great nineteenth-century commanders; Grant was a truly modern commander—a great manager of a modern war that foreshadowed the leadership of Eisenhower in World War II. The conservative tendencies in Southern leadership were compounded by the pernicious influences of Baron Antoine Henri Jomini (a nineteenth-century military theorist and contemporary of Carl von Clausewitz). According to Williams, the South fought a conservative war designed to guard the entire perimeter of the Confederacy against Union offensives. This fundamentally flawed strategy, which emphasized territorial objectives, was the principal reason for the defeat of the South. Williams recognized the offensive element in Jomini's idea but contended that the South, tied to a strategic defense, missed its chance to concentrate strategically and win a decisive military decision before 1863. After 1863 the South could not win independence on the battlefield. Any hope of Confederate success would now require the failure of Northern will.

Williams identified the problems of Southern generalship on another level in his biography of P. G. T. Beauregard. "Before a battle," Williams judged,

"[Beauregard] was often visionary and impractical"—his plans overly complicated or ill considered.[30] "Before and during the battle [of First Bull Run]," Williams explained by way of illustration, "he had demonstrated grave deficiencies as a general. His sense of logistics was weak. The plans of grand strategy he had presented to the government were impossible of execution because they were not based on the realities of available Confederate resources."[31] Nevertheless, he was popular with the Southern people: "When he spoke and when he acted, people thought of Paris and Napoleon and Austerlitz and French legions bursting from the St Bernard Pass onto the plains of Italy."[32]

In his military studies, as in his political writings, Williams revealed something fundamental about the Southern ethos. The South, in its peculiar way, had always been impractical, unrealistic, and romantic both in politics and in war, whether it was Davis or Lee or Beauregard.[33]

For a writer so popular with Southern audiences, Williams was remarkably critical of their Confederate heroes. Perhaps they never suspected the origins of Williams's criticism of the South: His father had been a nonconformist and a supporter of the great progressive Robert M. Lafollette, and Williams himself admitted that he inclined toward a Midwestern left-wing agrarian democracy. Like Huey, "T. Harry" was *sui generis.*

Williams's writings on war and politics stimulated high praise as well as calls for revision. His first book, *Lincoln and the Radicals* (1941), became one of the seminal works of Civil War scholarship. Paul M. Angle even included it in his selection for the *Shelf of Lincoln Books* (1946). In his analysis of the conflict between Lincoln and the radical leaders of the Republican Party, Williams pictured men such as Thaddeus Stevens, Ben Wade, Zachariah Chandler, and George Julian as "Jacobins," abnormal politicians. They constantly pressured the cautious, moderate Lincoln to take a forward position on slavery, to conduct the war according to their dictates, and to adopt a hard Reconstruction policy. These were the grim, humorless, impractical men who dominated national politics during "the savage years of the tragic era."[34] Eventually, his thesis was subjected to revisionist counterattacks. David Donald and Hans L. Trefousse, both consensus historians in this context, concluded that the differences between Lincoln and the Radicals were not as great as Williams contended. Later Williams conducted something of a strategic retreat: "It would indeed be an error, as we are in Professor Donald's debt for telling us, to make too much out of the conflict in the Republican Party over slavery. It would be a greater error to dismiss this unique episode and its unique issue as something normal or average and to treat it on the level of ordinary politics."[35]

Historian Mark E. Neely Jr. has criticized both the Williams thesis and the Williams style, noting that Williams's take on the Radicals and Lincoln was the "rashest statement of the case" and that Williams "often used similes best left in the barracks."[36] This latter comment was in reference to Lincoln's skillful manipulation of the Radicals as described by Williams: "The wily Lincoln surrendered to the conquering Jacobeans in every controversy before they could publically inflict upon him a damaging reverse. Like the fair Lucretia threatened with ravishment, he averted his fate by compliance."[37]

Williams continued his "Lincoln and" series with *Lincoln and His Generals* (1952), a Book of the Month Club selection, a best seller, and a Civil War classic. Williams and Lincoln appeared on the cover of the *Saturday Review of Literature;* Allan Nevins wrote the favorable review. Praise also came from the *New York Times* and the *American Historical Review.* What impressed Williams about Lincoln as a war leader was, again, his application of the political arts as commander in chief and his adherence to deeply held principle. But not all readers agreed with his thesis that Lincoln was a natural military genius. Critics have insisted that Williams exaggerated Lincoln's role and that the command organization he created was not truly the precursor to the modern American command system as Williams had argued.

Only three years later the LSU Press published *P. G. T. Beauregard: Napoleon in Gray.* Once again Williams was successful. Selected by the Civil War Book Club, it appeared in both hardback and paperback editions. Harnett Kane in the *Chicago Tribune,* David Donald, and Allan Nevins called attention to the biography's virtues.

T. Harry Williams continues to influence the course of Civil War scholarship and to cause historians to consider the import of his ideas. In *How the North Won: A Military History of the Civil War* (1983), Herman Hattaway (a Williams student) and Archer Jones initiated a respectful revision of Williams's theories concerning the reasons for the war's outcome. (The book in fact was dedicated to Williams.) They expanded their campaign in *Why the South Lost the Civil War* (1986). Here they, and two other authors, proposed a major, really radical, revision of Williams's interpretation of Southern strategy. Williams was not merely wrong, they claimed, but also misleading. He was wrong because he had seriously misinterpreted the Jominian theories of warfare and because he failed to see the essential similarities between Clausewitz and Jomini. But he was misleading because he had sent scholars down the wrong road. It was not, as Williams maintained, the failures of Southern strategy and generalship that explain the defeat of the Confederacy. The answer lies elsewhere, they argued, in Southern will and motivation. In his 2007 biography of Robert E. Lee, British historian Brian Holden Reid, for example, defended the general's reputation against Williams's charge that the Southerner was an "old fashioned general" and that British historians (Frederick Maurice, G. F. R. Henderson, and Cyril Falls) had a cultural bias in favor of

Lee, the "gentleman" soldier. On the contrary, being a Southern gentleman was a source of Lee's strength as a commander, not a weakness. Further, Lee possessed an imaginative strategic sense: "In the strategic game of poker that Lee played with Grant, he played an indifferent hand brilliantly."[38]

Legacy

That the works of T. Harry Williams still evoke favorable comment or provoke dissent is testimony to the enduring value of his contributions to political and military history. (*Lincoln and the Radicals, Lincoln and His Generals, P. G. T. Beauregard,* and *Huey Long* remain in print.) That he expressed his ideas with such verve and clarity, both in theme and style, explain his popularity. He understood the human element in history and was a gifted storyteller. He had a keen eye for the dramatic scene, the ironic comment, the vivid detail. These were the elements of his style—irony, directness, clarity, humor, and rich example. This sketch of Confederate general Braxton Bragg illustrates the point: "He was probably the ugliest and most disliked Southern general. Thin and stooped, he presented a cadaverous appearance; his plain features were distinguished only by high black eyebrows which met in a tuft above his nose and by a stubby iron-gray beard. Harsh in manner, sour in temper, he made few friends and many enemies."[39]

His lecture style reflected his virtues as an author. He paced across the stage lecturing to a large class of undergraduate and graduate students, his sleeves rolled up to his elbows, his arms flying about as he described a battle or imitated some character from the story of the Civil War. Years later, Harold McSween, one among a legion of admiring students, remembered Williams in an article in the *Virginia Quarterly Review:* "A natural and accomplished storyteller, he could take you back in time and hold you there."[40] All who enrolled in his famous Civil War course recall his description of the final surrender of the Confederate regiments, and many an LSU boy was brought to tears at the end of the class. The historian who preached the doctrine of pragmatism in the conduct of human affairs could evoke the most romantic emotions in his students. When Williams gave his last lecture at LSU, the hall overflowed with students, alumni, politicians, faculty, and the old guard of Louisiana society.

In the conclusion of his biography of P. G. T. Beauregard, we find the essence of the Williams approach to history. Here, in his masterful summery of the Creole general's will, is the rhythm and cadence of his prose at its best, the respectful disdain for the false romance of the antebellum South, the admiration for those leaders who could look through the moonlight and magnolias to a better South. T. Harry Williams—Pragmatic Historian:

The enigma of his life was in that inventory. There in the painfully listed columns was the sword which the ladies of New Orleans had presented to him after he captured Fort Sumter, and the little red-topped artillery general's cap which he had worn at Manassas and when he rode before the ranks the night before Shiloh, and the battle flag made by Hettie Cary in the exultant days of 1861—the faded and pathetic relics of the Old South. There too, and more numerous and significant, were the stocks, the real estate, the promissory notes, the speculative investments—the glittering symbols of the New South. And so, even to the last, he was a paradox. Despite all that he seemed and all that he fought for, he did not really look back to Contreras and the planting South and the mellow glories of the ancient regime, but forward to International House and the New Orleans industrial district and the bustling delta of tomorrow.[41]

Notes

Victor Slater, chair of the History Department at Louisiana State University, kindly arranged for the photocopying of selected letters dealing with Williams's early career.

1. *Washington* (DC) *Herald,* n.d., in T. Harry Williams Papers, Louisiana and Lower Mississippi Valley Collections, Special Collections, Hill Memorial Library, Louisiana State University Libraries, Baton Rouge (hereafter cited as Williams Papers).
2. William D. Williams to T. Harry Williams, Nov. 21, 1936, Williams Papers.
3. William E. Roth to Frank O. Holt, n.d., Williams Papers.
4. Mrs. Sherman Atkinson to T. Harry Williams, Nov. 14, 1936, Williams Papers.
5. G. S. P. Holland to T. Harry Williams, [Nov. 17, 1936,] Williams Papers.
6. T. Harry Williams to William B. Hesseltine, n.d. [1940?], Williams Papers.
7. Williams to Hesseltine, Aug. 16, 1943, Williams Papers.
8. Williams to Hesseltine, n.d. [1948?], Williams Papers.
9. Qouted in William Clemons, "T. Harry Williams, at Home Down South," *New York Times Book Review* (Nov. 1969): 2.
10. Estelle Williams, "A Biographical Introduction by Estelle Williams," in *The Selected Essays of T. Harry Williams: With a Biographical Introduction by Estelle Williams,* by T. Harry Williams and ed. Estelle Williams (Baton Rouge, 1983), 3.
11. Ibid.
12. Ibid.

13. T. Harry Williams, "The Louisiana Unification Movement," in *Selected Essays,* 94–95.

14. T. Harry Williams, "An Analysis of Some Reconstruction Attitudes," in *Selected Essays,* 109.

15. T. Harry Williams, *Romance and Realism in Southern Politics* (Athens, GA, 1961), 10.

16. Ibid., 63.

17. Ibid., 7.

18. Clemons, "T. Harry Williams," 2.

19. T. Harry Williams, *Huey Long* (New York, 1969), 414.

20. Ibid., 414–15.

21. "Trends in Southern Politics," in *The Idea of the South: Pursuit of a Central Theme,* ed. Frank E. Vandiver (Chicago, 1964), 58.

22. T. Harry Williams to Frank J. Wetta, personal conversation, n.d.

23. Williams, *Huey Long,* 704.

24. Williams, *Selected Essays,* 248.

25. *New York Times,* Nov. 2, 1969.

26. Hugh David Graham, "The Enigma of Huey Long: An Essay Review," *Journal of Southern History* 36 (May 1970): 206.

27. Alan Brinkley, *Voices of Protest: Huey Long, Father Coughlan, and the Great Depression* (New York, 1982), xi.

28. T. Harry Williams, *The History of American Wars, from 1745 to 1918* (New York, 1981), 254.

29. Joseph G. Dawson, "The First of the Modern Wars?" in *The American Civil War: Explorations and Reconsiderations,* ed. Susan-Mary Grant and Brian Holden Reid (New York, 2000), 126.

30. T. Harry Williams, *P. G. T. Beauregard: Napoleon in Gray* (Baton Rouge, 1955), vii.

31. Ibid., 93.

32. Ibid., 1.

33. T. Harry Williams, *Lincoln and His Generals* (New York, 1952), 314.

34. Paul Angle, *A Shelf of Lincoln Books: A Critical, Selective Bibliography of Lincolniana* (New Brunswick, NJ, 1946).

35. T. Harry Williams, "Lincoln and the Radicals: An Essay in Civil War History and Historiography," in *Grant, Lee, Lincoln and the Radicals: Essays on Civil War Leadership,* ed. Grady McWhiney (New York, 1964), 114.

36. Mark Neeley Jr., "Abraham Lincoln vs. Jefferson Davis: Comparing Presidential Leadership in the Civil War," in *Writing the Civil War: The Quest to Understand,* ed. James M. McPherson and William J. Cooper Jr. (Columbia, SC, 1998), 103.

37. Quoted in ibid.

38. Brian Holden Reid, *Robert E. Lee: Icon for a Nation* (New York, 2007), 222.

39. Williams, *P. G. T. Beauregard,* 47.

40. Harold B. McSween, "T. Harry Williams; A Remembrance," *Virginia Quarterly Review,* http://www.vqronline.org/articles/2000/autumn/mcsween-t-harry-williams/ (accessed Apr. 16, 2011).

41. Williams, *P. G. T. Beauregard,* 329.

General Robert Edward Lee. Library of Congress.

The Generalship of Robert E. Lee

Charles P. Roland

Machiavelli wrote that victory is the final test of skill in war. "If a general wins a battle," he said, "it cancels all other errors and miscarriages." Conversely, one may infer, if a general loses a battle, it cancels all other brilliance and daring. Experience in two world wars, followed by a growing insecurity in the modern age, heightens the American sense of nationalism today. Supreme excellence in all things (whether economic, intellectual, or military) must come of our peculiar political and social institutions, Americans are accustomed to believe. Rudely upset in the field of science by *Sputnik,* Gagarin, and Titov, this happy theme yet pervades much of the literature of American history, especially many recent treatises on the Civil War. Provincialism and conservatism restricted the Confederate military mind, say our nationalistic scholars, and assured victory to the Union. Here are the major problems in expounding the talents of Robert E. Lee: For he fought against the Union; and he is the only American general who has ever lost a war.

Fortunately, insofar as Lee's reputation is concerned, history sometimes flouts the inference from Machiavelli's rule: Occasionally a great genius in war—a Hannibal, a Charles XII, or a Napoleon—falls in defeat. These exceptions to such a law of success and failure in war demonstrate that generalship alone does not always prevail, however good it may be. Victory requires that one side overmatch the opposite in the sum of its generalship plus all other capabilities for waging war. Hence, judged fairly, a general's record must be weighed against the resources at his command.

Lee and the Confederacy opposed awesome superiority in the means of making war. "All else equal," said Clausewitz, "numbers will determine victory in combat. . . . In ordinary cases an important superiority of numbers, but which need not be over two to one, will be sufficient to ensure victory, however disadvantageous other circumstances may be." Early in the war,

Southern troops were outnumbered two to one; before war's end they were outnumbered three to one.[1] In industrial strength, the decisive weapon of modern war, the Confederacy was hopelessly overmatched. In 1860, for example, the North produced twenty times as much pig iron as did the South, and twenty-four times as many locomotive engines. At like disadvantage today, the United States would be pitted against an adversary manufacturing annually one billion tons of steel, along with comparable quantities of automotive and other industrial wares. In charge of the U.S. census, J. M. Edmunds wrote with candor in 1865 that the Confederacy fell for want of material resources, not for lack of will, skill, or courage. Forge and lathe, plow and reaper, rail and piston: All weighed in the balance against Lee and his associates.[2]

Since the South had to be invaded and conquered before Federal authority could reassert itself, the Confederacy held the strategic advantage of interior, or shorter, lines of communication. Theoretically, it was able more rapidly to concentrate troops upon points of decision than could the Union. Actually, this was seldom true. Possessing less than half the railway mileage the North had, and virtually no facilities for manufacturing or repairing locomotives and rolling stock, the Confederacy was unable to profit significantly from interior lines. Early in the war it lost the railroads of western and central Tennessee, including a long stretch of the vital Memphis and Charleston track. Command of these roads and of the upper Mississippi River and the lower Tennessee River gave to the Union forces the interior lines of communication within the broad Western Theater of the Confederacy. Unable to control the seas, the Confederacy fought with flank and rear continuously threatened with invasion.

Lee and the Confederate government had also to contend with the powerful influence of localism within the Confederacy. Asserting the rights of state sovereignty, many Southern governors withheld large numbers of men from the Confederate armies and demanded protection of all territory within their states. The institution of slavery aggravated this tendency; even the temporary appearance of Northern troops in any part of the South so disrupted the labor force and the economy that they could never be returned to normal. Hence, Confederate authorities were obliged to scatter many thousands of troops at scores of points having little strategic importance, if any.

Though Lee was not responsible for the general strategy of the defensive adopted by Jefferson Davis early in the war, Lee tacitly indorsed it. Some Confederate leaders urged a prompt invasion of the North, calling for a lightning stroke against the people of the Union, before its vast resources could be mobilized. Certain historians today support this strategy by pointing out that in a prolonged war of attrition, the South was foredoomed to defeat.

Critics speak with authority in disparaging Confederate strategy; they speak with uncertain voices in saying what it ought to have been. Offensive war against the North would seem to have been futile. Four years were required for the immensely more powerful Union to conquer the Confederacy; that the South could have conquered the North is inconceivable. Through the defensive, the South could conserve its lesser strength and exact of the North a heavier toll in blood and treasure. Doubtless unwittingly, Southern leaders followed Clausewitz's dictum, "Defense is the stronger form of war." Even that implacable critic of Confederate leadership, General J. F. C. Fuller, acknowledges that the defensive was the only sound policy for the South.[3]

Exigencies of Southern politics, society, and logistics caused Davis to adopt, and Lee to second, a strategy of territorial defense. Accordingly, the Confederacy was split into departments (or theaters), each with its own army, and each to be defended against invasion, with no territory to be yielded voluntarily to the enemy. Such a design fell short of the military rule "Unity of plan, concentration of force." Lee was aware that this strategy failed to achieve maximum concentration of force, that it thus violated the fundamental principle of war as set forth by the military theorist Henri Jomini, whom Lee is nowadays accused of following slavishly. But in fashioning this plan, Confederate leaders anticipated a principle of modern warfare not then generally recognized; they sought to provide what Cyril Falls describes as "that vital factor of the most recent times, the defence of the home base and civil population."[4]

In condemning this failure to concentrate, General Fuller says that the Confederacy ought to have yielded temporarily the state of Virginia and other areas of the upper South in order to mass its forces at the key rail center Chattanooga. By harassing Union communications and drawing Union armies away from base, he opines, the Confederacy may then have struck a decisive blow with its entire *grande armée*. As military science in the narrow sense, this may be sound, though it tempts the speculation that such an initial Confederate concentration would merely have caused a like Union concentration but in far greater strength. "Concentration *a priori* and without regard to enemy dispositions invites disaster," writes General de Gaulle in a perceptive comment on French operations in World War I. As strategy in the highest sense, strategy that blends military science with political science, social psychology, and economics, General Fuller's plan is folly. Abandonment of the upper South to the Shermans and Sheridans of the Northern army would have undone the Confederacy without a battle. "There is nothing in [Lee's] generalship," says Sir Frederic Maurice, "which is more striking than the manner in which he grasped the problems of the Confederacy and . . . adapted his strategy both to the cause for which the South was fighting and to the major political conditions of the time." Considering the circumstances of Southern life, territorial defense was probably the only strategy open to the leaders of the Confederacy.[5]

As adviser to President Davis early in the war, Lee did not decide strategy; he was in no sense general in chief of Confederate armies. "Broadly speaking," says biographer Douglas Southall Freeman, "Davis entrusted to [Lee] the minor, vexatious matters of detail and the counselling of commanders in charge of the smaller armies. On the larger strategic issues the President usually consulted with him and was often guided by his advice, but in no single instance was Lee given a free hand to initiate and direct to full completion any plan of magnitude."[6]

Restricted as he was by the character of his assignment, Lee nevertheless at this time showed deep insight into the nature of the war and urged certain measures that would greatly strengthen the South for the struggle ahead. In the early days after Fort Sumter, when many people of the South still predicted that there would be no war, and that, if it should come, it would be quickly won by Southern arms, Lee said that war was inevitable, and that it would be long and bloody. In the fall of 1861, when many thought that England was about to enter the war against the North because of the *Trent* Affair, Lee warned against such hope. "We must make up our minds to fight our battles and win independence alone," he wrote prophetically. "No one will help us."[7]

When in the spring of 1862, Forts Henry and Donelson fell, and the Confederate army in the West was threatened with destruction, Lee wisely advised stripping the Gulf Coast of troops in order to reinforce Albert Sidney Johnston and Beauregard at Corinth, Mississippi. To Johnston, Lee gave sound strategic counsel: Concentrate, said Lee, and strike the enemy at your front before the two wings of his army can be joined. The Battle of Shiloh, fought according to this plan, came within an inch of destroying the Union army there; neither side would again come so close to a total victory until exhaustion had overtaken the Confederacy at war's end.[8]

Lee's support of conscription to muster the manpower of the South indicated advanced military thinking and willingness to break with American precedent. As early as December 1861, Lee recommended state conscription by the government of Virginia, and after Confederate losses at Shiloh and New Orleans the following spring, Lee's endorsement of Confederate conscription helped to secure passage of the act by the Southern Congress. Lee's ideas on conscription offer proof of how far beyond Jomini he had gone during the first year of the Civil War. Jomini considered war an affair to be settled by professional armies; he refused to contemplate a people's war, and wrote, "[It] would be so terrible that, for the sake of humanity, we ought never to see it." Lee said, "Since the whole duty of the nation [will] be war until independence [is] secured, the whole nation should for a time be converted into an army, the producers to feed and the soldiers to fight." Not until the outbreak of World War I would the governments of the world grasp fully this principle of total mobilization laid down by Lee almost threescore years before.[9]

In the spring of 1862, as McClellan's powerful army moved to the Virginia Peninsula and threatened Richmond at close quarters, Davis leaned heavily upon Lee for support. Lee's talent as a strategist now began to emerge in his daring shift of Confederate troops to oppose McClellan's advance. But Lee saw the futility of meeting the Federal concentration with like concentration; he realized that the smaller Southern force must ultimately be overwhelmed if this were done. Instead, Lee adopted the more resourceful technique of weakening McClellan's army by threatening a blow at the North. "As to dividing the enemy's strength," wrote Machiavelli, "there can be no better way . . . than by making incursions into their country." From relatively unexposed points in the Carolinas and Georgia, Lee drew reinforcements piecemeal for the Confederate army on the Peninsula; in the meantime, Lee urged General Jackson in the Shenandoah Valley to strike the enemy there in order to divert Northern troops from McClellan. This was the genesis of Lee's later strategy for the entire Confederacy.[10]

On May 31, 1862, Confederate General Joseph E. Johnston fell wounded in the fighting on the Peninsula, and Davis named Lee to command the Army of Northern Virginia. Lee's mission was to defend Virginia, especially the Confederate capital, Richmond. He opposed the strongest of Union concentrations, which outnumbered his own force by two to one. For three years Lee would fulfill his mission against the heaviest odds ever faced by an American commander.

The wisdom of defending Richmond, to the relative neglect of other points in the South, has been seriously questioned. Defense of the capital to the bitter end cannot be justified, but there was reason for holding it as long as possible without sacrificing the army. Even if Richmond had possessed no intrinsic military value, as the capital it had great symbolic value. One may lightly disparage both Davis and Lincoln for waging long and bitter campaigns for the capture or protection of idle cities, yet both men sensed the psychological importance of being able to retain the seat of government. Winston Churchill recognized this principle when late in World War II he argued that Berlin was still an objective of great strategic importance, that nothing else would blight German morale so much as its fall. Moreover, Richmond was by no means an idle city: It contained the great parent arsenal of the South, the Tredegar Works, besides many other armories and factories. To the Confederacy, Richmond was Washington and Pittsburgh in one. Aside from symbolic and material values, northern Virginia possessed great strategic value for the Confederacy. It was a dagger pointed toward the heart of the enemy, a potential base for strikes against the Northern capital and the great northeastern centers of population, industry, and communication. A powerful, mobile Southern army in northern Virginia was the most effective instrument of the Confederacy for paralyzing the mind of President Lincoln and the will of the Northern people.

Lee preferred this command to all others, since it would keep him in his beloved Virginia. Though Davis made the decision to defend Richmond, Lee unquestionably approved of it. Once in command, Lee instantly did what he would always do as long as he had the strength for it: He seized the initiative in the campaign. His strategy for weakening McClellan's force had already borne fruit; Jackson's spectacular demonstration in the Shenandoah Valley (April 30–June 9) caused President Lincoln to divert McDowell's corps there. Ordering Jackson to Richmond by rail, Lee now attempted a concerted blow against McClellan. Faulty staff work and the derelictions of subordinates may have cost Lee a decisive victory. Nevertheless, in a series of fierce engagements (June 26–July 2) Lee persuaded McClellan to abandon the drive for Richmond.[11]

The blunting of McClellan's thrust enabled Lee to open what Davis called an "offensive-defensive" against the Union armies in Virginia. From the beginning, Lee knew that his army could not withstand a siege by the vastly stronger Northern numbers opposing it. Lee must keep the enemy forces divided; he could not afford for them to concentrate upon him. In order to prevent such concentration, he must constantly maneuver and confound his opponents with threats against Washington and with lightning blows against exposed fractions of their strength. Second Manassas was a brilliant demonstration of this technique.

In mid-July Lee learned that Federal troops were concentrating under General John Pope on the Rapidan River in northern Virginia. Lee had to decide quickly whether the next Union main effort was to be from the north or from the Peninsula. Sensing that it would be made by Pope, Lee started Jackson's corps north by rail; when on August 13 Lee learned that the Union force on the James was being reduced, he reasoned that these troops were being sent to Pope. Lee then rushed the remainder of his army up to strike Pope before McClellan's reinforcements could reach him. By dividing the Confederate army and sending Jackson around Pope's flank to threaten communications with Washington, Lee unsettled his adversary and forced him out of position. Reuniting Longstreet and Jackson on the battlefield, Lee then defeated Pope (August 29–30, 1862) and drove him back to the Washington earthworks.

Lee's decision to move his army from the James to the Rapidan showed seeming uncanny ability to anticipate the enemy; it has been called a supreme example of the manner in which judgment and boldness must supplement available information in shaping strategy. Lee's shift of force was a lesson in the use of interior lines of communication and the strategic employment of railroads. Dividing the Confederate army in the face of superior numbers violated the rules of warfare. Jomini warned against it; Lee was criticized for doing it. But Clausewitz says, "What genius does must be the best of all rules, and theory cannot do better than to show how and why it is so." Lee himself gave the explanation. "The disparity . . . between the contending forces rendered the risks unavoidable," he said.[12]

With the Federal army reeling under defeat, and his own troops flushed with victory, Lee now determined to carry the war to the enemy. He proposed to invade Maryland and Pennsylvania. Invasion of the North would extend Lee's war of maneuver, it would find provisions for his troops, and it would free Virginia of molestation during the harvest. A successful campaign across the Potomac might do much more than this. It might add Maryland to the Confederacy, it might sever communications between northeast and northwest, it might place the great cities of the East at Lee's command, and it might bring foreign recognition. It might even end the war, thought Lee, and he proposed that Davis offer peace with honor to the North at this time.

In early September Lee crossed the Potomac. Segments of his army were spread wide to cut the railroads and isolate McClellan from reinforcements. Here the fates deserted Lee. His appeal to the people of Maryland fell on deaf ears. Far worse, McClellan moved against him with disconcerting assurance. One of the traits of a great general is his insight into the character of the opposing general: the ability, as Colonel G. F. R. Henderson phrases it, "to penetrate the adversary's brain." In this faculty, Lee has had few peers. On the eve of marching into Maryland, he said, "McClellan's army will not be prepared for offensive operations—or he will not think it so—for three or four weeks. Before that time I hope to be on the Susquehanna." Ordinarily, Lee would have been right about McClellan, but something extraordinary happened on this occasion. Providentially supplied with a copy of Lee's plan of campaign, found wrapped around three cigars on the ground, McClellan struck Lee's divided army and came near to destroying it at Sharpsburg on September 16–17. Lee held McClellan off and won a tactical victory, but Lee was obliged to return to Virginia and abandon the campaign.[13]

In striking at the North and its capital, say some scholars today, Lee again was simply obeying the stale rules of warfare as set forth by Jomini, or by his chief American disciple, Professor Dennis Hart Mahan of West Point. Actually, Lee was using a strategy as old as war itself, and as modern, too. "If the defender has gained an important advantage," says Clausewitz, "then the defensive form has done its part, and under the protection of this success he must give back the blow. . . . Common sense points out that iron should be struck while it is hot. . . . A swift and vigorous assumption of the offensive—the flashing sword of vengeance—is the most brilliant point in the defensive." This principle was alike sound for Scipio Africanus, or Frederick the Great, or George Catlett Marshall. It was also sound for Lee.[14]

In retrospect, the grander aims of Lee's campaigns into the North seem visionary. Probably England and France would have remained neutral even if Lee had won a victory on Northern soil; that the Lincoln administration would have accepted a peace offer is unlikely. But Lee did not have the advantage of hindsight. The true goal in war, says Clausewitz, is to subject the enemy to one's will. Often this can be done only through destroying the enemy's armed forces. But this is not the sole method for accomplishing the object of war, continues Clausewitz. Moreover, when one lacks the resources to destroy the enemy's armed forces, he must resort to other means. He must then attempt to destroy the enemy's will through measures short of the destruction of his military power. Among such, says the German theorist, are the seizure of the enemy's capital or the inflicting of casualties beyond the enemy's expectations. Here was just Lee's situation.[15]

Lee knew that the South could not possibly destroy the war strength of the North, however successful in battle the South might be, and that, ironically, Southern victories in the field weakened the South in men and material resources relatively more than they weakened the North. Shortly after his greatest triumph (Chancellorsville), Lee wrote to Davis, "We should not . . . conceal from ourselves that our resources in men are constantly diminishing, and the disproportion in this respect between us and our enemies . . . is steadily augmenting."[16] Only by paralyzing the Northern will to victory could the South hope to achieve its war aims. Lee was aware that Washington had no intrinsic military value. But he knew also that President Lincoln and the Northern people had invested the city with great symbolic value, and he knew that defeat at home shakes a population more than defeat in a distant land. He believed that a successful invasion of the North by a victorious Confederate army was most likely to exalt his own people and to blight the morale of the enemy. Considered in this light, his decisions to invade the North are reasonable.

In Virginia again after the fruitless Maryland Campaign, Lee dispersed his army, recruited his strength, and braced for another Federal assault. It came in mid-December against the impregnable heights of Fredericksburg. Reconcentrating quickly, Lee met the attack point blank. Bloodily repulsed, the Northern army fell back across the Rappahannock to await a new commander and a new occasion.

The spring of 1863 found the lines of the Confederacy holding fast to the East but deeply pierced to the West. New Orleans was lost, Grant pressed upon Vicksburg, and Rosecrans was lodged in central Tennessee, threatening Chattanooga. Davis and his counselors sought desperately for a strategy that would restore the balance in the West. Many plans were offered. Most of them called for a shift of troops from relatively secure points elsewhere to the faltering armies of the West in the hope of concentrating sufficient strength there to win decisively over Grant or Rosecrans, or both. In early March, Lee told Davis that for some time he had hoped that the situation in Virginia would enable him to detach an entire corps of his army to the support of the West. Secretary of War Seddon strongly urged this move, and Generals Longstreet and Beauregard set forth variations of it. But the strength and activity of the Army of the Potomac, now commanded by General Joseph Hooker, prevented such an operation at this time, thought Lee. A month later, as affairs in the West grew worse, Secretary of War Seddon called upon Lee to consider sending one division there. Seddon's request for Lee's views on this measure caused Lee to formulate a general strategy for meeting the crisis.

In principle, the strategy now expounded by Lee was not new to him; rather, it was an elaboration of his ingrained philosophy of war as adapted to the peculiar needs of the Confederacy. Lee agreed with Davis and Seddon that the situation required boldness, that the Confederate armies in the West ought at once to take the initiative. Let Joseph E. Johnston concentrate and attack Grant in Mississippi, recommended Lee; let Bragg strike into Kentucky and threaten Ohio. But Lee cautioned against weakening the Army of Northern Virginia. Hooker would not stand idle, predicted Lee, but soon would strike a powerful blow against Virginia. An advocate of the maximum concentration of force against isolated segments of the enemy, Lee nevertheless felt that, in this instance, the distances were too great and the transport facilities of the South too feeble to justify such a move. The Confederacy could not match the Union in shifting troops from one department to another, he said; to rely on that method might render Confederate reserves always too late.

To prevent the North from transferring troops in order to concentrate at a given point, Lee said that all Southern commanders ought to take the offensive upon any weakening of the enemy on their fronts. Let Confederate armies in the major departments be reinforced from the less exposed departments of the Deep South, he advised—from the vicinity of Charleston, Savannah, Mobile, and Vicksburg. Lee's curious listing of Vicksburg came of an erroneous notion that Federal operations there would soon have to quit because of the pestilential Mississippi summer. Apparently Davis, whose home was but a few miles from Vicksburg, never disabused Lee of this idea.

Lee's prime recommendation was that he again strike at the North with his own army. "The readiest method of relieving pressure upon General Joseph E. Johnston," said Lee, "is for the [Army of Northern Virginia] to cross into Maryland. . . . Greater relief would in this way be afforded to the armies in middle Tennessee." To penetrate the enemy's vitals, or if this were impossible, to threaten them with Clausewitz's "flashing sword of vengeance"—this was the key to Lee's strategy.

True to Lee's prediction, in late April Hooker advanced in Virginia. Again Lee seized the initiative with great audacity. Splitting the Confederate force, Lee occupied the bulk of Hooker's powerful army with slightly above one-third of his own, and at the same time, he sent the remainder of his troops under the indomitable Jackson to fall upon Hooker's vulnerable flank and rear. Lee's victory at Chancellorsville (May 2–3), says Colonel Henderson, was one of the supreme instances in history of a great general's ability to outwit his adversary and direct the attack where it is least expected. The Army of the Potomac once more fell back across the Rappahannock, and Confederate leaders again took inventory of strategic resources.[17]

Anxious over the security of Vicksburg, Secretary of War Seddon again proposed the shift of troops from Lee's army to support Pemberton on the Mississippi. If necessary, replied Lee, order Pickett's Division to the West. But Lee warned anew that the great distance required by the move, plus the uncertainty of employment of Pickett's troops in Mississippi, made the venture inadvisable. Weakening of the Army of Northern Virginia, he felt, might force it to retire into the Richmond defenses, where it would cease to be a formidable instrument of Confederate strategy. Davis and Seddon met with Lee on May 15 and approved Lee's plan to invade the North again. This meant that Confederate armies in the West had to fend for themselves.

Already a part of Lee's army was on the move toward Pennsylvania. As he put his troops in motion, Lee searched the Confederacy for reinforcements and pondered other measures that would strengthen his blow. Earlier he had called upon Davis to bring idle troops from the Carolinas, Georgia, and Florida to the Army of Northern Virginia; if necessary, Lee had advised, strip the coastal garrisons except for enough men to operate the water batteries. He now repeated this plea and added another recommendation: Let General Beauregard come with these reserves to northern Virginia and there create a diversion in favor of the advance into Pennsylvania. The anxiety of the Northern government over the safety of Washington would cause a large force to be left for protection of the capital, Lee believed, and he thought Beauregard should command the diversionary column in person: "His presence would give magnitude to even a small demonstration and tend greatly to perplex and confound the enemy." A mere "army in effigy" under Beauregard would have good effect, thought Lee, if no more troops than this were available.

Thinking the North shaken by Chancellorsville and the threat of Confederate invasion, Lee again advised a Southern peace overture. The South ought not to demand peace unconditionally, he said; rather, it ought to encourage the peace party of the North to believe that the Union could be restored by negotiation. "Should the belief that peace will bring back the Union become general, the war would no longer be supported," he observed. Once hostilities ended, he believed that they would not be resumed, and that Southern independence would thus be achieved.

Gettysburg was Lee's debacle. Again fortune turned upon him; at Brandy Station, on the eve of the march into Pennsylvania, Federal cavalry seized Confederate correspondence indicating a northward move by Lee. Davis made no effort to bring up reinforcements or to create the army in effigy requested by Lee. Exceeding Lee's orders, Jeb Stuart rode amiss and deprived Lee of his "eyes," the cavalry, so that he groped his way into Pennsylvania without knowing the whereabouts of the Union army. General Ewell, recently elevated to corps commander as a result of Jackson's death, proved unequal to his responsibilities and failed to seize the key position, Cemetery Hill, early in the battle, when it probably could have been taken. Longstreet sulked and was sluggish in attacking Cemetery Ridge on the second day. Lee erred gravely in ordering the frontal assault against Cemetery Ridge on the third day, when it was impregnably held. After three days of carnage, Lee retreated into Virginia. The tide of the Confederacy was spent.[18]

That in the Gettysburg Campaign Lee was below his best goes without saying. His more severe critics see in the Gettysburg decision a narrow provincialism that blinded Lee to the war as a whole. In contrast to Lee's strategy, which the critics say was primarily a defense of Virginia, they see in the plan urged by Seddon, Longstreet, and Beauregard a truly comprehensive Confederate military design. It would have been a Jominian stroke on the grand scale, they say, taking advantage of the Confederacy's interior lines of communication and concentrating a maximum of Confederate strength for the destruction of Rosecrans's isolated army in Tennessee. Thus Lee becomes the culprit who squandered the Confederacy's one opportunity to win the war.[19]

This criticism is highly problematical. It rests upon the present knowledge that Lee's plan was tried, at least in part, and that it failed. The critics assume what cannot be known: that western concentration was more likely to succeed than was Lee's eastern offensive. Exponents of western concentration do not take into account the logistical weaknesses of the South, which Lee felt made the western venture impractical. After the war, Confederate

General E. P. Alexander had a vision of a powerful Confederate "army on wheels" using the interior lines of the South to shuttle rapidly back and forth between engagements East and West. Alas for the Confederacy, this could be but a vision. Southern troops could, of course, move somewhat more quickly from Virginia to Tennessee than could Northern troops, who had more than twice as far to go. But continued shifting of a large army to and fro across the South, as Alexander contemplated, was roughly the equivalent in time and effort of a like movement across Siberia today. Lee well knew the military significance of railroads; many of his campaigns had been skillful demonstrations in the strategic and logistical use of them. But he accurately sensed that Northern railroad superiority largely nullified the Confederacy's theoretical advantage of interior lines on a grand scale. General Alexander's plan was beyond the capacity of Southern transport and industry; it probably would have exhausted the Confederacy without a battle.[20]

Supporters of the western plan exaggerate the probability of decisive victory over Rosecrans and minimize the effect of weakening Lee's army as a major strategic weapon of the Confederacy. To achieve the purpose of the western effort, Confederate forces there had to do more than win a battle; they had to win so prodigiously as to cause the North to quit the war. That a western Confederate victory of any degree would have done this is questionable. Complete defeat or capture of Rosecrans's army would not have destroyed the war capacity of the Union; its major striking force was elsewhere. One may further question that a total victory over Rosecrans was likely, even granting the maximum Confederate concentration. Walter Millis has pointed out that the advent of railroad, steamboat, and telegraph ended the great battlefield decisions of finality.[21] No such victory was won by either side in the Civil War, regardless of numerical advantage, until the last stages of weakness and demoralization had come upon the Confederacy. If the South could, in any event, have won a western victory of such magnitude as to end the war, it could have done it probably only through three conditions: Rosecrans must obligingly remain exposed to destruction until the Confederacy could mass its strength against him; Hooker, with the most powerful of Union armies, must sit idle in the East all the while; and the western Confederate force, hastily assembled from all over the South, must operate free of the very kind of miscarriage that plagued Lee's veteran army—the varsity team—in its Pennsylvania offensive. That any of these circumstances would have prevailed seems doubtful; that all of them would have prevailed seems incredible.

Nevertheless, everything ought to have been hazarded for the West, it is said; the war was lost there. This appears to be only half truth. It obscures that the war was lost in both the East and West, and through a long process of exhaustion. The West was not intrinsically more valuable to the Confederacy than was the East, and once the East was taken, the West would surely fall. The Confederacy could not live without both.

Close examination of Lee's strategy refutes the accusation that it was merely a defense of Virginia. It was a comprehensive strategy for the Confederacy, however faulty it may have been. Interestingly, it was in some ways like Grant's later strategy for the Union. It employed Lee's seemingly invincible army, greatly strengthened, as the major Confederate striking force, and it called for simultaneous offensives by all major Confederate armies to prevent Northern concentration upon any one of them. It was designed, in part, to nullify the Northern advantages in transportation that enabled the Union to shift troops swiftly from one department to another. Lee's plan for an army in effigy under Beauregard was a superbly ingenious stratagem that might well have upset a nervous foe. It anticipated by almost a century General Patton's mock army threatening the Pas de Calais coast in World War II, which helped to deceive the German high command and to free the Normandy beachheads from heavy counterattack for many precious days.[22] Lee's request was worthy of strenuous effort to fulfill it.

Finally, Lee's plan would have cured the major ill in the deployment of Southern manpower; it would have drawn strategic reserves from the minor departments of the Confederacy to the main effort. Throughout most of the war, excessive numbers of Confederate troops were scattered at relatively idle stations about the South. In early 1863, total Confederate armies were outnumbered 2 to 1, but the major Confederate armies at this time faced odds of 2.5 to 1, while Confederate garrisons along the Atlantic Coast actually outnumbered the opposing Union armies. In the departments of the Carolinas, Georgia, and Florida, forty-five thousand Confederates opposed twenty-seven thousand Federals. From these troops, and others at various places in Virginia, Lee could have added an entire corps to his army, with enough left over to guard the coast and form Beauregard's army in effigy as well.[23]

In a word, Lee proposed to apply to the entire Confederacy the strategy that he had successfully employed within his own department. With offensives throughout the South, he would keep the total enemy force divided; with diversions in northern Virginia, he would confound and divide the local enemy force. Then, with the strongest, the most skillful, and the most cohesive army of the Confederacy, he would direct his main effort against the vital center of the North.

Lee asked for a diversionary force too late for Davis to create it, under the circumstances, even if he had attempted it. Lee proposed this ruse on June 23, only a week before Gettysburg. By now many of the troops from the Atlantic Coast had been sent, without Lee's certain knowledge, to Mississippi, where they would accomplish nothing. This suggests a further thought in weighing Lee's role in the Gettysburg decision. Lee was not general in chief of Confederate armies; he was still merely commander of the Army of Northern Virginia, with the primary mission of defending Virginia against invasion. He lacked the authority, the information, the point of vantage, and the breadth of mission for putting into effect such a plan as he expounded. The supreme weakness of Confederate operations in the summer of 1863 was not the offensive into Pennsylvania, it was the want of a unified command and strategy. As a result, no adequate strategic reserve was ever created out of the minor departments. The weak reserve that was formed was sent to Mississippi, while the main effort of the Confederacy was made in Pennsylvania. The right hand knew not what the left hand was about.

Let us deal the cards in Lee's favor, as they are often dealt in favor of the hypothetical plans that he opposed, and for a moment speculate on what might have been, had he been authentic general in chief in early 1863. Lee would have stripped the minor departments of troops, save for minimum defensive garrisons, and from this source would have strengthened the main effort of the Confederacy. He would have given Joseph E. Johnston full authority in Mississippi and would have ordered a concentrated effort against Grant there. Lee would have ordered Bragg to strike again into Kentucky in order to draw Rosecrans out of Tennessee and alarm the authorities and people of the North. He would have placed Beauregard with an army in effigy to threaten Washington from the South and paralyze his opponent. He would have led the Army of Northern Virginia, powerfully reinforced, into Pennsylvania. Lee would have kept his cavalry in hand and would have discovered and destroyed Meade's two advance corps at Gettysburg on July 1, before the rest of the Northern army could reach the battlefield. With his opponents scattered, confused, and demoralized, Lee would have struck the final psychological blow at the Northern will: He would have offered a negotiated peace with a hint that the Union might thus be preserved. Given all of these conditions, the Gettysburg Campaign was perhaps as likely to end the war successfully for the South as was any other strategy.

But enough of make-believe. Campaigns are seldom waged as critics afterward would have them waged. During the months after Gettysburg, Lee continued to believe that even yet he might be able to invade the North successfully. But defeat in Pennsylvania left its mark on him: When, upon Meade's failing to press Lee, Davis again desired to send a part of Lee's troops west, Lee consented. In early September he dispatched Longstreet with twelve thousand men to strengthen Bragg's army before Chattanooga. Victory at Chickamauga in mid-September was followed by disaster at Chattanooga in November. Weakened by Longstreet's absence, Lee made one unsuccessful offensive effort against Meade (Bristoe Station, October 14) then fell back on the defensive.

Lee now knew that the South was too weak to invade the North. The loss of Chattanooga moved him again to write Davis concerning the general Confederate military situation. The Union army at Chattanooga now threatens Georgia with its factories and provisions, Lee said; it must be stopped if the Confederacy is to survive. Place Beauregard in command of the Confederate army in Georgia and reinforce him with troops from Mississippi, Mobile, and Charleston, urged Lee. To defeat the coming Federal move, he explained, "the safety of points practically less important than those endangered by [it] must be hazarded. Upon the defence of the country threatened by [the enemy march] depends the safety of the points now held by us on the Atlantic, and they are in as great danger from [a] successful advance as by the attacks to which they are at present subjected." Written four months before Sherman set forth to destroy the war support of the lower South, these words show profound insight into the deficiencies of Confederate strategy. They were a prophecy of total war uttered out of season.[24]

Spring of 1864 brought face to face the military giants of the Civil War, Lee and Grant. Now came the heaviest sustained fighting that American troops have ever experienced. True to their natures and to their philosophies of war, both men attempted to seize the initiative in order to destroy the other. As Grant advanced below the Rapidan, Lee attacked fiercely. Had the two forces been equal in numbers, Lee may have achieved his aim, for he took Grant at disadvantage on the march in a country of woods and bramble. But the forces were not equal. For two days in the Battle of the Wilderness (May 5–6), the result trembled in the balance as both forces fought desperately for survival. Then the armies broke off action, neither of them victorious. Sensing his opponent's tenacity and purpose, Lee now moved unerringly to block Grant's circling advance against the flank and rear of the Army of Northern Virginia.

Failure to destroy or stop Grant in the Wilderness marked the beginning of a new phase in Lee's career. He continued to seek favorable opportunity to strike Grant, for Lee had long said that his army would be lost if ever it should be pinned down in the Richmond defenses. But the Wilderness was Lee's last general offensive action; the Army of Northern Virginia no longer had the power to attack. Hoping yet to demoralize the people of the North and place the peace party there in the ascendancy, Lee husbanded his waning strength and sought to exact of Grant the maximum toll in blood and energy. When one lacks the strength to destroy the enemy, says Clausewitz, then one ought, by skillful conservation of his own resources, to seek to exhaust the enemy's will by showing him that the cost of victory far exceeds his anticipation.[25] Lee's strategy was now the strategy of conservation.

For more than a week of fierce but intermittent fighting at Spotsylvania Courthouse (May 8–18), Grant hammered at Lee's line. Unable to break it, Grant moved again. Repeatedly he sideslipped to the left and inched forward in an effort to encircle Lee's flank, force him out of position, and destroy him. Repeatedly Lee anticipated his opponent's move and shifted athwart the flanking column. From Spotsylvania Courthouse to the North Anna River, and from there to Cold Harbor veered the deadly grapple. Earthworks went up at every position. At Cold Harbor (June 3), Grant again drove his battering ram against the Southern line. Reinforced with troops rushed from minor Confederate victories in the Shenandoah Valley and on the James River below Richmond, Lee repulsed the Northern assault with fearful punishment. Voices of censure began to rise against Grant "the butcher" among the civil and military population of the North. After a month of bloodshed such as the American people had never seen, the Army of the Potomac was still farther from Richmond than McClellan had been in the summer of 1862: Lee's gaunt army was still apparently invincible.[26]

Lee used his great talents to the utmost during this month of remorseless combat. His ability to foresee and counteract enemy strategy has become a part of universal military tradition. Carefully fitting together the shards of information collected from the battlefield, from prisoners, and from scouts and spies, Lee supplied the gaps from his own intellect and intuition. Out of the whole he created a true mosaic of enemy intentions. Then he was bold enough to trust his judgment and to act accordingly. Lee must be a great strategist, wrote a Michigan soldier, for everywhere the Northern army goes, it finds the Rebels already there. To friend and foe alike, Lee's skill seemed miraculous.[27]

With remarkable effectiveness, Lee made capital of the advantages inherent in the defense. His tactical employment of interior lines enabled him to move more quickly than did his opponent from one position to another. On a larger scale, he used interior lines to draw reinforcements from the Shenandoah Valley and the Virginia Peninsula; thus he partially offset the unavoidable handicap of fighting with flank and rear exposed to a sea controlled by the enemy. Relying upon the increased firepower of Civil War weapons, and ignoring Jomini's contempt for prepared positions, Lee developed the science of field fortification to a degree that significantly altered modern defensive tactics; he elevated axe and spade to near equality with musket and howitzer.

Lee's choice of position was unimpeachable, his eye for ground unerring. "When his eye swept a countryside it never betrayed him," says Cyril Falls. "From the ground or the map, or both in combination, [Lee] realized how to make the best use of every feature of the country, and the trace of every defensive position from his hand was masterly." Sound position, strengthened by field fortification, enabled Lee at critical moments to flout the tactical rule that one must always keep a reserve in being; he achieved maximum firepower by placing every regiment on the line. "If I shorten my lines to provide a reserve he will turn me," Lee told an observer at Cold Harbor. "If I weaken them to provide a reserve, he will break me." Audacity thus met the summons of necessity.[28]

Students of Lee's conduct in this campaign find it a brilliant lesson in defensive warfare. "[It] is a classical example in military history of how these objects [conserving one's own strength and taxing that of the enemy] ought to be sought," says Sir Frederic Maurice. "In method it was fifty years ahead of the times, and I believe that if the allies in August, 1914, had applied Lee's tactical methods to the situation . . . the course of the World War [I] would have been changed."[29]

Having failed to break Lee at Cold Harbor, Grant on June 12–16 marched around Richmond on the east and struck at Lee's communications by attacking the Petersburg rail junction below Richmond. As Grant half-circled Richmond, Lee warily moved along an inner half circle that kept his army between Grant and the city. This enabled Grant to pass south of the James River and fall with overwhelming force upon the defenders of Petersburg under Beauregard. Grant's move was daring in concept and skillful in execution. For several days Lee lost touch with the Army of the Potomac. But Grant's attack at Petersburg wanted the skill of his march. Beauregard held the Northern army at bay, and on June 18 Lee hastened the Army of Northern Virginia into the Petersburg trenches, where the great siege of the war began.

Lee shrewdly anticipated Grant's move south of the James; before Grant left Cold Harbor, Lee predicted such an attempt. Aware that he could not indefinitely withstand the full weight of Grant's numbers, which would grow with time, Lee sought again to weaken Grant's main body by creating a diversion elsewhere. Should he succeed in this, Lee hoped to be able to strike a telling blow at the force still opposing him. He hoped to repeat the maneuver that had caused a diversion of troops from McClellan's Peninsula army in the summer of 1862. Lee knew that Grant would not be shaken by this ruse. Lee's strategy was aimed above Grant's head; it was aimed at Lincoln himself. On June 13, the day on which Lee learned that Grant's army was no longer before him at Cold Harbor, Lee sent General Jubal Early with thirteen thousand men to threaten Washington from the Shenandoah Valley.

Notwithstanding Lee's foresight, and in spite of General Beauregard's many warnings and pleas for reinforcement, Lee responded slowly to Grant's move away from Cold Harbor. Lee's tardiness has some justification; it was the result of a narrow mission and of his want of information on the whereabouts of Grant's army. Lee's primary mission was to protect the capital, and without accurate knowledge of Grant's location, he thought it hazardous to uncover the direct route to the city. Confederate cavalry was absent, defending the Virginia Central Railroad against a massive Union cavalry raid. Beauregard's cries for help gave Lee no accurate information about the enemy; not until June 17 did Beauregard report that the Army of the Potomac was south of the James. Nevertheless, Lee did permit Grant to make the maneuver to Petersburg without striking him while on the march and vulnerable; and Lee did fail to checkmate the move at Petersburg until almost too late. Beauregard's determined resistance there saved the vital rail junction from capture. One must conclude that Grant was at his best in the passage of the James, while Lee's performance here was below that of the Overland Campaign from the Wilderness to Cold Harbor.[30]

The siege of Petersburg lasted almost nine months. It was so long and costly that it seriously blighted Northern morale and brought to the South a false hope of ultimate success. Sherman was now halted before Atlanta, and the end of the war appeared nowhere in sight. The peace movement in the North was growing. President Lincoln himself believed his reelection to the presidency was unlikely. If his Democratic opponent, General McClellan, should be victorious on a peace platform, said Lincoln, the Union probably could not be restored. Lee now learned that Davis was about to relieve Joseph E. Johnston from command of the Confederate army at Atlanta. Again Lee offered advice on general Confederate strategy. If Davis felt it necessary to remove Johnston, said Lee, then it must be done, but he made clear his own aversion to the decision. "It is a grievous thing to change the commander of an army situated as [the Army of Tennessee is]," he said. He had hoped that Johnston was strong enough to fight for Atlanta, wrote Lee, which was his way of saying that battle ought to be risked in an effort to save the city. If not, he counseled, concentrate all cavalry in the West on Sherman's communications and let the Confederate army fall back upon Augusta. This was probably as wise a move as the Confederacy was capable of making at this time.[31]

Lee's demonstration against Washington failed to break Grant's hold at Petersburg. The response of Union authorities showed that Lee's instinct was sound. As General Early crossed the Potomac and threatened Washington during the first week of July, General Halleck called upon Grant for troops, and on July 10, President Lincoln recommended, though he did not order it, that Grant himself come to the capital with a portion of the Army of the Potomac. But Lee lacked the strength to take advantage of his opponent's dispersals. Ultimately, Grant sent into the Valley enough troops to defeat Early, but Grant kept in the Petersburg entrenchments sufficient men to render an attack there by Lee impossible. Either Lee must hold his lines at Petersburg to the bitter end or he must abandon Richmond altogether.

Doubtless Richmond ought now, at all hazard, to have been given up. Atlanta was lost on September 2; its fall assured Lincoln's reelection to the presidency and doomed the Northern peace movement. Lee could not hope to destroy or seriously cripple Grant's army: Hood's effort to stop Sherman had ended in disaster. Perhaps the only remote chance of Confederate survival was for Lee to break away from Grant and attempt junction with Hood somewhere in the lower South for alternate blows, first against Sherman and then against Grant. That this would have brought deliverance to the stricken Confederacy is, of course, well-nigh inconceivable. It would have meant the immediate loss of the entire East, and Sherman's army could have been promptly reinforced to a strength that would have rendered him secure even against such combined attack. Lee saw the futility of trying to hold Richmond any longer. He had long said that a siege would destroy his army, that it must remain free to maneuver and strike if it were to live in the presence of so powerful a foe. In October, probably after the final defeat of Early in the Shenandoah Valley, Lee told his staff officers that Richmond was a millstone to his army. But the decision to abandon Richmond was not Lee's to make. Only Davis could make it, and Lee's exaggerated deference to the president and commander in chief would not permit him to suggest it as long as the city's defense was the first mission of his army.[32]

Hunger, cold, disease, and heartache over the plight of distant loved ones: These immeasurably assisted Grant's shells during the winter of 1864–65 to break Lee's army in flesh and spirit. Still his troops held grimly to the Petersburg defenses. In early February, under heavy public pressure, the Confederate Congress created the position of general in chief. Though Davis rightly interpreted this as a vote of censure against his leadership, he appointed Lee to the post.

As general in chief, Lee held dubious rank. President Davis had once written to Lee, "I have neither the [constitutional] power nor the will to delegate" to someone else the supreme command. In appointing Grant to command all Union forces, President Lincoln said to him, "The particulars of your plan I neither know nor seek to know. . . . I wish not to obtrude any constraints or restraints upon you." Such a letter as Lincoln's is unimaginable from Davis. When General Joseph E. Johnston heard of Lee's appointment as general in chief, Johnston wrote perceptively, "Do not expect much of Lee in this capacity. He cannot give up the command of the Army of Northern Virginia without becoming merely a minor official." No man could with impunity trespass upon Davis's authority; for Lee to attempt it would have been futile. Through tact and suggestion, Lee accomplished far more with Davis than he could have accomplished in any other way. Lee thus saved his talents, though circumscribed, for the Confederacy. Others, such as Beauregard and Joseph E. Johnston, who sought through sharper methods to influence Davis, wasted their faculties during most of the war in idleness and frustration. As long as Davis was president of the Confederacy he would be commander in chief in fact as in law.[33]

Only by the most drastic means could Lee have made his new authority tell. Only by a passionate appeal, in his own name, to the spirit of the South; only by commandeering railroads and provisions; only by abandoning Richmond, if possible, in order to concentrate against fractions of the enemy—in sum, only by making himself dictator in the manner of ancient Rome could Lee possibly have prolonged the life of the dying Confederacy. Prolonged it for a brief season, that is, for at this stage nothing could have postponed the final outcome for very long. Lee knew what measures were required. He discussed them with his staff and others. Doubtless the Congress and people of the South would have supported him in these moves. But Lee would not take them.

In accepting the appointment as general in chief, Lee made clear that he would continue to operate under Davis's authority. Lee is often censured for this subordination to Davis. Lee's adjutant general admitted that this deference robbed Lee of the qualities of a revolutionary leader.[34] But it is one thing to criticize Lee as a revolutionary and quite another to disparage Lee's generalship. Subordination of the military to the civil authorities is usually deemed a virtue among Americans. George Washington shunned the temptation to grasp the reins of government at dark moments during the War for Independence; nothing in Grant's career indicates that he would have led a coup d'état against President Lincoln if he had thought Lincoln a bungler. Indeed, Grant probably was as submissive to Lincoln as was Lee to Davis. To Grant's admirers, Lee's submissiveness was servility, while Grant's submissiveness was military statesmanship. Modern scholars who condemn Lee for his subordination to Davis look with indignation upon an American general who dared defy his president and commander in chief in a recent war. Lee was too American to play Napoleon.

Nevertheless, rather through suggestion than through command, Lee as general in chief attempted certain broad, coordinated strategic measures. He brought Joseph E. Johnston out of idleness and sent him to North Carolina to oppose Sherman, and he ordered Johnston to collect for this effort all the scattered troops of the Confederacy, except the Army of Northern Virginia. Lee advised the War Department that he must now unite his own force with that of Johnston, though this would forfeit the capital. Hoping to strike a concerted blow against Sherman, then one against Grant, Lee began to prepare supply depots for a march south.[35]

But such a move was impossible through the mud of winter and with horses near starvation. Lee had to wait for the roads to dry and for his livestock to regain strength. He also had to win Davis to the desperate plan. The president blew hot and cold on it: Previously he had hinted that all of the cities of the South might have to be given up in the waging of the war; now, in early March, he approved Lee's strategy of joining forces with Johnston. But Davis never gave unqualified consent to the abandonment of the capital; he never fully prepared himself to leave. On April 1, the day before Lee was driven from the Petersburg line, someone asked Davis whether Richmond would be held. "[Yes,] if we can," replied the indomitable Mississippian.[36]

As commander of the Army of Northern Virginia, Lee strove mightily during these last days just to keep his army alive. Hunger, exposure, demoralization, and constant attack by Grant's well-fed and well-clad army rendered this a burden beyond description. That under these conditions Lee was able to maintain a cohesive fighting force through the winter of 1864–65 is an enduring tribute to his leadership.

As general in chief, Lee devoted his thoughts to disengaging his army from Grant's tentacles and moving south to join Johnston. To combine the armies against Sherman would be a prodigious feat, requiring far more than simply moving the Army of Northern Virginia from Petersburg to North Carolina, though this alone would have taxed grievously the waning resources of the Confederacy. To accomplish the junction, Lee would have to free himself from Grant; then Lee's famished and exhausted troops would have to outmarch Grant's vigorous army. Moreover, since Grant's line enveloped Lee on the south, and the direct route to North Carolina (the Weldon Railroad) was in Grant's control, Lee needed to move farther to escape than did Grant to block the escape. Lee had to march west and then turn south, describing two sides of a triangle, while to intercept this movement, Grant needed only proceed along the third side of the triangle. Lee intended to do all in his power to make the junction, but he rightly sensed that it was well-nigh impossible. Since the coming of winter, quite likely no man or measure could have freed the Army of Northern Virginia from the Army of the Potomac, competently led.

On March 25, Lee made his move to escape and join Johnston. In an effort to force Grant to withdraw his encircling troops from the southern end of the line, Lee attacked Fort Stedman east of Petersburg. Lee planned then to slip away and gain a march on his adversary in the deadly race. Probably no better strategy could have been devised. But the attempt failed; Lee's army was too weak to break Grant's fortified line. Grant countered instantly with a successful thrust at Five Forks on the Southside Railroad (April 1), severing Lee's last line of supply. The next day Lee abandoned Petersburg and marched west for the Danville Railroad, which would carry him roundabout to junction with Johnston's army. Lee gained the railroad at Amelia Courthouse, only to lose a precious day there because his order for rations had gone awry. Before he could move south, Grant blocked the railroad at Burkeville. Lee then pushed west again, hoping somewhere to be able to turn the corner and get south of Grant's army. All was futile. Outpaced and surrounded, Lee ended the terrible drama on April 9 in the surrender of his army.[37] At last Lee's sword was sheathed.

* * *

For nearly a century, most students of the art of war have looked with unqualified admiration upon the generalship of Robert E. Lee. Early Northern historians of the Civil War lavished praise upon him: James Ford Rhodes attributed chiefly to Lee's talents the South's unsurpassed power of resistance; John C. Ropes said of Lee, "No army commander on either side was so universally believed in, so absolutely trusted. Nor was there ever a commander who better deserved the support of his Government and the affection and confidence of his soldiers." General Viscount Wolseley of England believed that Lee was the most skillful of American generals. Colonel G. F. R. Henderson, one of the nineteenth century's most perceptive military analysts, called Lee "one of the greatest, if not the greatest, soldier who ever spoke the English tongue." Sir Frederic Maurice, critic of strategy both ancient and modern, placed Lee among the most illustrious commanders of the ages. After studying the careers of the most renowned generals of the last hundred years, Cyril Falls concludes that Lee is the greatest of them all. "Lee alone in a century of warfare deserves to be ranked with Hannibal and Napoleon," he says. Dennis W. Brogan, keenest of the present European students of American history, says that Lee was the supreme military leader of the Civil War. Grant's solutions were adequate but seldom elegant, he says, whereas Lee's solutions were frequently elegant. The man who is perhaps today's greatest living scholar-warrior and surest connoisseur of military leadership seconds these exalted estimates of Lee. Winston Churchill writes, "Lee was one of the greatest captains known to the annals of war."[38]

Critics arise from time to time to challenge the grounds of Lee's fame. They have found human failings in him, but frequently their complaints against his generalship cancel one another out. Lee was too rash and combative, says one; Lee was excessively slow and cautious, says another. Lee did not take advantage of the South's interior lines, says one; Lee clung to the obsolete concept of interior lines, says another. Lee failed to concentrate the forces of the Confederacy, says one; Lee was preoccupied with the outworn principle of concentration, says another. Lee was a slave to Jomini, says one; Lee violated Jomini's fundamental principle of war, says another. Criticism of Lee thus often ends in a confusion of tongues.

Certainly Lee was mortal: Notwithstanding remarkable accomplishments, his military leadership fell short of the abstract yardstick of perfection. Major criticisms of Lee as a strategist have already been considered in this essay: He was too provincial to see the war as a whole and too conservative to break the fetters of the past. Without laboring all of the minor criticisms of Lee, a few may be scrutinized here.[39]

It has been said that Lee did not see the relationship between strategy and statecraft in modern war. This is true in that Lee deferred excessively to Davis and refused to seize dictatorial authority in a belated effort to save the Confederacy. But on a higher plane, the criticism is not true. Lee's foresight regarding the nature and magnitude of the war; his prescience in urging total mobilization; his prediction that Europe would remain aloof from the war; his adaptation of abstract military theory to the exigencies of Southern politics, economics, and logistics; his strategies aimed as well at President Lincoln's fears as at the weaknesses of opposing generals; his suggestions of peace overtures to encourage the Northern peace movement and split the mind of the enemy; and his advocacy of the employment of Negro troops and their subsequent emancipation—all argue that Lee saw far beyond the battlefield in waging war. Lee seasoned military strategy with a rich wisdom and insight into human affairs that transcended statecraft in its primal sense to become true statesmanship.

Lee is sometimes disparaged for the slack discipline of his command; certainly, by professional standards, or by twentieth-century standards in citizen armies, discipline in the Army of Northern Virginia was easy. Yet one may question whether any other method of managing the army would have accomplished as much. To be of value, discipline must be suited to the character of the men, says Sir Frederic Maurice. "Lee knew well that the discipline of Frederick [the Great's] grenadiers" would destroy his army of highly individualistic Southern planters and farmers. "The object of discipline in an army is to give bodies of men both cohesion and the instinct to suffer all for duty in circumstances of great stress and danger," explains Maurice. Few armies, if any, have ever endured more steadfastly the stress of privation and the danger of combat than did the Army of Northern Virginia.[40]

Lee's most unsparing critic, General J. F. C. Fuller, heaps scorn upon Lee as being a poor provider for his army. But General Fuller offers no promising remedy for the ills of the Confederate quartermaster and commissary. Lee kept every wheel turning and the wires hot with dispatches, he scattered his troops among the fields and flocks of the Southern countryside, often at the expense of combat efficiency, and he sometimes launched invasions of the well-stocked North, all in a ceaseless effort to feed and clothe his men. How, under the circumstances, anyone else in Lee's position could have done better is beyond convincing explanation.

Lee is sometimes taken to task for his extreme combativeness, his lust for battle for its own sake. "It is well that war is so terrible," said Lee while surveying the carnage before his position at Fredericksburg, "else we should grow too fond of it." This trait perhaps unsettled Lee's judgment on the third day of Gettysburg and caused him to attempt the impossible. But the will to fight is a fault easily forgiven in a warrior. Too often the critics believe that wars are won in some manner other than that by which they must be won, says Cyril Falls, which is by fighting. "Happy the army in which an untimely boldness frequently manifests itself," wrote Clausewitz. Lee's "fighting blood" (as Freeman calls it) was one of the qualities that made him formidable. If, on occasion, it betrayed him into unwise combat, on many others it saved him. It helped to make him, in the words of an opponent, "a very thunderbolt in war."

General Fuller believes that Lee failed to stamp his mind upon his military operations. Oddly, if Lee did not stamp his mind upon his own operations, he stamped it powerfully upon the operations of his enemy. "Among the many achievements of this remarkable man [Lee]," writes Bruce Catton, "nothing is more striking than his ability to dominate the minds of the men who were fighting against him." Lee's campaigns were the very product of his mind. One had as well say that the frescoes of the Sistine Chapel want the stamp of Michelangelo's mind as that the operations of the Army of Northern Virginia want the stamp of Lee's mind.[41]

Under the travail of his command, Lee sometimes made unaccountable errors of judgment regarding enemy capabilities outside his own department. His belief that the summer climate of Mississippi would stop Grant at Vicksburg, and his doubt that Sherman could march through the Carolinas, were wide of the mark. But they were offered as mere opinions. Significantly, they did not alter Lee's strategy: Notwithstanding his notions, Lee urged that Joseph E. Johnston concentrate and attack Grant in Mississippi without delay; and later, Lee ordered Johnston to oppose Sherman's drive in North Carolina with every man available to the embattled Confederacy.

Perhaps the chief flaw in Lee's generalship came of his boundless courtesy and humility. These traits heightened his deference to President Davis; sometimes they weakened Lee's supremacy over his army. Lee chose rather to lead through tact and orders of discretion than through iron discipline and positive commands. Freeman believes that at times Lee even permitted himself to be browbeaten by a stubborn subordinate. Yet the critic must be careful in scoring Lee on this count; some of Lee's most spectacular victories were the result of discretionary instructions to resourceful corps commanders. Ideally, Lee ought to have known to give Jackson his head but to keep tight rein on Stuart and Ewell, to stir Gordon with quiet suggestion but to impel Longstreet with sharp command. Here Lee made the mistake of attributing to all of his lieutenants his own great tactical insight and high code of gentlemanly attitude.[42]

Lee's theory of battlefield command did not always measure up to his other qualities of leadership. To fashion strategy and so manage his army as to bring it with maximum efficiency to the point of decision: this, felt Lee, was his primary function. Once the missions were assigned and the battle joined, he sometimes permitted control to drift. He was most guilty of this on the second day of Gettysburg. Here, for a time, says Freeman, the Army of Northern Virginia was virtually without a commander. Lee remedied this mistake during the later campaigns of the war.[43]

In dwelling upon Lee's particular weaknesses and misjudgments, both real and imagined, critics obscure his achievements as a whole. As commander of the Army of Northern Virginia, Lee's sole responsibility throughout most of the war, he earned the acclaim of history. Circumscribed in command, opposing overwhelming numbers, and fighting under every material disadvantage known to the science of war, Lee through his generalship largely sustained the Confederacy in one of the most prodigious military efforts of the modern age. What he could have accomplished as untrammeled general in chief must remain conjecture. His actual accomplishments, all things considered, were second to none in the American military experience. His virtues as a general transcended his faults.

Lee's prime quality, according to Freeman, was intellect; it was "the accurate reasoning of a trained and precise mind" and a "developed aptitude for the difficult synthesis of war." Intellect of the highest order enabled Lee to look into his opponents' minds and read their intentions, doubts, and fears, and then, with maximum efficiency, to capitalize upon this knowledge.[44]

Audacity enhanced intellect to make Lee the general. Boldness is the noblest of military virtues, says Clausewitz, the "true steel which gives the weapon its edge and brilliancy. . . . Boldness, directed by an overruling intelligence, is the stamp of the hero." Audacity enabled Lee repeatedly to seize the initiative from opponents commanding twice his strength; audacity moved him time and again to flout the established rules of warfare in order to strike the foe at the least expected times and places. "We must decide between the positive loss of inactivity and the risk of action," Lee once wrote in a terse but profound exposition of his theory of war. Lee's prowess came largely of a readiness to accept the risk of action.[45]

Character exalted intellect and audacity to make Lee one of the greatest leaders of men the world has known. "Alexander, Hannibal, Caesar . . . and Napoleon [had] the highest faculties of mind," says F. E. Adcock in a study on the outstanding generals of antiquity. "But . . . they possessed character in a still greater degree. To this list," continues Adcock, "I would add . . . Robert E. Lee." Character lights the moral flame of leadership, a quality indefinable and mysterious, one that Clausewitz says can be spoken of only in words vague and rhapsodical. Deep religious conviction united with the chivalric tradition of Virginia aristocracy to endow Lee with remarkable serenity and nobility of nature. "I have met many of the great men of my time," said General Viscount Wolseley, "but Lee alone impressed me with the feeling that I was in the presence of a man who was cast in a grander mould, and made of different and finer metal than all other men. He is stamped upon my memory as a being apart and superior to all others in every way: a man with whom none I ever knew, a very few of whom I have ever read, are worthy to be classed." Lee's sharpest critic eloquently tells the effect of Lee's leadership through character. "Few generals," writes General Fuller, "have been able to animate an army as [Lee's] self-sacrificing idealism animated the Army of Northern Virginia. . . . What this bootless, ragged, half-starved army accomplished is one of the miracles of history."[46]

Times are perilously late for Americans to permit the zeal of nationalism to blind them to excellence, no matter whence it may come. Lee's career teaches certain lessons for the military leadership of today. Jet airplanes, intercontinental missiles, and thermonuclear bombs make the weapons of Lee's era as obsolete as the tomahawk; they bring war to hypertrophy. But if today's "balance of terror" should continue to prevail, and mankind be spared the fiery bolts of extinction, then Lee's strategic and tactical concepts will again prove useful in the employment of conventional military forces. Victory through attrition, which has been the key to American strategy in the Civil War and the two world wars, is no longer possible for this nation; nor can the nation hope to destroy the war strength of its opponents without resort to thermonuclear weapons. It must again learn the skills of swift maneuver and the delivery of paralyzing blows by highly mobile forces upon lines of communication and points of decision. Armies of the future must be composed of semi-independent, self-contained units, says General Matthew Ridgway, units capable of operating over great distances on a fluid battlefield, and with a minimum of control from higher headquarters.[47] These words remind one of Lee's discretionary orders to the virtually independent commanders, Jackson, Stuart, Early, and, at the end, Joseph E. Johnston. In darker extremity, this nation must again learn to wage cunning defensive war for the conservation of weaker resources: war that destroys the enemy's resolve by taxing him beyond his anticipation.

Finally, if the American people must fight again, either with conventional arms or in the holocaust of thermonuclear war, then the nobler qualities of Lee's generalship will offer an even brighter example than his techniques of combat. The intellect to divine and cope with enemy capabilities and intentions; the boldness to strike when the occasion demands, however grave the risk; and, above all, the character to inspire purpose and sacrifice in the midst of supreme stress, hardship, and danger: These will be the imperatives of leadership for national survival. The art and science of war can yet profit from the genius of Lee.

Notes

"The Generalship of Robert E. Lee" was first published in *Grant, Lee, Lincoln and the Radicals: Essays on Civil War Leadership,* ed. Grady McWhiney, 31–71 (Evanston, IL, 1964), and is reprinted with permission of the Northwestern University Press.

1. Carl von Clausewitz, *On War,* 3 vols. (New York, 1940), 1:194–95, 3:170–71.
2. Charles P. Roland, *The Confederacy* (Chicago, 1960), 34–41.
3. J. F. C. Fuller, *Grant and Lee: A Study in Personality and Generalship* (Bloomington, IN, 1957), 262.
4. Cyril Falls, *A Hundred Years of War, 1850–1950* (London, 1953), 18; Archer Jones, *Confederate Strategy from Shiloh to Vicksburg* (Baton Rouge, 1961), 16–32.
5. Fuller, *Grant and Lee,* 39–40; Charles de Gaulle, *The Edge of the Sword* (New York, 1960), 93–94; Frederic Maurice, *Robert E. Lee the Soldier* (Boston, 1925), 76.
6. Douglas Southall Freeman, *R. E. Lee: A Biography,* 4 vols. (New York, 1934–35), 2:6–7.
7. Ibid., 1:621.
8. Lee to Albert Sidney Johnston, Mar. 26, 1862, in Albert Sidney and William Preston Johnston Papers, Mrs. Mason Barret Collection, Manuscripts Division, Howard-Tilton Memorial Library, Tulane University, New Orleans.
9. Freeman, *R. E. Lee,* 2:28.
10. Niccolo Machiavelli, *The Art of War* (Albany, NY, 1815), 233; Freeman, *R. E. Lee,* 2:39–50, 53–57.
11. Freeman, *R. E. Lee,* 2:199.

12. Clausewitz, *On War,* 1:100; Freeman, *R. E. Lee,* 2:302, 256–349.

13. G. F. R. Henderson, *The Science of War* (New York, 1905), 175; R. Ernest Dupuy and Trevor N. Dupuy, *The Compact History of the Civil War* (New York, 1960), 156–57.

14. David Donald, *Lincoln Reconsidered: Essays on the Civil War Era* (New York, 1956), 94; T. Harry Williams, "The Military Leadership of North and South," in *Why the North Won the Civil War,* ed. David Donald (Baton Rouge, 1960), 32; Clausewitz, *On War,* 2:154–55.

15. Clausewitz, *On War,* 1:35, 174.

16. Freeman, *R. E. Lee,* 3:34.

17. Henderson, *The Science of War,* 35.

18. Jones, *Confederate Strategy from Shiloh to Vicksburg,* 211–13; Freeman, *R. E. Lee,* 3:29–161.

19. Williams, "Military Leadership of North and South," 40, 46.

20. E. P. Alexander, *Military Memoirs of a Confederate* (New York, 1908), 364–65.

21. Walter Millis, *Arms and Men: A Study in American Military History* (New York, 1956), 111.

22. Gordon A. Harrison, *Cross Channel Attack* (Washington, DC, 1951), 76; Forrest C. Pogue, *The Supreme Command* (Washington, DC, 1954), 182–83. Both of these volumes are in the United States Army in World War II series, prepared by the Office of the Chief of Military History, Department of the Army.

23. Jones, *Confederate Strategy from Shiloh to Vicksburg,* 24–25.

24. Freeman, *R. E. Lee,* 3:206–7.

25. Clausewitz, *On War,* 1:35.

26. Freeman, *R. E. Lee,* 3:275–391; Bruce Catton, *A Stillness at Appomattox* (New York, 1958), 63–187.

27. Catton, *Stillness at Appomattox,* 152.

28. Falls, *Hundred Years of War,* 59–60; Alfred H. Burne, *Lee, Grant and Sherman: A Study in Leadership in the 1864–65 Campaign* (New York, 1939), 49.

29. Maurice, *Robert E. Lee,* 85.

30. Burne, *Lee, Grant and Sherman,* 55–61; Freeman, *R. E. Lee,* 3:392–425.

31. Freeman, *R. E. Lee,* 3:461–62.

32. Ibid., 441, 496n; Walter H. Taylor, *Four Years with General Lee* (New York, 1878), 145.

33. Jones, *Confederate Strategy from Shiloh to Vicksburg,* 232; Dupuy and Dupuy, *Compact History of the Civil War,* 281; Gilbert E. Govan and James W. Livingood, *A Different Valor: The Story of General Joseph E. Johnston, C.S.A.* (New York, 1956), 343.

34. Taylor, *Four Years with General Lee,* 148.

35. Govan and Livingood, *A Different Valor,* 347.

36. Varina Howell Davis, *Jefferson Davis: A Memoir by His Wife,* 2 vols. (New York, 1890), 2:579.

37. Freeman, *R. E. Lee,* 4:1–143.

38. Burne, *Lee, Grant and Sherman,* 207; John C. Ropes, *The Story of the Civil War,* 4 vols. (New York, 1933), 2:157–58; Garnet J. Wolseley, *General Lee* (Rochester, NY, 1906), 62; Henderson, *The Science of War,* 314; Maurice, *Robert E. Lee,* 293–94; Falls, *Hundred Years of War,* 48; D. W. Brogan, "A Fresh Appraisal of the Civil War," *Harper's Magazine,* Apr. 1960, 136; Winston Churchill, *A History of the English Speaking People,* 4 vols. (New York, 1958), 4:169.

39. The most sweeping criticisms of Lee's generalship are in Fuller, *Grant and Lee.* Other sharp criticisms are in Donald, *Lincoln Reconsidered,* 82–102; and Williams, "Military Leadership of North and South," 23–47.

40. Maurice, *Robert E. Lee,* 162–63.

41. Catton, *Stillness at Appomattox,* 48.

42. Freeman, *R. E. Lee,* 4:168.

43. Ibid., 168–69.

44. Ibid., 170–73.

45. Clausewitz, *On War,* 1:188–91; Freeman, *R. E. Lee,* 4:172.

46. F. E. Adcock, *The Greek and Macedonian Art of War* (Berkeley and Los Angeles, CA, 1957), 83; Clausewitz, *On War,* 1:178–79; Wolseley, *General Lee,* 60–61; Fuller, *Grant and Lee,* 280, 117.

47. Quoted in Millis, *Arms and Men,* 318.

General Robert E. Lee at the end of the Civil War. Library of Congress.

A "Confusion of Tongues": The Ebb and Flow of Robert E. Lee's Reputation since 1964

Brian Holden Reid

I was *almost* a student of T. Harry Williams. I had read (indeed, reviewed in an undergraduate essay) his *Lincoln and His Generals* (1952) and had been left dazzled by his vigorous literary skill and trenchancy of argument. When I contemplated serious research on the Civil War, his name appeared at the top of the list of the American scholars under whom I preferred to work; also, to a young man, Louisiana appeared to be an exotic place to work after the trim Sussex Downs. I received encouragement from and corresponded with the chairman of the department. Alas, it was not to be. The 1976 sterling crisis and subsequent cuts in public expenditure blighted all the transatlantic grants that previously could have been plucked from the trees like cherries. I went to King's College London instead and turned to British history, though I specialized in British military thought, 1914–45, a subject nourished by an umbilical cord stretching from Civil War history, and this choice of research topic facilitated my return to my first love from the late 1980s onward.

During these years, by an extraordinary coincidence, I forged the closest personal and professional links with a number of Williams's former students. At our frequent meetings, their reminiscences of their mentor fertilized my own impressions gained simply by reading his books. He sounded like a great character in a larger-than-life mold: a vibrant personality, a splendid teacher, as well as a shrewd, eloquent, and convincingly authoritative scholar of the Civil War. He was original in the sense of not being swayed by conventional wisdom; he bequeathed an enduring legacy in developing new perspectives on the Civil War, especially in the 1950s. Across the Atlantic I had felt this influence myself. He had challenged my own cozy and rather complacent attitudes about Robert E. Lee. British enthusiasts for Civil War military history tend to absorb the subject worshiping at the altar of the Lost Cause. Williams forced me to think about my hero in new ways. It is in acknowledgment of this enormous debt that I warmly welcomed the invitation to honor Williams in this posthumous *Festschrift* even though I never met him.

Lee's historical reputation had reached its apogee in the 1930s, before Williams undertook his research with the publication of Douglas Southall Freeman's *R. E. Lee* (4 volumes, 1934–35). But the seeds of its later decline had been planted just five years before that study's publication with the appearance of works by two British authors, Major General J. F. C. Fuller and Captain B. H. Liddell Hart. World War II, in various ways, proved to be the catalyst that reinforced the rapid diminution in Lee's overall standing as a modern-minded commander whose techniques and legacy were worthy of study and emulation by the generals of the future.[1]

The works of Kenneth P. Williams, Allan Nevins, and T. Harry Williams were enormously influential in shaping an approach to the war that has been dubbed the "Union" interpretation of the Civil War. This view stressed the importance of organization of resources, the creation of military institutions, and, especially, command structures capable of harnessing those resources in the field. By 1864, Union armies were being directed by commanders with the intellect, vision, and drive to secure victory in what T. Harry Williams always believed to be close to a "total war." Ulysses S. Grant and William T. Sherman were the favored sons of such a reappraisal, not Lee; by comparison, despite a certain flashy brilliance, Lee appeared limited, institutionally backward, provincial, and very old-fashioned.[2]

By the time of the Civil War Centennial in the 1960s, the Union interpretation had entered the mainstream of scholarly historiography. The most important defense of Lee's reputation and achievements was made by Charles P. Roland, initially in an address delivered at a centennial symposium held in 1961 at Northwestern University. Roland considered his participation in this event "the most exciting professional experience of my Tulane career." In rising to its challenges, he laid down the defensive lines for those who sought to resist the later and even more savage blows thrown in Lee's direction.[3]

Roland's defense is cast cleverly as a study of Lee's "generalship," a term already going out of favor in the 1960s with the demise of the view that history consisted of the doings of "great men." Yet Roland moves beyond the narrow confines of individuals' performance, as if they were Olympic athletes or football players. He acknowledges that generalship is just one of a series of components—mostly systemic—that contribute to "all other capabilities for waging war." Roland accepts the importance of the quiet revolution in military history that began in the 1960s, exemplified in the writings of Sir Michael Howard, which saw military events not as singular exertions, the fruits of unique genius—or incompetence, but as the reflection of the social structure of war-making polities. However, Roland insists on one significant point when weighing the balance of factors contributing to success or failure in the Civil War, namely, that Lee labored under severe disadvantages not usually encountered by American generals. He operated against opponents who enjoyed a significant degree of numerical and material superiority. Usually, American generals could be numbered among the "people of plenty." But Roland argues that "for three years Lee would fulfill his mission against the heaviest odds ever faced by an American commander."[4] But Roland does not indicate that Lee's predicament was exaggerated by Lost Cause special pleading.

Roland writes unapologetically of Lee's genius in a period before it became fashionable, after Vietnam and Watergate, to deride all claims to elevated distinction. Another singular feature of Roland's defense is that, writing before the Vietnam imbroglio, he emphasizes that "[Lee] is the only American general who has ever lost a war." The identification of the South as the only region of the United States that had experienced the humiliation of military defeat had a later historiographical impact when, after 1975, the entire country was shaken by the experience.[5]

In his essay Roland deploys a wide range of sources, though not the essential primary source, Clifford Dowdey and Louis H. Manarin's *Wartime Papers of R. E. Lee* (1961), because its publication and the delivery of the lecture occurred in the same year. Roland buttresses it with the works of military theorists, including Machiavelli and Carl von Clausewitz. Many of Lee's greatest champions had been British soldiers. Their works had often been used by American writers as a hedge against other American critics. Roland makes liberal use of the insights of Colonel G. F. R. Henderson, Major General Sir Frederick Maurice, Lieutenant Colonel A. H. Burne, and Captain Cyril Falls. He is notably judicious in countering the arguments of the soldier-historian whom he describes as "that implacable critic of Confederate leadership," Major General J. F. C. Fuller. Curiously, he does not mention Sir Basil Liddell Hart, probably the most famous military writer in the world at the time he was writing.[6]

The essay is so skillfully wrought that Roland anticipates many of the arguments used by later scholars, notably in his strong case for Lee's strategic insight and operational and tactical skill. Roland contends that Lee's strategic views were based on a desire to paralyze the enemy's "will to victory" by striking at Union psychological vulnerabilities, notably in the environs of Washington, D.C. Within this overall structure of a defensive-offensive strategy, Lee's two invasions of the North appear quite "reasonable," Roland argues, as Lee understood "that defeat at home shakes a population more than defeat in a distant land." Yet despite this favorable rendering of Lee's record, Roland does not fail to acknowledge the general's errors, including his belief that Union attempts on Vicksburg could be foiled by summer diseases. Regardless of this mistake, Lee developed a concept of the interdependence of the Eastern and Western Theaters. He was not unduly preoccupied by Virginia. His was "a comprehensive strategy for the Confederacy, however faulty it may have been."

The other strategic element depended on the concentration of force in the field armies, giving up the defense of secondary points when the primary were under attack or needed to switch over to the offensive. Thus Lee advocated for the Confederacy the methods he used in Virginia in 1862–63. He sought the division and fragmentation of Union strength followed by strong stabs at vital targets in the North. Such a strategy relied on commanders making the most of their opportunities. Lee may have enjoyed good luck, but he also made his own luck. His campaigns offered "supreme" instances, Roland argues, "of the manner in which judgment and boldness must supplement available information in shaping strategy." An element of special pleading enters the discussion when Roland attributes the failure of the Maryland Campaign in the autumn of 1862 to "the fates" deserting Lee rather than to his hasty errors.[7]

Some of the overall Confederate fumbling exhibited during the summer of 1863 Roland attributes to the weaknesses of the South's command system. Indeed, he identifies as its "supreme weakness" the lack of any unified command structure. The blame here rested with Davis, who consistently refused to appoint a general in chief until February 1865, when he was forced to appoint Lee. Roland judges that Lee held "dubious rank" because Davis remained the true general in chief. Roland is also critical of "Lee's exaggerated deference to the president" and feels that he should have imposed a dictatorship. But "Lee was too American to play at Napoleon." This comment has the feel of the posturing of 1960s escapism; in more sensible passages, Roland alludes to Lee's quiet measures, tact, and sober direction, an interpretation that has left a more enduring legacy.[8]

Roland completes his defense of Lee's generalship by paying tribute to his defensive skill, notably his tremendous eye for country. Lee chose and fortified positions of such strength that they compensated for his numerical inferiority and Union command of the sea. Of course, no commander's record sheet can be perfect. In the Virginia Campaign of 1864, Roland judges, Lee's performance during Grant's crossing of the James River in June was "below" that he exhibited from the Battle of the Wilderness to Cold Harbor.

He does not refer to the advantage Grant enjoyed in freeing himself from the burdens of army command. But Roland concludes by suggesting that Lee's role in sustaining the Confederacy virtually single-handedly after May 1864 was "one of the most prodigious military efforts of the modern age." Within a decade even this achievement would be assailed because of the human cost of prolonging the Civil War.[9]

In surveying the criticisms of Lee's generalship that were made before 1964, Roland remarks on their contradictory nature and the "confusion of tongues" that resulted. This confusion was never more marked than in the decade or so after the publication of Roland's seminal essay.[10]

The outpouring of Civil War books that occurred during the centennial did not materially alter the parameters of the discussion about Lee. The appearance at its conclusion of Clifford Dowdey's *Lee: A Biography* confirmed just how little modification had occurred in the proportions of his reputation among Southerners since the appearance of Freeman's biography. Dowdey's book served as the standard single volume "life" for some thirty years. It exhibits impeccable Lost Cause credentials, and though Dowdey intended the book to be "a fresh interpretation," it remains loyal to the interpretative tradition established by Freeman.

Clifford Shirley Dowdey Jr. (1904–1979) was a professional writer with a wide following. Born in Richmond, Virginia, his mother could trace her roots back to the Jamestown settlers, and four of his great uncles had fought as Confederate soldiers. He imbibed Lost Cause sympathies from his grandmother, who lived with his parents until her death, when Dowdey was nineteen. In 1925, he graduated from Columbia University and returned to Richmond to work for a year under Freeman's tutelage on the *Richmond News-Leader*, before returning to New York for the next decade to write for and edit various pulp magazines. In 1937, he published his first novel, *Bugles Blow No More,* which profited from an insatiable appetite for Confederate fiction after the success of *Gone with the Wind* (1938). It, too, became a best-seller and rendered him financially independent. Awarded a Guggenheim fellowship in 1938, he enjoyed a brief sojourn as a Hollywood scriptwriter. Gregarious and affable, Dowdey enjoyed the party circuit. "We wrote until noon," he recalled, and "then the parties began." But Dowdey felt the urge to apply himself more seriously and returned to Richmond. In all, he wrote nine novels, the last appearing in 1962. His fiction and historical works cross-fertilized one another. He produced ten works of history, including collaboration on the substantial edition of Lee's wartime correspondence noted above.[11]

Dowdey revealed considerable gifts as a historian, notably in working diligently at selecting, marshaling, and presenting his material. His true talent lay in description, enjoying a powerful narrative flow into which he would introduce serious arguments; he was no mere chronicler. His views were based on a thorough, impressive knowledge of the ground over which Lee fought. His style is never less than elegantly shaped, garnished with skillfully evoked atmospheres, both on and off the battlefield, and accompanied by finely etched character sketches that depict without hesitation the pettiness stemming from the clash of personalities. His battlefield accounts have been justly praised for their assurance and clarity. All of these skills are revealed in his biography of Lee, and the drama, excitement, and energy of Lee's career is summoned up with elegance and authority in one of his longest and most enduring books.

Dowdey's faults are as striking as his merits. As one of a group of professional writers who came to dominate popular history in the years of postwar prosperity, Dowdey exhibits jagged prejudices. He made no attempt to judge his material objectively, and his unabashed admiration for Lee appears in retrospect on a par with Freeman's "just this side of idolatry," to use Dowdey's own description. His portrait hardly differs from Freeman's essential outline; he embellished it with supporting detail. The familiar bugbears of the Lost Cause canon, James Longstreet especially, receive no more sympathetic treatment from Dowdey. Finally, his books lacked scholarly apparatus; his disdain for footnotes resembled Liddell Hart's. It is thus difficult to verify his sources on certain controversial points, and thus to evaluate his persuasiveness, which must be taken on trust. For Dowdey had no doubts; his account represented not a debate but the unvarnished truth. Bruce Catton, with whom Dowdey is sometimes compared, claimed shrewdly that Dowdey's vantage point resembles that "of the Unreconstructed Rebel."[12]

Dowdey judged Lee "the greatest soldier ever produced on the continent," but he sought to place him "in the context of the total history of the Republic," thus revealing his "eternal relevance." But his understanding of the latter remains firmly rooted in the 1930s and took no account of the extraordinary shift in the scholarly approach to slavery and Reconstruction that had occurred during the 1950s. A pessimistic Dowdey reflected bitterly on "the concept" held by vindictive Radical Republicans after 1865 "of the obliteration of a minority, or diverse society within the nation." His perspective has broader significance not only for his assessment of Lee's character but also on *how* he interprets Lee's generalship, and the issues which depended on its successful outcome. Dowdey's biography also reflected another feature of the pre-1941 "revisionist" outlook, one that would have a later resonance. "Americans have lost their illusions about war as a political resolution," he opined on the eve of large-scale military intervention in Vietnam, "and no longer believe a permanent pattern of good will result from mass killings and destruction, spreading ruin and misery." Dowdey had little faith in the utility of war.[13]

Surmounting these clouds of disenchantment and shattered hopes is the majestic image of Lee "as the single most perfected product" of "this Old America." In detail Dowdey's Lost Cause values are not our concern, but they do enjoy a direct connection with his discussion of Lee's generalship. Lee's earlier biographers, culminating in Freeman's great work, rely on an understanding of his Olympian personality as a means of validating the Confederate cause and simultaneously confirming Lee's military genius. General Fuller began the process of inverting this connection, that is, using Lee's personality as a tool to criticize his conduct in the field, but in the 1930s this technique had little influence. Dowdey restated the traditional view of Lee's "completeness" based on the opinions of some of his contemporaries, but later writers metamorphosed it "as a monumental design of moral concepts." On this grand but simply fashioned edifice rested ideas about Lee's military greatness.[14]

Dowdey's views were thus far from novel. He discussed Lee's preference for concentration at points of strategic significance to the Confederacy, but he also stressed the extent to which Lee's efforts to concentrate force were frittered away by a military system that found it difficult to allocate military priorities and stick to them. Lee gradually evolved what Dowdey termed a "cause and effect" strategy, involving catching the enemy's attention in a subsidiary theater in order to make progress in one of primary importance. Always he wanted to "engage the enemy as far from the capital as possible." He never deployed, as Joseph E. Johnston did, "for a purely defensive stand that could exert no effect on the enemy's arrangements." Lee's grasp of operational and strategic concepts were the fruit of an instinctive understanding of the defensive-offensive. Dowdey averred that "an aggressive initiative under some conditions gave the aggressor control of the enemy's mind." Lee was more preoccupied with "what *he* was going to do to upset the enemy" rather than with what disasters the enemy could inflict on him. Such self-confidence permitted Lee to impart "a boldness that had not appeared before in Confederate strategy."[15]

Dowdey's account of Lee's operational and tactical execution of these concepts resembles Freeman's not least in his discussion of Lee's clairvoyance in discerning his opponents' plans. He considers Lee's talent as "a deductive process whose results came to be called *genius* . . . the tireless evaluation of each detail." He could predict Grant's plans "as if he had read the battle orders." Lee sought to disrupt the enemy's schemes before they had evolved and thus reduce the benefit of numerical and material preponderance. Dowdey admits occasional errors, but he conceals them in the undergrowth of tactical detail. He certainly acquits Lee of any error in June 1864 during Grant's crossing of the James.[16]

The discussion of a more serious misreading of character by Lee, namely, James Longstreet's, follows a firm Virginian pattern. Longstreet's sense of "self-importance" dated from Second Manassas, when Longstreet counseled against an immediate attack on Major General John Pope's Union Army of Virginia. Longstreet concluded erroneously that he had established an ascendancy over Lee. This illusion was felt most disastrously at Gettysburg, when Longstreet's belated discovery that he lacked a favored position led to lethargy, surliness, and a failure to launch the concentrated, decisive blows that Lee's plans demanded on both July 2 and 3, 1863. Dowdey does not single out Longstreet as a scapegoat, but he does ask why Lee entrusted Longstreet with the conduct of these operations in the first place. But he does not ask whether the polemical debate built on this relationship was superfluous; nor does he censor Lee for entertaining, by his account, doubts about the hazardous enterprise on which he had embarked.[17]

Dowdey's biography thus devotes a lot of space to Lee's opportunism. From the Seven Days onward, Lee worked "within a master plan," but he simultaneously "worked at the details, one day at a time." Thanks to this combination, Lee succeeded in frustrating the purposes of a whole series of Federal generals. An important figure in this success was "his great collaborator," Stonewall Jackson, who "made possible the army's most brilliant maneuvers." After Jackson's death in May 1863, Lee assumed a larger tactical role (another theme anticipated by Freeman), especially during the Overland Campaign. The losses inflicted on Grant, equal to Lee's own strength when the campaign started, lay at the core of "Lee's achievement . . . his greatest achievement as a soldier." But his operational and tactical skills could not solve the strategic conundrum faced by the Confederacy. By July 1864, he had returned to the point where he started, "a static defense which doomed them by arithmetic."[18]

In Dowdey's opinion the person most responsible for the Southern defeat was Davis. He stressed the lost opportunities of the first year of the war before Lee took up command. Dowdey agreed with Roland that in March 1862 Lee did not wield the authority of a true general in chief. In marshaling his evidence, Dowdey makes a case against Davis that is very much his own and he does not mince his words. He judges Davis a neurotic obsessed with exerting rigid control over all decisions and the machinery that made them. But in important ways he refused to make use of the power at his disposal; he would plunge into detail, a protective cloak "against the threat of the unexpected that would be outside his control." Hence his addiction to charts indicating the military forces allotted to each of the Confederacy's departments. Not even Lee's skill could overcome Davis's obsession with maintaining his departmental boundaries inviolate. Lee thus failed to "intrude the dismal facts" into Davis's "fantasy world"—a judgment that occasionally offers reminders of Hitler's land of dreams in 1944–45. Dowdey attributes this failure to Lee's ingrained respect for constitutional authority but does not suggest that he should have tried to overturn it.[19]

Dowdey's biography combines a highly critical treatment of Davis with a slighting verdict on Grant's generalship all too characteristic of Lost Cause writers: "a nonmaneuvering direct hitter" who only won because of the enormous resources at his command. By such a sleight of hand, Dowdey avoids discussion of Lee's responsibility for Confederate defeat.[20]

At the end of the 1960s, a new school quickly came to the fore that made far fewer discreet criticisms of what it believed to be Lee's deficiencies as a strategist. A hint of this school's leading arguments had been offered in Archer Jones's 1961 account of Confederate strategy. Jones would take his place in the ranks, but the school's captain was Thomas L. Connelly (1938–1991). Connelly, like Roland, hailed from Tennessee, a native of Nashville. He had a conventional academic career, taking his postgraduate degrees at Rice University, where Frank E. Vandiver served as his dissertation adviser. Connelly taught at Mississippi State University before moving to the University of South Carolina, where, in 1971, he was promoted to professor. His academic reputation had been won with the publication of a two-volume history of the Army of Tennessee, *Army of the Heartland* (1967) and *Autumn of Glory* (1971), a splendid if censorious work from which no commander emerges with credit. Connelly cleverly employs the comparatively neglected state of Confederate history west of the Appalachians to lever his way into Lee historiography. His debut in *Civil War History*, an article on "Robert E. Lee and the Western Confederacy," stirred up a furor, perhaps not on the same scale as the 1913 Paris riots that followed the first performance of Stravinsky's *Rite of Spring*, but provoking probably more controversy than any other article published in that journal; a year later it published a fierce rebuttal by Albert Castel.[21]

The long-running controversy that Connelly ignited began the first wave of what might be termed the deconstruction of Roland's assessment of Lee. Connelly's article was reprinted unrevised, except for a new introduction and concluding paragraphs, in a substantial work, *The Politics of Command*, published four years later with Archer Jones.[22] As Connelly made no attempt to modify his views in light of criticism, it seems best to explore them within the context of this larger work. In their preface, Connelly and Jones deplore the degree to which Lee shaped Confederate strategy; of course, Jones bears the responsibility of joint authorship, but the style and tone of these remarks reveals Connelly's hand. They repeat the claim that Lee exhibited an "obsession" with affairs in Virginia. Further, they suggest Lee "succeeded in drawing Richmond's attention more often to the Virginia front" and thus achieved a "special status" for his army. A less polemical point of enduring value is the admission that Lee operated as a "theatre strategist," but the measures he employed, Connelly and Jones maintain, resulted from "an application of Napoleon and Jomini's principles."[23]

Discussion of the influence of the Swiss theorist Baron Jomini (1779–1869) on Civil War military operations had entered the debate in the 1950s. Indeed, T. Harry Williams later used his supposed influence as supporting evidence for his claim that Lee "was a product of a conservative culture, a culture that looked backward instead of forward." Williams and David Donald argue that Jomini advocated a "limited" form of warfare, preferred geometric solutions to military problems, and appeared preoccupied with the operational and tactical dimensions of warfare. Grant and Sherman, by comparison, grasped its vital social and political dimensions and seemed more akin to followers of Jomini's German contemporary, Clausewitz. The continual linkage of Jomini and the Confederacy damaged Jomini's reputation as a thinker, and such claims were rarely based on a deep knowledge of his writings. Connelly and Jones attempted a systematic survey based on his original works.[24]

Their explication is disappointing, though, with a diffuse opening chapter that is not always easy to follow. Connelly and Jones explore Napoleon's methods and Jomini's interpretation of them via the concepts of interior lines and central position in the *Précis de l'art de la guerre* (1838). On balance, Connelly and Jones make no further progress in illuminating the intractable relationship between military theory and practice than Williams; indeed, in some ways their approach is inferior. They merely assume that Jomini was read, and if it was read it *must* have been influential. "It thus seems likely," they speculate, "that Civil War generals whose basic military ideas were formed before the 1850s derived what Jominian instruction that they received from the *Traité*, either directly or through their instructors." As the United States lacked a staff college, then these instructors had to be found at the U.S. Military Academy at West Point, as "the influences within their own army must have been influential," and the teaching of Dennis Hart Mahan, in particular.

Yet such speculation begs an important question. Officer cadets often in their teens are not prepared mentally for such teaching, the content of which is, after all, often forgotten by maturity. The *Traité* in any case is a multivolume historical work, and the number of cadets who read it all was very small. In an unexplained, confusing conclusion, Connelly and Jones underline the influence of the Archduke Charles (who had worsted Napoleon at Aspern-Essling before going down to defeat at Wagram in 1809) on the leading intellects of the antebellum U.S. Army, Henry W. Halleck and P. G. T. Beauregard, neither of whom Connelly and Jones regarded as Jominian. These qualifications hardly inspire confidence in the book's broader thesis.

For Lee evinced only a slight acquaintance with Jomini's writings.[25] But such a shaky edifice did not discourage Connelly from claiming that nothing "better exemplifies the application of Napoleonic and Jominian concepts than Confederate operations on the Virginia front in 1861 and 1862." He concedes that "it is uncertain" whether the various commanders had any knowledge of these concepts, and he fails to establish whether Lee spent much time reading Jomini. He read biographies of Napoleon, but Napoleon was not Lee's hero; that palm belonged to George Washington. Lee's reading could just as equally have been designed to satisfy straightforward historical curiosity rather than any bid for professional instruction. But a presumed association with Napoleon allows Connelly to advance another argument that redounds to Lee's discredit, namely, that Lee's "frequent offensive thrusts and his almost invariable assumption of the offensive in battle suggest that he believed a stalemate could be avoided by the annihilation of the enemy's army." Connelly then completes this link of miscalculation with a characteristic speculation: "If Lee was pursuing the strategy of annihilation, he was disappointed."[26]

This latter assumption underwrites the remainder of the second chapter, which is devoted to Lee. At least the rather emotional flavor of the original 1969 article is pruned away, with indirect asides on Charles Roland's Tennessee roots but praise of Lee and references to the "colonial status" of Confederate western history. Forty years later the scholar cannot but be repelled by this polemical, shallow, and insular tone: the implication that a historian from Tennessee should support the West against the pretensions of the East.

Connelly's most striking argument was that "Lee actually supplied little general strategic guidance for the South." He had no grand strategy because he did not operate at this level "or else chose to remain silent on the subject." Yet whether or not he remained silent, Connelly nevertheless identifies "several factors" that "predominated his thinking." Connelly suggests that Lee concluded that the "prime Federal objectives" were the Mississippi basin and Richmond, but he failed to appreciate the disparity of resources between the theaters. Indeed, he made it worse. "Lee's interest in the West seemed limited to what the region could do to help Virginia." His overall perspective, Connelly argues, is determined by an ignorance of geography west of the Alleghenies; he failed to grasp the importance of munition supply areas in Georgia and Alabama.[27]

Within nine pages of arguing that Lee provided no grand strategic views, Connelly transforms Lee's opinions, mostly errors, into "Lee's strategic policies," and his discussion of these is sustained by a great deal of speculation.[28] Another inconsistency relates to Lee's place within the Confederate command system. Connelly rejects the arguments of Roland and Dowdey that Lee lacked any authority in this sphere.[29] Connelly contends that Lee enjoyed "a position of power." Yet in the absence of a dedicated Confederate general staff, Connelly could not sustain his conflation of power and influence because his focus had to be on personalities, not systems. No historian disputes that Lee had views, influence, and a voice; the point at issue is his ability to carry these out and his capacity to impose them on fellow commanders of comparable rank. In both cases influence was not enough. Furthermore, Connelly overlooks Davis's responsibility for these systemic weaknesses; grand strategy was ultimately the president's responsibility, not that of his advisers. Connelly cannot have it both ways: Lee either had a strategy or he did not; either he expressed his views or he did not. According to Connelly, he did both. But when he discusses the possibility that Lee sought to extend to the Confederacy the techniques he employed in Virginia, Connelly simply denies the practicability of his measures. He makes insinuations concerning the dominance in the Army of Northern Virginia of Virginian officers, including Lee's son and nephew.[30] Later research reveals clear reasons for this domination, including the relative efficiency of the Virginia militia and the greater proportion of officers and noncommissioned officers with a modicum of experience.[31] Connelly argues that Lee exercised only army command and that he entertained a "proprietary feeling" for his army, as most successful commanders tend to do. His point that Lee was as provincial as every other Confederate commander is really an indictment of the overall structure within which he had to work. Yet he does not provide clinching evidence that Lee's views were wrong.[32]

Connelly bequeathed one final argument that stresses the human cost of Lee's campaigns. The indictment here was vague but telling. According to Connelly, Lee "lost" more men in the Seven Days' Battles than Bragg did in the entire Kentucky Campaign; by September 1862, Lee had "lost" almost fifty thousand troops, a number that exceeded the field strength of the Army of Tennessee. Albert Castel challenged the veracity of the comparisons, but his objections did not blunt their impact, as the toll in the Vietnam War mounted in 1968–69. When the Confederacy should have assumed a "strategic defensive posture," Connelly concluded, "Lee's losses seem excessive." Elsewhere, the internal evidence of *Politics of Command* appears to justify Lee's zeal to concentrate Confederate forces. Of the 174,233 troops who surrendered by May 1865, only 59,048 could be found in the two key field armies.[33]

These arguments contain little new content; General Fuller had said it all before Connelly was born. Even Jones's convincing discussion of the departmental system as a strategic end in itself served to confirm Dowdey's view on the matter. But Fuller had only hinted at the distorting effect of Lost Cause literature, and Dowdey was part of it. Connelly's analysis of the Lost Cause provides his most enduring contribution to Lee scholarship. The greater part of his full-length study, *The Marble Man,* is first-rate intellectual history that charts the changing phases of Lee's image and reputation, assessing the motives of the soldiers, writers, clerics, and politicians who molded it. After this book's appearance, the subject could never be looked at in the same way again. But Connelly could not be content with this achievement. He felt compelled to press home his controversial arguments, and here his success has been short lived. Two valuable points, however, emerge from a reading of *The Marble Man.* The first is the importance of Stonewall Jackson as the South's premier hero until his death in May 1863.[34] The second is Connelly's treatment of Lee's personality "as a human being," which dwells on his complexity and contradictions as well as his moods, sense of failure, lack of fulfillment, and tendency toward depression. He also devotes space to the heavy demands that Lee made, not just on himself and subordinates but also on his family. Reiterations of the previous sanctification could never hope to convince, as Connelly presents a psychological portrait more amenable to modern taste.

In the round, such a clarification comes at a heavy price: a surge of narrow denigration and a highly polemical assessment of Lee's command. Connelly drew a direct connection between images of Lee's personality and images of his military career. These were placed in apposition to "reality"; hence the "need to re-examine . . . his image as a brilliant war strategist and overall war leader." Connelly argues that such an "image" only dated from Reconstruction. Consequently, he challenges Lee's claims to rank among the world's greatest generals and suggests instead that Lee has been "fashioned into what people have wished him to become, and consequently has become something that never was."[35]

Castel's rebuttal placed Connelly's criticisms in three categories: "unfounded, excessive or pointless." His arguments resemble mine in several ways. But his plain statement of military truths seems to have gone unheeded. Lee won in so many battles, Castel reminds us, because he attacked. The generals in the West were feeble at best, often incompetent. He asks for proof that a massive concentration in the West placed in such uncertain hands would have brought victory. Connelly does not provide it. So much of Connelly's Southern wish fulfillment rests on gaps in the documentary record into which he can insert special pleading rather than rely on what is actually there.

How can we know that Lee would not have been able to extend to the entire Confederacy his successful formula? He did not serve in the West and served all too briefly as commanding general. Certainly, Connelly fails to make an effective case that Lee sabotaged chances of a Confederate victory by diverting significant resources to Virginia. Connelly attempts to downplay the importance of the transfer of Longstreet's First Corps in the opposite direction, which Lee did not prevent or obstruct. Connelly fails to master his polemical passions and cannot avoid giving the impression that he is manipulating the evidence to support his prejudices. His entire approach represents the shrill cry of non-Virginian protest at the Old Dominion's appropriation of Confederate history. In a revealing aside, he considers that Virginian writers offer "interesting case studies in psychological motivation in historiography," and so does he.[36]

Connelly's prejudices appear as naked and crude as the "Virginia school" he criticizes so enthusiastically. Yet despite his limitations, his view rather than Castel's prevailed. Russell F. Weigley, in his important survey of American strategy and military policy, agrees with Connelly's assessment of Lee's parochialism. He titled his chapter on Lee "Napoleonic Strategy."[37] The reasons behind the appeal of Connelly's argument need to be assessed, as he inspired a host of imitators. The central reason was the continued dominance of the Union interpretation, the outlines for which Connelly provides ample justification. But the long-term appeal of his interpretation lay far distant from the undulating green vistas of Gettysburg, in the reaction to another defeat in the steamy jungles of Southeast Asia.

The full cost of the Vietnam War had made itself felt at the time Connelly was writing his initial essay on Lee. Combined fatalities in 1968–69 numbered 28,208, about half the war's total of 58,193; by 1973, they had fallen back to 168. An even greater influence over the next thirty years would be reflection on the defeat that became metamorphosed in American popular culture as the Vietnam Syndrome. Within a decade of the term's first appearance in 1972, a cluster of attitudes came to be associated with it. These came to influence military explanations of Civil War operations and the generals who directed them. The essential message of the syndrome stresses the fragility of public opinion, which would not tolerate heavy casualties in protracted operations and thus provided a new standard by which to judge both in 1861–65. American policy makers were fearful of "risk" in military operations, and they revealed a strong defensive outlook throughout the 1980s that percolated down to the "self-protection" of soldiers on the front line. Pessimistic views were expressed of the potential of military power to achieve set goals, and commanders seemed fearful of losing a single soldier.[38]

All of these attitudes are the reverse of the military qualities frequently singled out for praise in Lee's military record. Earlier scholarship supported some aspects of the later defensive outlook. The idea that the South had failed to develop a workable defensive strategy had been firmly established by

1970. Lee had been blamed for this, too, and by the 1980s his technique of seeking a decisive battle was judged unattainable and self-defeating because of the heavy casualties it entailed—mainly the result of ignoring advances in weapons technology that lent greater weight to the defensive. Hence the attraction of Connelly's striking conundrum at the end of his much criticized article as to "whether the South may not have fared better had it possessed no Robert E. Lee." Appeals on the grounds of Lee's military genius cut no ice either. The Seven Days' Battles might have prolonged the life of the Confederacy by almost three years, but the death and suffering this entailed could be construed, to put it mildly, as a mixed blessing for the South. The object of war had changed in the eyes of historians. It was no longer the defeat of the enemy but the saving of human life.[39]

Furthermore, the debate over the lessening utility of battle in the Civil War came to be reviewed through a Southern prism. Historians came to ask why the South lost. Why did the Confederacy fail to gain its independence? They did not ask why the North won. In short, the two prominent defeats in American history came to feed off one another, and this development had serious implications for Lee's reputation. Grady McWhiney and Perry D. Jamieson filled out the tactical background by arguing that the Confederacy had bled itself to death "by making more costly attacks more often than did the Federals." They assumed that the defensive is *always* inherently more economical than the offensive.[40]

The defensive question lay at the heart of the analysis. The operational problem could be solved by focusing on logistics, organization, and sustainability to get armies moving again. Edward Hagerman attempts to relate this question to later developments in *The American Civil War and the Origins of Modern Warfare* (1988). Lee emerges well from his judicious and meticulous study. Hagerman demonstrates that Lee's casualties were not as prodigious as Connelly implies. His operations in Virginia were part of "the strategy he had devised with Davis and [Joseph E.] Johnston to clear the Union army out of Confederate logistical territory on the East Coast." Hagerman is critical of Lee's attitude to his staff and argued that his staff procedures were too personalized and too easily eroded if casualty rates were high among middle-ranking officers.

Still, he is full of praise for Lee's efforts to grapple with the need to increase mobility. He argues that Lee anticipated William T. Sherman in his willingness to disperse his army while creating logistical structures that allowed his army to take supplies while on the move. He also centralized the command structure with three corps in 1862–63 (if the cavalry are included), four by June 1863. "That he achieved what he did toward his military objective of keeping the Union out of Virginia was a tribute to his logistical daring and insight," Hagerman notes. Nevertheless, Lee issued a warning that could not be ignored. Without an overhaul of the Confederacy's creaking war-making machinery, which strained the logistical system "beyond its limits," even if he achieved his objectives, "this type of strategy . . . would destroy that army."[41]

Hagerman's book did not gain the attention it deserved because it was overshadowed by two more scintillating books, both published before his, which had a greater impact on historiography. *How the North Won* (1983) by Herman Hattaway and Archer Jones and *Why the South Lost the Civil War* (1986) by the same two authors plus Richard E. Beringer and William N. Still Jr. held pride of place. Both profit from the post-1980 renaissance in American military thought and, on the whole, exhibit a better understanding of military ideas, especially those enshrined in Clausewitz's *On War*. The latter had appeared in 1976 in an authoritative, readable translation, which did much to illuminate an understanding of strategy and operational art.[42]

Curiously, a belated interest in operational art had little influence on Hattaway and Jones, who subscribed to a thesis that almost wrote out the significance of battle. The "relative insignificance of battle," they agree, "is simply another way of perceiving the primacy of the defense"; and throughout these books, they stress "the mid-nineteenth century army's virtual invulnerability to destruction in the open field." Such invulnerability, well represented by Lee's operations in Virginia, forced U. S. Grant in 1864 to resort to a "strategy of raids" in order to achieve his objectives by incremental attrition. Confederate collapse came on the home front, with disillusionment, feebleness, and pessimism, the consequence of a failure to evolve a coherent sense of Confederate nationhood. Southern moral failure rather than Northern resolve accounts for the war's outcome, not direct military action (even the naval blockade failed).[43]

Lee emerges from these two works as a technically skilled general, operationally more proficient than Grant, who compares well with the greatest masters in the art of war but was ultimately frustrated because of the limitations within which he worked. Other serious historians offered equally positive appraisals. For instance, Richard M. McMurry offered a ringing verdict: "[Lee] stands as a colossus of Confederate military history—the only southern commander to enjoy any degree of success."[44] But the detonation of Connelly's land mine continued to fracture Lee's reputation. From the mid-1980s a number of buffs (that is, members of other professions who studied the Civil War as a hobby) offered their own conclusions in print. Such books were not based on new source material and were often derivative. They imitated Connelly's methods without developing them in any significant way. Nonetheless, their ideas represent an important second wave in the deconstruction of Roland's view of Lee's generalship. A prominent member of their vanguard is Alan T. Nolan (1923–2008).[45]

Nolan was born in Evansville, Illinois, the son of a U.S. district attorney. He graduated from Indiana University and the Harvard Law School. In 1948 he returned to Indianapolis and practiced law for forty-five years, including a stint of seven years as chairman of the Disciplinary Committee of the Indiana Supreme Court. He had longstanding historical interests and published in 1961 his first Civil War book, a study of the Iron Brigade. He served as chairman of the Indiana Historical Society for twelve years. Nolan's prime targets were the myths sustaining the Lost Cause, with Lee as its paramount monument. His writings on Lee stirred outrage; one furious retired U.S. general entreated readers of *Civil War News* not to buy Nolan's book on Lee or to burn it if they had already purchased it. Neo-Confederates viewed him with the same horror with which they viewed the Antichrist.[46]

The offending work, Nolan's *Lee Considered* (1991), offers a measure of the depth to which Lee's popular reputation had sunk by the end of the twentieth century. Nolan dismisses the "excessive adulation" with which he had been regarded "as not the stuff of history." He sought to examine his motives and actions critically so as to "understand him rather than diminish him. . . . The historical process is not, after all, a neutral process." But Connelly had expressed similar objectives, and the end product does not appear very dispassionate in retrospect. The same stricture applies with even more force to Nolan. He made the same investment in his point of view as Dowdey had made in his; this return to sectional perspectives actually served to stimulate rather than dissipate neo-Confederate sympathy.[47]

Nolan borrowed from Connelly the technique of undermining confidence in Lee's military decisions by mounting a criticism of his personality laced with innuendo. He claims that Lee acted during the secession crisis craftily and dishonestly in resigning from the U.S. service and then transferring his loyalties to the Virginia service. Nolan calls it a "program," that is, "an arrangement that has been made and assented to by parties in advance." He also employs guilt by association, linking "Lee and the secessionists" as if he was one of their number when he was not. He admits that he has no new documentary evidence to support these charges and dismisses Lee's honor code as self-deluding. Honor, he snaps, "became Lee's word for what he wanted to do and what he had in fact done." This is hardly a charitable verdict: "Lee was honorable because he said so." Likewise Lee's reputation for magnanimity after 1865 gets short shrift. There is considerable truth in his view that Lee expressed very typical Southern sentiments on the causes of the war, blacks, and Reconstruction, but Nolan did not aid their acceptance by his reckless and indiscriminating form of argument.[48]

Nolan's sweeping arguments suit his polemical purpose but also raise doubts in the reader's mind about Lee's judgment and, by extension, the value of the cause he served. Nolan accepts that Lee's performance as a field commander was successful, often brilliantly so, though in practice his writing hardly ever sustains this judgment.[49] He distinguishes between grand and military strategy (what he calls "operational strategy") then proceeds to make a more tenuous distinction "between the true grand strategy" of both sides "and the[ir] *official* grand strategy"—in his opinion. He then relates grand strategy to the issue of whether the Army of Northern Virginia made "the maximum contribution towards the South's chances of winning the war." Nolan expresses no interest in pursuing the now-familiar theme of Lee's parochialism; his grand strategic interest thus gives the debate a new twist.[50]

The dimension that really seizes his attention is the claim that the Confederacy needed to defend to survive. He rests his forceful restatement of an old argument on two points. First, the North faced a major logistical challenge to the advance of large armies over even larger distances, and second, a successful defense could rest on what he termed "the rifled gun," presumably the rifled musket. He gives little attention to the influence of public opinion or morale. He thus does not offer answers to two further questions: What if Southern opinion demanded that Confederate armies attack, and what if Southern opinion lacked the resilience to "outlast" the North?[51]

As to the allocation of duties and responsibility for strategic direction, Nolan admits that Confederate grand strategy had never been defined. He is correct, and this state of muddle has been confirmed by recent research, though it does not blame Lee for it—on the contrary.[52] But the responsibility for a grand strategy lay with Davis and his Cabinet, and Davis consistently refused to appoint a general in chief. But Nolan is not interested in Davis, who lacks Lee's appeal and claim on American affections. Lee is therefore a better target on which to direct his complaints. Nolan has to fit this square peg into a circular hole defined by army command, and the result is not very happy. He must assess Lee's "sense of grand strategy in regard to his own army." The use of "sense" here begs many questions; indeed, it is difficult to understand how any single formation can constitute a grand strategy, as it is only a small facet of it. Nolan also fails to recognize that any commander faces insuperable dilemmas if he must "sense" what his government expects him to do.[53]

Nolan's terminological muddle is accentuated when he explores Lee's enthusiasm for the offensive. "The problem is *plain*," he declares forthrightly, but the answers seem less so. As Lee did not direct grand strategy until the end of the war, much of his discussion meanders past strategic issues and explores the operational level of war. The two levels are intimately connected, but Nolan's efforts to forge the link are not sure. He suggests that the Confederacy's grand strategy should have been defensive in nature, and via some cleverly lawyerly circumlocutions that are far subtler than Connelly's, he comes up with "Lee's grand strategy of the offensive." Such a policy, Nolan complains, "was not feasible to defeat the North militarily as distinguished from prolonging the contest until the North gave up." The case that offensive action might have lengthened the war is plausible, though equally, it might have rendered it shorter for the defensive sacrificed the initiative. Nolan's discussion of these controversial points is brief and as insular as Connelly's. It leads to a simple question—does Lee argue in the way that Nolan suggests, in a reckless, bull-headed manner?—and the answer must be in the negative.[54]

Nolan recognizes that the defensive requires more than the passive defense, that is, simply resisting attacks, and "can involve offensive operational strategy or the tactical offensive." But his argument downplays this reality. He assumes that the Confederates could always avoid battle or fight defensively when it suited them while raiding. Lee should "husband his strength" and avoid casualties (an argument that threatens to become circular); his offensive movements caused desertion, as in the autumn of 1862, but Nolan overlooks the reality that desertion often reached a pitch when armies did nothing. He offers no proof that Lee's casualties would have been diminished if he had fought exclusively on the defensive; counterattacks are always needed. In any case, Lee's casualties in the 1864 Overland Campaign were proportionately higher than Grant's. Casualties on this scale were the product of the *long war* that Nolan considers in the South's interest. But the stress placed on the defensive and the deprecation of risk indicates the powerful influence of the Vietnam Syndrome. Risk taking is surely unavoidable in war.[55]

Nolan's anachronistic tone is even more evident when he deals with Lee's tenacious Confederate loyalty, which he believes prolonged the war beyond sense. He dates Lee's recognition of eventual defeat at some point between mid-July and mid-December 1863, although the evidence is limited and based on speculation or conversations that were recorded long after the date at which they were supposed to have occurred. "Surely," Nolan claims, Lincoln's reelection in 1864 brought home to Lee "unconditionally that the war had been lost." Nolan then opens fire with both barrels. He dismisses the complex matrix of duty, commitment, and attachment, as well as the expectations of the led, and writes of Lee's persistence (again, not Davis's) in strictly rational terms. He regards Lee's persistence as "essentially an emotional commitment" to fight on "regardless of the cost," "the awful cost," he repeats, "long after [Lee] believed that it was futile to continue the contest." Lee held stubbornly to what he believed his duty demanded, even though "he personally believed" the cause lost. Nolan presents the matter as if the pursuit of any cause or policy is simply an aggregate of personal beliefs. But Nolan convinces himself that Lee ducked his responsibilities and thus should be held "accountable." Nolan's tone resembles that of a judge more than a historian. He excoriates Lee for failing to confront "the civilian authorities" and give his view "that the war should be ended." Lee's discretion is such that we cannot be sure that Nolan's criticism is correct. But the strictures once more avoid where the true responsibility lay—with Davis. Nolan's technique is the exact opposite of Clifford Dowdey's.[56] It also rests on questionable value judgments that ignore the military mores and values of the period, especially in relation to surrender, death, and sacrifice.[57]

Nolan attacks everybody else's view of Lee but fails to complete his own portrait. What he offers is a series of loosely connected episodes. In making sectional points against Lee, Nolan neglects the influence of earlier Northern writers on Lee, such as T. Harry Williams. His books are thought-provoking, and some of his arguments about Lee's attitudes to blacks and his magnanimity after 1865 have been sustained, but his military analysis is wayward, simplistic, and aimed at the wrong target. His books are lively, trenchant, and better written than Connelly's. His signal weakness is that Nolan was too good a lawyer to be an effective historian, and he employs a too brisk prosecutorial manner with cleverly concealed qualifying asides. It is also revealing of his dogmatism that he never considered the need to modify any aspect of his interpretation.[58]

By the mid-1990s, the foundations for a new interpretation of Lee, favorable but not uncritical, had been laid. From this date the reconstruction of Roland's approach, modified and amplified, begins. As the grounds for much of the earlier denigration rested on a sharp sketch of Lee's character, it was appropriate that this should first take a biographical form. Emory M. Thomas provided a one-volume biography that is "post-revisionist." He eschews earlier hagiography and provides a subtle psychological portrait that provides a convincing context for the personal roots of Lee's generalship. "Lee was a great human being," Thomas writes, "perhaps as great as Freeman believed, but not great in the ways that Freeman described." Thomas's understanding of Lee's elevated spirit is drawn from an understanding of his inner struggles. "Lee was great in his response to his tribulations and to his life in general." Thomas stresses Lee's resilience, his "incredible capacity to cope." He points to Lee's enigmatic quality and determination to conceal himself, always under control, and notes that he expressed a basically optimistic outlook and a desire to make the best of things. But Thomas's portrait is far from saintly and underlines Lee's asperity and sarcasm, especially when under pressure.[59]

Thomas cleverly redefines Roland's case for Lee's fertility of expedient and virtuoso execution of military technique. He explores the roots of Lee's "creative talent for turning adversity to his advantage." Thomas finds the source of Lee's audacity—his acute sense of the risks he took and his ability to pull them off—in his family heritage. His father "Light Horse Harry" Lee, had been a compulsive gambler. Lee kept such tendencies firmly in check in his own conduct in peace but found scope for them in war. The Civil War "brought resolution to the tension [in Lee's personality] between freedom and control that Lee seemed to feel so acutely." Thomas also illuminates Lee's desire to avoid confrontation in argument (as opposed to upbraiding subordinates) as a means of keeping matters restrained so that he gained his points by quiet persuasion. This technique served him best in dealings with Davis, aided by his son, Custis, who could monitor the president's shifting moods and inclinations while serving as a member of his staff. Thomas sees Lee as a typical Whig in his conservatism and horror of naked emotions. He is dismissive of Nolan's aspersions as a "pale" imitation of Connelly.[60]

Views on historical subjects are rarely unanimous, nor should they be. Steven H. Newton's assessment of Confederate operations before Richmond in the spring of 1862 argues that Lee did enjoy real authority as commanding general, an authority widely acknowledged throughout the army. His viewpoint seems to confirm the confusion over the command system and indicates once more an unwise conflation of power and influence. Just because others believed Lee enjoyed this authority does not mean he in practice exercised it. And if he had been invested formally as the Confederacy's commanding general, why did he not exert this authority after June 1862, when he took the field?[61]

Another work that remains loyal to the earlier critical perspectives is Michael Fellman's biography, published in 2000. He suggests that Lee's opponents were "critical blunderers"—an excessively harsh judgment. Fellman takes forward Thomas's views on Lee's bad temper and the fear he could inspire among his subordinates. He remarks that Lee's reputation was more as a disciplinarian than as a kindly man. He perhaps exaggerates the analogy made with the plantation regime, as generals can insist on punctuality and hard work without having run a plantation. But his portrait of Lee as "demanding, aloof and irritable" nevertheless rings true. Still, he presses matters too far when he argues that Lee's generalship embodied a "rage militaire," with Gettysburg as its climax, which reveals the relentless search for "a total victory that would vaporize the enemy army in one battle . . . a Napoleonic grand illusion of total victory," by now a well-worn theme.[62] Command is more than the sum of a general's personality, as Roland realized, and Fellman's formulation, though fascinating in some respects, is so overdrawn as to reduce Lee's generalship to a caricature.[63]

It is perhaps too soon to divine the overall impact of the more positive analysis of Lee's generalship. Yet its direction and the ways in which it verifies Roland's case is clear enough. The most important aspect that it addresses is Lee's relationship with Davis. Steven Woodworth's account *Davis and Lee at War* (1995) places Davis where he belongs: at the center of the discussion. Woodworth is far from blind to Davis's weaknesses, especially his indecisiveness and failure to impose a coherent grand strategy. He argues that the strength of the relationship can be located in Lee's political subtlety and sophisticated understanding of human nature. Lee displayed great skill at persuading Davis to accept the ideas he had suggested and adopt them as his own; in addition, he left Davis all-important room for political maneuvering. Woodworth also contends that political insight underlay Lee's dynamic strategy because he feared that most Southerners lacked the stomach for a long war. Woodworth believes that Lee and Davis disagreed over a response to this dilemma. He writes that the cautious Davis thought the Confederacy could win by not losing, while Lee held that it could avoid losing by its own, ultimately defensive-offensive exertions. But this represents only a difference in degrees of emphasis, not a fundamental disagreement in a relationship that reflects credit on both men.[64]

Joseph L. Harsh's study *Confederate Tide Rising* (1995) presents a fresh understanding of Lee's political skills as nourished by a reevaluation of Lee as a strategist. Harsh recognizes the vital relationship between the broad and the specific in Lee's outlook, planning, and opportunity, and apprehends that "opportunities led him forward, from success to success." This is a very different perspective from that of Connelly, Weigley, and Fellman, all of whom stress pre-programmed delusion. Harsh demonstrates the employment of strategic turning movements (which earlier had been highlighted by Hattaway and Jones) to protect Richmond and "baffle" his foes and "frustrate" their designs. For all the tactical errors and ill-disciplined muddle of the Seven Days' Battles, Lee showed that his strategy could work, that it rested on hard logic not "obsessions," and he thus bequeathed the "hope for victory" that a catalogue of earlier disasters in 1862 had almost extinguished.[65]

Gary W. Gallagher has unearthed important supporting evidence to buttress the altered perspective, especially in regard to the way in which Lee's strategy matched public expectations. Gallagher argues that Lee "formulated a national strategy predicated on the probability of success in Virginia and the value of battlefield victories." Gallagher further contends that this viewpoint rested on the strength of Confederate public opinion that manifested "a widespread tendency *during the war* to concentrate attention on Lee and Virginia." Lee appreciated the importance of Virginia to Southern morale, thanks to his wide reading among the public print, and such a point extends the debate well beyond Lee's personal inclinations. Lee grasped "that victories in Virginia were both more probable and calculated to yield larger results than whatever might transpire in the West." Gallagher thus effectively demolishes two of Connelly's most strident claims: Lee's "obsession" with Virginia "distorted" Confederate strategy and Lee's fame was a retrospective invention.[66] In his later short biography, written to refute the Connelly-Nolan approach, Roland emphatically agrees with Gallagher's conclusions.[67] Gallagher even puts in a good word for the Lost Cause tradition. Though it exaggerated Southern weakness, Gallagher contends that it conveyed a kernel of truth: The South and Lee *were* outnumbered and outgunned most of the time. As a native of Colorado, Gallagher has no sectional axe to grind in making such claims.[68]

The post-Connelly school is not afraid to criticize Lee. Joseph Harsh downplays the importance of the "Lost Order" in the Maryland Campaign. Instead he emphasizes Lee's errors in ordering Stonewall Jackson to "intercept" a supposedly fleeing Union garrison from Harper's Ferry, when a siege proved necessary. In turn, this requirement proved an obstacle to the rapid concentration of Lee's army once McClellan launched his counteroffensive.[69] Gallagher sides with Longstreet over the controversy at Second Manassas on August 29, when he counseled Lee against an immediate attack. Gallagher contends that Longstreet was right to offer his advice and Lee was right to accept it. The symbolic significance of his intervention is thus dismissed as a red herring. Similarly, Brian Holden Reid suggests that Lee had a "reasonable chance" of escaping to Lynchburg in April 1865, after the fall of Richmond, and must bear the responsibility for the staff errors that forced him to surrender his army.[70]

What does the future hold? An edited collection might indicate that Lee's operational opportunism could be a profitable theme for future study. William Miller's brilliant essay on Lee's intentions during the Seven Days disputes the claims made by so many historians that Lee sought to "destroy" the Army of the Potomac; he aimed to secure Richmond's safety, but he exceeded his expectations and thereafter sought a greater victory. Gordon C. Rhea doubts whether Lee exercised, in 1864, the clairvoyant powers claimed for him by Freeman and Dowdey. All such detailed studies cast doubt on any supposed "Lee's Search for the Battle of Annihilation," with all the defensive suppositions that accompany such arguments.[71]

Historians also will have to digest the conclusions of Elizabeth Brown Pryor's award-winning biography based on sources no biographer (including Freeman) had previously seen. She is most illuminating on his evolving technique as a leader, which only took its mature form after his unhappy experience as superintendent of West Point. The significance of such insights are best viewed in conjunction with institutional studies, such as Joseph T. Glatthaar's *General Lee's Army* (2008), a masterly survey of the Army of

Northern Virginia. Glatthaar reveals the strong links Lee's army had with slavery and corroborates Gary Gallagher's view that it had become the focal point of a proslavery nationalism fostered by its middle-ranking officers. Such arguments place the army's eagerness to carry out offensive operations in a broader, more authoritative context that relates to nonmilitary aspects, especially the state of Southern opinion and the views of the newspapers, to which Lee proved responsive.[72]

In sum, Lee's reputation since 1964 has experienced two waves of denigration and an insistent undertow of sympathetic but balanced appreciation that considers Lee one of the foremost of American soldiers. But the awe-struck reverence of earlier biographers has been banished forever. We might seek, as Marcus Cunliffe warns, "some sour antidote to so much saccharine,"[73] but the batting backward and forward of the same issues (that go back well beyond 1964) offers a warning of the dangers of jumping to extremes of argument; excessive denigration fosters a narrowing of focus and eventually a distortion of the case at issue. For instance, a contradiction of the claim that Lee was clairvoyant in his estimate of Union plans does not require biographers to reach the opposite conclusion. Lee was hardly deficient in a vital quality that Manstein sums up in a pithy phrase: "The only successful military commander is *one who can think ahead*."[74] Lee could do this with dexterity.

The broadening of the argument that has accompanied the undertow that has restored Lee's reputation benefitted from the technical advances of the "new military history." This has extended our knowledge and broadened our understanding; it also deprecates "league tables" of "great captains" as a way of understanding the military past. Lee and his command will profit from future studies of ideas and organizations that focus more on systems and less on personalities. Nevertheless, in the final reckoning, Lee remains a controversial figure: He *lost*, and his responsibility for defeat will invariably engender criticism.[75] Lee is an enigmatic figure, a noble man who led an ignoble cause (just like von Manstein). Charles Roland should have the last word, as he had the first. Lee "was a marvelously gifted soldier and an ardently devoted patriot, yet he defended the most unacceptable of American causes, secession and slavery, and he suffered the most un-American experience, defeat."[76] Alas, we must confront one of the realities behind the study of individuals both great and small. We might never be able explain everything about their lives, and thus we might never resolve the paradox of Lee's life.

Notes

I wish to thank Liz Triplett and her staff at the Richmond Public Library, Richmond, Virginia, for all their assistance, and to Roger J. Spiller for a close reading of an earlier draft.

1. Thanks to Freeman's popular success, this tendency was less marked among the war's senior participants. For George Marshall's admiration of Lee as "a soldier-statesman," see Forrest C. Pogue, *George C. Marshall: Education of a General, 1880–1939* (London, 1964), 67.

2. On the pre-1945 background, see Brian Holden Reid, "British Military Intellectuals and the American Civil War," in *Warfare, Diplomacy and Politics: Essays in Honour of A. J. P. Taylor*, ed. Chris Wrigley (London, 1986), 42–57. For Allan Nevins's attack on Lee's "parochial type of patriotism," see *The War for the Union*, 4 vols. (New York, 1959–71), 1:111. The term "Union interpretation" is taken from Ludwell H. Johnson, "Civil War Military History: A Few Revisions in Need of Revising," *Civil War History* 17 (June 1971): 115–30; also see Brian Holden Reid, "The Civil War, 1861–1865," in *A Companion to American Military History*, ed. James C. Bradford (Malden, MA, 2010), 1:99–122, but especially 104–7.

3. See Charles P. Roland, *My Odyssey Through History: Memoirs of War and Academe* (Baton Rouge, 2004), 109–10. Roland had worked as Williams's teaching assistant for a term at LSU, but his Ph.D. was directed initially by Bell I. Wiley and then Francis Butler Simkins (see 96–97).

4. Charles P. Roland, "The Generalship of Robert E. Lee," in *Grant, Lee, Lincoln and the Radicals: Essays on Civil War Leadership*, ed. Grady McWhiney (Evanston, IL, 1964), 31–32, 36–37 (a revised version of this article appears on pages 19–48 of this volume); Brian Holden Reid, "Michael Howard and the Evolution of Modern War Studies," *Journal of Military History* 73 (June 2009): 869–904. A later refinement of this approach is Eliot A. Cohen and John Gooch, *Military Misfortunes: The Anatomy of Failure in War* (New York, 1990).

5. Roland's uncompromising views on the "peace movement" and the Vietnam War can be found in Roland, *My Odyssey Through History*, 112–14.

6. Roland, "Generalship of Lee," 31, 69; also see Brian Holden Reid, "'A Sign-Post that Was Missed?' Reconsidering British Lessons from the American Civil War," *Journal of Military History* 70 (Apr. 2006): 386–414.

7. Roland, "Generalship of Lee," 38, 39–41, 42, 47–49, 51, 53. The reference to pestilence was self-serving, as Jefferson Davis's first wife had died in 1835 of it. See William C. Davis, *Jefferson Davis: The Man and the Hour* (New York, 1991), 74–75. The claim that the West was more important had been made by Archer Jones, *Confederate Strategy: From Shiloh to Vicksburg* (Baton Rouge, 1961). The preface to his second edition (1991) markedly qualifies this view.

8. Roland, "Generalship of Lee," 50, 57–59, 60, 63, 65–66. On Lee's subservience to Davis and neglect of the potential of his position, "to all intents and purposes dictator," see J. F. C. Fuller, *Grant and Lee: A Study in Personality*

and Generalship (London, 1933), 115–16, 234–35. Emory M. Thomas, *The Confederacy as a Revolutionary Experience* (Englewood Cliffs, NJ, 1971), explores this theme with varying degrees of persuasiveness.

9. Roland, "Generalship of Lee," 53–54, 56, 66.

10. Ibid, 63.

11. From 1938 Dowdey taught creative writing at the University of Richmond. Clifford Dowdey, *Lee: A Biography* (Boston, 1965; London, 1970), ix–x (all references are to the British edition); Richard D. Watson, "Clifford Dowdey : Contemporary Romance Novelist and Historian," *Richmond Quarterly* 4, no. 3 (Winter 1981): 19, 20, 21; Bill Millsaps, "Clifford Dowdey and the Sweet Life," *Richmond Times-Dispatch,* June 8, 1969; Welford D Taylor, ed., *Virginia Authors Past and Present* (Farmville, VA, 1972); Robert K. Krick, introduction to reprint of Clifford Dowdey, *Lee's Last Campaign: The Story of Lee and His Men against Grant—1864* (Lincoln, NE, 1993 [orig. pub. Boston, 1960]), xi, xii. I am very grateful to David Kilmon of the Richmond Public Library, Richmond, Virginia, for furnishing me with materials on Dowdey that are unavailable in Britain.

12. Guy Friddell, "A Tribute to Clifford Shirley Dowdey, Jr., 1904–1979," *Virginia Record* 101, no. 7 (July 1979): 6; Dowdey's attitude to footnotes is in *Lee,* xi, though his books sometimes contain detailed guidance to further reading; his comment on Freeman is in *Lee's Last Campaign,* 388; Catton is quoted by Watson in "Clifford Dowdey," 20; his indebtedness to Freeman is considered in ibid., 21.

13. See Bill Millsaps's observation (*Richmond Times-Dispatch,* June 8, 1969) that "Dowdey works amidst the graying, dusty evidence of the Lost Cause." Dowdey, *Lee,* 615. On the attitudes of the "revisionists," see Holden Reid, "Civil War," 101. Dowdey's bibliography contains Claude G. Bowers, *The Tragic Era* (1930), but no works of a more recent hue, such as those by John Hope Franklin.

14. Dowdey, *Lee,* ix. Such a view was by no means confined to Southerners; see Earl Schenck Miers's discussion of Lee's "wholeness . . . consistently the objective man" in his *Robert E. Lee* (New York, 1956), 52. Fuller, *Grant and Lee,* 106: "Heroism and self-sacrifice, and not generalship were the foundations of this cult." T. Harry Williams regrets that Fuller's book did not gain the attention that it deserved in the 1930s—"the first writer in modern times to call attention to Grant's greatness"—and welcomed the appearance of the second edition, even though Fuller was "too harsh in his strictures on Lee," in his review in the *Baton Rouge Morning Advocate,* Nov. 10, 1957.

15. Dowdey, *Lee,* 178, 189, 207, 229 (Dowdey's italics), 235.

16. Ibid., 428, 476–86.

17. Ibid., 291–92, 373, 375, 377; on Longstreet, 376; on Lee's doubts, 357–59; and on Dowdey's doubts, 384, 396–97.

18. Ibid., 215, 273, 354, 360, 381, 472, 486.

19. Ibid., 154, 182, 357, 451, 527. For the consistent anti-Davis tone in Dowdey's historical works, see Watson, "Clifford Dowdey," 20.

20. Dowdey, *Lee,* 414–15, 419.

21. Thomas L. Connelly, "Robert E. Lee and the Western Confederacy: A Criticism of Lee's Strategic Ability," *Civil War History* 15, no. 2 (June 1969): 116; it is reprinted in *Lee the Soldier,* ed.Gary Gallagher (Lincoln, NE, 1996), 189–207. Thirty-eight years after its appearance, a casual mention of Connelly's name during my Elizabeth Roller Bottimore Lecture at the University of Richmond during the Lee Bicentenary provoked hissing among the audience.

22. Thomas L. Connelly and Archer Jones, *The Politics of Command: Factions and Ideas in Confederate Strategy* (Baton Rouge, 1973).

23. Ibid., xi–xii.

24. Williams, "Military Leadership North and South," 37–42, 47, 48; David Donald, *Lincoln Reconsidered* (1956; New York, 2001), 89–103; T. Harry Williams, "The Civil War," in *Interpreting American History: Conversations with Historians,* ed. John A Garraty (New York, 1970), 304 (quotation), 315. An important turning point in the recovery of Jomini's reputation is John W. Shy, "Jomini," in *Makers of Modern Strategy: From Machiavelli to the Nuclear Age,* ed. Peter Paret (Oxford, 1986), 143–85.

25. See Douglas Southall Freeman, *R. E. Lee: A Biography,* 4 vols. (New York, 1934–35), 1:77, 354, 358.

26. For the previous three paragraphs, see Connelly and Jones, *Politics of Command,* 3–37, 20–21, 25, 27–28, 30; quotations, 15, 25, 29. On the Archduke Charles, see D. G. Chandler, *The Campaigns of Napoleon* (London, 1966), 46, 666–67, 700–706, 722–24.

27. Connelly, "Lee and the Western Confederacy," 116; Connelly and Jones, *Politics of Command,* 33, 38–39; also see 42, 193–95. Even Dowdey, *Lee,* 502, had criticized Lee's failure to appreciate the effect of the fall of Atlanta.

28. Connelly and Jones, *Politics of Command,* 42, 48. "However tenuous such a hypothesis may be, there may be truth in it" is a characteristic refrain, and so are the many sentences beginning, "If . . ."

29. Dowdey, *Lee,* 519.

30. Connelly and Jones, *Politics of Command,* 35, 46–47, 48.

31. Richard M. McMurry, *Two Great Rebel Armies: An Essay in Confederate Military History* (Chapel Hill, 1989), 77, 92–93, 103–4, 110.

32. Connelly and Jones, *Politics of Command,* 46–47, 93.

33. Ibid., 39, 92, 88.

34. An argument made more forcefully in Thomas L. Connelly, "The Image and the General: Robert E. Lee in American Historiography," *Civil War History* 19, no. 1 (Mar. 1973): 53.

35. Connelly, *The Marble Man: Robert E. Lee and His Image in American Society* (New York, 1977), xv, 197–205.

36. Albert Castel, "The Historian and the General: Thomas L. Connelly and Robert E. Lee," *Civil War History* 16, no. 1 (Mar. 1970): 50–63. It is reprinted, too, in Gallagher, *Lee the Soldier,* 209–23, from which all references are taken. For his treatment of Lee's attitude to the Western Theater, see Connelly, *Politics of Command,* 47–48; Connelly, "Lee and the Western Confederacy," 129; and Castel's criticisms, "Historian and the General," 213, 215–18.

37. Russell F. Weigley, *The American Way of War: A History of United States Military Strategy and Policy* (1973; Bloomington, IN, 1977), chap. 6; on the Connelly-Castel debate, see 497n63.

38. Roger J. Spiller, *In the School of War* (Lincoln, NE, 2010), 200–206; "Statistical Information about Casualties of the Vietnam War," http://www.archives.gov/research/Vietnam-War/casualty-statistics.html/ (accessed Sept. 30, 2010).

39. Weigley, *American Way of War,* 114–15, 117–18; Brian Holden Reid, "The Influence of the Vietnam Syndrome on the Writing of Civil War History," *RUSI Journal* 147, no. 1 (Feb. 2002): 44–46. A fair summary of the older view (and surely the most sensible) of the significance of the Seven Days' Battles can be found in J. F. C. Fuller, *The Decisive Battles of the Western World* (London: Eyre and Spottiswoode, 1956), 3:47.

40. Grady McWhiney and Perry D. Jamieson, *Attack and Die: Civil War Military Tactics and the Southern Heritage* (University, AL, 1982), xv, 157.

41. Edward Hagerman, *The American Civil War and the Origins of Modern Warfare* (Bloomington, IN, 1988), 115, 146–47, 148. This insight is built on earlier work; see Douglas Southall Freeman, *Lee's Lieutenants: A Study in Command,* 3 vols. (New York, 1942–44), 3:xiii; also see Clement Eaton, "The Confederacy," in *Interpreting American History: Conversations with Historians,* ed. John A Garraty (New York, 1970), 327–28.

42. Carl von Clausewitz, *On War,* ed. and trans. Michael Howard and Peter Paret (Princeton, NJ, 1976). On Howard's part in its appearance, and its aims, methods, and later criticisms of it, see Holden Reid, "Howard and the Evolution of Modern War Studies," 880–81, 891, 894–95.

43. Herman Hattaway and Archer Jones, *How the North Won: A Military History of the Civil War* (Urbana, IL, 1983), 230, 415, 420n91, 570, 692, 701; Richard E.

Beringer, Herman Hattaway, Archer Jones, and William N. Still Jr., *Why the South Lost the Civil War* (Athens, GA, 1986), 132, 192, 195, 201,300–305, 426–30, 432; Holden Reid, "Influence of the Vietnam Syndrome," 49–50.

44. Hattaway and Jones, *How the North Won,* 697; McMurry, *Two Great Rebel Armies,* 139.

45. See John D. Mackenzie, *Uncertain Glory: Lee's Generalship Reexamined* (New York, 1997); Edward H. Bonekemper III, *How Robert E. Lee Lost the Civil War* (Fredericksburg, VA, 1997); Michael A. Palmer, *Lee Moves North: Robert E. Lee on the Offensive* (New York, 1998).

46. "Alan T. Nolan," *Indianapolis Star,* Aug. 5, 2008, http://www2.indystar.com/cgi-bin/obituaries/index.php/ (accessed Oct. 19, 2010). Nolan's reaction to criticism is in his *"Rally Once Again!" Selected Writings* (Madison, WI, 2000), 61–62. Review by Richard Morris in H-Net Reviews, http://www2.h-net.msu.edu/reviews/home/ (accessed Oct. 19, 2010). Also see my review of his Lee book in the *Journal of American Studies* 27 (Apr. 1993): 113–14.

47. Alan T. Nolan, *Lee Considered: General Robert E. Lee and Civil War History* (Chapel Hill, 1991), xii, 8.

48. For a range of attacks, see ibid., 42–43, 44, 47–48, 50, 53, 111, 152. The plaudits that Nolan quotes are usually made without reference to the critical Northern tradition (which is relegated to the footnotes), thus setting up an "Aunt Sally" that is then blown away by Nolan's well-aimed salvoes. See ibid., 59–60. It is also striking in *"Rally Once Again!"* that Nolan never considers the need to modify any aspect of his discussion in the light of subsequent research; here is the "truth."

49. See Alan T. Nolan, "R. E. Lee and July 1 at Gettysburg," in *The First Day at Gettysburg: Essays on Union and Confederate Military Leadership,* ed. Gary W. Gallagher (Kent, OH, 1992), 1–29.

50. Nolan, *Lee Considered,* 61–62 (Nolan's italics).

51. Ibid., 70–71. Nolan dodges these queries in his response to criticisms in his *"Rally Once Again!"*14–15.

52. Donald Stoker, *The Grand Design: Strategy and the U.S. Civil War* (New York, 2010), 24–25, 26, 27, 123, 161, 232, 378, 413.

53. Nolan, *Lee Considered,* 72.

54. Ibid., 77–78, 79–80. There is some discussion of the international dimension in Nolan, *"Rally Once Again!"* 17.

55. Nolan, *Lee Considered,* 71, 76, 80, 82–86, 87, 91, 97, 98 (circular tendencies are evident on 88). All professional soldiers are trained to accept risks. See the response of Field Marshal Erich von Manstein in his Crimean Campaign of 1942: "But it is the last chance. . . . One must take the risk. God help us!"

Quoted in Mungo Melvin, *Manstein: Hitler's Greatest General* (London, 2010), 253. Lee is often compared with Manstein. See Castel, "Historian and the General," 209.

56. Nolan, *Lee Considered,* 115, 118, 119–21, 125–26, 130–31, 132, 161. Also see Mark A. Weitz's conclusion that a Fabian policy encouraged desertion in his *More Damning than Slaughter: Desertion in the Confederate Army* (Lincoln, NE, 2005), 172–73; thus the inference here that the morale and enthusiasm of Lee's army had been eroded by endless attacks needs to be severely qualified.

57. Nolan's Vietnam Syndrome–style of argument resonates with a "death-defying and youth worshipping culture" that goes "to great lengths of avoid facing even the smallest reminders of death." See Ernest Becker, *The Denial of Death* (1973; New York, 1997). Joseph Sharp, *Living Our Dying: A Way to the Sacred in Everyday Life* (New York, 1996), contends that far from destroying meaning, death is "a great giver of meaning." Also see M. Scott Peck, *The Road Less Travelled and Beyond: Spiritual Growth in an Age of Anxiety* (London, 1997).

58. Nolan, *Lee Considered,* 67, but especially 100.

59. Emory M. Thomas, *Robert E. Lee: A Biography* (New York, 1995), 14, 218; on self-control, 18, 112, 120, 151, 318; aloofness, 35, 145, 192, 316, 396; optimism, 46, 171, 414; and bad temper, 350, 351–53.

60. Ibid., 231, 353; on dislike of confrontation, 183, 222; persuasion, 256, 319; Whiggery, 79–80, 109, 137, 173; Nolan, 14; and Thomas continued to see Lee as antislavery, 183.

61. Steven H. Newton, *Joseph E. Johnston and the Defense of Richmond* (Lawrence, KS, 1998), 67–74.

62. Michael Fellman, *The Making of Robert E. Lee* (New York, 2000), 114, 116–24, 130, 131, 138.

63. See the argument of Holden Reid's Peter J. Parish Memorial Lecture, "William T. Sherman and the South," *American Nineteenth Century History* 11, no. 1 (Mar. 2010): 2–3.

64. Steven E. Woodworth, *Davis and Lee at War* (Lawrence, KS, 1995), 37, 158, 232, 234, 333; on Davis's caution, 157, 160, 161, 185, 197–98; on Lee's desire for an early victory, 157–58, 174, 179, 184, 214, 299, 330.

65. Joseph L. Harsh, *Confederate Tide Rising: Robert E. Lee and the Making of Southern Strategy, 1861–1862* (Kent, OH, 1998), xiii–xiv, xv, 96–97, 173; also see Appendix Three, "Notes on Lee's Strategy," 185–90.

66. Gary W. Gallagher, "Another Look at the Generalship of R. E. Lee," in Gallagher, *Lee the Soldier,* 280–82, 283, 284–85. In addition to his important anthology *Lee the Soldier,* also see Gallagher's two volumes of essays, *Lee and His Generals*

in War and Memory (Baton Rouge, 1998) and *Lee and His Army in Confederate History* (Chapel Hill, 2001).

67. Charles P. Roland, *Reflections on Lee: A Historian's Assessment* (Mechanicsburg, PA, 1995), 88. For Roland's assessment of their "tendentious and unbalanced" arguments, see Roland, *My Odyssey Through History,* 123.

68. Nolan's attacks on the Lost Cause tradition devotes hardly any space to the war itself; see Nolan, *"Rally Once Again!"* 63–74; Gallagher, *Lee and His Army in Confederate History,* 274.

69. Joseph L. Harsh, *Taken at the Flood: Robert E. Lee and Confederate Strategy in the Maryland Campaign of 1862* (Kent, OH, 1999), 186–87, 238, 252, 267–68, 315.

70. Gallagher, *Lee and His Generals in War and Memory,* 151–57; Brian Holden Reid, *Robert E. Lee: Icon for a Nation* (Amherst, NY, 2007), 236, 241.

71. Peter S. Carmichael, ed., *Audacity Personified: The Generalship of Robert E. Lee* (Baton Rouge, 2004), 1–25, 27–56, 57–81.

72. Elizabeth Brown Pryor, *Reading the Man: A Portrait of Robert E. Lee Through His Private Letters* (New York, 2007), 214–22, 412–14; Joseph T. Glatthaar, *General Lee's Army: From Victory to Collapse* (New York, 2008), 19–21, 309–14; Gary W. Gallagher, *The Confederate War* (Cambridge, MA, 1997), 58–59, 63, 66, 85, 86–89, 91–92, 95, 139.

73. Marcus Cunliffe, *George Washington: Man and Monument,* rev. ed. (New York, 1982), 3.

74. Quoted in Melvin, *Manstein,* 331.

75. A first stab at this is Ethan S. Rafuse, *Robert E. Lee and the Fall of the Confederacy,* 1863–1865 (Lanham, MD, 2008).

76. Roland, *Reflections on Lee,* 1.

Lieutenant General Richard Heron Anderson. Courtesy of Lawrence Lee Hewitt.

Lee's Most Maligned General: "Fighting Dick" Anderson

Lawrence Lee Hewitt

Seven men commanded infantry corps for lengthy periods in the Army of Northern Virginia. The first were James Longstreet and Thomas J. Jackson. When General Robert E. Lee reorganized the army following Jackson's death in May 1863, Richard S. Ewell took over Stonewall's 2nd Corps and Ambrose Powell Hill was promoted to head the newly constituted 3rd Corps. Longstreet's wounding on May 6, 1864, brought Richard H. Anderson to temporarily command the 1st Corps. Twenty-two days later, Jubal A. Early took over for the ailing Ewell. When Longstreet returned in October, a fourth demicorps was organized for Anderson. In December, Early remained in the Shenandoah Valley when the 2nd Corps, under Major General John Brown Gordon, rejoined Lee's army at Petersburg.

Anyone with a basic understanding of the Civil War knows that Jackson was the best of the seven. Even the most knowledgeable scholars of that conflict, however, disagree as to the relative merits of the remaining six, and an argument could be made that Gordon never had an opportunity to be fairly tested in corps command. All had tarnished records: Longstreet hesitated at Gettysburg and floundered in East Tennessee; Ewell, too, hesitated at Gettysburg and lost control of himself during the Spotsylvania Campaign; almost nonexistent at Gettysburg, Hill blundered at Bristoe Station; Anderson's command disintegrated at Sailor's Creek; Early's command was routed at Third Winchester (Opequon), Fisher's Hill, and Cedar Creek; and Gordon failed at Fort Stedman. Only one, however, has been maligned by historians.

Though the subject of two biographies, Richard Anderson is the least remembered of Lee's corps commanders. There are no statues of him. He never wrote his memoirs. Possibly his removal from command is why historians go out of their way to make erroneous comments about Anderson. Yet these same historians treat Early differently, though he, too, was relieved of command.[1] Anderson deserves a reappraisal.

Richard Heron Anderson was born at "Hill Crest" in Sumter County, South Carolina, on October 7, 1821. At sixteen, he secured an appointment to West Point, and he ranked fortieth out of fifty-six graduates in the Class of 1842. While serving in the 2nd U.S. Dragoons, Anderson was breveted for gallantry during the Mexican War, attempted to keep the peace in Kansas Territory, and participated in the expedition against the Mormons in Utah. Early in 1861 he resigned to defend his native state.[2]

Because Anderson was the senior U.S. Army officer from South Carolina to cast his lot with the Confederacy, Governor Francis W. Pickens reserved the colonelcy of the 1st South Carolina Regulars for him. When Anderson joined the regiment on March 16, he found himself commanding Fort Moultrie and the batteries on Sullivan's Island, part of Brigadier General P. G. T. Beauregard's forces constituting a "ring of fire" all but surrounding Fort Sumter. Upon its capture, Anderson and his regiment had the honor of garrisoning it. When Beauregard was relieved of duty in South Carolina on May 27, he left Anderson in command of all Confederate troops in the vicinity of Charleston.[3]

The former U.S. captain appeared to be on the fast track, as President Jefferson Davis had appointed only thirteen generals before May 27. By July 10, however, Davis had appointed another twenty-six. South Carolina's politicians took exception to Davis's overlooking of Anderson, and the president responded, appointing Anderson a brigadier general on July 19.[4]

On August 21, Anderson was ordered to report to Brigadier General Braxton Bragg at Pensacola, Florida. Anderson's second encounter with the enemy came on the night of October 8, when he led one thousand men on an expedition to Santa Rosa Island. The raid was successful, but during the withdrawal a musket ball struck Anderson in the left elbow. Bragg reported that Anderson had "conducted the expedition with a zeal and gallantry worthy of high commendation," and upon his recovery Anderson become Bragg's second in command.[5]

On the afternoon of January 1, 1862, the Yankees unexpectedly opened fire on Pensacola. Anderson was entertaining at home and already intoxicated. Absent at the time, when Bragg returned and discovered what had transpired on New Year's Day, he placed Anderson under arrest on January 8, confined him to Pensacola, and reported the matter to Richmond. Anderson admitted to having been drunk, promised it would never happen again, and was released from arrest on January 31.[6]

Anderson visited President Davis in Richmond to discuss his pending court-martial. Davis cut him off, saying, "I can suggest nothing but obedience." Considering their previous friendship and that his first cousin was married to Davis's sister-in-law, Anderson must have been taken aback but gave no indication of it. He politely thanked Davis for his time and excused himself. Anderson's behavior stunned the president, who had expected him to respond by pleading his case. Davis hardly slept that night. The next morning he admitted to his wife that his encounter with Anderson had upset him. Though there is no evidence that Davis intervened, Bragg, uncharacteristically, dropped the charges, and on February 12 Davis ordered Anderson to report to General Joseph E. Johnston at Manassas, Virginia, to take command of a South Carolina brigade in Major General James Longstreet's Division.[7]

He reported to Johnston on February 15 and joined his new command near Centreville. In March, the brigade withdrew south of the Rapidan River and in April it moved to the fortifications below Yorktown. The Confederates withdrew from the Yorktown defenses on the evening of May 3. The following evening, Longstreet assigned Anderson, with his own brigade and that of Brigadier General Roger A. Pryor, to occupy the fortifications east of Williamsburg as a rear guard while the army continued its withdrawal up the Peninsula.[8]

At 6:00 A.M. on May 5, the Battle of Williamsburg opened with the Yankees driving in Anderson's pickets. For the next seven hours, Anderson would hold back the enemy, eventually commanding five brigades before Longstreet arrived on the field in the afternoon and took charge. Johnston and Longstreet proclaimed Williamsburg a victory, and the latter reported that Anderson's "disposition of his forces and manner of leading them into action displayed great ability and signal gallantry and coolness." Eighty years later, however, Douglas Southall Freeman focused upon the redoubts Anderson had failed to occupy and concluded, "R. H. Anderson—perhaps not altogether careful in reconnaissance, but steady and capable of handling more than one Brigade with none of a beginner's uncertainty; possibly a bit negligent in watching small details." In 1999, Steven E. Woodworth opined, "Anderson is the enigma of the battle." Criticizing him for apparently disappearing during the engagement and intimating that he may have been drunk, Woodworth concluded, "At Williamsburg, Anderson had shown the darker side of his generalship." Three years later, Carol K. Dubbs found fault with most of the generals on both sides but had only one criticism of the South Carolinian: "Anderson should have been better acquainted with the field and adequately garrisoned the far left redoubts to defend that flank."[9]

Anderson occupied only two of the eight redoubts to his left: Redoubt 7, which he could see from Fort Magruder, and Redoubt 9, which, along with Redoubt 11 and possibly Redoubts 12 and 14, was discovered by Colonel

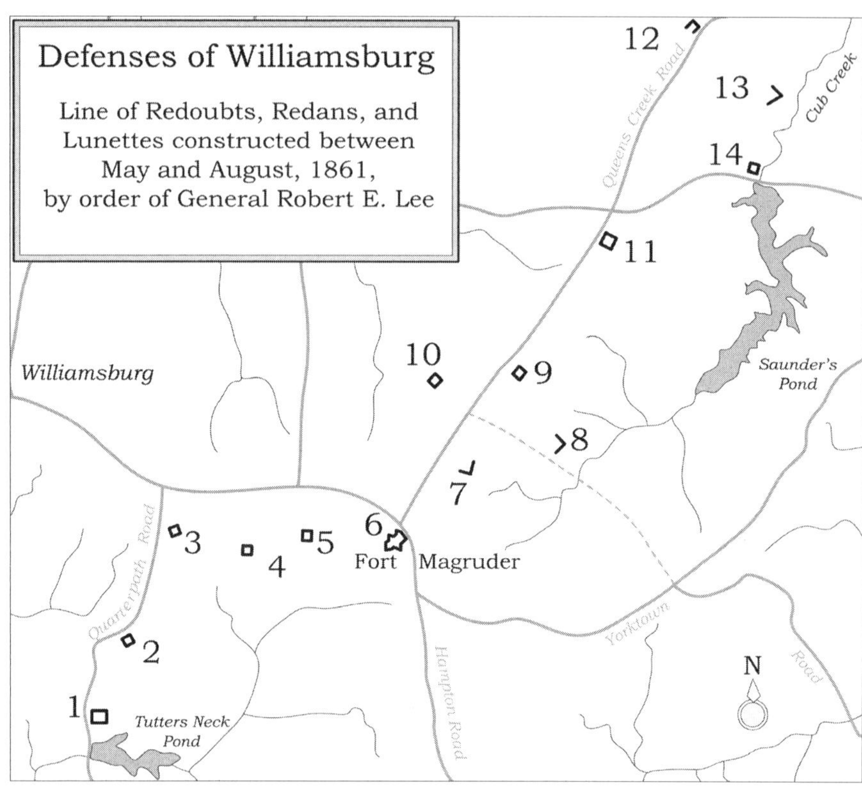

Defenses of Williamsburg, Virginia. Courtesy of Stuart Salling.

John Bratton during a reconnaissance along the road running northeast. Unaware that others existed, no one went looking for them in the darkness during a driving rain storm. Bratton suggested to Anderson that he "post at least a picket there [Redoubt 11], but was told that it was in charge of somebody else." Anderson thought his left was secure. Most historians have ignored Brigadier General James E. B. Stuart's troopers, who occupied Redoubt 11; Stuart, not Anderson, was responsible for guarding the roads that ran east and northeast from that redoubt. When Anderson left Fort Magruder in the morning to attend to his right, Stuart took responsibility for Fort Magruder and everything to its left. Stuart "frequently found it necessary to take the responsibility of dispatching re-enforcements of artillery, as well as infantry, to points obviously requiring them."

If someone was to blame for the Yankees turning the Confederate left in the afternoon, it was not Anderson. As to Anderson's "disappearance," Colonel Edward Porter Alexander stated that Anderson "in person had supervised all the movements of the morning." One reason for the confusion is Brigadier

General Cadmus M. Wilcox's claim: "Being the senior officer present on the field, I gave orders to the different brigades as they arrived and personally directed portions of these into positions." Between 10:30 A.M. and 12:30 P.M., Anderson remained along the line of redoubts and forwarded reinforcements in an attempt to extend his right. When these troops entered the woods, however, they found themselves on *Wilcox's field*. When the Confederates on the right advanced about 1:00 P.M., Anderson rode forward behind the 9th Alabama Infantry Regiment. As for drunkenness, all the evidence indicates that after giving his word not to do so, for the duration of the war Anderson never again consumed alcohol.[10]

The Confederate government also misjudged Anderson. On May 26, Ambrose P. Hill, a brigadier who had served under Anderson at Williamsburg, was promoted to major general. This was a slap in the face to Anderson, Wilcox, Raleigh E. Colston, and George E. Pickett, all of whom served in Longstreet's Division and outranked Hill. Hill's promotion didn't upset Anderson, but that can't be said of the others.[11]

The army's next engagement came at Seven Pines. When it was over, no one questioned who was the best brigadier. Anderson had led two brigades in support of Daniel H. Hill's Division and emerged with the soubriquet "Fighting Dick." Anderson, who hated paperwork, made no report of the battle, later claiming that he thought Longstreet would handle it for the division and Colonel Micah Jenkins for Anderson's Brigade. Nonetheless, Anderson was praised by Hill, Longstreet, and Johnston. In *R. E. Lee*, Freeman concluded that Anderson had become "the most brilliant but at that time the most erratic" of Longstreet's brigadiers. Less than a decade later, in *Lee's Lieutenant's*, Freeman wrote of Anderson: "No performance on the field had been more difficult or more admirably executed."[12]

Lee took command of the army on June 1. Five days later Longstreet wrote him, urging the promotion of Anderson. Lee followed up regarding Anderson the next day, writing President Davis:

> In reference to Genl. R. H. Anderson & your conception of his qualifications I enclose a note from Genl. Longstreet. I know little of Genl. A. personally except as Capt[.] of Dragoons. He was a favorite in his Regt[.] & was considered a good officer. I am told he is now under a pledge of abstinence, which I hope will protect him from the vice he fell into. . . . Unless [Major General Benjamin] Huger had other duty, I do not know where to get a division for Genl. A—yet awhile.

When Davis failed to act, Lee mentioned Anderson in a second letter on June 25. After agreeing with Davis that Major General John C. Pemberton needed to be relieved of command of the Department of South Carolina and Georgia, Lee suggested that Davis send Huger to replace Pemberton because Anderson could take command of Huger's Division.[13]

In accord with his usual practice, Anderson didn't file a report for the Seven Days' Battles. Undoubtedly, that is one reason his contribution at Gaines' Mill and Frayser's Farm (Glendale) continues to be overlooked. Some histories of the campaign don't even mention him, and the most recent regimental-level maps of the campaign omit Anderson *and his brigade* at Gaines' Mill.[14] Lee, however, recognized Anderson's contributions.

When the campaign ended, Lee set about reorganizing his command. "Of all the Brigadiers, R. H. Anderson, in his modest way," wrote Freeman, "probably had been the most definitely marked throughout the campaign by soldierly competence. At Frayser's Farm, he had been in charge of Longstreet's Division. . . . Jackson, too, had observed the 'gallant style' of the South Carolinian's advance on the 27th in support of Whiting." Lee wanted Anderson promoted. He prodded Davis for a fourth time on July 11: "In reference to my conversation with you when I had last the honour of seeing you, should Genl R. H. Anderson be promoted as then recommended, I would respectfully recommend Col[.] M. Jenkins to be made Brigadier General in his place." Learning that Huger had been relieved, on July 14 Lee wrote Secretary of War George W. Randolph requesting that Anderson be promoted and assigned to command Huger's Division. Davis did so that same day.[15]

Anderson, commanding the brigades of Brigadier Generals Lewis A. Armistead, William Mahone, and Ambrose R. "Rans" Wright, joined the fighting at Second Manassas on August 30. Late that day, the Confederates were driving the Yankees toward Henry Hill when Mahone was wounded and the attack faltered. To regain the momentum, Anderson ordered Wilcox, whose brigade had arrived on the scene, and Armistead to relieve Wright and Mahone. Brigadier General Thomas F. Drayton's Brigade had arrived and it went forward as well. Longstreet put Brigadier General Robert Toombs in charge of the final advance. As the three brigades represented three different divisions and three different states, possibly Longstreet thought that the well-known, popular Georgia politician could better inspire the men than Anderson. The sun had already set before Toombs's men made a feeble effort to gain the crest; darkness ended the attack.[16]

Later that night, Major General Stuart urged Armistead to renew the attack in order to prevent the enemy from escaping. Armistead declined. Stuart then communicated with Lee, but the attack was not made, and as result, the Yankees escaped. Some Confederate general must have been responsible. Longstreet, who praised Anderson, gave three reasons for failing to seize Henry Hill: Wilcox moved to the right with one brigade instead of three, the unauthorized use of Drayton's Brigade to guard the extreme right delayed its participation in the assault, and Jackson was slow to advance. Lee at the time, and Freeman in 1943, faulted no one, and the journalist praised Anderson, Hood, and Stuart.

In 1993, John Hennessy, the expert on Second Manassas, concluded that those who did less than they could have on the thirtieth were Brigadier Generals Winfield S. Featherston and Roger A. Pryor, Colonels Eppa Hunton and George T. Anderson, "and (especially) R. H. Anderson." In 2008, Joseph Glatthaar blamed only Anderson: "The onset of darkness, some confusion in the mind of division commander Maj. Gen. Richard H. Anderson over Longstreet's intention, and a failure to recognize the critical nature of the Union forces combined to convince Anderson not to press the enemy too strongly." Either the historians have been unduly critical of Anderson or the South Carolinian hoodwinked Lee, who rewarded his performance by increasing his division to six brigades, making it the strongest in the army.[17]

Anderson had little chance to distinguish himself during the invasion of Maryland. He served under Major General Lafayette McLaws during the investment of Harpers Ferry. At Sharpsburg, Anderson's Division constituted Lee's last reserve. After detaching Armistead's Brigade to his left flank, at 10:30 A.M. Lee ordered Anderson to advance his division to support D. H. Hill in the Sunken Road. Anderson was wounded before he could deploy his men, and with only one brigadier present, things quickly fell apart. Robert K. Krick concluded in 1999, "Much of the reinforcements' ineptitude can be traced to the loss of command. General Anderson, of modest competence that might have met the needs of the hour, was wounded 'severely . . . in the thigh' before his troops closed to musketry range."[18] Clearly, if Krick, the leading authority on the Army of Northern Virginia, is being fair to Anderson, then he is using the Lee Scale. With Marse Robert a 10 and Stonewall a 9, "modest competence" might equal a 5.

Anderson's wound kept him away from the army for two months. During his absence, Lee reorganized his army, making several changes to Anderson's Division. Most significantly, because it was the largest in Longstreet's Corps and Pickett's the smallest, Lee transferred Armistead's Brigade to Pickett. With his revamped division, Anderson held the extreme left of the Confederate line at Fredericksburg, guarding against a Yankee crossing upstream from the town. Consequently, his men saw little action during the battle.[19]

That changed when the Union army crossed the Rapidan River above Fredericksburg in the spring of 1863. Rushing to Chancellorsville on the evening of April 29, Anderson had three brigades deployed by sunrise. Learning that the enemy was approaching in overwhelming numbers, Anderson pulled back, fending off Union cavalry along the way. At the intersection of the

Orange Turnpike and Plank Road, Anderson met Lee's chief engineer, who had orders to lay out a line of fortifications for Anderson's men to construct. Facing four corps, Anderson was lucky that Union Major General Joseph Hooker chose not to attack on the thirtieth. Instead, at 11:00 A.M. on May 1, Jackson ordered an advance. Anderson, with two brigades, moved forward on the Plank Road. Initially followed by Jackson's entire corps, soon only one brigade was behind him. Holding the enemy's attention with two brigades, he sent Wright's off to his left to turn the enemy's flank. Wright surprised the enemy, who fell back before Anderson's advance until darkness ended the fighting. The next morning, Anderson held the Plank Road with three of his brigades. When the enemy attacked the rear of Jackson's flanking column, Anderson sent Brigadier General Carnot Posey's Brigade to drive them back. When Union reinforcements arrived, he sent Wright to support Posey, holding the Plank Road with only Mahone's Brigade until Brigadier General Edward A. Perry rejoined him after dark. At sunrise on the third, Anderson discovered that the enemy had withdrawn and Lee ordered his division to advance. Driving the Yankees from their earthworks, Anderson's men were the first to reach Chancellorsville.[20]

Shortly after noon, Anderson was ordered to send Mahone's Brigade to McLaws, and at 4:00 P.M., Lee ordered Anderson to move with three brigades to threaten Hooker's line of retreat. Anderson found the enemy already there and it was too late to attempt an assault. Shortly after daylight on the fourth, Lee ordered Anderson to withdraw as soon as Jackson's men relieved him and report to McLaws at Salem Church. At noon, Lee ordered Anderson to move toward Fredericksburg and link up with Major General Jubal A. Early. At 6:00 P.M., Early and Anderson attacked the enemy, driving them toward Banks' Ford. Darkness ended the fighting, and the Yankees escaped across the river during the night. Except for some marching, the campaign was over for Anderson's men. In his report, Anderson commended all his brigadiers.[21]

Lee praised only six generals for their conduct during the campaign: Jackson, Stuart, Brigadier General Robert E. Rodes (at Jackson's request), Early, Anderson, and Wilcox. The official record noted that "Maj. Gen. R. H. Anderson was also distinguished for the promptness, courage, and skill with which he and his division executed every order," and Freeman wrote that Anderson had been "admirably efficient, despite the tradition that Longstreet only could elicit his full powers." Giving Anderson credit for coming up with Wright's flanking movement, Freeman concluded, "Always it was Anderson's nature to take the largest blame and the least praise. At Chancellorsville, as previously, he merited far more than ever he would have thought of claiming. He never seemed to realize that his side-slipping [of Wright] to the left and his subsequent attack to the northward exhibited tactics of the first order." Ignoring Anderson, Gary Gallagher described Wright's movement as "spectacularly successful" and claimed that it "gave impetus to the hope that more could be accomplished," a reference to Jackson's flanking march the following day.[22]

In 2008, Anderson descended from being ignored to being criticized. Regarding his actions on May 4, Joseph Glatthaar wrote in *General Lee's Army: From Victory to Collapse,* "Sensing an opportunity to crush Sedgwick's command, Lee rushed R. H. Anderson's division over to collaborate with the two veteran commanders. By the time Anderson got in position, forming the third side of a box, it was near 6:00 P.M., about the time of Jackson's flank attack several days earlier. This time, however, Early struck aggressively, Anderson half-heartedly, and McLaws barely budged." Glatthaar implies that Anderson was the novice in comparison to Early and McLaws. Yet Anderson had more years of service in the U.S. Army than Early, outranked him by more than six months as a major general, and had commanded multiple brigades in five major engagements to Early's two before Chancellorsville. Glatthaar raised his opinion of Anderson eighty-nine pages later, declaring, "In the Battle of Chancellorsville, [Anderson] and his men fought extremely well." As to Anderson's performance on May 4, Lee wrote McLaws that very night, "Generals Anderson and Early drove the enemy handsomely from the positions on Downman's Hill beyond the Plank road." Notably, when Lee wrote Davis on May 20 recommending the promotion of Ewell and A. P. Hill, he added, "R. H. Anderson and J. B. Hood are also capital officers. They are improving, too, and will make good corps commanders, if necessary." Neither Early nor McLaws was mentioned.[23]

Lee clearly held Anderson in high esteem. No one could take issue with Ewell's promotion, but the choice of Hill remains questionable. Longstreet speculated that Hill received the promotion because he was a Virginian. Whatever his reasoning, Lee's selection of Hill made it easier to create a third corps. Transferring Hill's old division from the 2nd Corps, Lee removed two brigades from it and added two brigades new to the Army of Northern Virginia to create a division. The third division had to come from Longstreet's Corps, and its commander would be the ranking major general under Hill. Lee chose Anderson's.[24]

At Gettysburg on July 2, after deploying his infantry, Anderson received orders that Longstreet was going to attack on his right and Hill had been ordered to cooperate "with such of my brigades from the right as could join in with his troops in the attack." When Longstreet's assault reached Anderson, he was to advance his brigades in echelon; Major General William D. Pender's brigades would follow. The Confederates were on the verge of winning a decisive victory when the attack fell apart. The last of Anderson's brigades failed to attack. When Anderson learned about it, he sent a staff officer to order Mahone to advance. But still the brigadier refused, and Pender was mortally wounded while riding to check on Mahone. The brigadier's refusal led directly to Pickett's Charge the following day. Anderson advanced two brigades to support Pickett, but Longstreet ordered him to halt, "the assault having failed."[25]

Mahone should have been court-martialed for disobeying a direct order and Anderson and Hill reprimanded for failing to get Mahone's Brigade engaged on July 2. With the campaign lost and so many generals having failed him, Lee took no action against them. But it left the first black mark against Anderson in Lee's mind. The South Carolinian performed competently in the Bristoe Station and Mine Run Campaigns that fall, but it was not until the following spring that Anderson had an opportunity to shine.

About noon, May 6, 1864, a volley from the Virginians of Mahone's Brigade severely wounded Longstreet. When Lee learned what had happened, he sent for Anderson. Now commanding three divisions, Anderson prepared to renew the assault when the Yankees attacked his left. After repulsing that assault, he made little headway advancing eastward. Then, at 6:00 P.M., a second attack struck his left. Anderson's men repulsed the enemy, and darkness ended the fighting.[26]

At sunrise on May 7, Lee called Longstreet's adjutant general, Lieutenant Colonel G. Moxley Sorrel, to his headquarters to discuss a temporary commander for the 1st Corps. Pointing out that neither Charles W. Field nor McLaws were suitable, and never mentioning Pickett, Lee said that he had narrowed his choice to three—Early, Edward Johnson, and Anderson—and asked for Sorrel's opinion. The adjutant responded "probably Early would be the ablest," but he had previously alienated Longstreet's men, and Johnson "is quite unknown to the corps." Regarding Anderson, "We *know him* and shall be satisfied with him." That afternoon Lee relieved Anderson of divisional command, put him in command of the 1st Corps, and ordered, "As soon after dark as you can effect it, withdraw Longstreet's Corps from the lines as quietly as possible, so that the movement will not be discovered by the enemy. When you have done this, march the troops a little way to the rear and let them have some sleep. A guide will report to you this evening. At 3 o'clock punctually, march towards Spotsylvania Court-House."[27]

About dark, Brigadier General William N. Pendleton, Lee's chief of artillery, personally delivered Anderson's guide. After Anderson learned the condition of the road, he determined to rest his men at the end of the march and so informed Pendleton, who reported, "Here a circumstance occurred which should be specially noticed. General Anderson stated that his orders were to march by 3 next morning. He was preparing to start at 11 that night. Those four hours anticipated proved of incalculable value next day." The myth that he only marched that far because he could not find a suitable place for his men to rest sooner is based on two private letters written by the ever self-effacing Anderson long after the war. Freeman wrote in 1944, "The modesty of [Anderson's] nature kept him from asserting anything more concerning his march to Spotsylvania than that, after starting, he kept moving because he did not find a suitable place at which to rest. This may have been the literal fact, but behind it was the soldierly spirit which applies almost instinctively this sound principle: when on the march, the best insurance against the accidents of the road is an early start. An extra hour allowed at the beginning will compensate for an hour unexpectedly lost en route." Thirty years later, William W. Hassler concluded that by this "brilliant performance" Anderson had earned his promotion within twenty-four hours of receiving it. Yet some historians still contend that Anderson's "brilliant performance" was a mere "accident."[28]

Before his column had closed up, Anderson learned that Yankee infantry were about to overwhelm Confederate cavalry on the Brock Road, thereby blocking Anderson's route, and Union cavalry were threatening to drive Rebel troopers from Spotsylvania Court House. Anderson immediately sent two brigades of Kershaw's Division to both locations. The reinforcements arrived in time to retain the position on Brock Road, but those ordered to the court house had to fight to regain it. Anderson's men repulsed every assault until after 5:00 P.M., when the arrival of Ewell's Corps caused the Yankees to pull back. Though the Confederates were unaware of it, another factor contributed to Anderson's achievement. Gordon Rhea summed it up best: "If Anderson had followed Lee's instructions and delayed his march, or if the Union army's machinery had worked with even moderate efficiency, [Major General Ulysses S.] Grant would have won the race . . . placing Lee at a serious disadvantage." Freeman claimed that "Anderson maintained after the 8th the excellent rating he won that day, but his opportunities and his risks" were few at Spotsylvania.[29]

Discovering the enemy leaving his front on May 21, Lee responded by sending off Ewell's Corps. Not until 7:00 P.M., however, did he order the remainder of his army to move. Within an hour the last of Anderson's Corps had departed, with Lee riding in the vanguard. Three days later at the North Anna River, dysentery prevented Lee from overseeing the destruction of the Union 2nd Corps. His adjutant, Lieutenant Colonel Walter H. Taylor, thought Lee's illness was brought on by fatigue caused by his corps commanders. Anderson was not a detail person, and Lee naturally looked out for his greenest senior officer. Surviving documents indicate that Lee believed Anderson's major weaknesses were carelessness with his pickets and pushing his men too hard.[30]

When the Federals failed to attack along Totopotomoy Creek on May 30, Lee determined to launch his own assault with Ewell's Corps, now under Early, supported by Anderson. At the least, Anderson was to occupy the fortifications vacated by Early, and, if possible, some of his men should join in the attack. Anderson moved Kershaw's and Field's divisions into Early's trenches and even abandoned a section of his own so that he could send all of Pickett's Division to join in Early's attack. Pickett's assault failed to aid Early, and it brought about a confrontation between the two temporary corps commanders. At 8:00 P.M., Anderson sent Early a message: "General Field reports having come upon an intrenched line of the enemy, and owing to that circumstance, and the approach of darkness I have suspended his movement and have drawn my whole line back to the left again, so as to connect with General Breckinridge, between whom and the left of my line a very wide gap had been made."[31]

An expert on Early, Gary Gallagher deemed the Battle of Bethesda Church "a bloody fiasco . . . where young Stephen Dodson Ramseur persuaded [Early] to make a rash attack." Some in the army blamed Early, *who used only two brigades instead of three divisions,* but Early blamed Anderson: "I gained the position I mentioned to you, drove the enemy back, and established the batteries, from which I opened on him. I met with no cooperation from your force except the artillery, which opened on my request. I could find neither General Pickett nor yourself on the line." Left unsupported, Early reported that he could do nothing but withdraw. The ever-forgiving and unflappable Anderson no doubt surprised Early when he shot back, "If you mean by cooperation, committing equal folly with yourself, I grant that I did not cooperate; but if you mean that I did not proceed to carry out the instructions of General Lee, your statement is false. Your opinion as to the best point for attacking the enemy, and the manner of conducting the attack, is very obligingly given. I have not, however, a high appreciation of your judgment, and I decline to be guided by it." Anderson closed by telling Early that if he had another cooperative movement to propose in the future to "communicate it to the Commanding General, instead of me." Gordon Rhea's contention that "Anderson's half-hearted showing on May 30 poisoned his future relations with Early and raised serious questions about his fitness for corps command"[32] is correct only as it applies to Early's unwillingness to cooperate with Anderson afterward.

Sometime after 4:00 P.M. on May 31, the 1st Corps began marching toward Cold Harbor. Additionally, Major General Robert F. Hoke's Division had been rushed from the Bermuda Hundred defenses to reinforce Lee. At 7:00 P.M., Anderson reported to Lee that Hoke was on his right within a half mile of Cold Harbor. He ended the message, "P.S.—Will General Hoke be under my command, or is his a separate and co-operating force?" Later that night Adjutant Taylor responded, "General Hoke will, whilst occupying his present relative position to you, be under your control. He was directed to see you and arrange for co-operation to-morrow." Things did not bode well. Hoke had not reported to Anderson, and apparently Taylor failed to instruct him to do so. The order Hoke received from Taylor has not been found, but his response to it was, "The instructions of General Lee have been attended to."[33]

Anderson fared no better with the bureaucrats in Richmond. Though unaware of it—*maybe forever*—Anderson's promotion did not go according to Lee's plan. On May 30, Congress passed an act allowing for temporary brigadier, major, and lieutenant generals. The following morning, Davis nominated Early to temporary rank and informed Lee, who immediately replied, encouraging the promotion of Anderson as well. Davis's letter nominating Early to rank from date of confirmation reached the Senate that day and was promptly confirmed. Lee's telegraphed request prompted the president to have Secretary of War James A. Seddon immediately draft a letter nominating Anderson to rank from May 31. That letter wasn't received by the Senate until the following day, when it was promptly approved. Consequently, Early, who had assumed command of the 2nd Corps on May 27, officially outranked Anderson, who had twenty days seniority over the cantankerous Virginian. If Lee knew the truth, he kept it to himself, and the two lieutenant generals operated for the remainder of the war under the impression that Anderson outranked Early.[34]

Kershaw's Division led Anderson's column on June 1, with Colonel Lawrence M. Keitt's brigade in front. Anderson issued orders for Hoke to simultaneously advance on Cold Harbor, but he "did not become engaged." Rhea's conclusion that, "as neither Anderson nor Hoke evidenced much skill in cooperative operations on other occasions, it is impossible to determine the source of the confusion" is based solely on a postwar account by one of Hoke's brigadiers whose only evidence was an alleged conversation he had with Hoke. While Hoke failed to cooperate on several occasions, only Early ever accused Anderson of such behavior. Moreover, later that day Lee reported that "General Anderson and General Hoke attacked the enemy in their front this forenoon and drove them to their intrenchments." Either Lee deliberately lied or he based his report on an earlier message from Anderson stating that was his intention and Lee assumed it had been done.[35]

Ordered to find the enemy, Kershaw pressed forward. Keitt's men came under fire as they approached Beulah Church. Inexperienced in fighting outside fortifications, Keitt hastily formed his command into a column with a narrow front, deployed skirmishers only on his left flank, and rode forward with his men. He was killed and his men nearly routed before the following brigade could deploy and move forward in support. Seeing Keitt repulsed and Hoke's failure to advance, Kershaw called off the attack. At 8:45 A.M., he notified Anderson of what had occurred, and Anderson notified Hoke that the assault was over. The Confederates began digging in, but Kershaw left a gap between his right and Hoke's left, where a ravine penetrated their line. Hoke attempted to secure this weak spot by advancing Brigadier General Johnson Hagood's Brigade in front of the gap.[36]

Yankee gunners opened on Anderson's position at 4:00 P.M., and the Confederates could see the enemy moving to Cold Harbor. When Hoke saw the Union line extending south beyond his front, he shifted Hagood's Brigade to his right, neglecting to inform Kershaw or his now leftmost commander, Brigadier General Thomas L. Clingman, that the gap between them was once again undefended. At 6:00 P.M., the Yankees advanced, moved through the ravine, and easily penetrated the Confederate line. To the north, one brigade broke, followed by part of another, while south of the ravine, Clingman's Brigade slowly gave way. The Rebels moved quickly to seal the breach. Learning of the breakthrough, Anderson knew Hoke would need reinforcements, and he dispatched two brigades. Hearing nothing from Hoke, he sent Sorrel to check on the situation. Before Sorrel returned, Anderson informed Lee that he believed the enemy would renew the attack at first light and requested reinforcements. He also informed Lee that it would be necessary to drive the Yankees from some of his works or construct a new line. Anderson adopted the latter course, building a horseshoe-shaped line around the ravine that formed a continuous connection with Hoke manned by four brigades. Anderson's prediction was off by twenty-four hours; the attack came at 4:30 A.M. on June 3. Three Union brigades entered Anderson's horseshoe, losing a third of their men.[37]

Ten days later, Early's Corps departed for the Shenandoah Valley to drive the Yankees out and threaten Washington. Grant had already left Cold Harbor, stealing a march on Lee under cover of darkness. Lee reacted quickly, and Anderson marched his corps across the Chickahominy River and bivouacked near Frayser's Farm (Glendale). Locating Grant the following afternoon, it remained to be determined if Grant was going to cross the James River. As a precaution, that night Lee ordered Hoke's Division to move to the pontoon bridge over the James above Drewry's Bluff.[38]

Union troops advanced on Petersburg on the morning of June 15. Hoke immediately departed for the city, and Beauregard began moving troops from Bermuda Hundred to Petersburg. After dark, he abandoned Bermuda Hundred altogether, leaving it up to Lee to deal with the Union Army of the James. Anderson received orders at 3 o'clock the following morning to move a division into the works abandoned by Beauregard. Anderson and Pickett left immediately, leading one of Pickett's brigades. The remainder of Pickett's troops and Field's Division followed. Finding the fortifications in Yankee hands, Pickett deployed his men to attack the left of the line. It was around sunset before Field got his troops in position to assault the center and right. The Confederates charged and regained the left of the main line of earthworks, as well as the secondary line in the center and right, before darkness halted their advance.[39]

Lee arrived on the scene the following morning and, after reconnoitering the area, ordered Anderson to attack at 2:00 P.M. to regain the remainder of the main line. After issuing the order, Lee instructed his engineers and Anderson to examine the position currently held by Field to see if it would suffice. With Field present, Anderson determined that his line was adequate and sent word to Pickett not to advance. Pickett did not receive the order in time, however, and his division attacked. Seeing Pickett charging on their left, many of Field's troops disobeyed orders and joined in the assault, and Anderson then ordered Field to go forward with his entire division. Lee was elated with the performance of Anderson's men: "I believe that they will carry anything they are put against."[40]

Kershaw's Division joined Anderson on the evening of June 17, and was immediately ordered to proceed to Petersburg at 3:00 A.M. the next day. The division, accompanied by Anderson, arrived there later that morning, in time to relieve Beauregard's exhausted soldiers. Field's Division followed and reached the city about noon. Pickett's Division was left to man the Bermuda Hundred defenses. Little of consequence occurred during the ensuing weeks for Anderson's men as they adjusted to siege warfare.[41]

On the morning of July 23, Kershaw's Division departed Petersburg for Chaffin's Bluff, which fell within the Department of Richmond, commanded by Ewell. At 1:30 P.M. on July 27, Anderson was ordered to move his headquarters to Chaffin's and "take command of the troops belonging to this army there," which included Major General Henry Heth's and Kershaw's divisions. Anderson could not command Ewell's troops, and when Ewell was present, he was subject to Ewell's orders. The following day, Anderson attacked the enemy on the Long Bridge Road with four brigades with indecisive results. After receiving a message from Ewell that night, Lee responded, "What is the enemy's force of cavalry? What do you propose to do? Are you directing operations?" Ewell replied, "I consider myself as directing operations as much as circumstances permit. . . . I have not seen Anderson since last night." Ewell's intrusion into the Army of Northern Virginia's command structure would plague Lee for months.[42]

On August 6, Anderson went to Richmond to meet with Lee and President Davis. They determined to create a diversion by having Anderson threaten Washington. By August 12, he had Kershaw's Division, Cutshaw's artillery battalion, and Major General Fitzhugh Lee's Division of cavalry at Culpeper Court House. That afternoon, Anderson received a request from Early for reinforcements. By 4:00 P.M., Anderson had his entire command moving toward the Blue Ridge Mountains. Lee wrote Anderson that day that it appeared the enemy was trying to gain Early's rear by way of Luray Valley and ordered him to "move up to Sperryville and be governed by circumstances." Anderson didn't stop at Sperryville but marched on and arrived at Front Royal on the fourteenth, effectively blocking the northern entrance to the Luray Valley.[43]

Anderson had notified Early in advance that he was coming so that Early could "arrange a combined attack upon the enemy before he discovered the extent of the force suddenly making its appearance in the valley." But no one from Early was at Front Royal when he arrived, and no one appeared the following day. Seeing the opportunity slipping away, Anderson sent Fitz Lee to meet with Early on the sixteenth, but it was too late. Having learned of Anderson's arrival, Major General Philip H. Sheridan (commanding Union forces in the Shenandoah Valley since August 7) began retreating that night.[44]

On August 17, Anderson moved his forces across the Shenandoah River and advanced toward Winchester, where he met with Early on the eighteenth. Early later wrote, "General Anderson ranked me, but he declined to take command, and offered to co-operate in any movement I might suggest." Early departed the following morning for Bunker Hill, and Anderson remained in Winchester until August 21, when he marched his infantry and artillery toward Charlestown and sent Lee's cavalry to Berryville. After a minor skirmish, the main column camped at Summit Point at 3:30 P.M., while Lee's cavalry drove a division of Yankee cavalry through Berryville and bivouacked a mile beyond. As Early saw it, Anderson's failure to press on prevented them from attacking the Union army south of Charlestown. Had Anderson continued, however, he would have left a division of Yankee cavalry free to attack his rear, attack Lee's rear who already faced one division, or ride into Winchester unopposed and gain Early's rear. The next day, Anderson met with Early in Charlestown.[45]

On August 25, Early moved toward Martinsburg and Fitz Lee took most of the cavalry toward Williamsport, and Anderson moved Kershaw's men into Early's vacated position. Jeffry Wert concluded that Sheridan "let the tactical opportunity of the campaign slip by" when he failed to destroy Anderson. Sheridan ordered Major General George Crook to make a strong reconnaissance against Anderson's right at 4:00 P.M. on the twenty-sixth. Crook's reconnaissance force outnumbered Anderson's entire command. Two infantry brigades struck Anderson's right, a third one made a feint on his front, and a brigade of cavalry joined in as well. Anderson realized that instead of chasing Early, Sheridan's army had remained at Halltown and could destroy him at will. Learning that night that Early was not within supporting distance, Anderson decided to retreat at dawn and informed Early that he was retiring behind Opequon Creek.[46]

The men in the ranks knew that something was odd about the way Early and Anderson had maneuvered for the past two weeks. Captain Francis W. Dawson summed it up best: "It was a strange business anyway. General Anderson ranked General Early, but did not wish to take command of his troops, as he would necessarily have done had the two commands operated together. The result was that the two commands swung corners and chasse'ed in every direction to no good purpose, that any of us could see. It was a delightful sort of military pic-nic, and in that sense everybody enjoyed it."[47] Anderson, however, didn't find it humorous, having made it clear to Early that he would not supersede him.

Early had expressed his concern to Lee on August 23, writing that Anderson's actions on the twenty-first had prevented him from crushing Sheridan. On August 26, Lee responded,

> I am aware that Anderson is the ranking officer, but I apprehend no difficulty on that score. . . . He crossed the mountains at your suggestion, and, I think, properly. If his troops are not wanted there he could cross into Loudoun or Fauquier and return to Culpeper. It would add force to the movement of cavalry east of the Blue Ridge. I am in great need of his troops, and if they can be spared from the Valley, or cannot operate to advantage there, I will order them back to Richmond. Let me know.

Early shared the contents of Lee's letter with Anderson, and the two agreed that Anderson should move east of the Blue Ridge with his entire command.[48]

The Confederates knew that Sheridan had advanced his army to Charlestown on August 28, and that on September 2 "the enemy was reported moving in force toward Berryville." Two Union cavalry divisions spent the night at Berryville and early on the third moved to the Front Royal Turnpike, threatening Early's communications. Having finally located the "force," Fitz Lee rode to Newtown in the morning to protect the Confederate rear. At noon, Anderson departed Winchester headed for Berryville, rather than taking the direct road to Ashby's Gap. Possibly he thought he might be able to squeeze the Union cavalry between Kershaw's infantry and Lee's cavalry as he moved east toward the Blue Ridge. What Anderson didn't know was that he was marching toward Sheridan's entire army. Earlier that morning, Sheridan managed to move forty thousand infantry without Early learning of it. Over fifteen thousand infantry under Crook marched from Halltown to Berryville, with the thirteen-thousand-man 19th Corps following. The 6th Corps, over twelve thousand strong, moved from Charleston to Clifton.[49]

Lacking cavalry, Anderson ran head on into Crook four miles west of Berryville about an hour before sunset. One of Anderson's staff recalled, "It was at this time that the whole command could have been gobbled up . . . and General Anderson reached the conclusion that nothing but audacity would save us." While Kershaw deployed his infantry in line of battle, Cutshaw's cannon began firing. Anderson even brought his wagon train up to Kershaw's line. Then the Confederates charged across the open ground that separated them from the Yankees, who were firing from behind stone walls. A Union regiment broke, then another, and at least two more gave way as well. Instead of being able to outflank Anderson with his superior numbers, Crook had to use his second division to shore up the first. T. Harry Williams wrote, "The impromptu little battle had been a real slugging match, fought by both sides with lethal tenacity, much of it in darkness with friend indistinguishable from foe." Crook retired, leaving Anderson in possession of the high ground, less than a mile from Berryville.[50]

Prisoners informed Anderson that the 6th Corps was only three miles away, but apparently the whereabouts of the 19th Corps remained unknown. Anderson informed Early of his situation and urged him to join him by daylight on the fourth. Early arrived with three divisions about 9:30, claiming muddy roads had delayed him. By then, Crook had fallen back and Sheridan placed his three corps in a continuous fortified line. Anderson and Early decided that while Anderson demonstrated in Sheridan's front with two divisions, Early would take two divisions and attempt to turn the Union right. But the Yankee line was too long and well fortified for even the rash Early to attempt an assault. Anderson concurred with Early's decision, and the two commanders moved west of Opequon Creek on September 5.[51]

Sheridan was unwilling to cross the Opequon in force, so after quiet had reigned in the Valley for a week, Anderson and Early conferred again as to what the latter should do. They decided that Lee's cavalry should remain in the Valley and Anderson would take Kershaw's infantry and Cutshaw's artillery east of the Blue Ridge. Brigadier General James Connor wrote afterward, "Had Early been less selfish and more harmonizing [Kershaw's] Division need never have left Winchester. If he had told Anderson that he needed it Anderson would have left it, but they did not harmonize."[52]

Anderson was about to depart on September 13 when Union cavalry surprised and captured his pickets on the Berryville Road. This activity by the enemy caused Anderson to postpone his departure. When Sheridan failed to follow up and attack, Anderson departed Winchester on the fifteenth and arrived at Culpeper on the morning of the nineteenth.[53]

Unaware of Anderson's departure, Lee wrote Early on September 17,

> I have been very anxious to recall General Anderson with Kershaw's division to me. But a victory at this time over Sheridan would be greatly advantageous to us, and I feared that your corps would be insufficient for the purpose. General Anderson is more necessary here than in the Valley, and I have written to him to return with his staff if circumstances permit, and to direct General Kershaw with his division to report to you for the present. Should you and he decide that Kershaw's division is unnecessary in the Valley, I wish it to return with General A.

In a similar message to Anderson that day, Lee added, "Should you and General Early agree that the presence of Kershaw's division in the Valley is unnecessary you can bring it to Gordonsville with you. . . . Let me know what is your determination."[54]

At noon on September 20, Anderson proceeded to Rapidan Station. The next two days his men labored to rebuild the bridge while he received a series of messages from Lee stating that Early had been defeated and would probably be calling upon him for reinforcements. When the bridge was finished on the twenty-third, having heard nothing from Early, Anderson moved to Gordonsville. Awaiting Anderson when he arrived that night were fresh orders from Lee: "Early has again met with a reverse. . . . Send Kershaw's division with battalion of artillery through Swift Run Gap to report to him at once. You had best report here in person with your staff."[55]

Anderson arrived in Richmond on the twenty-sixth and reported to Lee's headquarters at Petersburg the next day. After dining with Lee, Anderson proceeded to Pickett's Division at Bermuda Hundred. Two brigades of Field's Division were north of the James, while the remaining three formed Lee's mobile reserve. On September 28, Lee ordered Anderson to assume command of the troops north of the James.[56]

Anderson departed early the next morning for Chaffin's Bluff, reaching there at 11:00 A.M. He met with Ewell, who informed him that Fort Harrison had been captured along with the exterior line of defenses east of it. Anderson took command of Brigadier Generals John Gregg's and Henry Benning's brigades on Ewell's left, as they struggled to hold the earthworks between Fort Harrison and Fort Gilmer. Later that night, Field encountered Lee and informed him of his intention to attack Fort Harrison immediately, "but [Lee] thought it better to remain where I was for the present."[57]

Between 10:00 P.M. and daylight, Major General Robert Hoke arrived with three of his brigades and one from the 3rd Corps. Lee commenced his attack on Fort Harrison at 1:45 P.M. It was his plan, and he remained on the field, but Anderson was placed in command of the two divisions. Richard Sommers described the plan as "complicated [hinging] on timing and tactical skill to offset the dangers of concentrating distant columns at the actual point of battle. Lee . . . felt sure his veteran infantry had that skill." The attack fell apart when Brigadier General George T. Anderson's Brigade, the first to advance, failed to lie down in a depression as planned. Brigadier General Anderson had neglected to inform his subordinates of this critical detail. To support Anderson's Georgians, Field ordered his remaining two brigades to advance immediately. Hoke, however, refused to budge until 2:00 P.M., and the respective locations of Hoke, Anderson, and Lee prevented Hoke from receiving orders to advance immediately. Field's Division was fought out before Hoke moved forward with only two of five brigades. The fiasco cost twelve hundred casualties, and Lee rode out to rally the survivors in a scene reminiscent of Pickett's Charge.[58]

On October 7, Lee and Anderson watched their troops advance along the Charles City and Darbytown roads. Initially successful, Field's Division then advanced southward along the outside of the Confederate's old exterior line of fortifications, while Hoke's men moved parallel to it on the inside. They encountered Union infantry near the New Market Road. Anderson reported: "Field's Division advanced. . . . Hoke's Division did not become engaged on the right. . . . By direction of the commanding General, who had in person conducted the attack, the troops were withdrawn." Hoke had left Field's men hanging for the second time in nine days. In his report, Lee credited Anderson with the victory on the Charles City Road and with failing to dislodge the enemy on the New Market Road.[59]

On October 10, Anderson began to construct a new line of fortifications that ran from Fort Gilmer to the Charles City Road, where it tied into the old exterior line. Union troops moved against the extreme left of Anderson's new line near the Darbytown Road on the thirteenth. They were repeatedly repulsed by Field's Division. This was Anderson's last action as commander of the 1st Corps. Longstreet, having sufficiently recovered to return to duty, resumed command of the corps on October 19.[60]

Wanting to keep Anderson with him as a lieutenant general, Lee created a fourth corps out of Beauregard's old command. Known as Anderson's Corps, it officially consisted of the divisions of Major Generals Robert Hoke and Bushrod R. Johnson and four battalions of artillery. In reality, Anderson seldom commanded more than Johnson's division and several battalions of artillery. He was responsible for the fortifications east of Petersburg, from the

Appomattox River to Rive's House. Longstreet held the left flank north of the James because he outranked Ewell. With Pickett south of the James and Kershaw in the Valley, Longstreet only had Ewell's reserves and Field's Division, so Hoke was detached to him. In December, Hoke's Division departed for Wilmington, North Carolina.[61]

When Anderson took command of his new corps, Johnson's Division was significantly larger than any other in the army. Except for a minor action in late October and the death of Brigadier General Archibald Gracie Jr. on December 2, little occurred of consequence until March 25, 1865, when two of Anderson's brigades participated in the futile attack on Fort Stedman. Four days later, Anderson fought the indecisive Battle of Lewis's Farm.[62]

When Grant attempted to cut the Southside Railroad, Lee countered by concentrating more than ten thousand men, including two of Anderson's brigades, at Five Forks under Pickett. On March 31, Lee attempted to turn the Union left flank with four brigades, including Anderson's remaining two. Lee directed the operation, with Anderson in tactical command. The Yankees attacked first, however, but three Confederate brigades routed three Union brigades, then routed two more. A. Wilson Greene concluded, "Thus, three undersized and organizationally unrelated brigades had combined to drive two veteran Union divisions from the field. It was a remarkable tactical achievement." Anderson drove the Yankees one and a half miles, but the outnumbered Confederates eventually had to withdraw.[63]

That same day Pickett attacked Dinwiddie Court House, but he withdrew that night to Five Forks. Lee was with Anderson on April 1, when they heard firing from Five Forks at 4:00 P.M. Pickett's command was quickly overrun, suffering three thousand casualties. Learning of the disaster about 5:30, Lee instructed Anderson to move to Pickett's relief. Anderson met with Fitz Lee at Church Crossing early on April 2, but there was no word from Pickett. News arrived at 11:00 A.M. that the Yankees had broken through the lines at Petersburg, along with orders for Anderson "to retire behind the Appomattox crossing at Bevill's Bridge." Anderson's men moved out at noon, with Lee's cavalry covering his rear.[64]

Anderson found Pickett at Bevill's Bridge, who informed him that Brigadier General Matt W. Ransom's and William H. Wallace's brigades had been virtually wiped out at Five Forks. Before crossing the Appomattox, Anderson received orders from General Lee to remain south of the river and march toward Amelia Court House with Johnson's and Pickett's divisions. The two divisions numbered fewer than eight thousand men, having lost half their strength in five weeks.[65]

Marching west about four miles on April 4, the Confederates came to an intersection with the road leading south occupied by Union cavalry.

Anderson could have continued marching west, but as William Marvel pointed out, if Anderson had failed to hold this intersection, Yankee troopers could "gallop northward to intercept the rest of the army on the Goode's Bridge Road. The security of Lee's line of retreat therefore depended on Anderson holding that crossroads." He did so until the following morning.[66]

At 4:00 A.M. on the fifth, Anderson's men headed north and reached Scott's Shop at 8:40 A.M. After resting there a couple of hours while Mahone's Division marched past, Anderson's troops pushed on to Amelia Court House, where Lee began reorganizing his army. When A. P. Hill had been killed on April 2, Lee had put Longstreet in temporary command of that portion of Hill's Corps that had been east of the breakthrough at Petersburg. Shortly after noon, Lee made Longstreet's command of the reunited 3rd Corps permanent, telling Hill's division commanders, "I give notice of my purpose to dimish [diminish] the number of Corps and division commanders in this army."[67]

It was after dark when Lee's infantry resumed their march. Field's Division, flanked by two cavalry divisions, headed the column, followed by the divisions of Cadmus M. Wilcox and Henry Heth. Instead of following Heth as ordered, Mahone mistakenly turned to the right, taking the road to Paineville. Pickett followed, and the error was not discovered until Mahone caught up with a wagon train. The two divisions had to retrace their steps and then drive away enemy cavalry that had seized the road during the interim.[68]

Once on the correct route, Mahone and Pickett were followed by Johnson, Major General G. W. Custis Lee, Kershaw, Gordon's 2nd Corps, and finally Major General William H. F. "Rooney" Lee's cavalry. Longstreet outstripped the column and reached Rice's Station early on April 6; the rear of the column was fifteen miles back. Moreover, the wagon train was merging with the infantry near Deatonsville, further slowing the pace. Mahone was having breakfast with Pickett at Little Sailor's Creek when he received orders from General Lee to move his division past the ordnance wagons and artillery currently ahead of his men and hasten to join Longstreet. After marching about one mile, Mahone encountered General Lee at an intersection. Lee "requested" Mahone to detach a brigade to guard the road leading south before proceeding to Rice's Station. Instead of leaving his strongest brigade, Mahone left *only half* of his second weakest, approximately 250 men instead of 1,000.[69]

Pickett was still at Little Sailor's Creek when Johnson's Division was attacked at Holt's Corner. Pickett headed back and deployed on Johnson's right as Custis Lee came up and deployed on Johnson's left. Chris M. Calkins, the expert on the Battle of Sailor's Creek, wrote in 1997, "The reason for what

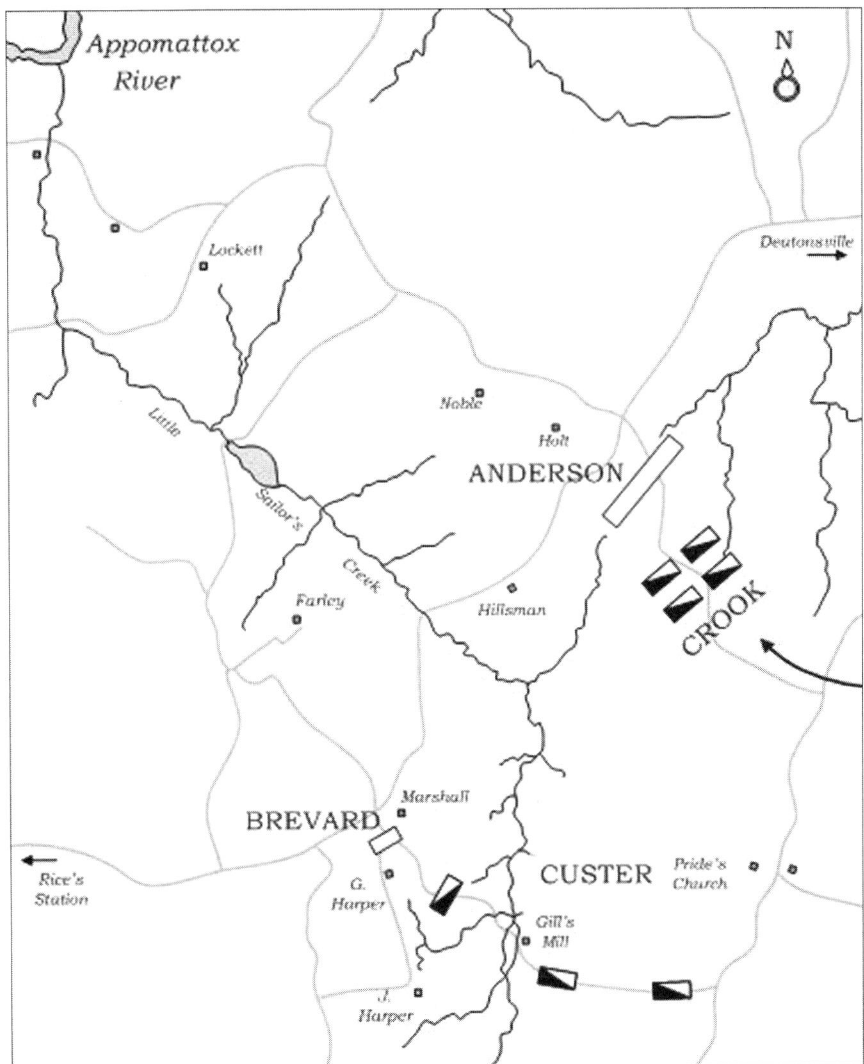

Deployment near Little Sailor's Creek about noon, April 6, 1865. Courtesy of Stuart Salling.

became a two-mile gap was that Anderson was being attacked by George Crook's cavalry at Holt's . . . Corner." More recently, William Marvel concluded, "The long line of slow-moving wagons . . . occluded any view of the trouble at Mahone's rear: the officers at the tail of his column failed to detect that Pickett's division had stopped to fight, so they marched on, oblivious to the gap developing between the two infantry divisions." Neither historian held any Confederate general responsible for the gap.[70]

While Crook held Anderson at Holt's, Brigadier General George A. Custer's Division rode on. Crossing Little Sailor's Creek at Gill's Mill, Custer's troopers captured most of Mahone's detachment before striking the Rice's Station Road at Marshall's Corner. The lead brigade turned right toward Holt's Corner, gobbling up wagons and artillery. Hunton's Brigade, resting behind Anderson's right flank, immediately charged across Little Sailor's Creek. Pickett followed with the remainder of his division and drove Custer's lone brigade back half a mile. Hearing the firing about 2:00 P.M., Anderson immediately dispatched Johnson with two brigades. As Johnson crossed the creek, two more brigades of Union cavalry arrived.[71]

Anderson had remained near Holt's with two of Johnson's brigades and Custis Lee's ad hoc division. Lee later reported, "General Anderson seemed anxious to push on, and said to me that he must move on to support General Pickett. . . . As soon as General Gordon closed up on General Ewell's rear (Kershaw), General Anderson moved forward towards [Little] Sailor's Creek."[72]

Having been informed of Anderson's situation, Ewell hurried to confer with him. Anderson suggested they either unite and break through or move off through the woods to their right and attempt to reach Farmville. Ewell later claimed that he recommended the second alternative but left the decision to Anderson, who chose to fight. Ewell returned to his command and told Custis Lee that "General Anderson wished us to unite with him and drive the enemy out of the way." Anderson ordered Johnson's men to shift to Pickett's right while Lee closed on Pickett's left. Before the attack commenced, however, word arrived that the enemy had closed on Ewell's rear, a consequence of Gordon having followed the wagon train instead of Ewell. "General Anderson told General Ewell that the latter would have as much as he could do to take care of the rear," recalled Lee, "and that he (General Anderson) would endeavor to drive the enemy out of the way in front." Ewell agreed. Lee pulled his division out of line between Kershaw and Pickett, moved behind Kershaw, and formed on his left.[73]

Within five minutes of advancing, Anderson's men were repulsed. While Anderson hurried to rally his troops, Ewell rode off to rejoin his command, only to be captured en route. Anderson's line collapsed when Union cavalry penetrated between Johnson's and Pickett's divisions. Then Yankee troopers broke through Pickett's front at several points, capturing Brigadier Generals Hunton and Montgomery D. Corse, along with hundreds of their men. It was now every man for himself.[74]

About 1:00 P.M., Lee learned that Yankee cavalry had struck the wagon train about two miles away. Learning nothing more, at 3:00 P.M. Lee headed back with Mahone's Division. From a hilltop, Lee saw Ewell's men surrender in the distance while Anderson's fled toward him. Mahone recalled,

> I saw in the tale [*sic*] end of the fleeing herde [*sic*] my old division commander. . . . I rode down and met Genl Anderson. I discovered at once that he had lost his heart in the cause. He was the picture, the sad picture, of a man who was whipped. I said Genl Lee wished to see you Genl Anderson. When he had come up to Genl Lee I said Genl Lee here is Genl Anderson, where upon turning his head toward Genl Anderson, he said with severe emphasis Genl Anderson, take command of these straglers [*sic*] and to the rear—signaling the emphasis by a violent sling of his left hand. Genl Anderson rode on[,] the herde [*sic*] following him.[75]

"Could Lee have prevented the disaster at Sayler's [*sic*] Creek? Was he to blame for it? Probably not," asked and answered Freeman. "Neglect of his orders rather than a defect in them opened the two gaps through which the Federals struck in front and in rear," claimed the biographer, who contended that the gap in front resulted from the failure of Anderson and Pickett to notify Mahone that Pickett had halted, but "Mahone, also, must take his share of the blame." Ten years later in *Lee's Lieutenants,* however, Freeman blamed only Anderson.[76] Since Lee ordered Mahone to march on and sent no similar orders to Pickett, and Mahone was with Pickett when he received the orders, Lee, Mahone, and Pickett all knew that a gap would occur in the line. Anderson, waiting for Ewell's arrival at Holt's Corner, was unaware of Mahone's departure. Moreover, Anderson's only means of closing the gap would require him to abandon Holt's and allow Union cavalry to cut off Ewell, Gordon, and the wagon train moving between them.

After leaving Lee, Anderson moved westward with the army, gathering and organizing his troops on the march. The following day, Lee temporarily attached Pickett's Division to Mahone's Division and Johnson's Division to Gordon's Corps. Then, on the afternoon of April 8, Lee relieved Anderson, Pickett, and Johnson of their commands and ordered them from the army. The three could go where they wished and then report their location to Secretary of War John C. Breckinridge. Lee never gave a reason for their removal.[77]

Freeman speculated in 1934 that Lee either concluded that Anderson was too despondent to remain on duty or that he was responsible for the debacle at Sailor's Creek. He offered no opinion regarding Pickett and Johnson. Ten years later he concluded that all three generals were relieved because "they did not have commands that fitted their rank. To assign them to head other troops would entail the displacement of officers who had done their full duty and had not suffered defeat. On the other hand, to call on the three Generals to remain with the Army and to have no part in its battles was a humiliation." Freeman was less than candid. More recently, another of Lee's biographers, Emory Thomas, concluded that "this trio felt Lee's wrath, and Lee's righteousness endured to the end of his tenure in command."[78]

Freeman's claim that "they did not have commands that fitted their rank" rings hollow. Pickett managed to remain in command of his division, only the second smallest. Though not its commander, Johnson surrendered with his division, the fourth largest. By rank and previous service, Anderson should have replaced the fallen Hill. Yet Lee had decided otherwise prior to Sailor's Creek. Lee wanted his infantry consolidated under Longstreet and Gordon. The 3rd Corps was assigned to Longstreet because two of its division commanders outranked Gordon. Conversely, Gordon outranked Johnson and Custis Lee.[79] Undoubtedly, Lee would have relieved Ewell as well had he not been captured.

Anderson was still gathering the fragments of his command when he received the order relieving him. Departing promptly, he escaped the encircling Yankees and headed south, probably intending to report to Breckinridge in person. Unable to do so, Anderson went home.[80]

More than any other Confederate officer, Richard Heron Anderson was responsible for the Confederate victory at Williamsburg. He was the superstar at Seven Pines and Spotsylvania. He was the first man promoted to major general in the Army of Northern Virginia following the Seven Days' Battles, and after his performance at Second Manassas, Robert E. Lee doubled the size of his division, making it the strongest in the army. Following Anderson's performance at Chancellorsville, Lee deemed him a "capital officer" capable of commanding a corps. In June 1864, the South Carolinian rode at the head of his vanguard when his troops restored the line across Bermuda Hundred and when they prevented the fall of Petersburg. On his own initiative, he entered the Shenandoah Valley to secure Early's rear even after Old Jube had blamed him for his own shortcomings at Bethesda Church. He routed a Yankee corps with barely a fourth its numbers at Berryville. At White Oak Road his ad hoc command of three undersized brigades routed two divisions, and four days later he held the intersection that enabled the Army of Northern Virginia to escape the pursuing Yankees and concentrate at Amelia Court House.

Anderson was wounded at Sharpsburg before he could demonstrate his competence, which he was able to do at Fredericksburg, Bristoe Station, Mine Run, the Wilderness, North Anna River, Bethesda Church, Charlestown, Lewis's Farm, and throughout the siege of Petersburg. The breakthrough at Cold Harbor was Robert Hoke's fault, and Anderson quickly sealed the breech. Hoke also failed the South Carolinian at Darbytown Road, and it was Hoke, along with Robert E. Lee and G. T. Anderson, who were responsible for the fiasco at Fort Harrison. Without abandoning Holt's Corner, and with it Ewell's ad hoc command, Gordon's 2nd Corps, and the principal wagon train, there was little Anderson could have done to prevent the disaster at Little Sailor's Creek. His exhausted, hungry men, many lacking weapons, were no match for the more numerous Yankee cavalrymen who had ridden to the battlefield with full stomachs, many carrying repeating carbines.

But there was that black mark earned at Gettysburg. Inexplicably, those same historians who have maligned Anderson for his conduct on other battlefields fail to criticize him for the one event that warranted it. With so many to fault at Gettysburg, the South Carolinian's failure deserves to be overlooked.

In his writings on Civil War generals, T. Harry Williams demonstrated that to be a great battle captain in that conflict one had to be willing to fight. What general on either side could claim to have a more aggressive—and successful—record in battle than "Fighting Dick" Anderson? He was no Robert E. Lee or Stonewall Jackson, but how many generals in the Army of Northern Virginia deserve to be rated between Jackson and Anderson on the Lee Scale? Certainly no more than a handful, if you ask *only one historian.*

Notes

I am eternally grateful to Edwin C. Bearss, Chief Historian Emeritus of the National Park Service, for sharing with me his opinion of Lee's lieutenant generals before I began researching this essay. Prior to our conversation, I was ready to write Anderson off as the worst of the lot. I sent a copy of my finished essay to Ed, and though it was unsolicited, he carefully edited it and returned it to me, leaving me doubly indebted to him. I also wish to thank Stuart Salling of Opelousas, Louisiana, for having the patience to put up with me while producing the maps.

1. C. Irvine Walker, *The Life of Lieutenant General Richard Heron Anderson of the Confederate States Army* (Charleston, SC, 1917); Joseph Cantey Elliott, *Lieutenant General Richard Heron Anderson: Lee's Noble Soldier* (Dayton, OH, 1985), 157; Douglas Southall Freeman, *Lee's Lieutenants: A Study in Command,* 3 vols. (New York, 1942–44), 3:635–36.
2. Walker, *Life of Lieutenant General Richard Heron Anderson,* 10, 25; George W. Cullum, *Biographical Register of the Officers and Graduates of the U.S. Military Academy at West Point, N.Y., from Its Establishment, in 1802, to 1890, with the Early History of the United States Military Academy,* vol. 2, 3rd rev. ed. (Boston, 1891), 147; Elliott, *Lieutenant General Richard Heron Anderson,* 30, 43.

3. Gov. F. W. Pickens to Secretary of War Leroy P. Walker, July 11, 1861, Brig. Gen./Maj. Gen. Richard H. Anderson File, Compiled Service Records of Confederate General and Staff Officers, and Nonregimental Enlisted Men, National Archives and Records Administration, Washington, DC (hereafter cited as NARA); Walker, *Life of Lieutenant General Richard Heron Anderson,* 58; U.S. War Department, *War of the Rebellion: The Official Records of the Union and Confederate Armies,* 128 vols. (Washington, DC, 1880–1901), ser. 1, vol. 1:36 (hereafter cited as *OR;* all references are to series 1 unless otherwise indicated); ibid., vol. 53:176.

4. Cullum, *Biographical Register,* 147; Marcus J. Wright, comp., *General Officers of the Confederate Army, Officers of the Executive Departments of the Confederate States, Members of the Confederate Congress by States* (New York, 1911), 21, 46–56; Brig. Gen./Maj. Gen. Richard H. Anderson File; Colonel R. H. Anderson File, 1st (Butler's) South Carolina Regulars, Compiled Service Records of Confederate Soldiers Who Served in Organizations from the State of South Carolina, M267, NARA, Washington, DC.

5. *OR,* vol. 51, pt. 2:245; ibid., vol. 6:458–59, 753–54; Elliott, *Lieutenant General Richard Heron Anderson,* 34.

6. *OR,* vol. 6:497–98; Elliott, *Lieutenant General Richard Heron Anderson,* 37; Bragg, S.O. No. 8/2, Army of Pensacola, Jan. 8, 1862, and S.O. No. 40, Department of Alabama and West Florida, Jan. 31, 1862, both in Brig. Gen./Maj. Gen. Richard H. Anderson File.

7. Quoted in Elliott, *Lieutenant General Richard Heron Anderson,* 152; *OR,* vol. 9:430; ibid., vol. 5:914, 1074.

8. *OR,* vol. 5:1074; ibid., vol. 11, pt. 1:275, 441, 564.

9. *OR,* vol. 11, pt. 1:564–65, 567, 568, 580–81; Freeman, *Lee's Lieutenants,* 1:192; Steven E. Woodworth, *No Band of Brothers: Problems of the Rebel High Command* (Columbia, MO, 1999), 24, 29–30, 35–36; Carol Kettenburg Dubbs, *Defend This Old Town: Williamsburg during the Civil War* (Baton Rouge, 2002), 197.

10. *OR,* vol. 11, pt. 1:570–71, 582, 591; John Bratton, "The Battle of Williamsburg," *Southern Historical Society Papers* 7 (1879): 299; E. P. Alexander, "Sketch of Longstreet's Division—Yorktown and Williamsburg," *Southern Historical Society Papers* 10 (1882): 42; Edmund D. Patterson, *Yankee Rebel: The Civil War Journal of Edmund DeWitt Patterson,* ed. John G. Barrett (1966; reprint, Knoxville, 2004), 20; Elliott, *Lieutenant General Richard Heron Anderson,* 37; Douglas Southall Freeman, *R. E. Lee: A Biography,* 4 vols. (New York, 1949), 4:111n25.

11. Wright, *General Officers,* 27, 56, 62–63, 67, 69, 71; Gerald A. Patterson, *From Blue to Gray: The Life of Confederate General Cadmus M. Wilcox* (Mechanicsburg, PA, 2001), 36.

12. Janet E. Hewett, ed., *Supplement to the Official Records of the Union and Confederate Armies,* 100 vols. (Wilmington, NC, 1994–2004), 2:428 (hereafter cited as *SOR;* all citations are to part 1 unless otherwise indicated); Elliott, *Lieutenant General Richard Heron Anderson,* 45–46, 47; *OR,* vol. 11, pt. 1:941; Freeman, *R. E. Lee,* 2:91; Freeman, *Lee's Lieutenants,* 1:249.

13. Longstreet to [Lee], June 6, 1862, Brig. Gen./Maj. Gen. Richard H. Anderson File; Robert E. Lee, *Lee's Dispatches: Unpublished Letters of General Robert E. Lee, C.S.A., to Jefferson Davis and the War Department of The Confederate States of America, 1862–1865,* ed. Douglas Southall Freeman, new ed. by Grady McWhiney (1915; New York, 1957), 10; Jefferson Davis, *The Papers of Jefferson Davis,* vol. 8, *1862,* ed. Lynda L. Crist, Mary S. Dix, and Kenneth H. Williams (Baton Rouge, 1995), 271.

14. Joseph E. Cullen, *The Peninsula Campaign, 1862: McClellan and Lee Struggle for Richmond* (New York, 1973); Richard Wheeler, *Sword Over Richmond: An Eyewitness History of McClellan's Peninsula Campaign* (New York, 1986); map of the Battle of Gaines Mill, Civil War Trust website, http://www.civilwar.org/battlefields/gainesmill/maps/gainesmillmap.html/ (accessed May 3, 2010).

15. Freeman, *Lee's Lieutenants,* 1:652; Lee, *Lee's Dispatches,* 33; Brig. Gen./Maj. Gen. Richard H. Anderson File; *Journal of the Congress of the Confederate States of America, 1861–1865,* 7 vols. (Washington, DC, 1904–5), 2:298, 343, 374; *OR,* vol. 11, pt. 3:642. Anderson was confirmed on the twenty-seventh, though his service record states the twenty-sixth.

16. John Hennessy, *Return to Bull Run: The Campaign and Battle of Second Manassas* (New York, 1993), 309, 421–24, 561; John Hennessy, *Second Manassas Battlefield Map Study,* 2nd ed. (Lynchburg, VA, n.d.), 426–27.

17. Hennessy, *Return to Bull Run,* 462; *OR,* vol. 12, pt. 2:737; James Longstreet, *From Manassas to Appomattox* (Philadelphia, 1896), 191; Freeman, *Lee's Lieutenants* 2:139; Joseph T. Glatthaar, *General Lee's Army: From Victory to Collapse* (New York, 2008), 162; Walker, *Life of Lieutenant General Richard Heron Anderson,* 96.

18. *OR,* vol. 19, pt. 1:145; Stephen W. Sears, *Landscape Turned Red: The Battle of Antietam* (New York, 1983), 240, 241–42; Robert K. Krick, "It Appeared as Though Mutual Extermination Would Put a Stop to the Awful Carnage: Confederates in Sharpsburg's Bloody Lane," in *The Antietam Campaign,* ed. Gary W. Gallagher (Chapel Hill, 1999), 239.

19. *OR,* vol. 19, pt. 2:674, 683; ibid., vol. 21:569, 571.

20. *OR,* vol. 25, pt. 1:796–800, 849–51, 995.

21. Ibid., 851–53.

22. Ibid., 803; Freeman, *Lee's Lieutenants,* 2:655, 665; Gary W. Gallagher, *Lee the Soldier* (Lincoln, NE, 1996), 365.

23. Glatthaar, *General Lee's Army,* 254, 343; Wright, *General Officers,* 28, 32; *OR,* vol. 25, pt. 2:810–11, 860.

24 Freeman, *Lee's Lieutenants,* 2:696, 697; *OR,* vol. 25, pt. 2:840.

25. *OR,* vol. 27, pt. 2:608, 613–15.

26. Ibid., vol. 36, pt. 1:1062, 370, 372; Gordon C. Rhea, *The Battle of the Wilderness, May 5–6, 1864* (Baton Rouge, 1994), 371, 374n41, 381, 400–401; *SOR,* 6:696.

27. G. Moxley Sorrel, *Recollections of a Confederate Staff Officer,* ed. Bell I. Wiley (Jackson, TN, 1958), 238–39; *SOR,* 6:656.

28. *OR,* vol. 36, pt. 1:1041; Freeman, *Lee's Lieutenants,* 3:379n22, 380n24, 444; Walker, *Life of Lieutenant General Richard Heron Anderson,* 162–63; William W. Hassler, "'Fighting Dick' Anderson," *Civil War Times Illustrated* 12, no. 10 (Feb. 1974): 41; William A. Blair, "Grant's Second World War: The Battle for Historical Memory," in *The Spotsylvania Campaign,* ed. Gary W. Gallagher (Chapel Hill, 1998), 243.

29. Freeman, *Lee's Lieutenants,* 3:384–87, 444; Gordon C. Rhea, "Lee, Grant, and 'Prescience' in the Overland Campaign," in *Audacity Personified: The Generalship of Robert E. Lee,* ed. Peter S. Carmichael (Baton Rouge, 2004), 68.

30. Gordon C. Rhea, *To the North Anna River: Grant and Lee, May 13–25, 1864* (Baton Rouge, 2000), 216, 248–49, 345, 354; Glatthaar, *General Lee's Army,* 375; *OR,* vol. 36, pt. 3:814, 823–24, 828, 834, 838, 858; *SOR* 3:542.

31. Gordon C. Rhea, *Cold Harbor: Grant and Lee, May 26–June 3, 1864* (Baton Rouge, 2002), 125, 148; *OR,* vol. 36, pt. 3:851, 854.

32. Gary Gallagher, introduction to reprint of Jubal A. Early, *Lieutenant General Jubal Anderson Early, C.S.A.: Autobiographical Sketch and Narrative of the War Between the States* (Wilmington, NC, 1989 [orig. pub. 1912]), x; quoted in Rhea, *Cold Harbor,* 157–58; *OR,* vol. 51, pt. 1:245.

33. Rhea, *Cold Harbor,* 188, 198; *OR,* vol. 36, pt. 3:858; ibid., vol. 51, pt. 2:974, 975.

34. *Journal of the Congress of the Confederate States* 4:127, 128, 135–36; Jefferson Davis, *The Papers of Jefferson Davis,* vol. 10, *October 1863–August 1864,* ed. Lynda L. Crist, Kenneth H. Williams, and Peggy L. Dillard (Baton Rouge, 1999), 442–43.

35. Rhea, *Cold Harbor,* 196, 445n4; *OR,* vol. 36, pt. 1:1031, 1059.

36. Rhea, *Cold Harbor,* 199–200, 202.

37. Ibid., 228, 232, 234, 249–50, 253, 264–65, 350, 359–60; *OR,* vol. 51, pt. 2:976; ibid., vol. 36, pt. 1:1032.

38. Freeman, *Lee's Lieutenants,* 3:528–29; *SOR,* 7:249.

39. Freeman, *Lee's Lieutenants,* 3:529–31; *SOR,* 7:250; *OR,* vol. 40, pt. 1:760.

40. *SOR,* 7:250; quoted in Freeman, *Lee's Lieutenants,* 3:532.

41. *OR,* vol. 40, pt. 1:760–61; Freeman, *Lee's Lieutenants,* 3:537; *SOR,* 7:251.

42. *OR,* vol. 40, pt. 1:762; *SOR,* 7:252; *OR,* vol. 40, pt. 3:813.

43. *OR,* vol. 42, pt. 1:873; *SOR,* 7:253; *OR,* vol. 43, pt. 1:997.

44. *SOR,* 7:597.

45. *OR,* vol. 42, pt. 1:873–74; Early, *Lieutenant General Jubal Anderson Early,* 408; *OR,* vol. 43, pt. 1:516.

46. *OR,* vol. 42, pt. 1:874; Jeffry D. Wert, *From Winchester to Cedar Creek: The Shenandoah Campaign of 1864* (Carlisle, PA, 1987), 38; *OR,* vol. 43, pt. 1:360, 920; *SOR,* 7:254.

47. Francis W. Dawson, *Reminiscences of Confederate Service, 1861–1865* (Charleston, SC, 1882), 123.

48. *OR,* vol. 43, pt. 1:1006; Early, *Lieutenant General Jubal Anderson Early,* 411.

49. *OR,* vol. 43, pt. 1:156, 426, 974, 1026; Early, *Lieutenant General Jubal Anderson Early,* 411.

50. *OR,* vol. 43, pt. 1:360–61; *SOR,* 7:256; Dawson, *Reminiscences,* 122–23; T. Harry Williams, *Hayes of the Twenty-third: The Civil War Volunteer Officer* (New York, 1965), 241–42.

51. *OR,* vol. 42, pt. 1:875; *SOR,* 7:256; *OR,* vol. 43, pt. 1:361.

52. *OR,* vol. 43, pt. 1:156; ibid., vol. 42, pt. 2:1257; Early, *Lieutenant General Jubal Anderson Early,* 413; quoted in Wert, *From Winchester to Cedar Creek,* 41.

53. *SOR,* 7:257.

54. *OR,* vol. 42, pt. 2:1257; ibid., vol. 43, pt. 2:876.

55. *OR,* vol. 43, pt. 2:877, 878; ibid., vol. 42, pt. 1:875.

56. *OR,* vol. 42, pt. 1:875; Dawson, *Reminiscences,* 125; Richard J. Sommers, *Richmond Redeemed: The Siege at Petersburg* (New York, 1981), 24–25, 28.

57. *SOR,* 7:258; *OR,* vol. 42, pt. 1:875; C. W. Field, "Campaign of 1864 and 1865," *Southern Historical Society Papers* 14 (1886): 556.

58. *OR,* vol. 42, pt. 1:876; Sommers, *Richmond Redeemed,* 137, 139–40, 143, 145, 146–47.

59. *OR*, vol. 42, pt. 1:876; *SOR*, 7:259–60; Robert E. Lee, *The Wartime Papers of R. E. Lee*, ed. Clifford Dowdey and Louis H. Manarin (Boston, 1961), 861.

60. *OR*, vol. 42, pt. 1:876; *SOR*, 7:260; Field, "Campaign of 1864 and 1865," 558.

61. F. Ray Sibley Jr., *The Confederate Order of Battle*, vol. 1, *The Army of Northern Virginia* (Shippensburg, PA, 1996), 149–50, 158, 166–68, 175–76, 185–86, 194–95, 204–5, 214–15; *SOR*, 7:462, 818; A. Wilson Greene, *The Final Battles of the Petersburg Campaign: Breaking the Backbone of the Rebellion*, 2nd ed. (Knoxville, 2008), 14–15, 21–22.

62. Walter H. Taylor, *Four Years with General Lee*, rev. ed. (New York, 1962), 179–86; *SOR*, 7:745, 818–19, 820; William C. Davis, ed., *The Confederate General*, 6 vols. (Harrisburg, PA, 1991), 3:22.

63. Greene, *Final Battles*, 154, 165, 170, 172; *SOR*, 7:745–46, 779, 820.

64. Greene, *Final Battles*, 186; *SOR*, 7:780–82, 820; *OR*, vol. 46, pt. 1:1288.

65. *OR*, vol. 46, pt. 1:1289, 1300; William Marvel, *Lee's Last Retreat: The Fight to Appomattox* (Chapel Hill, 2002), 41; *SOR*, 7:821.

66. *OR*, vol. 46, pt. 1:1289; Marvel, *Lee's Last Retreat*, 45.

67. *SOR*, 7:747, 811; William Mahone, "On the Road to Appomattox," ed. William C. Davis, *Civil War Times Illustrated* 11, no. 9 (Jan. 1971): 8.

68. Marvel, *Lee's Last Retreat*, 63–64, 65; *OR*, vol. 46, pt. 3:1385; *SOR*, 7:747.

69. Chris M. Calkins, *Appomattox Campaign, March 29–April 9, 1965* (Conshohocken, PA, 1997), 57, 106; *OR*, vol. 46, pt. 1:389; "Paroles of the Army of Northern Virginia," *Southern Historical Society Papers* 15 (1887): 303–57; Mahone, "Road to Appomattox," 9; J. J. Dickison, *Confederate Military History Extended Edition*, vol. 16, *Florida*, ed. Clement A. Evans (Wilmington, NC, 1999), 160.

70. *OR*, vol. 46, pt. 1:1289–90; Marvel, *Lee's Last Retreat*, 78–79; Calkins, *Appomattox Campaign*, 105.

71. Marvel, *Lee's Last Retreat*, 79, 81–82.

72. "Report of General G. W. C. Lee, from the 2d to the 6th of April, 1865," *Southern Historical Society Papers* 13 (1885): 258.

73. *OR*, vol. 46, pt. 1:1294, 1298; Calkins, *Appomattox Campaign*, 111.

74. *OR*, vol. 46, pt. 1:1295; *SOR*, 7:747; Calkins, *Appomattox Campaign*, 112; Henry A Wise, "The Career of Wise's Brigade, 1861–5," *Southern Historical Society Papers* 25 (1897): 17–18.

75. Campbell Brown, *Campbell Brown's Civil War: With Ewell and the Army of Northern Virginia*, ed. Terry L. Jones (Baton Rouge, 2001), 282; Mahone, "Road to Appomattox," 10.

76. Freeman, *R. E. Lee,* 4:91n11; Freeman, *Lee's Lieutenants,* 3:701.

77. Freeman, *R. E. Lee,* 4:111–12.

78. Ibid., 3:721; Emory M. Thomas, *Robert E. Lee: A Biography* (New York, 1995), 360.

79. "Paroles of the Army of Northern Virginia," 70; *OR,* vol. 46, pt. 1:1277–78; Wright, *General Officers,* 33, 35, 38, 40.

80. Walker, *Life of Lieutenant General Richard Heron Anderson,* 212–13.

Major General James Ewell Brown Stuart. Library of Congress.

Jeb Stuart, R. E. Lee, and Confederate Defeat at Gettysburg

Joseph G. Dawson III

The Battle of Gettysburg was the Civil War's biggest battle, and it produced numerous controversies. Some swirled around Major General J. E. B. Stuart, leader of the Cavalry Corps of the Army of Northern Virginia and one of the Confederacy's most significant and successful generals. Stuart revealed that at Gettysburg on July 3, he led most of General Robert E. Lee's cavalry around the Union army's right flank, where he "*hoped to effect a surprise upon the enemy's rear.*"[1] Despite historians' assessments of the Gettysburg Campaign, Stuart's move against the Federal rear remains underappreciated, even though it can be connected to the most famous Confederate assault of the war, Pickett's Charge, on July 3.[2] This essay examines Stuart's generalship during his raid through Pennsylvania as well as his decisions in the cavalry battle east of Gettysburg on July 3. In Pennsylvania Stuart failed to obtain significant results from his actions, demonstrating that even highly respected generals confront problems or make mistakes they cannot overcome.

Stuart's Background

The Lee-Stuart connection began at the U.S. Military Academy in the 1850s. Stuart entered the academy in June 1850, graduating with the Class of 1854, and Lee served as the institution's superintendent from 1852 to 1855. Lee made a strong impression on West Point cadets while he was superintendent. A West Pointer himself (Class of 1829), Lee displayed a gentlemanly personality and imposing physical presence. He had established a lofty reputation as a military engineer and member of Major General Winfield Scott's staff during the Mexican War. Stuart was a good friend to one of Lee's sons, Custis, and was often an invited guest at the superintendent's home. Lee and Stuart renewed their connection in 1859, when Stuart stayed with Lee at his home while in Washington, D.C., to confer with the U.S. Patent Office. Later that year, Stuart was Lee's aide when Lee led U.S. Marines responding to the raid by abolitionist John Brown, who had hoped to inspire a slave uprising by seizing the U.S. Arsenal at Harpers Ferry, Virginia. Only a lieutenant at the time, Stuart delivered the ultimatum for Brown to surrender. Brown rejected surrender and the Marines, along with Stuart, stormed the arsenal, and captured the abolitionist.[3]

Both Lee and Stuart were Virginians who resigned from the U.S. Army in April 1861, when Virginia seceded from the Union. Stuart accepted a colonelcy and command of a Virginia cavalry regiment, while Virginia's governor appointed Lee to command all state troops. Both soon were appointed Confederate officers. Stuart was tapped for promotion to brigadier general in command of a cavalry brigade in September, and Lee was the third ranking general in the Confederate army and military adviser to President Jefferson Davis. Outside Richmond on May 31, 1862, General Joseph E. Johnston was badly wounded. Davis turned to Lee to replace Johnston as leader of the largest Confederate field army. Later that year Stuart rose to command Lee's Corps of Cavalry with the rank of major general.

Lee entrusted one of his sons, W. H. F. "Rooney" Lee, and his nephew, Fitzhugh Lee, to Stuart as brigade leaders in his corps, and Stuart became like a surrogate son to the army commander. Like a proud father, Lee closely monitored Stuart's several successes. During the Peninsula Campaign in the spring of 1862, Stuart led a spectacular raid around Major General George B. McClellan's Union army, obtaining valuable information about McClellan's troop dispositions while disconcerting the enemy commander. A few weeks later, during the Second Battle of Manassas, Stuart and his horsemen captured some of Union Major General John Pope's documents, enabling Lee to order the commander of one of the wings of his army, Lieutenant General Thomas J. "Stonewall" Jackson, to strike the rear of Pope's army with devastating effect, helping the Confederates win the battle. Taking some of the sting out of the Confederate strategic defeat in the invasion of Maryland in September, in October Stuart performed a gallant raid to Chambersburg, Pennsylvania, again flamboyantly riding completely around the Union army and capturing twelve hundred horses. Stuart's exploits firmly cemented his relationship with Lee. They also established Stuart's reputation among Confederates as a dashing commander who gathered reliable intelligence, produced substantial results, and boosted national morale.

At Chancellorsville in May 1863, Stuart provided Lee with just the information he needed. The right wing of Major General Joseph Hooker's Federal army was dangerously exposed—it hung "in the air"—unprotected by terrain, supporting troops, or a cavalry screen. Confirming his audacious reputation, Lee authorized Jackson to take his entire corps and deliver a crashing blow on this exposed flank; it sent the Federal army reeling in defeat.[4]

Suddenly, the winning team dissolved. Jackson took staff officers to conduct a personal reconnaissance but did not send someone ahead to warn pickets they were reentering Confederate lines. Unfortunately for the Confederacy, Stonewall was mortally wounded when his own soldiers fired on him by mistake. Jackson's death left Lee with questions to answer—about replacing him and choices to make about his army's organization—and re-emphasized how significant subordinates are to an army leader.

Prior Developments at Fredericksburg

Sometimes an army commander's success partly depends on how clearly the commander and his subordinate generals understand one another, and how effectively subordinate generals execute the commander's designs and orders. For instance, Lee and Jackson demonstrated an exceptional cooperation and communication that may develop between a commander and a subordinate. By talent or intuition, Jackson seemed to know what Lee intended or wanted.[5] Among the Civil War's army commanders, no one would ever mistake Robert E. Lee for Union Major General Ambrose E. Burnside. The two men contrasted in numerous ways, but they also had a point in common: They were seriously let down by their subordinates in their hallmark battles—Burnside at Fredericksburg, Virginia, in the winter of 1862 and Lee at Gettysburg the following summer.

In December 1862, Burnside made plans outlining coordinated multiple attacks on formidable Confederate defensive positions, anchored on Marye's Heights, above Fredericksburg. Burnside's design collapsed when one of his subordinates, Major General William B. Franklin, failed to press home the assaults he wanted. Burnside zeroed in on the enemy's right flank. Franklin, however, failed to recognize how significant it was to attack strongly and threaten to outflank or turn Lee's right at about the same time as Federal assaults started toward the Confederate center. Upon reflection, it may appear that Lee's defenses on Marye's Heights were nearly impregnable, but the Federal drives on his center could threaten to break Lee's defenses if other serious Federal actions were coordinated well enough to *pose serious threats elsewhere.*[6]

Franklin's failures to turn Lee's right placed the burden on frontal attacks by other Union units against Marye's Heights. These frontal assaults on Lee's center were stigmatized by the forlorn images of Union soldiers who recognized their low chances of surviving the battle. They had printed their names on slips of paper and pinned the papers to their jackets so their bodies could be identified. This was also the assault that brought General Lee to say, "It is well that war is so terrible—[else] we would grow too fond of it."[7]

In America's Civil War, such attacks often resulted in high losses for the attackers, such as Lee at Gaines' Mill—eight thousand casualties, Lee at Malvern Hill—five thousand casualties, Ulysses S. Grant at Cold Harbor—seven thousand casualties, and John Bell Hood at Franklin, Tennessee—six thousand casualties. As others have emphasized, at Fredericksburg the Union attack on the center had little chance of a breakthrough without being supported. Public criticism and blame fell on Burnside for Fredericksburg's high Federal casualties. The next month, the disastrous effects of the army's "Mud March" further debilitated Burnside's status. Critics questioned not only his generalship but also his common sense: How could any reasonable general with regard for his soldiers have sent his men across open ground to be slaughtered and failed so miserably to maneuver his army effectively? Politicians and public reached a clear verdict: Burnside deserved to be sacked. President Abraham Lincoln banished Burnside to an administrative assignment in Ohio, though he resumed field command later in the war. No matter that Burnside previously led Union forces to a notable victory at Roanoke Island, North Carolina, in February 1862 and later commanded the successful Union defense of Knoxville, Tennessee, in the winter of 1863–64. Burnside's name was forever associated with the failed attack against Marye's Heights at Fredericksburg.[8]

In contrast to Burnside, Lee was one of the two great generals of the Civil War (Grant was the other) and arguably one of the great generals of American history.[9] As an army commander, Lee accomplished much with modest resources. Burnside accomplished nothing with vast resources. Another contrast between the two was Burnside's disappointing relationship with Lincoln; Lee nurtured a respectful, productive relationship with Confederate president Jefferson Davis. Buoyed by the high regard of his president, battlefield victories, and his soldiers' devotion, Lee marched into Pennsylvania.

Lee's Goals and Subordinates, Spring 1863

Lee's offensive into Pennsylvania in 1863 was his greatest gamble. Lee developed specific campaign objectives designed to result in significant strategic outcomes. The objectives included capturing a capital of a Union state, cutting east-west railroad connections, threatening Washington, D.C., taking some of the pressure off of Confederate forces in the Western Theater at Vicksburg, gathering supplies to assist the Confederate war effort, and breaking the spirit of the Union. Achieving some combination of those goals might result in improved chances for diplomatic recognition of the Confederacy from Britain and France, and perhaps a greater grand strategic result.[10]

Above all, Lee hoped that a crowning victory in Pennsylvania would lead to Confederate independence.[11] To achieve such a stunning result, much depended on the effectiveness of Lee's subordinates. Jackson's death on May 10 forced Lee to make a series of decisions about his corps commanders and the organization of his army. It appeared logical for Lee to consider replacing the fallen Stonewall with Jeb Stuart. After Jackson's wounding at Chancellorsville, Stuart had done well temporarily filling in to command Jackson's corps, though critics noted the high casualties the corps suffered under Stuart's leadership.[12] Thus arose one of the controversies about Stuart and Gettysburg: Should Stuart have replaced Jackson to command Lee's Second Corps?

Lee had to weigh a number of pros and cons about the best place for Stuart. Obviously, Lee thought highly of Stuart. Fitzhugh Lee later wrote that his uncle had paid Stuart a high compliment: "A more zealous, ardent, brave and devoted soldier than Stuart the Confederacy cannot have." Although the Confederacy had other good cavalry generals, Stuart was the South's greatest "wizard of the saddle," and a sound argument could persuade Lee to retain Stuart with the Cavalry Corps. Also retained was Lieutenant General James Longstreet (age forty-two, West Point Class of 1842), commander of Lee's First Corps. One its senior artillery officers, Colonel Edward Porter Alexander, probably spoke for others when he contended, "I always thought it an injustice to Stuart and a loss to the army that he was not . . . *continued in command of Jackson's corps*. He had *won* the right to it."[13]

By May 23, after weighing various choices, Lee responded to a letter from Stuart. He told his cavalry leader, "I am obliged to you for your views as to the successor of the great and good Jackson. Unless God in his mercy will raise us up one [a successor], I do not know what we shall do." Actually, by the twenty-third Lee had decided that Stuart was not the sole candidate to replace Jackson. Critics could have pointed to Stuart's youth (thirty years old), but other youthful Confederates officers held high commands. A less likely possibility for the command, infantry officer John Bell Hood (age thirty-three, West Point Class of 1849), led an infantry division in the Pennsylvania Campaign, commanded a corps in the Army of Tennessee in the spring of 1864, and later commanded that entire army. Another possibility was Major General Richard H. Anderson (age forty-two, West Point class of 1842), whom Lee regarded highly. But an analytical comment from John Esten Cooke, a fellow Virginian, one of Stuart's staff aides and his ardent admirer, may suggest the reason Lee made his decision. Cooke concluded: "At

Chancellorsville, when he [Stuart] succeeded Jackson, the troops, although quite enthusiastic about him, complained that he led them too recklessly against artillery. . . . Fighting was a necessity of his blood, and the slow movements of infantry did not suit his genius." If Cooke's assessment was valid, perhaps Stuart was too immature or aggressive to handle the complexities of deploying an infantry corps.[14]

Instead of picking Stuart to replace Jackson, Lee decided on a drastic step, to reconfigure his army from two corps to three. Lee picked infantry officers as his new corps commanders, two Virginians with lengthy service in the Eastern Theater, Richard S. Ewell and Ambrose Powell Hill. Lee's army had little time to adjust to this significant reconfiguration, and Ewell and Hill, assuming their commands on May 23 and May 24, respectively, had only about a month to get familiar with responsibilities of corps command. Another important factor to take into account was health. Stuart was physically fit, but Hill and Ewell both had serious medical problems. Hill (age thirty-seven, West Point Class of 1847) suffered from the recurring effects of venereal disease, which afflicted him with chronic prostatitis. On some days Hill's condition made it too painful for him to ride a horse. Hill had to travel to combat in an ambulance, not an inspiring sight to his troops. His compatriot, Richard Ewell (age forty-six, West Point Class of 1840), had been severely wounded in action nine months earlier, and doctors had amputated his right leg. Ewell could not mount a horse without assistance and, once assisted, had to be strapped to his saddle.[15]

Lee's selections showed how shallow was the pool of Confederate officers available to be corps commanders in the East, or the narrow limits Lee put on his choices. Lee chose Ewell and Hill over Stuart, even with their debilitating medical conditions. Evidently, he did not consider other senior officers, such as those in the Army of Tennessee, for Jackson's replacement. Lee's choice of Ewell and Hill instantly installed them among his most significant subordinates and on a par in importance to Longstreet and Stuart.

Brandy Station and Cavalry Plans

Stuart did not let Lee's decision distract him; he threw himself into plans for holding a series of formal reviews of the cavalry. Consequently, on June 9, Stuart was caught unaware when nearly ten thousand Federal cavalry under Brigadier General Alfred Pleasonton made a reconnaissance in force and conducted an exceptionally bold attack on Stuart's cavalry at Brandy Station, Virginia. It was the war's biggest cavalry battle. Fought to the edge of defeat, Stuart redeemed himself by extraordinary personal bravery and his troopers' determination to carry the day. Although the Federals withdrew, leaving the

Cavalry fight near Aldie, Virginia. Library of Congress.

field to the Confederates, Brandy Station marked a drastic departure. During the following two weeks, Stuart and his horsemen fought the Federals in three other cavalry engagements in Virginia at Aldie, Middleburg, and Upperville. The Union cavalrymen demonstrated remarkable improvement since 1861. They were more aggressive and displayed better tactics. Better mounted, better armed (some carried repeating carbines), and better led than ever before, they were no longer awed by either Stuart or Southern horsemen. Although Stuart's staff officer, Major Henry B. McClellan, contended that Brandy Station had "made" the Union cavalry into an effective fighting force, neither Lee nor Stuart appeared to acknowledge these differences when they began planning for the Pennsylvania Campaign.[16]

Based on Stuart's previous successful raids, which had made him and his cavalry famous among Confederates and infamous in the North, at the start of 1863's summer campaign Stuart planned to conduct another raid that could yield potential benefits. The prospects included causing distress and confusion to the Union army's field commander (Joseph Hooker), raising havoc and doubts among Union leaders about Lee's objectives, disrupting Federal communications by ripping up railroad tracks and tearing down telegraph lines, posing threats to Baltimore, lifting Confederate morale while undermining Union spirits, and capturing useful supplies. Stuart wanted to take his best brigades, Wade Hampton's, Fitz Lee's, and Rooney Lee's, allocating for General Lee's use the brigades of Brigadier Generals John D. Imboden and Albert G. Jenkins. The brigades of Brigadiers Beverly Robertson and W. E. ("Grumble") Jones were to guard the Blue Ridge passes until they left Virginia to join Lee. Imboden and Jenkins both planned to ride with or near Ewell's corps. Thus Stuart and his staff believed that Lee would have adequate cavalry until Stuart rejoined the army. As the army commander, Lee had to judge the prospects of such allocations and deployments versus the risks involved.[17] If Lee were going to alter Stuart's preferences for allocating units, he needed to adjust cavalry assignments at that juncture. For example, directing that Wade Hampton and his brigade remain with the army would have provided the army commander with an officer more likely to be in tune with his needs than either Imboden or Jenkins.

On June 22, Lee dispatched orders to Stuart. As usual, his orders permitted discretion to his subordinate, but they also gave some obvious and clear directives, steps for Stuart to take during the army's march inside the Union states of Maryland and Pennsylvania. Lee directed: "If you find that [Hooker] is moving northward, and that two [cavalry] brigades can guard the Blue Ridge & take care of your rear, you can move with the other three [cavalry brigades] into Maryland & [1] *take position on General Ewell's right,* [2] *place yourself in communication with him,* [3] *guard his flank,* [4] *keep him informed of the enemy's movements &* [5] *collect all the supplies you can for the use of the army.*" Lee stated that the Confederate army "probably" was going "to move toward the Susquehanna" River, to create political turmoil by threatening the railroad center at Pennsylvania's capital Harrisburg. The cavalry raiders could threaten Washington, D.C.[18]

Stuart took his orders directly from Lee, but Longstreet followed up Lee's orders by sending a note expressing his own views. He had read Lee's orders to Stuart, he said, and asked that Stuart "order General [Wade] Hampton—whom I suppose you will leave here [at the army's camp] in command, to report to me at Millwood [Virginia]." Longstreet also emphasized his concerns that a big raid by Stuart's cavalry might reveal Confederate plans to Hooker, and therefore Longstreet wondered if Stuart "had better not leave us." Stuart disregarded all of these suggestions.[19]

Adding fuel for potential controversy, Lee sent supplemental orders to Stuart late in the afternoon of June 23. These orders confirmed permission for Stuart to take three brigades into Maryland. Lee's supplemental orders contained a distinctive phrase about the possibility of the Federal army hindering Stuart's venture northward, burdening Stuart to anticipate fluid conditions of the near future: "You will, however, be able to judge whether you can pass around their army *without hindrance*, doing them all the damage you can, and cross the [Potomac] river east of the mountains." Lee ordered once more that Stuart "must . . . feel the right of Ewell's troops [while] collecting information, provisions, &c." Lee also *ordered* Stuart to order Robertson's and Jones's brigades guarding the passes to soon ride north, "closing upon the rear of [Lee's] army." Striking an odd note of caution to his raiding specialist, Lee's orders concluded, "Be watchful and circumspect in all your movements."[20]

Stuart had not made his reputation by being circumspect and such orders permitted him to do anything he wanted. Several aspects of cavalry operations interconnected: the number of days Stuart devoted to his raid, how clear he made his orders to Robertson and Jones and their energy in responding them, and the actions Imboden and Jenkins took to gather intelligence for the army.

For his own part, Stuart stated his expectations clearly to Robertson, who, along with Jones, acknowledged them but then failed to act. After holding the Blue Ridge Mountain passes at Ashby's Gap and Snicker's Gap, they were ordered to ride to Lee, "follow the army, keeping on its right and rear," and to "harass [Hooker's] rear if you find he is retiring. Be always on the alert." That Stuart did not possess full confidence in Robertson's initiative may be seen by his adding the obvious: for Robertson to watch the Federals and "report anything of importance to . . . Longstreet." Lee assumed that Stuart's orders were enough to prompt Robertson and Jones to join the army as it moved deeper into Pennsylvania. Neither brigade leader acted as Lee and Stuart intended. Both brigades—totaling about three thousand men—stood idle too long in Virginia. Robertson did not report Federal actions to Longstreet, did not harass Hooker's rear, and did not rejoin Lee's army until he received specific orders from Lee to do so, depriving Lee of cavalry he needed.[21]

Lee's supplemental orders did not alter the commander's intent for Stuart's raid, and thus notable portions of Lee's first order to Stuart plainly indicated Lee's priorities for his cavalry. The Federal army indeed moved northward, paralleling Lee's army: Thus Stuart was to raid northward, as Lee and Stuart anticipated. Lee's orders authorized Stuart to ride into Maryland—but at the same time Lee expected Stuart to "take position on General Ewell's right" flank and maintain communication with Ewell as well as "guard his flank [and] keep him informed of the enemy's movements." Lee also asked Stuart to "collect all the supplies you can," a familiar task for Stuart. Collecting supplies came last in the list of Lee's directives. Maintaining communication with Ewell, and by extension keeping in touch with Lee, guarding Ewell's right flank—which was also the vanguard of Lee's army—and keeping Ewell informed of the enemy's actions all came before gathering supplies.[22]

On Stuart's previous mounted raids, Lee's loose orders had permitted him operational discretion, and Stuart had delivered results in a short time. On other raids Stuart had been away from the army for only three or four days before rejoining it. Federal units, cavalry in particular, had not created a serious "hindrance" to Stuart. With some logic, Lee and Stuart were counting on similar results again in 1863. Perhaps after gallivanting more than one hundred miles across two enemy states, Stuart would rejoin Lee's army as it moved northward, perhaps in about three or four days, perhaps near Harrisburg, Pennsylvania.[23]

But the summer of 1863 was a different time in the war. Lee's Confederates were going to operate deeper inside hostile territory than before. Brandy Station had revealed a reinvigorated Federal cavalry, while at the same time the Confederate mounted units had reached a plateau of effectiveness. Suffering a surprise and coming close to a defeat at Brandy Station, Stuart felt the stings of public criticism. Another flamboyant, successful raid would reconfirm his reputation.[24] Although General Hooker had been befuddled at Chancellorsville, his army remained strong, capable, and larger than Lee's. President Lincoln possessed greater self-confidence in making decisions and appointments than in the first two years of the war. Moreover, since 1861 Federal troops had intruded into all of the Confederate states. The Confederacy clearly was losing the war in both the Trans-Mississippi and the Western Theaters. Only winning, or at least maintaining the operational initiative, in the Eastern Theater allowed the Confederacy an edge in the war.

To maintain that edge, Lee was ultimately responsible for leading his army, picking his subordinates, and assuring that they understood his directives. Lee's pattern of giving discretionary orders to subordinates worked well with Jackson when he and Lee went up against mediocre Federal commanders, such as McClellan and Pope. Now Ewell and Hill were untested as corps commanders; additional guidance or a firmer hand might be required. In this instance, Lee and Stuart also may have been guilty of one of the serious errors of any senior commander—underestimating his opponent. Lee and Stuart counted on not only facing the volatile Hooker as commander of the Army of the Potomac but also facing the caliber of Federal cavalry Confederates had come to expect prior to Brandy Station. Furthermore, Lee and Stuart underestimated potential problems in this campaign: It did not seem obvious for Lee to have to remind Stuart to return to the army within a certain number of days or by a certain date.

Once Lee let Stuart loose in the Union rear, Stuart was on his own.

Stuart's Raid through Maryland and Pennsylvania

Before 1:00 on the morning of June 25, Stuart began his raid, leading approximately six thousand troopers in brigades belonging to Wade Hampton, Fitz Lee, and Rooney Lee, the latter under Colonel John R. Chambliss due to Rooney's having been wounded. Lee's three infantry corps, supported by the cavalry brigades of Imboden and Jenkins, already had proceeded north. Riding through Glasscock Gap, Stuart's horsemen moved toward the right of Hooker's army. Stuart sent out a messenger to notify Lee of the cavalry's movement, but he did not reach the commander. Rather than being able to form a screen between Lee and the Federals, on June 25 at the town of Buckland, Virginia, Stuart encountered Federal infantry of Major General Winfield Hancock's II Corps. This encounter deflected the cavalry due south, pushing Stuart away from Lee's army and further out of touch with Ewell's right flank. Proceeding south through Bristoe Station and Brentsville, Virginia, Stuart and his riders turned east, camping near Wolf Run Shoals on the Occoquan River on June 26. Stuart's troopers suffered sharp disappointment to find the area had been picked clean of forage for their horses.[25]

June 27 was a long day of hard riding. Still in Virginia, Stuart's troopers fought skirmishes at Fairfax Court House and Burke's Station. Turning north before reaching the Potomac, the Confederates spurred their tired horses to Dranesville and crossed the river into Maryland at Rowser's Ford around midnight. Stuart had dispatched another rider to Lee, but this messenger also failed to find the army. On that day Lee's adjutant, Major Walter Taylor, recognized that "with the exception of the cavalry, the army was well in hand. The absence of that indispensable arm of the service was most seriously felt by General Lee," who had wanted Stuart "to maintain communication with the main column and especially directed to keep the commanding general informed of the movements of the Federal army."[26]

By that time, Lee's army was already in Pennsylvania: Longstreet at Chambersburg, along with Hill's corps, and Ewell in Carlisle, only a few miles from Harrisburg. Taylor was justified in his caustic comment because, making matters worse as far as cavalry support was concerned, Imboden's Brigade had just moved into Maryland, out of contact with Ewell and too far away to do any direct service for Lee.[27]

Allowing his men and horses some rest, Stuart did not put his raiders on their way until after midmorning on June 28. They rode toward Rockville, Maryland, where a gift fell into their hands—a huge Federal supply train of 150 army wagons. In an odd twist, rather than surrendering immediately, as the Confederates assumed he would, the convoy's leader made a remarkable effort to escape capture, rushing pell-mell down the road toward Washington.

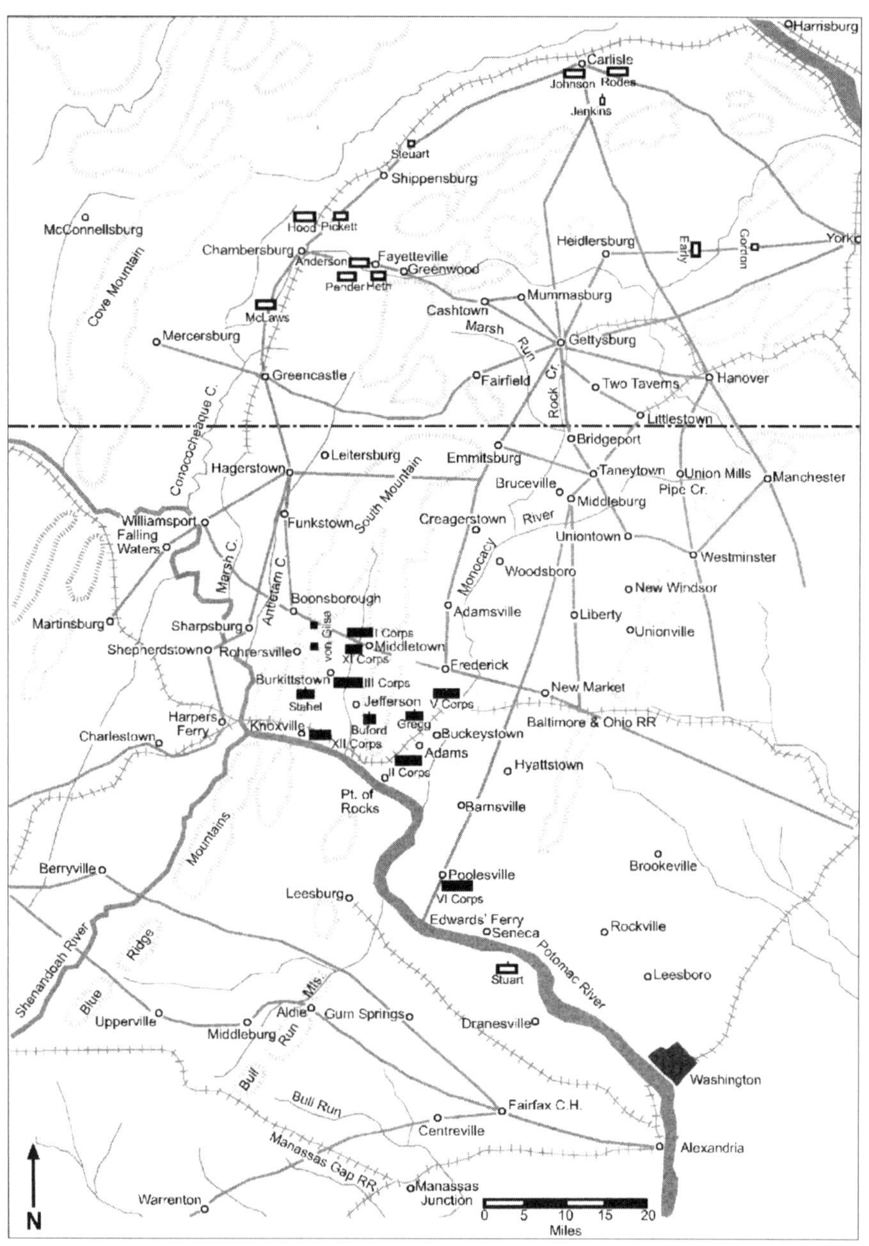

Gettysburg Campaign, June 27, 1863. From Bradley M. Gottfried, *The Maps of Gettysburg: An Atlas of the Gettysburg Campaign, June 3–July 13, 1863* (New York: Savas Beatie, 2007); courtesy of Ted Savas.

To capture these valuable wagons and the food and fodder they carried, Stuart's men consumed time and energy giving chase, going "for six more miles or more" *away* from Lee's army, drawing near to Georgetown and throwing Washington City into a temporary panic but posing no real threat. Making a belligerent stab toward Washington appeared attractive, but Stuart realized such a gesture would take more time and energy.[28]

Twenty-five wagons eluded the raiders, but they retained a substantial prize of 125 wagons with four hundred soldiers as prisoners, along with civilian teamsters, among whom were former slaves, African American men—"contrabands," as Major General Benjamin F. Butler had called them. Stuart now had options. One was to send the wagons to the safety of Virginia, detaching a regiment to usher them about twenty miles back to Rowser's Ford and into the Confederacy. He decided that the rations the wagons carried would be valuable to feed Lee's troops and, though they had an undetermined number of miles to go northward, the wagons might be used to haul away other supplies found in Pennsylvania. Plus Stuart would reap the benefit of delivering the wagons to Lee in person. Determined to retain the wagons as his trophies and contact Lee by finding an opening between the Union corps, Stuart kept his column moving well into the night, halting near Cooksville, Maryland.[29]

By the evening of June 28, Colonel A. L. Long, Lee's military secretary, recalled that "when General Lee arrived at Chambersburg he had received no intelligence from Stuart for several days, consequently he had no information of the movement of the Army of the Potomac." Not having heard from the brigades of Robertson and Jones, left at the Blue Ridge passes, Lee, according to Long, had been "deprived of the use of that portion of his force which has been named 'the eye of the army.'" Both of these officers had failed to understand their orders, and Lee now ordered them to join the army. By not leaving the passes until June 29 Robertson and Jones deprived Lee of two cavalry brigades to boost Lee's offensive in Pennsylvania.[30]

Lee, without word from Stuart for four days, had to get news from others. Longstreet's civilian "scout," known as "Harrison," had come into Lee's camp with word that the entire Federal army was moving northward parallel to Lee's line of march. Although Lee had anticipated that the Union army would move north sooner or later, he wanted to be nearer to Harrisburg before the Federals drew close. Harrison had more news: Hooker was no longer commanding the Army of the Potomac. After sending a stream of complaints to Lincoln, he had resigned from command of the army on June 28. The president accepted Hooker's resignation and replaced him with Major General George G. Meade, an acerbic Pennsylvanian respected by his fellow corps commanders. Meade was a stable general, not given to flash, who in Lincoln's pithy vernacular might "fight well on his own dunghill" in his home state. Lee immediately appreciated the implications for the campaign. He had counted on again putting Hooker under pressure, when he was more likely to make a hasty decision. The deliberate Meade would be less prone to error. The whole outlook of the campaign was different.[31]

The next day, June 29, rather than press ahead and find Lee, Stuart succumbed to the temptation of wrecking the Baltimore & Ohio Railroad. Delaying their advance, the raiders devoted hours to ripping up tracks, cutting telegraph wires, and setting fire to a bridge before riding east to Eldersburg and then striking northeast. Near Westminster, Stuart's troops met another delay. The Federal 1st Delaware Cavalry Regiment put up an unexpectedly good fight, bowing out of the way after suffering sixty-three casualties. Gathering some supplies, but not lingering at Westminster though evening approached, the Confederates pushed on toward Union Mills. Showing signs of being tired, the Confederates were slowed down by the captured wagons. Every time Stuart wanted to cut through the Federal line of march, he found no gaps in the solid phalanx of Federal infantry. Lee's army had advanced, in Longstreet's phrase, "as a man might walk over strange ground with his eyes shut."[32]

On June's last day, Stuart headed almost due east, toward the road junction at Hanover, Pennsylvania. From there a major road led west toward Gettysburg and Cashtown, and another northeast, across country, toward Heidlersburg and Carlisle. Around 10:00 A.M., however, Stuart encountered a Union cavalry screen, fronting a substantial force of mounted troops. The Federal regiments attacked, bringing on an engagement lasting much of the day. One of the most aggressive Federal units was a Michigan cavalry brigade, led by Brigadier General George A. Custer (West Point Class of 1861). Although he graduated last in his class, Custer had parlayed impetuous battlefield actions into promotions and impressed influential senior officers. Just one day earlier he had been promoted as the youngest volunteer general in the Union army. The fighting at Hanover caused an uncertain number of casualties, perhaps two hundred Federals and one hundred Confederates. Stuart's staff officer, Captain William Blackford, acknowledged that they met Brigadier General Judson "Kilpatrick's division of cavalry and had a hot affair with them"—so hot for Stuart that he was almost captured and narrowly escaped.[33]

For a small battle, Hanover was significant on several counts. Captain Blackford later observed, "We were just opposite Gettysburg and if we could have made our way direct, the fifteen miles to that place . . . we would have affected [*sic*] a junction with General Lee the day before the battle began." Major Henry McClellan agreed. But Blackford then highlighted what had become a sticking point among the Confederates: "It was here [at Hanover] that the wagon train began to interfere with our movements, and if General Stuart could only have known what we do now it would have been burned." From the other side of the hill, Captain James H. Kidd of Custer's brigade, grasped the meaning of the battle: "The result of the day at Hanover was that Stuart was driven *away from a junction with Lee. He was obliged to turn to the east,* making a wide detour by the way of . . . Dover."[34]

Confederates also admitted that the Federals had improved their mounted troops. Captain Blackford recalled that the "cavalry of the enemy were steadily improving and it was all we could do sometimes to manage them." Lieutenant G. W. Beale of the 9th Virginia Cavalry acknowledged "the enemy fought well." In other words, the Union cavalry was stronger by the summer of 1863 than in previous years, and Confederates had generally underestimated their opponents at the start of the campaign.[35]

The Federals at Hanover had slowed Stuart from reaching Lee by at least one full day, but considerable responsibility also rests with Major General Jubal A. Early, who had arrived at Heidlersburg, Pennsylvania. One of Ewell's experienced division commanders, Early had heard gunfire from the direction of Hanover but failed to send scouts to investigate or send a rider to Lee to report the gunfire. Early had expected Stuart's brigades in his vicinity and should have confirmed what the firing meant. This was yet another important missed opportunity of the campaign for the Confederates.[36]

Fought to a standstill by Kilpatrick's cavalry at Hanover, Stuart decided by nightfall that the Federals had blocked him from going west. Once again, Stuart had been deflected away from Lee's army, riding east to the town of Jefferson, Maryland. In order to try to circle around the obstructing Federal cavalry, Stuart decided to ride all night to reach Dover by daybreak. Unfortunately for Lee, Stuart was unable to contact Ewell's right flank. Rather than keeping Ewell informed of Federal movements, Stuart himself was in the dark about the enemy army. The only order Stuart fulfilled was collecting supplies, which once collected impeded execution of the other, more important parts of his orders. Moreover, the Confederate cavalry brigades were utterly exhausted.

Ordering only a four-hour rest for his bone-tired men and horses on July 1 and still shepherding his captured wagons, Stuart was unaware that Confederate infantry were about to encounter Federals at Gettysburg. Putting his column into motion and sharply turning north, Stuart aimed toward Carlisle, Pennsylvania. Around 4:00 P.M., the Confederate advance elements sighted Carlisle, where more than two thousand state militia confronted them. State militia units were notoriously uneven in training, leadership, and arms, and it was logical for Stuart not to take the Pennsylvanians too seriously. At the start of the campaign, Stuart and his veteran troopers would have swept aside such a laughable obstruction, but the Confederates had been on the march for eight days, covered 160 miles or more, and fought several engagements. As one lieutenant wrote home, "It is impossible for me to give you a correct idea of the fatigue and exhaustion of our men and beasts at this time." To the Confederates' surprise the militia fought well. Three times Stuart issued demands for his Federal opponents to surrender. Each time they refused. Stuart had the option of giving up on Carlisle; there was nothing so valuable there to warrant a further delay to locate Lee and Ewell. But frustrated by obstreperous Union militia, Stuart consumed more time to deploy his artillery and bombard the town, setting fire to buildings at the U.S. Army's Cavalry School. He also sent out two more riders to locate the Confederate army.[37]

Carlisle was a good place for Stuart to take stock of his situation. Nearly exhausted and out of contact with Lee for more than a week, Stuart had reasons for concern. None of Stuart's messengers had returned to tell him of Lee's whereabouts. Obviously he had not been in communication with Ewell. Although he had collected a major supply train, it had become a time-consuming burden of questionable value, according to his staff officer McClellan. To have maintained a grip on these wagons, Stuart must have recalled the credit that Stonewall Jackson had received after seizing two hundred Federal wagons at Harpers Ferry in 1862 during the Maryland Campaign.[38]

In the meantime, Lee was near Cashtown. His adjutant, Taylor, reemphasized the distressing point that an "army without cavalry in a strange and hostile country is as a man deprived of his eyesight and beset by enemies." Beyond receiving only partial information about the enemy, Lee also appeared anxious about Stuart himself. According to Major General Henry Heth, the day before Lee had inquired, "Any news to give me about General Stuart?" Around noon, as the army commander approached Gettysburg, he spoke to Major Campbell Brown, one of Ewell's staff officers. According to Brown, Lee "asked me with a peculiar searching, almost querulous impatience, which I never saw in him before . . . whether Gen'l Ewell had heard anything from Gen'l Jeb Stuart, & on my replying in the negative, said that he had heard nothing from or of him for three days—& that Gen'l Stuart had not complied with his instructions." Although there was no reason why Lee needed to offer explanations to Brown, Lee then summarized those instructions and worried over the lack of information about Meade's army and its movements. "This from a man of Lee's habitual reserve surprised me," Brown concluded. Longstreet recalled learning of a similar conversation Lee reportedly had with Major General Richard H. Anderson, with Lee concluding, "I cannot think what has become of Stuart; I ought to have heard from him long before now."[39]

At Gettysburg, July 1

Lee's dealings with his three infantry corps commanders also had a bearing on when, if, or how Stuart's cavalry would engage the Union army during the Battle of Gettysburg. Lee's problems with subordinates began early as controversy flared between Lee and one of his new corps leaders on the battle's first day. Ewell failed to order his troops to attack Union defenses on Cemetery Hill on July 1. Lee appeared to want Ewell to seize Cemetery Hill, but it was a hallmark of Lee's orders to allow discretion to his general on the spot. Lee's directions to Ewell included the important qualifying phrase to take Cemetery Hill "if he found it practicable." This discretion allowed Ewell to exercise his judgment and make the decision on the battlefield. Ewell decided not to attack. Critics speculated that Stonewall would have understood Lee's intent and attacked, at least to test the Federal defenses there. (It is further speculation to postulate what the aggressive Stuart would have done in Ewell's place.) Dislodging the Federals from either Cemetery or Culp's Hill could have changed the course of the battle, perhaps even fragmented Federal defenses and forced them to withdraw from the field and relocate elsewhere. In other words, seizing either hill created the possibility of giving the Confederates a resounding victory on July 1 that might have been the opening battle in a longer campaign.[40]

Ewell's decision not to attack allowed Culp's Hill to anchor the Union's right flank, and the battle played out in other ways. For instance, on the Union left flank, at the lower end of the battlefield on July 2, Longstreet's Confederates tangled with soldiers of the corps of Union Major General Daniel Sickles, who had made an unorthodox advance off of Cemetery Ridge and into the Peach Orchard. On the same day at Little Round Top, a key hill in the Union's defensive perimeter, a desperate struggle ensued between soldiers of the 20th Maine Regiment and Alabama troops.

Confederate efforts had failed to dislodge the Federals during the first two days in July, exposing differences between Lee and senior corps commander James Longstreet, another a key subordinate. Longstreet urged him to break off the battle and renew the fighting elsewhere or attempt outflanking the Federal left with a turning movement. Not inclined to disengage, Lee wanted to arrange other attacks.

After Lee rejected Longstreet's advice to bring on battle away from Gettysburg, Longstreet appeared disappointed, uncooperative, and sullen. Actually, Lee and Longstreet had failed to see eye to eye since the time Confederate leaders held a discussion seven weeks earlier in Richmond about an offensive into the Northern states. The generals' disagreements had lingered and crystallized on the evening of July 2, when Lee evidently decided that he was going to order a big assault the next day, supported by secondary attacks. Units from both Longstreet's corps and Hill's corps, even some that had already been engaged at Gettysburg, would make that big assault.[41]

Stuart from Carlisle to Gettysburg, July 2

Major Andrew Venable, a member of Stuart's staff, was one of several riders sent to locate Lee. The major found General Lee just west of Gettysburg on the afternoon of July 1. Sometime after midnight carrying a dispatch from Lee, Venable found Stuart at Carlisle. The dispatch notified Stuart that the armies were locked in combat at Gettysburg. The army commander required Stuart to report there "at once." Stuart left within the hour and arrived at Lee's headquarters in the early afternoon.[42]

The meeting of Lee and Stuart on the afternoon of July 2 is legendary in Confederate history. Only the two of them were present, no one else to record what they said. That has not stopped all sorts of speculation about the tone of the meeting and the attitudes of both officers. After several days apart, it would have been natural for Lee to request Stuart's report on the raid—who he had fought, what had he done, where he had been, why he was late—and describe the condition of his brigades. Lee could have asked what additional intelligence Stuart had gleaned from his contacts with the enemy. Possibly Stuart hoped to gain credit for the 125 captured wagons, and possibly he explained the reasons that had kept him from contacting Ewell.[43]

Soon enough the urgency of the army's circumstances meant discussion of the ongoing battle, how Stuart's mounted brigades could contribute in the hours remaining of July 2, and the most effective ways to deploy the cavalry the next day. As the Cavalry Corps neared Gettysburg, hundreds of Hampton's troopers helped turn back a Union cavalry probe near Hunterstown. While Stuart praised his men's performance, these necessary engagements caused casualties and wore down horses that would have benefited from resting that afternoon. Nevertheless, Stuart sent scouts eastward down the York Pike, where they conducted observations around 6:00 P.M. near Cress Ridge, some three miles from Culp's Hill.[44]

Plans for July 3

Lee was determined to attack on July 3, but controversy and confusion enveloped the time of day when Lee intended that Hill's and Longstreet's units were to attack—around dawn, in the morning hours, or afternoon? In his postcampaign report, Lee stated he wanted a morning attack. Support can be found for all of those times, based on records and recollections of officers.

Longstreet denied that his troops were slow off the mark for his attack, turned aside implications that Lee intended an early morning attack, and rejected assertions that he failed to give his beloved commander his full support.[45]

Moreover, disputes arose among the Confederate on such matters as how soon after dawn they were prepared to attack. For some units it was difficult to have been in place prior to noon. And which portion of the Union defensive line would be their primary objective—the enemy left flank or the center-right? Additionally, artillery units required time to prepare and move to the best positions to deliver supporting fire before noon. It remained unclear if Lee's subordinates understood what he wanted done on these matters, and Lee's exact orders for the time of attack may not have been put in writing directly to Longstreet, depending instead on verbal exchanges the army commander and his corps commanders may have had on July 2. After dawn on July 3, with no attacks underway or immediately forthcoming, Lee had to adjust his plans again for attacks to be made that afternoon.[46]

In an effort to coordinate his subordinates for the attack, Lee called a meeting early on the morning of July 3 at Longstreet's headquarters, about four miles from Lee's own headquarters. Attending were Lee, Longstreet, Powell Hill, division commander Henry Heth, and two members of Lee's staff, Colonel A. L. Long and Major Charles S. Venable. Stuart was not present, nor was Ewell, who had already initiated an attack on Culp's Hill. Major General George Pickett's division of Virginians from Longstreet's corps formed the nucleus of the main attacking force. Hill attended because Lee had picked several units from his corps to join the attack. These included numerous North Carolina brigades as well as regiments of Alabama, Tennessee, and Mississippi soldiers from Heth's division, under Brigadier General James J. Pettigrew (because Heth had been wounded) and additional North Carolinians under Major General Isaac R. Trimble. Other regiments from Florida rounded out the attacking forces. Ideally, these senior subordinates needed to be acting in accord with one another. But Longstreet and Hill harbored longstanding mutual animosity dating back to the Peninsula Campaign in 1862. On this morning, Hill was dissatisfied with troop dispositions, and in the next few hours the two corps commanders had to iron out important details of troop alignment.[47]

According to Longstreet, at this meeting he again recommended a remarkable change in the Confederate dispositions; he recommended canceling the planned assault and making a "move around to the right of Meade's army, and maneuver him into attacking us." Expressing himself in the strongest terms, Lee responded, "The enemy is there [Cemetery Hill, not the Ridge], and I am going to strike him." Longstreet answered in one of the most quotable remarks about any Federal forces ever opposed to the Army of

Northern Virginia: "'General, I have been a soldier all my life . . . and should know, as well as any one, what soldiers can do. It is my opinion that no fifteen thousand men ever arrayed for battle can take that position,' pointing to Cemetery Hill." Whether or not the generals pointed in the vague direction of *both* Cemetery Ridge *and* Cemetery Hill or specifically only at Cemetery Hill is unclear.[48] However, it appeared that the meeting concluded with uncertainty as to timing of the attacks and in what ways Longstreet and Hill, still unable to put aside their animosities, were to cooperate. Notable also is that neither Longstreet nor Colonel Long recalled Lee's indicating any parts that Stuart and Ewell were to play that day.[49]

No matter where Confederate units aimed their attacks on July 3, Lee had designated units from Ewell's corps to assault Culp's Hill. That way the Confederates would be acting against at least two portions of the Federal lines simultaneously. Ewell did not coordinate his units effectively. Combat began at Culp's early in the morning, continued until around noon, and never forced Meade to reassign significant units to Culp's that might have weakened his center.[50]

Cavalry Action July 3

A great general—and Lee was a great general—was not going to order a single unsupported attack when other units were available. Involving about thirteen thousand soldiers from six states, Pickett's Charge was not going to be the same type of attack that ruined Ambrose Burnside at Fredericksburg. To provide additional support for Pickett, a third Confederate strike took shape against Meade's army.[51]

On the morning of July 3, acting "pursuant to instructions from the commanding general," Stuart led most of the available cavalry in the Army of Northern Virginia east on the York Pike and around the Federal right flank, aiming for the northern tip of Cress Ridge, about three miles from Gettysburg. Stuart evaluated this significant terrain feature as "a commanding ridge [that] completely controlled a wide plain of cultivated fields," crisscrossed by wooden rail fences. Cress Ridge overlooked two road junctions that "commanded a view of the routes leading to the enemy's rear." The Hanover Road joined the Low Dutch Road, and a quarter-mile west of that junction, the Bonaughton Road branched off of Hanover Road. Bonaughton Road led to the Baltimore Pike, allowing direct access into the rear of Federal positions on Culp's and Cemetery Hills.[52]

Riding with Stuart were participants of the recent raid—the brigades of Fitz Lee, Wade Hampton, and Rooney Lee—plus Jenkins's Brigade. Allowing for losses among the three raiding brigades, Stuart probably commanded between forty-five hundred and five thousand men; other estimates put the total lower, based on calculations for higher casualties among troopers as well as horses exhausted on the recent raid. He may have led about 8 percent of the Army of Northern Virginia fit for duty at Gettysburg on July 3, a substantial portion of Lee's available soldiers.[53]

Timing was important for this mission. Stuart left his camp so as to reach Cress Ridge around 12:30 P.M., after hooking around the right of the Federal perimeter. Stuart's brigades did not deploy in a defensive screen but remained one large cohesive force. Aggressive as usual, he reached the ridge and assumed an offensive posture, ready to conduct "further operations." Based on Lee's orders, Stuart "hoped to effect a *surprise upon the enemy's rear*" by acting in coordination with other Confederates. His adjutant, Major McClellan, also stated that Stuart's move was executed with the "*intention of attacking the rear* of the Federal right flank."[54] Stuart's troopers were ideally placed to support Pickett, Pettigrew, and Trimble, whose massed infantry were preparing to attack, after Porter Alexander's artillery barrage, to commence about 1:00 P.M.

In previous battles senior generals of the Army of the Potomac had suffered from lapses in rear security or left gaps between units, and depending on what Meade had arranged (or failed to arrange), it would have been to Stuart's advantage to gain Cress Ridge without being seen by the Federals. But at Gettysburg things were different. About noon Federal observers on Cemetery Hill flashed a message to the leader of the Second Cavalry Division, Brigadier General David M. Gregg, whose tired troopers recently had been paralleling Stuart's raid across Maryland. Anticipating a possible threat, Meade had stationed about four thousand cavalry, including Gregg and two of his brigades, on his right rear. The message warned Gregg "that large columns of the enemy's cavalry were moving toward the right of our line." Gregg figured that the Confederates could approach his position in less than an hour. Based on this signal, Gregg asked Brigadier General George Custer and his brigade to remain attached to him near the junction of the Hanover Road and Low Dutch Road, about a mile from Cress Ridge's north edge. Custer's brigade rounded out the Second Division because Gregg's 2nd Brigade had been posted elsewhere. Major General Pleasonton recently had ordered Custer to return to his parent unit, located across the battlefield on the Union left. Not wanting his command decreased by one-third, Gregg asked Custer to stay with him, and Custer replied that he was "only too happy" to assist Gregg if the division commander ordered it. Gregg issued the order and Custer prepared for battle.[55]

The two mounted forces had contrasting missions. Gregg contended that "Stuart's cavalry was moving to our [Union] right with the evident intention of passing to the rear, to make a simultaneous attack there." Captain William Miller of the 3rd Pennsylvania Cavalry Regiment asserted the same point—that Stuart was not conducting a "mere reconnoissance [*sic*]" but his presence in such strength meant his "object was to strike the rear of the Federal army in cooperation with Pickett's grand attack upon its center." Few developments on a battlefield are as distressing as having enemy forces appear to one's rear, and Lee had delivered such unexpected attacks in other battles. Therefore, Gregg's objective was to prevent Stuart's cavalry advance onto the Bonaughton Road. No matter what their casualties, Gregg and Custer would be the winners if they blocked Stuart from gaining access to the rear of the Union army. On the other hand, Stuart would be defeated if he were turned back before he created a threat by advancing down the Bonaughton Road to Culp's Hill and Cemetery Hill. As Gregg contended in summary, Stuart's objective "was to do; ours was to prevent."[56]

An odd scene played out when Stuart reached the ridge. He ordered an artillery battery that had accompanied him to detach one cannon. It unlimbered around 12:30 or 12:45 and, for some obscure purpose, fired four consecutive shots. Was Stuart signaling to Lee that he had taken position on Cress Ridge? These shots came shortly before Porter Alexander's preassault bombardment got underway after 1:00. Certainly these cannon shots now indicated no worries by Stuart about being heard or seen by the Federals.[57]

After the cannon's shots, Gregg watched a Confederate skirmish line form. Some of Jenkins's troopers advanced on foot from the woods atop Cress Ridge. The skirmishers occupied buildings of the Rummel farm, giving them protection and affording fields of fire into the plain. Confederates remained at the Rummel farm most of the day. Gregg surmised that these Confederates presented a direct threat, "preparing to gain the rear of our [Federal] line of battle," and responded by ordering elements of two of his regiments to deploy into dismounted skirmish formations. Battle was moments away.[58]

Back on Cress Ridge, hundreds of troopers from Hampton's and Fitz Lee's brigades received orders to dismount and walk forward to engage the Federals, supported by cannon fire from Stuart's artillery. Federal artillery under Gregg's direction delivered accurate counterbattery fire. The battle intensified. Commanding some of the most heavily engaged dismounted Federal troopers, Colonel John B. McIntosh of Gregg's 1st Brigade did all he could to hold his position along a creek called Little's Run. Other Union units, including Colonel Russell A. Alger leading the 5th Michigan Cavalry Regiment, reinforced McIntosh. If Stuart and his men were to support Pickett, they had to scatter the hasty defenses set up along the fence lines and Little's Run and then seize the road junctions.

It was time for some mounted units to dash down and rout the Federals. Stuart picked the 1st Virginia Cavalry to spearhead the attack. Pennsylvania's Captain Miller complimented Stuart's horsemen: "A more determined and vigorous charge than that made by the 1st Virginia it was never my fortune to witness." Stuart recorded that soon the "hand-to-hand fighting involved the greater portion of the command till the enemy were driven from the field."[59]

Hoping to spoil this success, which threatened to reach the Hanover Road, Custer responded rashly. Custer called out to the troopers of the 7th Michigan Cavalry Regiment: "Come on, you Wolverines!" The Virginians, some of whom had stopped at a fence line, blasted the 7th Michigan as it approached, and soon Custer's men came under fire from three directions. Taking casualties, Custer avoided being trapped and galloped back to Gregg's lines along Hanover Road. Eager to produce a rout, other Confederates pursued Custer, joined by men from two nearby regiments. General Hampton described what happened: "In their eagerness, they followed him too far, and encountered his reserve in heavy force." Other units from the brigades of Hampton and Lee joined the attack. Hampton himself was wounded in the ensuing melee before the fighting broke off. The time now approached three o'clock. Gregg, McIntosh, and Custer had done well so far by delaying Stuart's offensive probes toward Hanover Road.[60]

A few minutes later, Alexander's cannonades ended on the main battlefield; Pickett, Pettigrew, and Trimble were about to attack. The cavalry action had reached a crucial point. To support Pickett's Charge, Stuart ordered several available regiments to attack. Formed into a column rather than line of battle, perhaps two thousand riders moved forward like a huge pile-driver, aiming to break the Union cavalry lines. "In these charges," Stuart recalled, "the impetuosity of those gallant fellows, after two weeks of hard marching and hard fighting on short rations, was not only extraordinary, but irresistible." But not quite.[61]

Colonel J. Irvin Gregg, in charge of General David Gregg's 3rd Brigade, called on Colonel Charles Town of the 1st Michigan to prepare his men for a countercharge. For the second time that day, Custer stepped forward and shouted to his fellow soldiers from Michigan, "Come on you Wolverines!" The Michigan regiments formed up and counterattacked. Custer and Colonel Town led the way.[62]

Meantime, the Confederate pile-driver smashed ahead. As it neared Little's Run, Colonel McIntosh retreated out of its way. The Rebel column splashed across the creek and thundered onward toward Hanover Road. Then Confederates leading the column realized that other mounted men were riding to meet them—but it seemed to be a diminutive response, perhaps one thousand men. How could those Federals hope to stop Stuart's horsemen, the finest cavalry in North America?

Keeping remarkably cohesive formations across nearly five hundred yards, the Michigan cavalry squadrons delivered their full weight. The impact of the Michigan and Virginia horsemen created a "crash" audible to soldiers across the field. According to Captain Miller, "So sudden and violent was the collision that many of the horses were turned end over end and crushed their riders beneath them. The clashing of sabers, the firing of pistols, . . . and cries of the combatants filled the air." But it wasn't just the Michiganders. Inspired by Custer's counterattack, hundreds of other Federals—individuals, squadrons, and regiments—turned and reentered the fight or left their positions and rushed forward to attack. Sabers flashing, some of the Union horsemen slashed the gray riders on the flanks of the Southern columns, shredding their formations. Union artillery batteries poured blasts of cannon fire into the packed gray column. The Confederate attack faltered as casualties mounted, but more men in blue than gray lay scattered across the plain.[63]

The cavalry collision stopped Stuart's regiments in their tracks. The Federals had gained no ground; they had not advanced to secure the Rummel farm or driven Stuart off of Cress Ridge, but that was not their purpose. Gregg's brigades and Custer's Wolverines had blocked Confederate access to the road junctions. Later that afternoon, it must have been a tremendous satisfaction to the Union horse soldiers to see the Confederate cavalry abandon the Rummel farm and ride away from Cress Ridge.

Back on the main battlefield, in the center and on the right of the Federal defenses came echoes of Fredericksburg. The charge by Pickett, Pettigrew, and Trimble crossed one mile of open ground and brushed against the stout Union positions on Cemetery Ridge. The Federals rejected their attacks with heavy losses—some nine thousand Southerners killed, wounded, and captured. As the Confederate survivors streamed back in defeat toward Seminary Ridge, a taunting chant rose up from the Union soldiers: "Fredericksburg! Fredericksburg!"[64]

Conclusions

For such an intense engagement, the reported losses seem modest. Stuart admitted casualties of 8 officers killed, 17 officers wounded, and 2 officers missing, 21 enlisted men killed, 117 enlisted men wounded, and 61 enlisted men missing or made prisoner. This total, 226, meant casualties of perhaps less than 5 percent of Confederates engaged. Gregg listed a total of 254 killed, wounded, and missing, but he omitted Custer's losses, which are unknown. Lieutenant William Brooke-Rawle of the 3rd Pennsylvania Cavalry Regiment concluded Union losses totaled 9 officers and 69 enlisted men killed, 25 officers and 207 enlisted men wounded, and some 225 missing or made prisoner. If accurate, the Federals lost about 14 percent of men engaged, a small price for keeping Stuart from gaining Meade's rear. Stuart did not set up a defense or remain overnight at Cress Ridge. Instead he abandoned the field.[65]

Some Union officers made striking assertions about the cavalry fighting that took place between June 20 and July 3, especially between Cress Ridge and Hanover Road. David Gregg claimed that the Union horse units did their "full share in winning the great victory that crowned our [Union] arms in the Gettysburg Campaign." Lieutenant William Brooke-Rawle claimed even more: "We [Union] cavalrymen have always held that we saved the day at the most critical moment of the battle of Gettysburg." A Michigan officer, Captain James H. Kidd, came to a similar conclusion, contending that the Federal army relied on the "invaluable services which the second cavalry division and Custer's Michigan brigade rendered at the very moment when a slight thing would have turned the tide of victory the other way." Kidd awarded his highest praises to his own Michigan Wolverines, whose second charge "coincided in point of time with the failure of Pickett's assault upon the [Union] center, and was a contributing cause in bringing about the later result." Given all of the other matters that went right or wrong on both sides during July 1–3, Brooke-Rawle's and Kidd's arguments can seem overdrawn but may not have been appreciated widely enough.[66]

Many in the nineteenth century would have agreed with General David Gregg's contention that "the cavalry of an army are its eyes and ears." This contention relates to some of the Gettysburg Campaign's most enduring controversies—the wisdom of Stuart's extensive cavalry raid and the decreased effectiveness of the Confederate cavalry during the Pennsylvania Campaign, including the Battle of Gettysburg itself.

In postwar writings, Confederate Major General Henry Heth agreed with Gregg that "the eyes of any army are its cavalry" and left no doubt that, in his opinion as an infantryman, the Confederate cavalry was most at fault in the campaign. Without Stuart and his cavalry brigades, the "eyes of the giant [Lee's army] were out" and "the failure to crush the Federal army in Pennsylvania in 1863 . . . can be expressed in five words—*the absence of our cavalry.*" Fellow Confederate Porter Alexander later characterized Stuart's cavalry ride across Maryland as a "useless raid," a remark that seemed persuasive to many. Charles Marshall, Lee's military secretary, wrote that Stuart "left General Lee without any information as to the movement of the enemy from the time he crossed the Potomac river until July 2nd." So "the movement toward Gettysburg was the result of the want of information which the cavalry alone could obtain for us." Marshall's postwar views can be understood as part of the acrimonious exchanges of blame and criticism among Southerners embittered by the Confederacy's failure to win independence, but Captain Charles Blackford, brother of William Blackford of Stuart's staff, expressed a similar sentiment only a few days after the battle: "General Stuart is much criticized [among Confederates] for his part in our late campaign. . . . [Cavalry] played a small part in the great drama either as the 'eyes of the army' *or any other capacity*. . . . In his anxiety to 'do some great thing,'" Blackford added, "General Stuart carried his men beyond the range of usefulness and Lee was not thereafter kept fully informed as to the enemy's movements as he should have been, or as he would have been had Stuart been nearer at hand."[67]

Some may see Blackford's opinion being too much influenced by his being a member of Longstreet's staff, but R. E. Lee himself appeared to arrive at similar conclusions. In his postcampaign report, dated January 20, 1864, Lee leveled a clear and weighty criticism: "The movements of the army preceding the battle of Gettysburg had been *much embarrassed by the absence of the cavalry*." In the next sentence Lee mentioned the brigades of Robertson and Jones, and may only have meant to criticize them. But by using the broader term "*the cavalry*" Lee appeared to encompass Stuart and the brigades with him as well as those of Robertson, Jones, Imboden, and Jenkins. All were at fault for not conducting themselves more effectively, as they routinely did before June and July 1863. Lee had a chance to revise this negative part of his report; his staff officer, Walter Taylor, no friend of Stuart's, had drafted the report, but Lee made no revisions.[68]

However, Lee's own decisions contributed to the cavalry's failures. He permitted Stuart to take options during his raid that deprived the army of three brigades and Stuart's presence for a week. Stuart's decision to exercise the discretion Lee gave him to ride around Hooker's army appeared more flawed after Lee and the Confederates lost the battle and the war. Until Stuart returned, Lee failed to recognize that Imboden or Jenkins needed to remain close by. When Robertson and Jones lagged, the army commander should have ordered them to join him sooner. Stuart implied as much in his postcampaign report and also criticized Jenkins, stating that his "brigade was not as efficient as it ought to have been." But Lee was probably missing Stuart himself. Two members of Stuart's staff and one of his friends thought so. Major McClellan asserted "it was not the want of cavalry that General Lee bewailed, for he had enough of it had it been properly used. It was the absence of Stuart himself that [Lee] felt so keenly; for on him had he learned to rely to such an extent that it seemed as if his cavalry were concentrated in his person, and from him alone could information be expected." In similar words, William Blackford concurred with McClellan. Stuart's friend, John Mosby, also stressed that "it was the *personality* of Stuart that was needed [by Lee]—not cavalry."[69]

Only a few years after Lee's death in 1870, Gettysburg assumed greater importance. Union cavalryman William Brooke-Rawle called the battle "the turning point of the war." In the following decades Northerners and Southerners were drawn to Gettysburg. It was near Washington, D.C., in a dramatic setting preserved as a national historic site where more than twenty thousand casualties had been inflicted on both armies. Thousands of visitors arrived annually to see the place where Lincoln had given a historic public address. By contrast, the cavalry fight east of Gettysburg got lost, overshadowed by Pickett's Charge rather than connected to it.[70]

Recognized as the Confederacy's premier cavalryman, Stuart commanded the cream of Southern horse units. That made his efforts in the Pennsylvania Campaign all the more disappointing. Absent written orders from Lee or one of his staff officers, the specific goals of Stuart's presence at Cress Ridge may never be clarified. Since Stuart took only offensive actions after arriving at Cress Ridge, his presence there can be linked to Pickett's Charge. Stuart's failure at Cress Ridge meant that he had failed Lee, reduced Pickett's chances to break the Union line, and contributed to reducing the chances for Confederate victory on July 3.

Stuart's headquarters. From the *Illustrated London News*, 1862.

Stuart did not help his own case in the weeks following his return from Pennsylvania. In his postcampaign report, Stuart proclaimed a record of nearly continuous accomplishment during the campaign. Prior to July 1 he "realized the importance of joining our army in Pennsylvania," but one thing and then another meant making forced night marches and taking detours, nearly exhausting his men and horses. His attention turned from tearing up railroad tracks to capturing wagons to threatening Washington, D.C. He admitted that "the whereabouts of our army was still a mystery" for eight days, but in hindsight he described just missing linking up with elements of Ewell's corps at one town or another. In Stuart's estimation, the results of his raid sustained "the utility of the move."[71]

In letters to his wife, Stuart bragged, "I had a grand time in Pennsylvania and we [the Cavalry Corps] returned without defeat." Stuart contended that "my Cavalry has nobly sustained its reputation and done better and harder fighting than it ever has since [the start of] the war." Leaving aside Hanover, he listed selected escapades: "I shelled Carlisle and burnt the barracks. I crossed [the Potomac] near Dranesville and went close to Georgetown and Washington, cutting four important railroads, joining our army in time for the battle at Gettysburg, with 900 prisoners and 200 wagons and splendid teams." He embellished further: "I have been blessed with great success on this campaign." His claim of "great success" did not match the outcome of the cavalry battle east of Gettysburg on July 3.[72]

Many factors—no one overriding factor—converged to result in the Confederate defeat and the remarkable Union victory at Gettysburg. It can be argued that Lee tried to accomplish too many goals in one campaign but failed in all of them. Instead, he lost one-third of his army, retreated to Virginia, and never took the offensive again. Lee's retreat meant that he was no nearer to Confederate independence. Combined with Grant's capturing Vicksburg, Gettysburg greatly enhanced Lincoln's chances to restore the Union and avoid what the president called the "national destruction" of the United States. Gettysburg was the second significant turning point in the Eastern Theater (the first was the Union strategic victory at Antietam the year before).[73]

The mediocre performance of Lee and his top infantry commanders were significant factors in the Pennsylvania Campaign. Lee's choice to restructure his army by dividing Jackson's corps and placing Ewell and Hill in charge of the two new corps was one of his crucial decisions. The other obvious option, one Lee rejected, was to replace Jackson with Stuart, an assertive, offensive-minded commander. Ewell's failure to attack the heights south of Gettysburg on July 1, Longstreet's reluctance to wholeheartedly endorse Lee's tactical offensive choices on July 2 and 3, and Hill's petulance toward Longstreet all compounded the postwar disappointments of former Confederates.

Mistakes by the cavalry brigade commanders further complicated how the campaign was conducted and reduced Lee's chances for success. Stuart, Robertson, Jones, Imboden, and Jenkins all contributed to the campaign's outcome. Like his other raids, Stuart's 1863 venture displayed inspiring bravado, dynamic energy, and remarkable stamina, and he sought ways to meet Confederate logistical needs. However, the raid lasted too long and lacked results worth its great effort. Moreover, despite what seemed to be Stuart's clear guidance, Robertson and Jones disappointed Lee and Stuart by their inaction, and neither Imboden nor Jenkins temporarily replaced Stuart until he returned to the army.

Finally, another major factor was out of Lee's hands: The Federal army's determined fighting played a decisive part in the outcome of the Pennsylvania Campaign. George Pickett confirmed this when asked why his famous charge failed: "I think the Union army had something to do with it."[74] Applied to the Union cavalry, the same observation explains the result of the cavalry action on July 3. The tremendous actions of George Custer, David Gregg, John McIntosh, and their troopers had much to do with Stuart's failure to break through into the rear of Union lines and cause chaos while Pickett's Charge threatened the Federal front.

One of the main purposes of the Federal war effort was the defeat of the Confederate armies. As Lincoln said in his second inaugural address, it was "the progress of our arms, upon which all else chiefly depends."[75] It was crucial for the Federals to defeat the Southern armies not only in the Western Theater and Trans-Mississippi Theater but also in the East, taking on Lee and his best subordinates. On July 3, 1863, that is just what happened. Federal infantry on Culp's Hill and Cemetery Ridge and cavalry deployed along Hanover Road defeated the best units in the Confederate army. When Lee began his retreat on the evening of July 4, he changed the perceived pattern of war in the Eastern Theater.

Helping to establish a new pattern toward the Union was Jeb Stuart's performance in the Pennsylvania Campaign. Major William L. Royall, a Virginian who had served in the antebellum army, fought for the Union. An experienced cavalry officer, Royall succinctly concluded, "Stuart ought not to have exercised the discretion conferred upon him [to conduct an extensive raid]. His hard horse sense ought to have told him to stick to Lee. That was the place where he was wanted."[76]

Notes

1. Stuart's postcampaign report, Aug. 20, 1863, in U.S. War Department, *War of the Rebellion: The Official Records of the Union and Confederate Armies,* 128

vols. (Washington, DC, 1880–1901), ser. 1, vol. 27, pt. 2:687–710, quote on 697 (emphasis added) (hereafter cited as OR; all references are to series 1 unless otherwise indicated).

2. Numerous historians have focused on Stuart in June and July 1863. Among the sharpest assessments are Emory M. Thomas, "Eggs, Aldie, Shepherdstown, and J. E. B. Stuart," in *The Gettysburg Nobody Knows,* ed. Gabor S. Boritt (New York, 1997), 101–21; Warren C. Robinson, *Jeb Stuart and the Confederate Defeat at Gettysburg* (Lincoln, NE, 2007); and Tom Carhart, *Lost Triumph: Lee's Real Plan at Gettysburg—and Why It Failed* (New York, 2005). More favorable toward Stuart are Eric J. Wittenberg and J. David Petruzzi, *Plenty of Blame to Go Around: Jeb Stuart's Controversial Ride to Gettysburg* (New York, 2006) and Mark Nesbitt, *Saber and Scapegoat: J. E. B. Stuart and the Gettysburg Controversy* (Mechanicsburg, PA, 1994). Other notable studies dealing with Stuart and the Gettysburg Campaign include Douglas S. Freeman, *R. E. Lee,* 4 vols. (New York, 1934–36), 3:40–48; Douglas S. Freeman, *Lee's Lieutenants: A Study in Command,* 3 vols. (New York, 1942–44), 3:354–60; Edwin B. Coddington, *The Gettysburg Campaign: A Study in Command* (New York, 1968), 107–12; Jeffry D. Wert, *Cavalryman of the Lost Cause: A Biography of J. E. B. Stuart* (New York, 2008), 253–90. Several works introduce the interactions among the senior commanders at Gettysburg. Notable among them is Brooks D. Simpson, "'If Properly Led': Command Relationships at Gettysburg," in *Civil War Generals in Defeat,* ed. Steven E. Woodworth (Lawrence, KS, 1999), 161–89.

3. Emory M. Thomas, *Bold Dragoon: The Life of J. E. B. Stuart* (New York, 1986), 25, 28–29, 55–59; Wert, *Cavalryman of the Lost Cause,* 37.

4. William P. Snow, *Lee and His Generals* (New York, 1867), 380–89.

5. James I. Robertson Jr., *Stonewall Jackson: The Man, the Soldier, the Legend* (New York, 1997), 452, 546–47, 509, 631, 644, 649, 714–15; Frank E. Vandiver, *Mighty Stonewall* (New York, 1957), 329, 337, 438; Joseph T. Glatthaar, *Partners in Command: The Relationship between Leaders in the Civil War* (New York, 1994), 7–8, 27–28, 47–49; Clifford Dowdey, *The Seven Days: The Emergence of Robert E. Lee* (Boston, 1964), 72. See also Paul D. Casdorph, *Lee and Jackson: Confederate Chieftains* (New York, 1992), 218–19, 239, 393–96.

6. William Marvel, "The Making of a Myth," in *The Fredericksburg Campaign: Decision on the Rappahannock,* ed. Gary W. Gallagher (Chapel Hill, 1995), 1–25.

7. Edward Porter Alexander, *Military Memoirs of a Confederate, by General E. P. Alexander* (1907; reprint, Bloomington, IN, 1962), 302; Gary W. Gallagher, ed., *The Fredericksburg Campaign: Decision on the Rappahannock* (Chapel Hill, 1995), xxii, n1.

8. A. Wilson Greene, "Morale, Maneuver, and Mud: The Army of the Potomac, December 16, 1862–January 20, 1863," in Gallagher, *Fredericksburg Campaign,* 171–227.

9. An excellent brief assessment of Lee and Grant is T. Harry Williams, *Lincoln and His Generals* (New York, 1952), 310–14.

10. For discussions of Confederate goals and objectives, see Coddington, *Gettysburg Campaign,* 5–9; Stephen W. Sears, *Gettysburg* (Boston, 2003), 7–17; Lee's correspondence collected in Robert E. Lee, *The Wartime Papers of R. E. Lee,* ed. Clifford Dowdey and Louis Manarin (Boston, 1961), 482–533; William Allan, "Memoranda of Conversations with Robert E. Lee," in *Lee the Soldier,* ed. Gary W. Gallagher (Lincoln, NE, 1996), 13–14; and Gary W. Gallagher, ed., *The First Day at Gettysburg: Essays on Confederate and Union Leadership* (Kent, OH, 1992), 10–13.

11. Offering a postwar reflection on Confederate hopes for the result of the Pennsylvania Campaign fourteen years after the events, Jefferson Davis mused that "a victory over the army of Meade would have ensured peace on the only basis we were willing to accept it—Independence." Jefferson Davis to Dabney H. Maury Dec. 17, 1877, quoted in Jefferson Davis, *The Papers of Jefferson Davis,* vol. 9, *January–September 1863,* ed. Lynda Crist, Mary S. Dix, and Kenneth H. Williams (Baton Rouge, 1997), 259 (dash added for emphasis).

12. Thomas, *Bold Dragoon,* 210–23; Wert, *Cavalryman of the Lost Cause,* 227–32.

13. Lee to his wife, Mary Lee, May 16, 1864, in Lee, *Wartime Papers,* 730–31, quote on 731; Fitzhugh Lee, *General Lee* (New York, 1904), 337; Bennett H. Young, *Confederate Wizards of the Saddle* (Boston, 1914); E. Porter Alexander to H. B. McClellan, May 16, 1885, in H. B. McClellan, *The Life and Campaigns of Major General J. E. B. Stuart, Commander of the Cavalry of the Army of Northern Virginia* (Boston 1885), 256.

14. R. E. Lee to Stuart, May 23, 1863, *OR,* vol. 25, pt. 2:820–21, quote on 821; John Esten Cooke, *Wearing of the Gray* (1867; reprint, Bloomington, IN, 1959), 20. See the discussions in Thomas, *Bold Dragoon,* 131, 211–15; and Wert, *Cavalryman of the Lost Cause,* 225–36.

15. Born in the District of Columbia, Ewell was a longtime resident of Virginia. On officers' medical situations, see James I. Robertson Jr., *General A. P. Hill: The Story of a Confederate Warrior* (New York, 1987), 11–12, 206, 209, 240, 249–50, 260, 272, 299, 311–12; Donald C. Pfanz, *Richard S. Ewell: A Soldier's Life* (Chapel Hill, 1998), 257–59, 263–65, 345–47; and Jack D. Welsh, *Medical Histories of Confederate Generals* (Kent, OH, 1995), 63–65, 99–100. Based on their medical records, it is unlikely that either Ewell or Hill would have

received field assignments in the rank of lieutenant general in the U.S. Army in the twentieth or twenty-first century.

16. McClellan, *Life and Campaigns,* 294; Stephen Z. Starr, *The Union Cavalry in the Civil War,* 3 vols. (Baton Rouge, 1979–85), 1:376–95; Freeman, *Lee's Lieutenants,* 3:53.

17. See the views of Stuart's adjutant, Major McClellan, *Life and Campaigns,* 333–35, and a Confederate cavalry officer who was not at Gettysburg, Stuart's friend, John S. Mosby, *Memoirs of Colonel John S. Mosby* (Bloomington, IN, 1959), 208. Mosby also defended Stuart with articles in *Century* magazine, reprinted in *Battles and Leaders of the Civil War: Being for the most part contributions by Union and Confederate officers based upon "The Century War Series" edited by Robert Underwood Johnson and Clarence Clough Buel, of the editorial staff of The Century Magazine,* 4 vols., ed. Robert U. Johnson and Clarence C. Buel, (New York, 1884–88), 3:251–52, and in the *Philadelphia Times,* later reprinted in *Battles and Leaders of the Civil War,* vol. 6, ed. Peter Cozzens (Urbana, IL, 2004), 281–90, as well as a separate book in the style of a legal brief, John S. Mosby, *Stuart's Cavalry in the Gettysburg Campaign* (New York, 1908). R. E. Lee's adjutant, Walter Taylor, emphasized that neither Imboden nor Jenkins were directly attached to Lee. Walter H. Taylor, *Four Years with General Lee* (Bloomington, IN, 1962), 113.

18. Lee to Stuart, June 22, 1863, *OR,* vol. 27, pt. 3:913. Lee also directed Stuart, "You will, of course, take charge of [Albert G.] Jenkins' brigade, and give him necessary instructions."

19. Longstreet to Stuart, June 22, 1863, ibid., 915. Having admonished Stuart to stay with the army *before* the campaign began, in the postwar Longstreet berated Stuart but also implied criticism of Lee when he asserted, "General Stuart should not have been permitted [by Lee] to leave the general line of march, thus forcing us to march blindfolded into the enemy's country." General James Longstreet, "Lee in Pennsylvania," in *Annals of the War Written by Leading Participants,* ed. Alexander K. McClure (1879; reprint, Dayton, OH, 1988), 433. Freeman supported Longstreet's contention, agreeing that Lee was "blinded by the absence of Stuart." Freeman, *Lee's Lieutenants,* 3:170.

20. Lee to Stuart, June 23, 1863, *OR,* vol. 27, pt. 2:923. Recalling Stuart's reaction to the order is Stuart's adjutant, McClellan, *Life and Campaigns,* 316–19. A thoughtful discussion of Lee's two orders is Nesbitt, *Saber and Scapegoat,* 57–68.

21. Beverly H. Robertson, "Confederate Cavalry in the Gettysburg Campaign," in Johnson and Buel, *Battles and Leaders,* 3:253. Condemning the "inactivity" of Robertson and Jones was Stuart's staff engineer, W. W. Blackford, *War Years with Jeb Stuart* (New York, 1945), 229. McClellan, *Life and Campaigns,*

335–36, estimated that Robertson's and Jones's brigades totaled three thousand men.

22. Gallagher, *First Day at Gettysburg,* 16–20.

23. Stuart's postcampaign report, *OR,* vol. 27, pt. 2:707.

24. Freeman, *Lee's Lieutenants,* 3:51–52.

25. Ibid., 3:63. A Union officer saw a main purpose of the Federal cavalry "to push him [Stuart] as far away as possible, so that he might be delayed in communicating with his chief [Lee]." William E. Miller, "Cavalry Battle near Gettysburg," in Johnson and Buel, *Battles and Leaders,* 3:397.

26. Taylor, *Four Years with General Lee,* 92; also found in Walter H. Taylor, "Campaign in Pennsylvania," in *Annals of the War Written by Leading Participants,* ed. Alexander K. McClure (1879; reprint, Dayton, OH, 1988), 306.

27. James Longstreet, *From Manassas to Appomattox* (1896; reprint, Bloomington, IN, 1960), 359, 546.

28. Chasing wagons "six miles or more," G. W. Beale to Dearest Mother, quoted in G. W. Beale, *A Lieutenant of Cavalry in Lee's Army* (1918; reprint, Baltimore, 1994), 112; mentioning temporary panic in Washington in John Abbott, *History of the Civil War in America,* 2 vols. (New York, 1863, 1866), 2:401; Stuart's postcampaign report, *OR,* vol. 27, pt. 2:694.

29. Capturing black teamsters in Beale, *Lieutenant of Cavalry,* 112; Cooke, *Wearing of the Gray,* 239; Wittenberg and Petruzzi, *Plenty of Blame,* 35–41.

30. A. L. Long, *Memoirs of Robert E. Lee* (New York, 1886), 274, 280.

31. Longstreet, *From Manassas to Appomattox,* 346–47; Longstreet, "Lee in Pennsylvania," 419; Lincoln quoted in Freeman Cleaves, *Meade of Gettysburg* (Norman, OK, 1960), 123; Charles Marshall, *An Aide-de-Camp of Lee: Being the Papers of Colonel Charles Marshall,* ed. Frederick Maurice (Boston, 1927), 218; Freeman, *R. E. Lee,* 3:60–61.

32. Longstreet, "Lee in Pennsylvania," 419; Wittenberg and Petruzzi, *Plenty of Blame,* 42–60.

33. Blackford, *War Years with Stuart,* 225; George R. Prowell, *Encounter at Hanover: Prelude to Gettysburg* (Shippensburg, PA, 1962), 38–82; Wittenberg and Pettruzi, *Plenty of Blame,* 65–117.

34. Blackford, *War Years with Stuart,* 225; McClellan, *Life and Campaigns,* 325; J. H. Kidd, *Personal Recollections of a Cavalryman with Custer's Michigan Cavalry Brigade* (Ionia, MI, 1908), 69; Starr, *Union Cavalry,* 3:428–29. Arriving at Gettysburg on June 30 could have put Stuart into combat on July 1 against Brigadier General John Buford's cavalry, which did such a good job handling the advance of Confederate infantry.

35. Blackford, *War Years with Stuart,* 233; Beale, *Lieutenant of Cavalry,* 116; Arthur J. L. Fremantle, *Three Months in the Southern States* (New York, 1874), 274–75.

36. Wittenberg and Petruzzi, *Plenty of Blame,* 296. As these authors point out, it is ironic that Early became one of Stuart's most severe postwar critics.

37. Beale, *Lieutenant of Cavalry,* 114; Freeman, *Lee's Lieutenants,* 3:137–38.

38. McClellan, *Life and Campaigns,* 325; Robertson, *Stonewall Jackson,* 606; Freeman's chapter, "The Price of 125 Wagons," in *Lee's Lieutenants,* 3:51–72; Wittenberg and Petruzzi, *Plenty of Blame,* 139–55.

39. Taylor, *Four Years with General Lee,* 281, also found in Taylor, "Campaign in Pennsylvania," 307; Henry Heth, *Memoirs of Henry Heth,* ed. James L. Morrison (New York, 1974), 174; Campbell Brown, *Campbell Brown's Civil War: With Ewell and the Army of Northern Virginia,* ed. Terry L. Jones (Baton Rouge, 2001), 204–5; Longstreet, "Lee in Pennsylvania," 420.

40. Lee's postcampaign report described his order to Ewell (*OR,* vol. 27, pt. 2:318), and Ewell's postbattle report (ibid., 445) stated his option to use his discretion. Pfanz, *Richard S. Ewell,* 307–13; Gary W. Gallagher, *Lee and His Generals in War and Memory* (Baton Rouge, 1998), 165–69, 175–81.

41. Sears, *Gettysburg,* 6–12, 17; Earl J. Hess, *Pickett's Charge: The Last Attack at Gettysburg* (Chapel Hill, 2001), 16–19, 58–62, 68–70.

42. Blackford, *War Years with Stuart,* 229.

43. An influential, albeit fanciful, account of the meeting on July 2 is found in John W. Thomason, *Jeb Stuart* (New York, 1930), 440, who contended that Lee met Stuart "austerely," exclaiming "Well, General Stuart, you are here at last!" Depending on Lee's tone of voice, that exclamation could be one of relief and joy or sharp rebuke. Having Lee employ the same phrase is Freeman, *Lee's Lieutenants,* 3:139, and Thomas, *Bold Dragoon,* 246. Wert, *Cavalryman of the Lost Cause,* 282, notes the absence of an account by any attendee at the meeting and reports Lee's remark as something he "purportedly" said. Analyses of the meeting are in Carhart, *Lost Triumph,* 137–42, and Nesbitt, *Saber and Scapegoat,* 89–91.

44. Carhart, *Lost Triumph,* 142–44; Wade Hampton's report, Aug. 13, 1863, *OR,* vol. 27, pt. 2:724; Wittenberg and Petruzzi, *Plenty of Blame,* 162–75. Seeing Confederate scouts at Cress Ridge in Miller, "Cavalry Battle near Gettysburg," 3:400.

45. Lee's postcampaign report stated his expectation for a morning attack, *OR,* vol. 27, pt. 2:320. Longstreet, "Lee in Pennsylvania," 414–46; General James Longstreet, "Mistakes of Gettysburg," in *Annals of the War Written by Leading Participants,* ed. Alexander K. McClure (1879; reprint, Dayton, OH, 1988),

619–33; James Longstreet, "Lee's Right Wing at Gettysburg," in Johnson and Buel, *Battles and Leaders,* 3:339–54, especially 342 regarding a morning attack. See also William Allan, "Reply to General Longstreet," in Johnson and Buel, *Battles and Leaders,* 3:355–56; and Longstreet's memoir, *From Manassas to Appomattox.* Some ex-Confederates, who adhered to the Democrats, were antagonistic toward Longstreet because after the war he openly criticized Lee following the commander's death in 1870 and he joined the Republican Party. Explaining postwar attitudes toward Longstreet is William G. Piston, *Lee's Tarnished Lieutenant: James Longstreet and His Place in Southern History* (Athens, GA, 1987), 129–36, 142–48, 154–57.

46. William G. Piston, "Cross Purposes: Longstreet, Lee, and Confederate Attack Plans for July 3 at Gettysburg," in *The Third Day at Gettysburg and Beyond,* ed. Gary W. Gallagher (Chapel Hill, 1994), 31–55; Simpson, "If Properly Led," 161–89.

47. Long, *Memoirs of Lee,* 288; Freeman, *Lee's Lieutenants,* 3:180–85; Robertson, *General A. P. Hill,* 95–97, 193.

48. Longstreet, "Mistakes of Gettysburg," 429. See also Longstreet, *From Manassas to Appomattox,* 386.

49. Longstreet quoted in Longstreet, "Mistakes of Gettysburg," 429; Longstreet, *From Manassas to Appomattox,* 386–87; Long, *Memoirs of Lee,* 288. See also Troy D. Harman, *Lee's Real Plan at Gettysburg* (Mechanicsburg, PA, 2003).

50. For Ewell's contributions at Culp's Hill, see Harry W. Pfanz, *Gettysburg: Culp's Hill and Cemetery Hill* (Chapel Hill, 1993), 284–327.

51. James M. McPherson, *Battle Cry of Freedom* (New York, 1988), 663; Sears, *Gettysburg,* 391; Coddington, *Gettysburg Campaign,* 520.

52. Stuart's report, *OR,* vol. 27, pt. 2:697, 699, but copies of Lee's orders evidently have not survived.

53. Estimates of the number of horsemen with Stuart on July 3 is yet another controversy of the battle. According to Stuart, on his raid he lost only 117 troopers to all causes, killed, wounded, missing, prisoners, and accident. *OR,* vol. 27, pt. 2:713–14.

54. Stuart's report, *OR,* vol. 27, pt. 2:697; McClellan, *Life and Campaigns,* 341 (emphasis added).

55. David M. Gregg's postbattle report, July 25, 1863, *OR,* vol. 27, pt. 1:956; David M. Gregg, *The Second Cavalry Division of the Army of the Potomac in the Gettysburg Campaign* (Philadelphia, PA, 1907), 11; Custer's postbattle report is not in the *OR,* but a contemporary version, dated August 22, 1863, is in Frank Moore, ed., *Rebellion Record,* 11 vols. plus supplement (New York, 1862–69), 7:398.

56. David M. Gregg, "Union Cavalry at Gettysburg," in *Annals of the War Written by Leading Participants,* ed. Alexander K. McClure (1879; reprint, Dayton, OH, 1988), 378; Miller, "Cavalry Battle near Gettysburg," 3:401; Gregg, *Second Cavalry Division,* 13; Carhart, *Lost Triumph,* 224.

57. Stuart's orders to the artillerists "perplexed" Major McClellan (*Campaigns of Stuart,* 338). Stuart did not mention ordering the cannon shots in his postcampaign report.

58. Gregg's postbattle report, July 25, 1863, *OR,* vol. 27, pt. 1:956.

59. *OR,* vol. 27, pt. 2:698; Miller, "Cavalry Battle near Gettysburg," 3:404.

60. Stuart's report, *OR,* vol. 27, pt. 2:698; Wade Hampton's report, Aug. 13, 1863, *OR,* vol. 27, pt. 2:724–25; Custer's report, in Moore, *Rebellion Record,* 7:398; Gregory J. W. Urwin, *Custer Victorious: The Civil War Battles of General George Armstrong Custer* (Rutherford, NJ, 1983), 75–78.

61. Stuart's report, *OR,* vol. 27, pt. 2:698.

62. William Brooke-Rawle, "Right Flank at Gettysburg," in *Annals of the War Written by Leading Participants,* ed. Alexander K. McClure (1879; reprint, Dayton, OH, 1988), 481; Custer's report, in Moore, *Rebellion Record* 7:398; William Brooke-Rawle, "Gregg's Cavalry Fight at Gettysburg," *Journal of the U.S. Cavalry Association* 4 (Sept. 1891): 270–71.

63. Miller, "Cavalry Battle near Gettysburg," 3:404; Kidd, *Personal Recollections,* 88–89; Custer's report, in Moore, *Rebellion Record,* 7:398; Brooke-Rawle, "Gregg's Cavalry Fight," 271; Urwin, *Custer Victorious,* 79–81.

64. George C. Rable, *Fredericksburg! Fredericksburg!* (Chapel Hill, 2002), 1–2.

65. Casualties in Stuart's report, *OR,* vol. 27, pt. 2:714–15; McClellan, *Life and Campaigns,* 345–46; Gregg, *Second Cavalry Division,* 12–13; Custer's report, in Moore, *Rebellion Record,* 7:398–99; William Brooke-Rawle, "Further Remarks on the Cavalry Fight on the Right Flank at Gettysburg," *Journal of the U.S. Cavalry Association* 4 (June 1891): 160.

66. Brooke-Rawle, "Gregg's Cavalry Fight," 274; Kidd, *Personal Recollections,* 90. See, for examples, Paul D. Walker, *The Cavalry Battle that Saved the Union: Custer vs. Stuart at Gettysburg* (Gretna, LA, 2002); and David F. Riggs, *East of Gettysburg: Stuart vs. Custer* (Bellevue, NE, 1970).

67. Gregg, *Second Cavalry Division,* 3; Henry Heth, "Why Lee Lost at Gettysburg," [*Philadelphia Times,* Sept. 22, 1877], in Cozzens, *Battles and Leaders,* vol. 5, 367; Alexander, *Fighting for the Confederacy,* 228 (quote), 231; Marshall, *Aide-de-Camp of Lee,* 223, 220; Charles M. Blackford to his wife, July 18, 1863, in *Letters from Lee's Army,* comp. Susan L. Blackford (New York, 1947), 195 (emphasis added).

68. R. E. Lee's report, Jan. 20, 1864, in *OR,* vol. 27, pt. 2:321 (emphasis added); Sears, *Gettysburg,* 502.

69. Stuart's report, *OR,* vol. 27, pt. 2:708; McClellan, *Life and Campaigns,* 232; Blackford, *War Years with Stuart,* 232; Mosby, *Memoirs,* 230 (original italics).

70. Brooke-Rawle, "Right Flank at Gettysburg," 467.

71. *OR,* vol. 27, pt. 2:697, 707, 708.

72. Stuart to "My Darling Wife," July 10, 1863, and Stuart to "My Dearest Wife," July 13, 1863, in James E. B. Stuart, *Letters of Major General James E. B. Stuart,* ed. Adele H. Mitchell (n.p., 1990), 326, 327–28.

73. Lincoln, message of July 4, 1861, in Abraham Lincoln, *The Collected Works of Abraham Lincoln,* 9 vols., ed. Roy P. Basler (New Brunswick, NJ, 1953–55), 4:421–41, quote on 424. Sears, *Gettysburg,* 497–504. For contrasting views, that the outcome and aftermath of Gettysburg was not so dire as asserted here, see Gary W. Gallagher, *Lee and His Army in Confederate History* (Chapel Hill, 2001), 83–114; and Richard M. McMurry, "The Pennsylvania Gambit and the Gettysburg Splash," in *The Gettysburg Nobody Knows,* ed. Gabor S. Boritt (New York, 1997), 200–202. See also Richard Beringer, Herman Hattaway, Archer Jones, and William N. Still Jr., *Why the South Lost the Civil War* (Athens, GA, 1986), 97, 264, 268.

74. Pickett quoted in Carol Reardon, "'I Think the Union Army Had Something to Do with It': The Pickett's Charge Nobody Knows," in Boritt, *The Gettysburg Nobody Knows,* 122.

75. Lincoln, second inaugural address, Mar. 4, 1865, in Lincoln, *Collected Works,* 8:332–33, quote on 332.

76. William L. Royall, *Some Reminiscences* (New York, 1909), 25.

General Pierre Gustave Toutant Beauregard. Courtesy of the U.S. Army Military History Institute, Carlisle, Pennsylvania.

P. G. T. Beauregard and the Petersburg Campaign

A. Wilson Greene

September 7, 1864, dawned cloudy and cool along the trenches ringing Petersburg and Richmond. Except for the usual picket firing and occasional exchange of artillery, the opposing armies remained quiet in their elaborate fortifications, welcoming the respite from a campaign that had already witnessed four bloody Union offensives. In the Confederate capital, General Pierre Gustave Toutant Beauregard paid little heed to events along the earthworks that day. "I leave tomorrow for Wilmington," he wrote his adjutant general, Brigadier General Thomas Jordan. "I am here performing the play of Hamlet with that character left out 'by special request.' Wishing you success in your Herculean task of endeavoring to take an actual role in the present struggle for the life and death of our country, I remain yours truly." [1]

This sarcastic note, penned by the second highest ranking Confederate general in the Virginia Theater, reflected its author's frustration with his subordinate role at Petersburg. Once considered the preeminent military hero in the Confederacy and recently the independent commander of a military department responsible for hundreds of square miles of territory in North Carolina and Virginia, by the late summer of 1864 Beauregard found himself under the respectful but firm control of General Robert E. Lee, his ability to dictate operations and exercise discretionary authority all but evaporated. Beauregard's mercurial Civil War career had ebbed once more, as it had so often since the spring of 1861.

Beauregard's near irrelevance now stood in stark contrast to his early-war profile. Born on May 28, 1818, to a Creole family below New Orleans,

Beauregard entered West Point at the age of sixteen, graduating second in the class of 1838. He served with distinction in the Mexican War, skillfully superintended the construction of defenses around New Orleans in the 1850s, and rose to command of the United States Military Academy in January 1861, a post he held for less than a week when his pro-secession sentiments led to his dismissal. Beauregard returned to Louisiana, expecting to be named commander of state forces, only to learn that Braxton Bragg had received the post. His pride wounded, Beauregard declined a lesser position and volunteered to serve as a private soldier. Soon, however, the influence of his brother-in-law, former Senator John Slidell, landed him a commission as brigadier general in the Confederate army and a posting at Charleston, South Carolina. Beauregard presided over the surrender of Fort Sumter in April and then moved to Manassas Junction, Virginia, in command of the gathering army confronting the Federals moving south from Washington. The Confederate victory at Manassas on July 21 cemented his stature as the most famous and revered military figure in the South.

The Confederate Congress rewarded Beauregard with one of only five full-general commissions in national service, but soon his pen undid much of what his sword had accomplished. Beauregard publicly criticized the Davis administration for failing to exploit his victory at Manassas, a course of action the Creole naïvely predicted could have resulted in the capture of Washington. The president, although outwardly tolerant of Beauregard's indiscretion, grew resentful of his outspoken general, feelings exacerbated by rumors that Davis's political enemies intended to run Beauregard for president. Eventually Davis rid himself of the troublesome officer by sending him to the Western Theater, where he served as second in command to General Albert Sidney Johnston. When Johnston received a mortal wound on April 6, 1862, at the Battle of Shiloh, Beauregard assumed army command. He failed to deliver the knockout blow that many at the time thought possible and, in fact, would order his forces back to Corinth, Mississippi, the following day. When he evacuated Corinth in late May and moved south to safety at Tupelo, actions viewed as further evidence of Beauregard's leadership deficiencies, the Louisianan took an unauthorized leave of absence to restore his chronically shaky health.

By this time Beauregard's military star had begun to descend, and the administration held him responsible for the reversal of fortunes that had marked the army's course since Sidney Johnston's death. His failure to ask for permission to leave the army provided the excuse Davis needed to relieve Beauregard and name the president's friend, Braxton Bragg, as his replacement. Nevertheless, Beauregard continued to enjoy public popularity, and this, combined with his high rank, compelled Davis to find him a new billet. In September, Beauregard again assumed authority at Charleston, where during the next twenty months he performed well, repelling several Federal attempts to capture the "cradle of the rebellion."

Although the south Atlantic Coast was more significant than historians have generally acknowledged, Beauregard grew restless and despondent over what he considered a lackluster assignment. By February 1864, he was giving serious consideration to resigning his commission, and in April he sought an extended leave to restore his health and spirits. Then orders arrived to repair to Virginia and assume command of the vast military department extending from the James River south to the vital port of Wilmington, North Carolina. Beauregard accepted the transfer and arrived at department headquarters in Petersburg on May 10. He then presided over an offensive that drove Major General Benjamin Butler's Army of the James into a fortified camp at Bermuda Hundred, a peninsula between the James and Appomattox rivers.

By late May, with Butler's army apparently checked, General Lee called on Beauregard to send reinforcements to his Army of Northern Virginia, which faced Union General-in-Chief Ulysses S. Grant and Major General George G. Meade's Army of the Potomac a few miles northeast of Richmond. The Creole reluctantly loaned Lee one of his two infantry divisions and with his remaining troops guarded the railroad running south from the Confederate capital, along with the eastern defenses surrounding the vital transportation hub at Petersburg. Lee's victory at Cold Harbor on June 3 ended Grant's immediate efforts to bull his way into Richmond and set the stage for Beauregard's most important service during the subsequent campaign.[2]

Modern students of Beauregard's wartime performance express a variety of opinions regarding his military skills. His biographer, T. Harry Williams, admitted that "as a general [Beauregard] had his defects—the penchant for grand planning, the disregard of logistics, the exaggeration of results to be attained—but his general strategic sense was often sound, especially where enemy intentions were involved."[3] At no time would this analysis be better illustrated than during the middle of June 1864 as Grant undertook the Petersburg Campaign.

In addition to outnumbering the Confederates by more than three to two in central Virginia, the Federals maintained the operational initiative and enjoyed unity of command. Grant's objective was to destroy Lee's army as an effective fighting force, a goal he might accomplish by continuing to pound the enemy north and east of Richmond at a great human toll, or by secretly moving south of the James River, at a point below the mouth of the Appomattox River, and targeting Petersburg. Capture of the Cockade City, twenty-three miles south of the Confederate capital, promised to choke off all but one reliable rail supply line feeding Richmond and Lee's army, a circumstance that would likely compel Lee to either come out from behind his odds-evening fortifications and confront the Federals or submit to a siege with predictable consequences. All that stood between Grant and Petersburg was the James River and Beauregard's small army.

As early as June 7, Beauregard warned Braxton Bragg, now serving as Jefferson Davis's military advisor, that "Grant . . . doubtless intends operations against Richmond along James River, probably on the south side. Petersburg being nearly defenseless would be captured before it could be reinforced."[4] Grant, indeed, planned just such an operation by ferrying a portion of his forces back to Bermuda Hundred and marching the rest across a massive pontoon bridge, erected at a point sufficiently downstream to avoid the notice of Lee's cavalry. Butler's bungled raid on June 9 seemed to Beauregard evidence of the Federals' plans, but Lee replied to his excitable comrade that "no troops have left General Grant's army . . . and none could have crossed the James River without being perceived. I think it is very improbable . . . that Grant would diminish his force."[5]

Lee was right about the nature of the June 9 attacks but entirely wrong in his assessment of Grant's intentions and capabilities. An increasingly nervous Beauregard deployed most of his diminished army at Bermuda Hundred—behind the fortifications, blocking Butler's access to the Richmond & Petersburg Railroad—placed one veteran brigade supplemented by militia in the eastern portion of Petersburg's permanent defenses, and persistently warned Richmond of his precarious position, pleading for the return of Major General Robert Hoke's Division and other troops sent to Lee prior to Grant's attack at Cold Harbor.[6]

On June 14, Beauregard's scouts positioned along the James reported the presence of troop transports moving up that river, filled, according to deserters, with units from Butler's army returning to Bermuda Hundred from Cold Harbor.[7] Lee interpreted this movement as merely the restoration of Butler's brigades to their original assignment—not evidence of a massive movement of the Army of the Potomac. This intelligence did, however, prompt Lee to shift Hoke's Division opposite Drewry's Bluff, at the north end of a pontoon bridge spanning the James seven miles downstream from Richmond, in position to go to Beauregard's aid if necessary. The Virginian guessed that the disappearance of the Federals at Cold Harbor meant that they were concentrating somewhere on the north bank of the James, perhaps in preparation for an advance along the river or with the eventual intention of operating against Petersburg. Neither Beauregard nor Lee had definite knowledge of Grant's whereabouts or plans or any conception of how swiftly the Federal commander could bring an overwhelming force to bear against Petersburg.[8]

Between June 15 and 18, Grant would commit the entire Army of the Potomac and most of the Army of the James to an offensive against Beauregard's lines. Beauregard would confront enormous odds, which at times approached nearly six to one, and manage to hold the Federals out of Petersburg for more than seventy-two hours. Not until the morning of June 18 did the first reinforcements from the Army of Northern Virginia reach Petersburg. With Lee's veterans on the scene, the final Federal offensives failed and Grant commenced operations against Petersburg's supply arteries, a process that would require another 288 days.[9]

Students of the campaign have wrestled with the question of why it took Robert E. Lee so long to realize that Grant's true target was Petersburg and by so doing risk the viability of the Confederate capital and its primary army. Beauregard's actions during those critical three days are crucial to unraveling this mystery.

It is important to reiterate that neither Lee nor Beauregard grasped Grant's operational plan or the Federal commander's ability to shift so many troops across the James River in so short a time. When Beauregard dispatched a volunteer aide, Colonel Samuel B. Paul, to meet with Lee in the predawn hours of June 15, he instructed his emissary only to request the return of Hoke's Division and to emphasize the threat he faced from Butler's reinforced army at Bermuda Hundred. At 7:00 A.M. Beauregard wrote Bragg that the "return of Butler's forces sent to Grant, and the arrival of the latter at Harrison's Landing renders my position more critical than ever; if not reinforced immediately enemy could force my lines at Bermuda Hundred Neck . . . or take Petersburg."[10]

Lee also miscalculated Grant's capabilities. At 12:10 P.M. on June 14, the Confederate commander wired President Davis that he guessed that Grant was "preparing to move South of James River. . . . It may be Gen. Grant's intention to place his army within the fortifications around Harrison's Landing . . . where by the aid of his gunboats, he could offer a strong defence. . . . He could then either refresh it or transfer it to the other side of the River without our being able to molest it. . . . We ought therefore to be extremely watchful & guarded." A few hours later, Lee modified his thinking to inform the president that his best information suggested that Grant's forces had moved to the James at both Westover and Wilcox's Landing and that "his facilities for crossing the river and taking possession of Petersburg are great."[11]

Wilcox's Landing provided the northern anchor for the pontoon bridge that Union engineers constructed on the afternoon and evening of June 14. Remarkably, none of Beauregard's river scouts witnessed this phenomenal engineering achievement, preserving the secrecy of Grant's operation. Confederate reactions to the unfolding Union offensive remained speculative

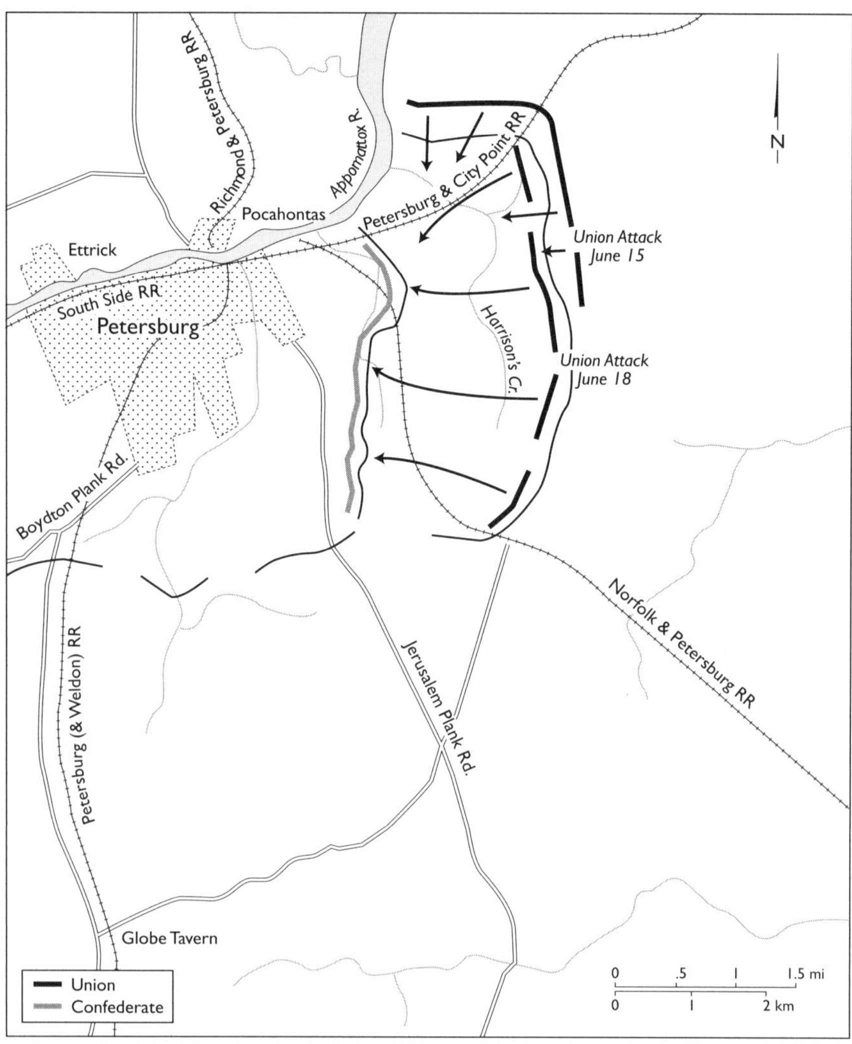

Petersburg, Virginia, June 15–18, 1864.

and were confined to the shifting of Hoke's Division and Brigadier General Matt Ransom's Brigade, of Major General Bushrod R. Johnson's Division, across the James late on the morning of June 15 with orders to report to Beauregard.[12]

In hindsight it is evident that Beauregard more accurately predicted the imminence and seriousness of the threat to his position than had Lee. Both commanders conceded that Grant might cross the James, but neither assumed that the Federals could move fast enough to require more than the return of Beauregard's own troops until Beauregard requested an additional division on the afternoon of June 15, just hours before the Union assaults commenced. The blow fell on Petersburg's eastern defenses, a series of artillery redans connected by infantry works, resulting in the capture of more than a mile of the Confederate line. Hoke's lead elements arrived just as troops from Major General William F. Smith's Eighteenth Corps of Butler's army and Major General Winfield S. Hancock's Second Corps consolidated their gains—too late to redeem the disaster.

Beauregard swiftly reacted to the crisis that threatened to doom Confederate fortunes in Virginia. He ordered Johnson's Division, save for a few pickets, to abandon its trenches at Bermuda Hundred and report south of the Appomattox. Joined by Hoke's arriving reinforcements, Beauregard skillfully deployed Johnson's troops behind a new defensive line behind Harrison's Creek, the soldiers frantically clawing the earth with bayonets and tin plates to create a defensible breastwork. By dawn the Confederates rested behind a formidable position anchored on the Appomattox River and connecting with their original ramparts south of the zone controlled by the Federals.[13]

Beauregard notified Bragg shortly after 9:00 P.M. of the loss of a portion of his Petersburg defenses, his intention to abandon the Bermuda Hundred works, and the need for Lee to "look to the defenses of Drewry's Bluff and the lines across Bermuda Neck." Two hours later, the Louisianan wired Lee, apprising him of the tactical situation south of the James and of his plan to hold his pickets at Bermuda Hundred until dawn. "Cannot these lines be occupied by your troops?" Beauregard inquired. "The safety of our communications requires it. Five thousand or 6,000 men may do." A staff officer awoke Lee at 2:00 A.M. with this message, which failed to identify the troops who had attacked Petersburg. Lee quickly dispatched Major General George E. Pickett's Division of forty-five hundred men to cross the James and occupy the nearly empty entrenchments abandoned by Johnson's brigades.[14]

By 9:40 A.M. on June 16, Lee had established his new command post south of the James at Drewry's Bluff, having accompanied Pickett's Division across the river. Shortly thereafter, Lee heard from Beauregard for the first time that morning, reporting that the Federals at Petersburg were "pressing us in heavy force" and asking that Pickett's Division be sent across the Appomattox while another division replace Pickett at Bermuda Hundred.[15]

Beauregard's 9:45 A.M. message was not, however, the first he had directed to Lee that day. Two hours earlier the Creole had informed Lee that a Union prisoner had identified himself as a member of the Second Corps and revealed that Hancock's men had crossed the James on June 14. Unfortunately for the Confederates, this telegram had been directed to Lee's headquarters north of the James, a location that Lee had abandoned early that morning. For some reason the message never caught up with the army commander at Drewry's

Bluff, so Beauregard's first positive report of the presence of a portion of Meade's army in front of Petersburg eluded Lee. Thus the commander of the Army of Northern Virginia replied to Beauregard's message by admitting, "I do not know the position of Grant's army, and cannot strip the north bank of James River. Have you not force sufficient?"[16]

Lee would ask Beauregard four times that day for information on the whereabouts of the Army of the Potomac, but not until 7:00 that night would Beauregard again mention the presence of Hancock's corps in his front. It is possible, of course, that he assumed that his early morning telegram had reached Lee and that the Virginian's questions pertained only to the missing three Federal corps (the Fifth, Sixth, and Ninth). Still, Beauregard's failure to reiterate what he had learned about the location of a portion of the Army of the Potomac in response to Lee's multiple inquiries speaks poorly of his communication skills during the crisis.[17]

To make matters worse, Beauregard wrote Lee at 12:45 P.M. in a tone that, for the first time, brimmed with optimism. "We may have force sufficient to hold Petersburg," he enthused. "Pickett will probably need reinforcements on the lines of Bermuda Hundred Neck." Lee replied about 3:00 P.M., shortly after this telegram reached him at Drewry's Bluff: "Am glad to hear that you can hold Petersburg. Hope you will drive the enemy."[18]

Thus by midafternoon June 16, based on the information that Beauregard had supplied, Lee concluded that the Louisianan faced only the Army of the James, that he had sufficient force to hold his new line of works at Petersburg, and that the only remaining danger point south of the James stretched along the abandoned works at Bermuda Hundred. There, Lieutenant General Richard H. Anderson, commander of Lee's First Corps, who had accompanied Pickett across the river during the morning, reported that he was engaged with the enemy near Chester Station, combat that would in short order restore the Confederate defenses blocking access to the railroad.[19]

Beauregard's midday ebullience stemmed from his repulse of probes by Hancock and Smith designed to locate favorable positions against which to launch a serious attack later in the day. Elements of Major General Ambrose E. Burnside's Ninth Corps began filing in from the pontoon crossing late that morning, but Meade, in operational command of the offensive, opted to wait until more of Burnside's men arrived before ordering an assault. Thus no Ninth Corps troops engaged in combat during the afternoon and therefore their presence remained unknown to Beauregard and the Confederates waiting in their front.

In Beauregard's 7:00 P.M. message to Lee he reported, "There has been some fighting today without result." He also revealed that he had laid out a third line of defense that he intended to occupy sometime on the seventeenth, "the only objection to it is its proximity to the city." He concluded by admitting that he had no "satisfactory information" regarding Grant's crossing of the James, although he casually repeated that Hancock and Smith's corps had provided the opposition all day. Of course, this was the first Lee had heard of Hancock's presence south of the James. Ironically, it must have been only minutes after Beauregard's message reached the wires that Meade's major attack exploded in front of Johnson and Hoke. Units from Smith's, Hancock's, and Burnside's corps charged along a wide front—perhaps sixty-seven thousand Federals against Beauregard's fourteen thousand. Although the graycoats fought with remarkable tenacity from advantageous positions Beauregard had designated, Meade's overwhelming numbers should have carried the day. Why Beauregard prevailed on June 16 had more to do with the poor tactics of the Federal commanders and the exhaustion and demoralization of the Union rank and file than with any particular brilliance on the part of the Confederates.[20]

Similarly, Butler's incompetence allowed Pickett to easily dislodge the Army of the James from its tenuous position along the trenches abandoned earlier by Beauregard. Lee had committed another First Corps division south of the James, that of Major General Charles Field, and had moved Major General Joseph Kershaw's Division to the north end of the bridge opposite Drewry's Bluff. Thus as the action abated on June 16, Lee was back in control of Bermuda Hundred and Beauregard had held his ground against repeated Union attacks at Petersburg. Half of the Confederate infantry was now south of the James, but neither Lee nor Beauregard could locate three entire corps of the Union army. Consequently, Lee continued to hedge his bets, speculating that Hancock's presence in front of Beauregard might be a ruse to draw him south and expose Richmond to a sudden lunge from the left bank.

Lee opened the correspondence with Beauregard at 6:00 A.M. on June 17, expressing "delight" at the Creole's repulse of the Federal assaults the previous day, urging Beauregard to recover his lost lines, and inquiring again about Grant's movements. Beauregard replied three hours later, explaining that he had insufficient troops to assume the tactical initiative and asking that Lee supply the needed reinforcements in order "to take the offensive [and] thus get rid of the enemy here." He professed no additional knowledge of Grant's whereabouts. "Enemy has two corps in my front, with the advantage of position," he told Lee.[21]

Inexplicably, Beauregard remained unaware of the presence of Burnside's corps at Petersburg. At dawn, Brigadier General Robert Potter's Ninth Corps division had attacked Johnson near the Shand House on Beauregard's right in what a close student of the campaign called "one of the most remarkable assaults of the entire Civil War." At the same time, Major General Gouverneur K. Warren's Fifth Corps arrived behind Burnside but did not participate in the early morning offensive. Beauregard not only failed to identify the presence of Burnside's and Warren's corps at Petersburg but also, at 11:15 that morning, wired Lee suggesting that the Fifth Corps had marched well into the Virginia Piedmont to counter a Confederate offensive unfolding there. "If so, can we not be suddenly re-enforced here, thus enabling us to crush the enemy in our immediate front?" he asked. Despite displaying tactical competence along his hard-pressed lines, Beauregard remained tragically clueless about the nature of the enemy that confronted him.[22]

Understandably, Lee, who had moved his command post halfway between Richmond and Petersburg, assumed from the tone of Beauregard's correspondence that his comrade maintained full control of the situation at Petersburg. He would concentrate on locating the Fifth, Sixth, and Ninth Corps to evaluate the remaining threat north of the James. "Until I can get more definite information of Grant's movements," he advised Beauregard at noon, "I do not think it prudent to draw more troops to this side of the river."[23]

By early in the afternoon, Lee had satisfied himself that Warren had not left the Richmond-Petersburg Theater and so informed Beauregard. At nearly the same time, a message arrived from Petersburg that turned the tactical situation there on its head. "The enemy carried this morning another of the weak points in the old lines," Beauregard reported. "I am collecting all available troops to resist until night, when I hope to be able to occupy new lines. We greatly need reinforcements to resist such large odds against us. The enemy must be dislodged or the city will fall."[24]

Whereas a few hours earlier Beauregard had requested fresh troops to crush his chastened opponents, he now described a crisis that threatened to sacrifice Petersburg. While Lee considered the import of this latest Beauregard bombshell, the Louisiana commander sent another telegram north relaying word from his cavalry commander, Brigadier General James Dearing, that some thirty thousand Federals had crossed the James River near Fort Powhatan with Petersburg as their destination. Lee replied at 4:30 P.M. that despite having no confirmation of this portentous news, he would shift Lieutenant General Ambrose Powell Hill's Third Corps troops to the north side of the pontoon bridge across from Drewry's Bluff in position to cross the James and come to Beauregard's rescue if circumstances required. Shortly thereafter Major General W. H. F. "Rooney" Lee, commander of one of his father's cavalry divisions, confirmed the existence of the pontoon bridge and the Federal crossing to the south side.[25]

Beauregard seemingly lifted the veil on whatever mystery remained regarding the location of the Federals in a message sent Lee at 5:00 P.M., June 17:

"Prisoners just taken represent themselves as belonging to the Second, Ninth, and Eighteenth Corps. They state that the Fifth and Sixth Corps are coming on. . . . They say that Grant commanded on the field yesterday." Lee churned through the import of this news, the most positive information regarding Grant's whereabouts in more than a week. Beauregard had based his conclusions on the reports of prisoners and scouts interrogated by unidentified officers. Were such sources adequate rationale for stripping the capital of its defenders? As Lee weighed his options, the final message from Beauregard that day reached his headquarters. Sent at 6:40 P.M. but arriving more than three hours later, Beauregard calmly explained that "the increasing number of the enemy in my front, and inadequacy of my force to defend the already too much extended lines, will compel me to fall within a shorter one, which I will attempt to effect tonight. This I shall hold as long as practicable but without reinforcements I may have to evacuate the city very shortly. In that event I shall retire in the direction of Drewry's Bluff, defending the crossing at Appomattox River and Swift Creek."[26]

This dispatch contained none of the histrionics that characterized much of Beauregard's rhetoric, thus its calm, reasoned tone increased its credibility. Combined with the evidence provided by his cavalry, Lee now felt confident that the time had come to shift his army to Petersburg. He sent orders to Kershaw to march his division southward at early dawn, while instructing Hill to cross the river at Drewry's Bluff and prepare to march to the Cockade City as well. Late that night, Captain A. R. Chisholm of Beauregard's staff found Lee at his headquarters and provided the army commander with a detailed and accurate summary of the tactical situation below the Appomattox, confirming Lee's decision to commit his army to Petersburg.[27]

That situation was proving perilous for the Confederates. Early in the afternoon of June 17, Burnside sent a fresh Ninth Corps division against the Confederate line somewhat north of the morning's attack zone. Elements of both Johnson's and Hoke's divisions, supported by expertly placed batteries, poured a devastating fire upon the charging bluecoats, inflicting nearly 50 percent casualties. Again at 6:00 P.M., another of Burnside's divisions launched the corps' third offensive of the day. This assault pierced the Confederate line, but Beauregard organized a determined counterassault that restored the defensive perimeter, the firing continuing until almost midnight.

While Beauregard's brigades fought for their very lives, his brilliant engineer, Colonel David B. Harris, and his chief of artillery, Colonel Hilary P. Jones, laid out a new line closer to Petersburg. They examined each fold in the ground, identified proper locations for artillery positions, and drove stakes in the soil to document their work. Once they completed their survey Harris and Jones showed staff officers from Beauregard's two infantry divisions their men's destinations, once instructions to fall back were delivered after dark. The prolonged fighting that evening delayed those orders until the wee hours of June 18, when Beauregard's weary warriors silently withdrew to their new positions, leaving blazing campfires in their wake to bemuse the nearby Federals. After a taxing day of combat, during which the Confederates launched numerous surgical assaults to regain lost positions and keep the numerically superior Federals—now nearly eighty thousand strong—at bay, the exhausted Rebels spent the predawn hours of June 18 constructing works along the lines so carefully identified the day before. No matter how uneven Beauregard's communications with Richmond and Lee had been during the previous forty-eight hours, the performance of his troops, officers, and staff could not have been better.[28]

Kershaw's Division appeared around 7:30 A.M. on June 18 following a four-hour trek through Chesterfield County and across the Appomattox River bridge. Two hours later Charles Field's Division arrived and the two First Corps units extended Beauregard's vulnerable right. Meade discovered the Confederate withdrawal at dawn and ordered a renewal of the attacks that had come so close to victory the previous evening. But a combination of attrition in his officer ranks, fatigue and deflated morale among the soldiers who had grown quite reluctant to attack fortifications, and the fresh troops from Lee's army led to frustration and failure for the Federals. None of Meade's disjointed offensives succeeded, with one particularly tragic assault resulting in the largest regimental loss suffered by any unit in a single engagement during the entire war.[29]

Lee arrived in Petersburg about 11:30 that morning, when, accompanied by Beauregard, he rode to the heights on the south end of the city, providing the two officers a panoramic view of the opposing lines. The visionary Beauregard now urged Lee to assume the initiative by sweeping around Grant's exposed left flank and driving the Federals back toward the James. Lee dismissed this notion, citing the enemy's superior strength, the fatigue of his own troops, and the need to devote attention to defending Petersburg, Richmond, and communications between the two cities. Alfred Roman, whose name is attached to Beauregard's military memoirs, suggested that had Lee assented to Beauregard's plan, "he might have crushed one-half of General Grant's army," an assessment that all students of the campaign dismiss out of hand.[30]

With Lee's arrival at Petersburg, Beauregard's tenure as an independent department commander came to an end. Special Orders Number 139, dated June 15, had specified that "all officers exercising separate commands in the States of Virginia and North Carolina will report to and receive orders from General R. E. Lee," but Beauregard's authority at Petersburg had not terminated until Lee's physical arrival south of the Appomattox.[31]

How, then, should the Louisianan's performance be evaluated during these fateful three days when he operated without supervision? Although at least one analyst finds Beauregard's tactical leadership unequal to the praise it has received, most observers agree with Douglas Southall Freeman, who asserted that "Beauregard's troops made a splendid fight in front of Petersburg and were handled by him with great skill and boldness. Nobody could have done better." Thomas Howe and T. Harry Williams considered the first three days at Petersburg the finest performance of Beauregard's Civil War career. "He demonstrated that in a crisis he was a fine combat officer," wrote Williams. "He might be theoretical before a fight, but when he went in he went in hard. Seldom in war has a general contended successfully so long against such odds."[32]

There is much less unanimity regarding the interplay between Lee and Beauregard from June 14 through 17, an issue Williams calls "one of the great historical controversies of the war." Williams makes the best case for Beauregard while Freeman argues that Lee should not be criticized for exercising prudence in the gradual transfer of his army toward Petersburg. While it is tempting to cite Beauregard's many warnings about the vulnerability of the Cockade City and his attempts to convince Bragg and Lee to bolster the thin defenses south of the James, as evidence of the Creole's strategic prescience, the facts do not sustain such a judgment. Beauregard's intelligence network failed miserably during these critical days in mid-June. Not only did the presence of the Ninth and Fifth corps at Petersburg escape Beauregard's notice for more than twenty-four hours (even while his outnumbered brigades were locked in combat with them), but Beauregard's scouts along the James allowed the existence of one of military history's longest pontoon bridges to go undiscovered for nearly three full days.

Moreover, the quality of Beauregard's communications with the Richmond authorities and with General Lee left much to be desired. He neglected to identify the troops that opposed him while vacillating between breathless predictions of disaster and sudden bursts of optimism. Williams argues that "having put himself on record [Beauregard] seemed to feel his responsibility was ended. Let Lee and Bragg figure out the obvious. He had to take care of his own line." Such leadership hardly merits admiration. Grant unquestionably stole a march on Lee and deceived the great Virginian for nearly seventy-two hours, Freeman's protests to the contrary notwithstanding. Still, Lee acted reasonably given the information he had available—no thanks to P. G. T. Beauregard. In the final analysis, Grant's operational plan worked to perfection, providing him with the opportunity to capture Petersburg between June 15 and 17. Neither Beauregard nor Lee understood the true nature of affairs during this time, a lapse for which the Creole general is the more culpable. Only a markedly lackluster performance by the enervated Army of the Potomac and stellar combat and engineering work by Beauregard and his little army allowed the Petersburg Campaign to extend beyond mid-June.[33]

Rumors quickly circulated in Richmond that Beauregard was in trouble with the War Department, fueled by a request from Bragg that the Creole explain the circumstances under which he had ordered Johnson to abandon Bermuda Hundred's entrenchments. By June 21, however, such gossip had disappeared. "Gen. Beauregard has not been removed from his command," noted one famous Richmond diarist. "It would be too great a shock to popular sentiment."[34]

The next day, Grant's second Petersburg offensive targeted the Petersburg Railroad which connected the Cockade City with Weldon, North Carolina, but spirited Confederate counterattacks inflicted heavy casualties on June 22–23, forcing the Federals back to positions astride the Jerusalem Plank Road. Lee and Beauregard now perceived an opportunity to strike the Union works along the south bank of the Appomattox River and threaten Grant's supply line back to City Point, where the Appomattox entered the James. Brigadier General Johnson Hagood's Brigade of Beauregard's command spearheaded the attack on June 24 but met a quick and bloody repulse. Blame descended on Beauregard, for his troops were the ones that failed, but Hagood heatedly pointed a finger at Field's First Corps division, which had not appeared in support of his men as envisioned by the plan of attack. An opportunity thus arose for a bitter schism between Lee's forces and Beauregard's, but Lee doused the controversy two weeks later by ascribing the setback to "some misunderstanding as to the part each division was supposed to have performed."[35]

Beauregard and Lee had observed the aborted June 24 offensive together from a perch on the north side of the Appomattox River, not far from where each established his headquarters no more than three hundred yards apart. Beauregard now functioned as the head of the smallest infantry corps in Lee's army, although the Virginia general paid his proud subordinate more than the usual amount of rhetorical deference in recognition of Beauregard's technical status as a department commander. Lee and Beauregard maintained cordial and functional relations under these difficult circumstances, although Beauregard quietly chafed at his reduced authority.[36]

Grant would spend the next nine months methodically extending his tentacles to envelop the remaining supply lines feeding Petersburg, Richmond, and the Army of Northern Virginia. The one exception to this operation occurred on July 30, when the explosion of a mine under a Confederate fort along the eastern defenses created the opportunity to storm into Petersburg and capture the city in a coup de main. Beauregard's name is rarely as-

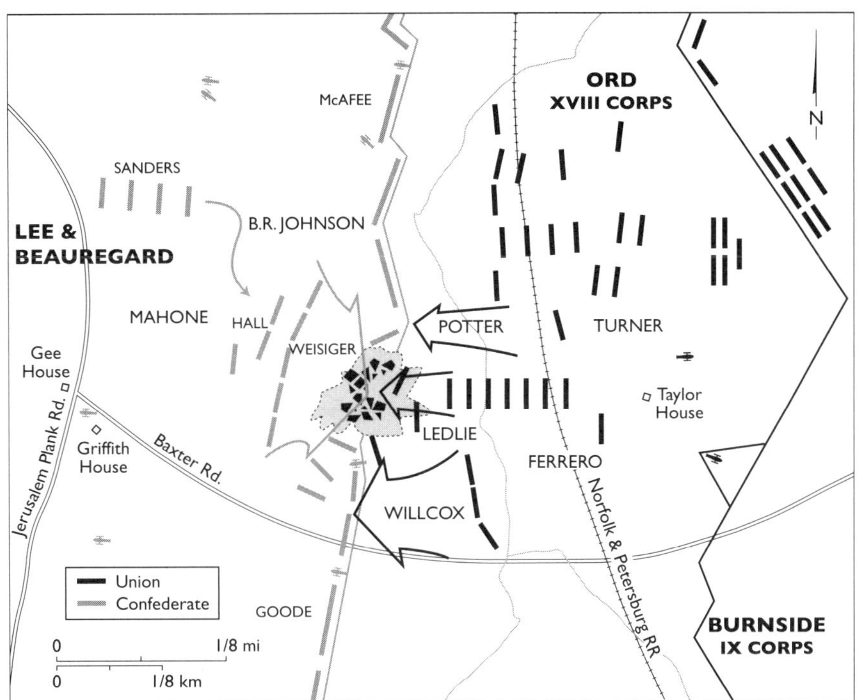

Battle of the Crater, July 30, 1864.

sociated with the ensuing Battle of the Crater, although the breach occurred along his lines at a strong point variously called Pegram's or Elliott's Salient.

Rumors of the Federal mining had circulated among the Confederates for weeks before the blast. Three salients along Beauregard's front, including Elliott's, provided the most logical targets for such a clandestine operation. Beauregard ordered the construction of cavaliers—reserve embankments at the base of the salients—as secondary defenses should the forward fortifications be breached. He emplaced artillery at key locations behind the threatened areas and instructed his brigade commanders to concentrate on any point compromised by an explosion or attack, leaving merely a picket line in their own fronts. "General Beauregard's . . . reputation as an engineer officer went largely to compose the fears of all," added Major General William Mahone, a division commander in Hill's corps, "when it was understood that under his direction a 'countermine' was underway." Indeed, Confederate engineers sunk shafts at all the threatened points, but none of them at Elliott's Salient penetrated deeply enough to intercept the Federal tunnel.[37]

The Yankees had buried eight thousand pounds of gunpowder beneath the unsuspecting South Carolina infantrymen and Virginia artillerists, and when they detonated it shortly before 5:00 A.M., the reverberations could be felt north of the Appomattox, where Beauregard was jolted out of a sound sleep. In short order, Colonel Paul rushed into Beauregard's tent with a sketchy report of the crisis along Elliott's front. Calming the excitable staff officer, Beauregard instructed Paul to repair to Lee's command post, relate events as he knew them, and request that Lee meet him at Bushrod Johnson's headquarters on Cemetery Hill, half a mile northwest of the mine.

While Paul provided the Confederate commander with his first detailed understanding of the unfolding drama, Beauregard rode across the Appomattox and met with Johnson, in whose division Elliott's Brigade served, taking time to scribble a hasty explanatory note to A. P. Hill, who commanded the only other Confederate infantry south of the Appomattox that morning. He then continued south along the Jerusalem Plank Road to the Gee House, located a mere 530 yards due west of the mine, where he personally observed the chaotic situation. Beauregard then returned to Johnson's headquarters, met with Lee, and learned that his superior had ordered Mahone to dispatch two of his brigades to repair the breach. Dutifully instructing Johnson to subordinate himself to Mahone, whom Lee had designated to direct the counterattacks, Beauregard suggested that he and Lee return to the Gee House from where they could watch the action. The two officers took position in the basement of the one-story frame structure, fearlessly peering out a window as Union shot and shell peppered the building.[38]

Four separate attacks executed by three of Mahone's brigades settled the outcome at the Crater. Tactical control of the battlefield remained with "Little Billy" Mahone, who emerges from this notable episode as the primary Confederate protagonist. Lee receives credit for his prompt reaction to the crisis and for his inspirational presence near the battlefield. Beauregard, in the words of his biographer, "epitomized his position in Lee's army. He was somebody else's agent, in this case almost an onlooker."

That assessment may be slightly unfair. Beauregard, through the pen of Alfred Roman, claimed that he, along with Lee, ordered the artillery concentration that initially froze the Federal attackers and that he sent some of the infantry reinforcements that eventually descended on the Crater and reclaimed the corpse-strewn landscape for the Confederacy. The evidence seems irrefutable that Beauregard insisted that Hoke reinforce Johnson's line, resulting in the deployment of the 61st North Carolina of Brigadier General Thomas L. Clingman's Brigade, and that he attempted to obtain help from Brigadier General Alfred H. Colquitt's and Hagood's brigades as well.[39]

Beauregard played a more prominent role in the postcombat negotiations to retrieve the wounded and bury the dead. The parley began on the afternoon of July 30, when Ninth Corps division commander, Brigadier General Orlando B. Willcox, sought permission to request a truce to recover the "large number of our wounded men between our line and the crater." Meade hesitated. The Union commander remembered that on June 19 Beauregard had disingenuously declined to grant a truce to succor the wounded and bury the dead from the previous day, an act that one of Meade's staff called "a specimen of his mean creole blood" and an example of Beauregard's "dirty spite. Lee does not [do] such things." Moreover, military protocol held that a commander seeking a cessation of hostilities tacitly admitted defeat, a humiliation Meade wished to avoid. On the morning of the thirty-first, the Union commander requested that Burnside seek an informal truce that would allow him to save face, but failing that, he drafted a formal request to General Lee for a "cessation of hostilities . . . that the sufferings of our wounded may be relieved and that the dead may be buried."[40]

Alabama Brigadier General John C. C. Sanders received Burnside's request for an unofficial truce and passed it up the chain of command. At noon, word returned that only a formal appeal from Meade to Lee, in accordance with normal military usage, would be considered. Burnside promptly forwarded the contingent document that Meade had provided. Lee received Meade's communication in due course but then passed it down to Beauregard for his consideration on the grounds that the area in question was under the jurisdiction of Beauregard's department. All of this took time. When Beauregard at last penned his reply the sun had grown too low in the western sky to allow enough daylight to complete the grim task at hand. "Your proposition is acceded to, and hostilities will be suspended for the purpose to-morrow morning at 5 o'clock," Beauregard told Meade. The truce was to last four hours.[41]

Beauregard was as good as his word. Promptly at 5:00 A.M. on August 1, all firing ceased and a Federal burial detail advanced as throngs of spectators from both armies watched the grisly proceedings. Among the onlookers were Brigadier General Archibald Gracie, a brigade commander in Johnson's Division, and Beauregard himself, dressed in privates' uniforms to hide their identities. So much time had elapsed since the battle, however, that the surviving wounded numbered only a handful, dwarfed in volume by rows of the dead, "as if the terrible artillery fire had been a mighty scythe and had mown them down." The bodies had roasted in the summer sun for nearly two days, turning the skin of the slain "a purplish black. Their faces are swollen and disfigured beyond all hope of recognition," remembered one horrified witness, and "some of the bodies have burst open . . . the black, thick blood . . . oozing from the congested veins." This was not the first instance when the hubris of generals inflicted unspeakable suffering upon the wounded, a fact that does little to absolve Meade, Lee, and, to a lesser extent, Beauregard of shameful insensitivity.[42]

The unhappy outcome at the Crater convinced Grant to return to more conventional means for reducing Petersburg. Once again he targeted the Petersburg Railroad, on August 18 sending the Fifth Corps toward the tracks south of the city. As he had done in July, the Federal general in chief had lured a large portion of Lee's forces north of the James by launching an offensive against Richmond a few days earlier. Once again, Beauregard at Petersburg found himself the senior Confederate officer charged with repulsing a major Union offensive.

Four Confederate infantry divisions—Johnson's and Hoke's of Beauregard's department and Major General Henry Heth's and Mahone's of Hill's corps—deployed south of the Appomattox, occupying the lengthy Petersburg fortifications from the river below the city to a point southwest of the city limits, although two of Mahone's five brigades had joined Lee north of the James River. Dearing's cavalry picketed the Petersburg Railroad while "Rooney" Lee's troopers ranged beyond the army's right flank and as far south as Reams's Station. The Eighteenth and Ninth Corps held the Federal lines opposite Beauregard while, early on the morning of August 18, four divisions of Warren's Fifth Corps sallied west and interdicted the railroad near Globe Tavern, six miles south of Petersburg.

Dearing notified Beauregard in midmorning of the blue-clad incursion, intelligence that Beauregard immediately conveyed to Lee, requesting additional troopers to deal with the undefined threat. By noon, the Creole took matters into his own hands. He ordered two of Heth's brigades to confront the Federal raiders near a dwelling close to the tracks called the Davis House. In contrast to the ambiguity of his correspondence with Lee in June, Beauregard quickly identified his opponents as the Fifth Corps and by 7:00 P.M. had told the Confederate commander that Heth's counterthrusts had repulsed the enemy, adding with accuracy that he needed more troops to finish the job in the morning.[43]

Beauregard also informed Hill that he would have field responsibility for managing the infantry forces Beauregard designated for subsequent counterattacks, admonishing Hill to "watch and feel closely the enemy during the night, and report any change in his position." He further directed that Hill use a brigade from Mahone's Division, supplemented by Colquitt's Brigade of Hoke's Division, all under the command of Mahone, to support Dearing's horsemen in advance of the Confederate trenches but not to place Mahone "too far beyond our lines as his services may be needed at night in the event of an assault on our works."[44]

No attack materialized that night or early the next morning from either Warren or the Federals confronting the trenches east and south of Petersburg. At 8:00 A.M., therefore, Beauregard informed Lee that he intended to "dislodge" the enemy astride the railroad, using the troops then available to him, although he reiterated that the "result would be more certain with a stronger force of infantry." He conveyed the attack orders to Hill indicating that Clingman's Brigade would join Colquitt's and the Virginia brigade from Mahone's Division to form the assaulting force. Mahone and Hill refined Beauregard's instructions to include a two-pronged advance. Two of Heth's brigades would move straight down the tracks, as had occurred the previous day, while Mahone's strike force would hit the seam between Warren's exposed right and the termination of the permanent Federal lines to the east. Despite Mahone's preference for commanding troops entirely from his own division—an arrangement that Beauregard could not accommodate—the Rebels smashed into Warren's vulnerable flank, rolling it up and snaring some twenty-seven hundred prisoners. Union reinforcements arrived in time to stem the Confederate juggernaut, and despite the overwhelming tactical success of Mahone's assault, the day ended with the Federals still astride the vital rails.[45]

As Grant withdrew most of the troops north of the James, Lee released reinforcements to Petersburg, including the two missing brigades of Mahone's Division. Beauregard reminded Hill on the night of the nineteenth that "the prompt dislodgment of the enemy is of the highest importance," but unfavorable weather and the need to sort out the fresh units while relieving those exhausted by the previous two days' combat conspired against a renewal of the attacks on August 20. The last of the Confederate counterthrusts along the Petersburg Railroad proceeded without Beauregard's direct involvement, beyond his competent marshaling of seven brigades for the offensive—the largest effort yet to drive Warren off the tracks. Once again Mahone led the assaults, this time focused on the Union left flank, but the Northerners were ready and easily repulsed him, inflicting particularly severe casualties on Hagood's Brigade of Beauregard's command.[46]

President Davis leveled thinly veiled criticism of Beauregard's management of the fighting at the Petersburg Railroad in an August 23 letter to Lee. "I cannot say I was surprised that the enemy have been able to break through the Weldon railroad, though I regret they should have had time to fortify themselves as a consequence of feeble attacks made upon them at the time of their first occupation of it," snarled the president. The enmity of the chief executive and his military advisor, Braxton Bragg, toward Beauregard had not abated during the summer. For his part, Lee ascribed the loss of his direct communications with the south to the enemy's "superiority of numbers" and reiterated his doubts that defending the Petersburg Railroad was ever feasible. At no point did Lee imply that Beauregard's generalship lacked competence or sufficient aggressiveness.[47]

Despite Lee's refusal to encourage the hostility evinced toward Beauregard in Richmond, the Louisiana general continued to feel that he "had been placed in an unworthy position, was wasting his powers upon work that, under the guidance of General Lee, almost any subordinate general could have performed." He also felt aggrieved at not being selected to command the army in the Shenandoah Valley led by Lieutenant General Jubal Early, and by Lieutenant General John Bell Hood's promotion to replace General Joseph E. Johnston as commander of the Army of Tennessee. Thus by the end of August, Beauregard was anxious to take any position that would provide some degree of independence, an instinct that Lee appreciated and hoped to gratify.[48]

With the capture of Mobile Bay in August, the port of Wilmington, North Carolina, took on special importance. Wilmington comprised a part of Beauregard's department, and his district commander there, Major General William Henry Chase Whiting, requested on August 31 that Beauregard repair to the port city to examine Whiting's preparations to meet the anticipated Federal offensive. Beauregard replied on September 2 that he would visit Wilmington soon. Governor Zebulon Vance of North Carolina added his voice to the matter three days later, urgently requesting Lee to assign Beauregard to Wilmington "because of the great confidence felt in him." Beauregard left Petersburg for the coast on September 8, and two days later Lee replied to Vance, informing the governor that it was his desire to give Beauregard command at either Wilmington or Charleston, depending upon which city seemed most threatened. The looming crisis along the south Atlantic coast thus provided a tailor-made opportunity to relieve Beauregard of his anomalous position in Virginia while sending a competent officer to a critical theater.[49]

While Beauregard was in Wilmington, the Confederacy reeled from disaster at another vital point. On September 2, Hood abandoned the railroad hub at Atlanta and a clamor arose from the anti-Davis faction of the government to relieve Hood and replace him with either Johnston or Beauregard. As Beauregard returned to Petersburg from Wilmington, President Davis journeyed to Georgia to gauge the mood of the people and the army relative to the confidence felt in General Hood. Davis inquired of Lee as to Beauregard's willingness to serve in Georgia, eliciting a lengthy reply from the Virginian on September 19. "Should you deem . . . a change in the commander of the army in Georgia advantageous, and select General Beauregard for that position," Lee advised, "I think you may feel assured that he understands the general condition of affairs, the difficulties with which they are surrounded, and the importance of exerting all his energies for their improvement."[50]

Davis ordered Beauregard to go to Charleston on September 25, ostensibly to evaluate the defenses there and referee a dispute between local commanders. However, the president had something more in mind than a mere inspection trip. While in Charleston, Beauregard received a message from Davis asking him to come to Augusta, Georgia, for a meeting. There, on October 3, Davis placed Beauregard in charge of a new jurisdiction called the Military Division of the West, embracing the departments commanded by Hood and Lieutenant General Richard Taylor, and encompassing troops in Georgia, Alabama, Mississippi, and eastern Louisiana. The assignment, a "master stroke" of political and military personnel management by Davis, proved less prestigious than it seemed. Beauregard was to exercise command over troops in the field only when he felt his personal presence was required, which everyone understood to be as infrequently as possible. In essence, Beauregard would preside over a paper empire. Nevertheless, the Creole accepted his new assignment and by doing so terminated his part in the campaign for Petersburg.[51]

Beauregard's departure from Virginia elicited scant reaction from the rank and file, although one admiring Confederate soldier thought that Major General William T. Sherman would find Beauregard "a hard mule to ride." He had taken leave of General Lee on good terms with that good man, but the literature is almost barren of comments expressing either regret or relief that the Louisianan was leaving the Old Dominion. Much like today, Beauregard was the forgotten man of the Petersburg Campaign in the autumn of 1864.[52]

Beauregard commanded troops at Petersburg during three of the four initial Federal offensives and the first of three Confederate attacks. Little is remembered about his contributions at most of these engagements, a legacy that is commensurate with the limited role in which he was cast.[53]

Such is not the case with the fighting that occurred east and south of the Cockade City between June 15 and 18. Most of the students covering this phase of the operation credit Beauregard with heroic fighting and unique knowledge about the whereabouts and intentions of the Union army—knowledge that Robert E. Lee ignored until the last of those critical days. While Beauregard's engineering skill, tactical competence, and leadership ability allowed his outnumbered troops to defy staggering odds, let us put an end to the nonsense that Beauregard's sound advice fell on deaf ears at Lee's headquarters. The Louisiana general delivered inconsistent, incomplete, and contradictory correspondence from June 14 through the evening of June 17 and understood little more about Ulysses S. Grant's operations than did Lee. Grant fooled Lee as well, but Beauregard was in a better position to decipher the true intentions of his Federal opponents and thus deserves the lion's share of the blame for the potentially fatal delay in concentrating the gray armies at Petersburg.

In the end, of course, Petersburg would survive in Confederate hands for more than nine months after these initial assaults. By the time the Union army reached the city's iconic courthouse on April 3, 1865, P. G. T. Beauregard's efforts to defend the city from May through September 1864 were consigned to one of the darker corners of Civil War history, where they rest today.

Notes

1. Beauregard to Thomas Jordan, Sept. 7, 1864, P. G. T. Beauregard Papers, Manuscripts Division, Library of Congress, Washington, DC (hereafter cited as Beauregard Papers). The four Union offensives at Petersburg through early September included the initial assaults against Petersburg, June 15–18; the attacks against the Jerusalem Plank Road, June 22–23; the mine explosion of July 30; and the capture of the Petersburg Railroad, August 18–21.
2. The best treatment of Beauregard's Civil War career is T. Harry Williams, *P. G. T. Beauregard: Napoleon in Gray* (Baton Rouge, 1955). A reprint edition of Alfred Roman, *The Military Operations of General Beauregard in the War Between the States, 1861 to 1865: Including a Brief Personal Sketch and a Narrative of His Services in the War with Mexico, 1846–8,* 2 vols. (New York, 1994), should be read as Beauregard's virtual autobiography and valued for its insightful introduction by T. Michael Parrish (all references are to volume 2). Stephen D. Engle covers the Shiloh and Corinth operations succinctly in *Struggle for the Heartland: The Campaigns from Fort Henry to Corinth* (Lincoln, NE, 2001). Beauregard's performance at Charleston is brilliantly analyzed by Stephen R. Wise, *Gate of Hell: Campaign for Charleston Harbor, 1863* (Columbia, SC, 1994). Steven E. Woodworth addresses Beauregard's generalship during the Bermuda Hundred Campaign in an essay published in his *Leadership and Command in the American Civil War* (Campbell, CA, 1996), 197–230.
3. Williams, *Beauregard,* 225–26.
4. U.S. War Department, *The War of the Rebellion: A Compilation of the Official Records of the Union and Confederate Armies,* 128 vols. (Washington, DC, 1880–1901), series 1, vol. 36, pt. 3:878–79 (hereafter cited as *OR;* all references are to series 1 unless otherwise indicated).
5. Roman, *Military Operations,* 566.
6. See, for example, *OR,* vol. 36, pt. 3:889, 895–96; Roman, *Military Operations,* 228; P. G. T. Beauregard, "Four Days of Battle at Petersburg," in *Battles and*

Leaders of the Civil War: Being for the most part contributions by Union and Confederate officers based upon "The Century War Series" edited by Robert Underwood Johnson and Clarence Clough Buel, of the editorial staff of The Century Magazine, 4 vols., ed. Robert U. Johnson and Clarence C. Buel (New York, 1884–88), 4:540; P. G. T. Beauregard, "The Battle of Petersburg," in *Battles and Leaders of the Civil War*, vol. 6, ed. Peter Cozzens (Urbana, IL, 2004), 408–11.

7. *OR*, vol. 51, pt. 2:1012; ibid., vol. 40, pt. 2:653.

8. Robert E. Lee, *Lee's Dispatches: Unpublished Letters of General Robert E. Lee, C.S.A., to Jefferson Davis and the War Department of The Confederate States of America, 1862–1865*, ed. Douglas Southall Freeman; rev. ed. Grady McWhiney (New York, 1957), 226–33.

9. The best overview of the Petersburg Campaign is Earl J. Hess, *In the Trenches at Petersburg: Field Fortifications and Confederate Defeat* (Chapel Hill, 2009). The opening battles of the campaign between June 15 and 18 are admirably outlined in Thomas J. Howe, *Wasted Valor, June 15–18, 1864* (Lynchburg, VA, 1988).

10. Williams, *Beauregard*, 228; Beauregard, "Battle of Petersburg," 411–12; *OR*, vol. 40, pt. 2:655; Roman, *Military Operations*, 573–74.

11. Lee, *Lee's Dispatches*, 226–33.

12. Roman, *Military Operations*, 573; *OR*, vol. 40, pt. 2:655, 658, 677; Lee, *Lee's Dispatches*, 235–36. Roman claims that Beauregard issued orders to Hoke to join him in Petersburg on the fourteenth while Lee reported that he sent orders to Hoke to march to Petersburg on the morning of the fifteenth. Hoke reported at 11:30 A.M. on the fifteenth that he had just received orders to cross the river and report to Beauregard, suggesting that either Roman was mistaken or that Beauregard's orders failed to reach Hoke.

13. Howe, *Wasted Valor*, 21–41; Hess, *In the Trenches at Petersburg*, 18–20. Controversy still swirls around the decision by Smith and Hancock to halt their attacks at dark, allowing Beauregard to develop his new line and position his reinforcements behind it.

14. *OR*, vol. 40, pt. 2:656–57, 677; Roman, *Military Operations*, 570, 574–75; Douglas Southall Freemen, *R. E. Lee, A Biography*, 4 vols. (New York, 1934–35), 3:409–10 (all references are to volume 3).

15. *OR*, vol. 40, pt. 2:659; ibid., vol. 51, pt. 2:1078.

16. *OR*, vol. 51, pt. 2:1078; Roman, *Military Operations*, 571; *OR*, vol. 40, pt. 2:659; Freeman, *R. E. Lee*, 412. References to "Grant's army" reflect the assumption by many contemporaries and modern students that the Army of the Potomac belonged to Grant, not its actual commander, Major General George G. Meade.

17. Lee inquired of Beauregard as to Grant's whereabouts at 10:30, 1:15, 3:00, and 4:00. See *OR*, vol. 40, pt. 2:659; and Roman, *Military Operations*, 571.

18. *OR*, vol. 51, pt. 2:1078; ibid., vol. 40, pt. 2:659.

19. Ibid., vol. 51, pt. 2:1079.

20. Ibid., 1078–79. See Howe, *Wasted Valor*, 42–61, for a summary of the combat on June 16.

21. Robert E. Lee, *The Wartime Papers of R. E. Lee*, ed. Clifford Dowdey and Louis Manarin (New York, 1961), 787; *OR*, vol. 40, pt. 2:664; ibid., vol. 51, pt. 2:1079.

22. *OR*, vol. 51, pt. 2:1079–80; Howe, *Wasted Valor*, 62–70.

23. Lee, *Wartime Papers*, 788; *OR*, vol. 40, pt. 2:664.

24. *OR*, vol. 51, pt. 2:1079.

25. Ibid., 1080; Lee, *Wartime Papers*, 789.

26. *OR*, vol. 51, pt. 2:1080; Roman, *Military Operations*, 572, 234–35; Beauregard, "Battle of Petersburg," 418; Freeman, *R. E. Lee*, 420–21.

27. Freeman, *R. E. Lee*, 422–23; *OR*, vol. 40, pt. 2:663, 665.

28. For accounts of the fighting after noon on June 17, see Howe, *Wasted Valor*, 75–105; and Hess, *In the Trenches at Petersburg*, 26–29.

29. For the action on June 18, see Howe, *Wasted Valor*, 106–35; and Hess, *In the Trenches at Petersburg*, 29–37. The 1st Maine Heavy Artillery suffered the unprecedented losses that afternoon.

30. Roman, *Military Operations*, 247; Howe, *Wasted Valor*, 117; Freeman, *R. E. Lee*, 425; Douglas Southall Freeman, *Lee's Lieutenants: A Study in Command*, 3 vols. (New York, 1942–44), 3:537, 544 (all references are to volume 3); Beauregard, "Battle of Petersburg," 423; Beauregard, "Four Days of Battle," 544; General G. T. Beauregard to General C. M. Wilcox, *Papers of the Military Historical Society of Massachusetts*, 14 vols. and index (Wilmington, NC: Broadfoot, 1989–90), 5:123. In this letter Beauregard claims that Lee at first was inclined to make the attack as Beauregard suggested but then changed his mind.

31. *OR*, vol. 40, pt. 2:654.

32. Howe, *Wasted Valor*, 138; Williams, *Beauregard*, 235. The contrarian view belongs to Lieutenant Colonel Alfred H. Burne, *Lee, Grant, and Sherman: A Study in Leadership in the 1864–65 Campaign* (New York, 1939), 64.

33. Williams makes his case in *Beauregard*, 232–35; Freeman's defense of Lee is in *R. E. Lee*, 438–46. For the thoughtful analysis of a contemporary, see Edward Porter Alexander, *Fighting for the Confederacy: The Personal Recollections of General Edward Porter Alexander*, ed. Gary W. Gallagher (Chapel Hill, 1989), 429.

34. Freeman, *Lee's Lieutenants,* 554; John B. Jones, *A Rebel War Clerk's Diary at the Confederate States Capital,* 2 vols. (Philadelphia, 1866), 2:236; *OR,* vol. 40, pt. 2:675–78.

35. Johnson Hagood, *Memoirs of the War of Secession* (1910; reprint, Germantown, TN, 1994), 270–78; Freeman, *Lee's Lieutenants,* 554–55; *OR,* vol. 40, pt. 1:799, 804–5; Williams, *Beauregard,* 236–37.

36. Freeman, *Lee's Lieutenants,* 555; Williams, *Beauregard,* 236; Hagood, *Memoirs of the War,* 276; Earl J. Hess, "Into the Crater: The Mine Attack at Petersburg,"170, manuscript provided by the author in advance of publication.

37. Roman, *Military Operations,* 259–63; William Mahone, "The Battle of the Crater," Virginia Historical Society, Richmond. Hess expresses doubt as to Beauregard's responsibility for designing the cavalier trenches in "Into the Crater," 47. The other two salients on Beauregard's front, Gracie's and Colquitt's, were north of Elliott's Salient near Hare's Hill.

38. Many accounts summarize the Confederate reaction to the mine explosion on the morning of July 30. See Hess, "Into the Crater," 170–73; Richard Slotkin, *No Quarter: The Battle of the Crater, 1864* (New York, 2009), 211–14; John F. Schmutz, *The Battle of the Crater: A Complete History* (Jefferson, NC, 2009), 205–8; Michael A. Cavanaugh and William Marvel, *The Battle of the Crater: "The Horrid Pit"* (Lynchburg, VA, 1989), 53–55. The various primary sources from which these narratives are written disagree in detail as to the sequence of events that morning. Some have Beauregard meeting Mahone at Johnson's headquarters, others have Lee riding alone to join Beauregard at the Gee House, which is sometimes described as a two-story house with Lee and Beauregard occupying the second floor, not the basement.

39. Williams, *Beauregard,* 237; Freeman, *R. E. Lee,* 475; Roman, *Military Operations,* 267–68; Robert F. Hoke Papers, North Carolina Department of Archives and History, Raleigh.

40. *OR,* vol. 40, pt. 3:667, 691; Theodore Lyman, *Meade's Army: The Private Notebooks of Lt. Col. Theodore Lyman,* ed. David W. Lowe (Kent, OH, 2007), 216–17. Summaries of the truce negotiations may be found in Schmutz, *Battle of the Crater,* 312–17; Slotkin, *No Quarter,* 296–307; Hess, "Into the Crater," 295–96, 309–16; Cavanaugh and Marvel, *Battle of the Crater,* 104–5.

41. *OR,* vol. 40, pt. 3:821.

42. Hess, "Into the Crater," 313; Henry G. Thomas, "Twenty-two Hours Prisoner of War in Dixie," in *War Papers Read Before the Commandery of the State of Maine, Military Order of the Loyal Legion of the United States,* 4 vols. (Portland, ME, 1898), 1:29. Schmutz estimates that only a dozen wounded Federals were found alive.

43. John Horn, *The Destruction of the Weldon Railroad* (Lynchburg, VA, 1991), 55; *OR*, vol. 42, pt. 2:211. Beauregard's August 18 telegrams to Lee may be found in *OR*, vol. 42, pt. 2:1186–87; ibid., pt. 1, 857–58; and *Southern Historical Society Papers*, 52 vols. (Richmond, 1876–1919), 7:346–47.

44. Beauregard to Hill, Aug. 18, 1864, Beauregard Papers.

45. Ibid.; *OR*, vol. 42, pt. 2:1190; Horn, *Destruction of the Weldon Railroad*, 76–89.

46. For the course of events August 20–21, see Horn, *Destruction of the Weldon Railroad*, 90–113.

47. *OR*, vol. 42, pt. 2:1198, 1194; Freeman, *R. E. Lee*, 487. For a summary of the relationship between Beauregard and Bragg, see Judith Lee Hallock, *Braxton Bragg and Confederate Defeat*, vol. 2 (Tuscaloosa, 1991), 211–13.

48. Roman, *Military Operations*, 273–74; Williams, *Beauregard*, 238–39.

49. *OR*, vol. 42, pt. 2:1212, 1232, 1234–35, 1237, 1242; Freeman, *R. E. Lee*, 493; Williams, *Beauregard*, 239–40; Roman, *Military Operations*, 274–75.

50. *OR*, vol. 39, pt. 2:846; Williams, *Beauregard*, 240; Roman, *Military Operations*, 274–75; Thomas Lawrence Connelly, *Autumn of Glory: The Army of Tennessee, 1862–1865* (Baton Rouge, 1971), 471–72.

51. *OR*, vol. 35, pt. 2:630; ibid., vol. 39, pt. 3:782; Roman, *Military Operations*, 275–79; William J. Cooper, *Jefferson Davis, American* (New York, 2000), 492; Williams, *Beauregard*, 242–43; Connelly, *Autumn of Glory*, 472–73.

52. Henry Duplessis Wells to "Dear Carrie" [his sister], Sept. 5, 1864, Henry Duplessis Wells Papers, Southern Historical Collection, Wilson Library, University of North Carolina at Chapel Hill.

53. Earl Hess has divided the Petersburg Campaign into nine Union offensives and three Confederate offensives. Hess, *In the Trenches at Petersburg*, xvii–xxi.

Lieutenant General Thomas Jonathan "Stonewall" Jackson. Library of Congress.

Stonewall Jackson: The Christian Soldier in Life, Death, and Defeat

George C. Rable

"That crazy old Presbyterian fool," was how Major General A. P. Hill in the fall of 1862 described Lieutenant General Thomas J. Jackson. At the time Hill was ailing and had been feuding with Jackson off and on for the last two months, though other soldiers in Jackson's corps might have agreed with Hill's description. But by this time the eccentric Jackson had also acquired a reputation as one of General Robert E. Lee's most trusted lieutenants, and indeed his rock-ribbed Presbyterianism was one of his most widely known traits—and, to many devout Confederates, the key to his success. Even Hill perhaps agreed that God had often smiled on Jackson in battle, but he also predicted that might soon end: "The Almighty will get tired, helping Jackson after awhile, and he'll get the damndest thrashing."[1]

This last statement carried a certain irony because Stonewall Jackson wholeheartedly believed that the Lord held the fate of men and nations in his hands. Jackson viewed not only all human history but his own life as well as the lives of his family and his country as part of a slowly unfolding and vast providential design. The Civil War was simply a part of this history, and only God fully understood its purpose and direction. Jackson's life and death were part of the story, offering lessons for the living, comfort for the sorrowing, and eventually an explanation for the collapse of the Confederacy.

The divine will could often appear most inscrutable and at times hardly beneficent; Jackson's own life had been a case in point. Born on January 21, 1824, at Clarksburg in western Virginia, Jackson had faced a proverbially hardscrabble early life. By age two, his father and baby sister had died, leaving a widow and three children with a burden of debt and largely dependent on public charity. Young Thomas was eventually sent away to live with an uncle, Cummins Jackson, a hard-driving miller who had neither the temperament nor the time to devote much attention to an emotionally starved nephew. But as a teenager Jackson struck up a friendship with Joseph A. J. Lightburn, whose father owned a nearby mill, and under the influence of the Lightburn family became quite a reader. He reveled in stories of the American Revolution but also became an avid student of the Bible. Joining the Lightburns in worship at a local Baptist church and reportedly once walking three miles to hear a Methodist spellbinder, Jackson became increasingly pious. Nightly prayers and deep introspection led him to consider becoming a minister, but he had never formally joined a church and deeply felt the defects of a very limited education.[2]

"The subject of becoming a herald of the Cross has often seriously engaged my attention," Jackson later wrote to an aunt. Regarding the ministry as the "most noble of all professions," he had even fantasized about dying "upon a foreign field, clad in ministerial armor, fighting under the banner of Jesus."[3] As a West Point cadet and especially while serving in the Mexican War, Jackson became a religious seeker, showing considerable curiosity as he inquired into various branches of Christendom. Whether the mild Episcopalianism at the academy left much of an impression is difficult to say. During his service under Major General Winfield Scott, the young officer talked with monks and even consulted with the archbishop of Mexico on several occasions before deciding that Catholicism was not for him. All the while, he was combing the Bible and praying regularly.[4]

A posting at Fort Hamilton on Long Island, New York, in 1849 might well have marked a religious turning point because there Jackson was baptized into the Episcopal Church. Whether he then embraced the doctrines of that faith remains open to question, but chronic health problems and more than a touch of hypochondria undoubtedly shaped his evolving religious views. "My afflictions," he informed his sister Laura, "were decreed by Heaven's Sovereign, as a punishment for my offences against his *Holy Laws:* and have probably been the instrument of turning me from the path of eternal death, to that of everlasting life." And to Jackson like so many other Americans, "everlasting life" came to mean a heavenly reunion with parents and siblings—a not surprising hope for an orphan boy.[5]

Jackson's piety was truly extraordinary. He would not write or mail a letter on Sunday, he avoided small pleasures such as dancing and theater, and one tale later circulated that he had given up whiskey because he enjoyed it too much. Extreme, fanatical, or merely eccentric, such careful observance of what Jackson deemed biblical mandates appeared odd even to close friends and family. "My life is not one of privation, as you sometimes see among

Christians," he explained to Laura. Yet he also appeared to be deflecting her fear that he had grown excessively ascetic. "I enjoy the pleasures of the world, but endeavor to restrict them within the limits which Nature's God has assigned to them." And not surprisingly he connected upright behavior to improved health: "I believed that God would restore me to perfect health, and such continues to be my belief." Therefore the righteous path appeared crystal clear: "Rather than willfully violate the known will of God I would forfeit my life; it may seem strange to you, yet nevertheless such a resolution I have taken, and I will by it abide."[6]

If, as Jackson repeatedly avowed, all religious faith and practice must be measured against the Bible, the question then became which church most closely conformed to God's word. After becoming a professor at the Virginia Military Institute (VMI), Jackson tried the Episcopal, Methodist, and Baptist churches before joining the Presbyterian Church in Lexington. There he sat bolt upright in his pew, though he often dozed through much of the sermon. He read the New Testament daily, along with various devotional books, and began tithing; with considerable effort and no little discomfort, he even overcame his early, halting efforts at public prayer. Of course, even Jackson found it hard to fathom the harder teachings of Presbyterianism—especially predestination—and his own life became a struggle both to grasp and accept the decrees of providence.[7]

In 1853, Jackson wed Elinor Junkin, the daughter of a Presbyterian minister and a devout believer in her own right, but after they had been married for a little over a year she died in childbirth. The day after her death, Jackson wrote that it was God's will that his wife and child be taken from him but that God "will overrule this sad, sad bereavement for good." But however well he appeared to be holding up, like many a grieving soul, he at times longed to join his beloved Ellie in the grave. Eventually the promises of Christ, the tenets of his faith—no matter how painfully expressed—provided both comfort and consolation: "Religion is all that I desire it to be. I am reconciled for my loss and have joy and hope of a future reunion where the wicked cease from troubling and the weary are at rest." Surely the Lord intended to use this sorrow to teach Jackson a lesson, so he tried to be a better Christian and in 1857 married Mary Anna Morrison, another Presbyterian minister's daughter. Under instruction of his pastor, William S. White, he pored over the church's Westminster Shorter Catechism; Jackson and his wife later recited passages together in the evening.[8]

The Shorter Catechism already played a central role in another religious enterprise. In 1855, Jackson had proposed to Reverend White that a Sabbath school for slaves be created, and soon the class attracted between eighty and one hundred pupils each Sunday afternoon. There would be singing, prayer, a brief exposition of scripture, and oral instruction from the catechism, the whole exercise lasting no longer than forty-five minutes. As was his wont, Jackson emphasized punctuality, order, and obedience; he compiled monthly reports of attendance followed by visits to the owners of those slaves whose attendance had been spotty. He even awkwardly led the singing on occasion. Like many devout white people, Jackson viewed slavery as an institution at least permitted if not blessed by divine providence and so he was simply doing the Lord's work in promoting the "colored Sunday school." During the spring of 1858, Jackson apparently ran into some local opposition and had a sharp exchange of words on the streets of Lexington with local officials who accused him of promoting an "unlawful assembly."[9]

Here was a classic confrontation between evangelical duty and slaveholder interests that occurred naturally enough during a period of heightened sectional tensions. In the wake of Lincoln's election, Jackson expressed a consistent hope that somehow the Union could still be maintained, but his unionism was always of the qualified variety so characteristic of upper-South conservatives. "I desire to see the state use every influence she possesses in order to procure an honorable adjustment of our troubles," he advised his sister. "But if after having done so the free states, instead of permitting us to enjoy the rights guaranteed to us by the Constitution of our country, should endeavor to subjugate us, and thus excite our slaves to servile insurrection in which our families will be murdered without quarter or mercy, it becomes us to wage such a war as will bring hostilities to a speedy close." Jackson along with a detachment of VMI cadets had witnessed John Brown's execution, and these comments clearly echoed from the fears evoked by that devout fanatic's failed raid on Harpers Ferry. With the Deep South states leaving the Union one by one, Jackson hoped the "Christian people of this land" would respond heartily to President James Buchanan's call for a day of humiliation, fasting, and prayer. Perhaps the petitions of the righteous could yet pull back the country from brink of civil war, but if not, God remained sovereign. After listening to a sermon lamenting the nation's troubles, Jackson gave the orthodox response: "Why should Christians be at all disturbed about the dissolution of the Union? It can only come by God's permission, and will only be permitted, if for his people's good, for does he not say that all things shall work together for good to them that love God?"[10]

From this belief, Jackson seldom if ever wavered. He naturally viewed the ensuing war as a providential judgment against a sinful people but believed that the Lord surely favored the Confederacy. Therefore the smallest incidents became portents for the future and signs of divine blessing on both himself and the new Southern nation. After receiving a slight finger wound at Manassas and obtaining the sobriquet "Stonewall," Jackson decided that the Lord had preserved his life just as certainly as he had brought the Confederates a "glorious victory."[11] A sovereign God literally decreed victories and defeats, and whatever course the war took, it reflected the divine will. One young Virginian noted in the summer of 1862 that "God has Jackson in his special favor," thus explaining the risks that the general took and his great success when defeat seemed inevitable. Jackson might appear to be a fatalist, but in fact he poured himself into the war with a relentless sense of duty to serve his country and his God. Even Confederate ordnance chief Josiah Gorgas, who hardly shared Jackson's stern theology, wrote of the general, "Jackson is a just and upright man, and in earnest. Providence will help the righteous man who puts his shoulder to the wheel." Some deemed Jackson a Gideon or a Joshua, but the most common comparison was to Oliver Cromwell, surely ironic in light of the widely held notion of a yawning gulf between Southern cavaliers and Northern Puritans. Yet if the Episcopalian Robert E. Lee embodied the gentlemanly cavalier, the Presbyterian Jackson seemed to resemble the stern old Puritan Cromwell. Lieutenant General Richard Taylor, who was no admirer of Jackson, later recalled the general as a man with "ambitions as boundless as Cromwell's and as merciless," who perhaps had been fortunate enough to die before the Confederacy perished and before his reputation had suffered in defeat. At the time, however, Ohio congressman James Garfield worried about Confederate troops being "inspired" by "a kind of Cromwell spirit which make their battalions almost invincible."[12]

As a pious general who kept preachers on his staff, Jackson adopted an almost seventeenth-century model of the Christian soldier. He often prayed in his tent—morning and evening—or went off into the woods. Like Cromwell, Jackson hoped that his men would not only be good soldiers in the field but also good soldiers of the cross; he once publicly prayed that God would baptize the whole army with his Holy Spirit. Major General Lafayette McLaws complained in early 1863 that Jackson "panders to the zeal of a puritanical Church, and has numerous scribes writing fancy anecdotes of his peculiarities." Even during the war, he insisted on Sabbath observance and continued to protest the transportation of mail on Sunday because "no nation that thus arrays itself . . . against God's holy day, can expect to escape His wrath." And the Almighty's stern judgment would not be long delayed because "the punishment of national sins must be confined to this world, as there are no nationalities beyond the grave."[13]

Not surprisingly, Jackson could be difficult and rigid—a man reluctant to take into account weaknesses in himself or others. Such religious zeal reinforced Confederate civil religion because Jackson believed it vital that the government recognize the Lord's sovereignty. "Let our Government acknowledge the God of the Bible as its God, and we may expect soon to be a happy and independent people," he wrote to fellow officers. The old Union had "occupied an extreme position in the means it took to prevent the Union of Church and State," and he hoped that Confederates could more openly declare themselves a Christian people living under a Christian government. The benefits would be both obvious and immediate. When the president, Congress, and the people had prayed to the Almighty, the Lord had answered their prayers with victories. After the Battle of Port Republic, Jackson remarked to Major General Richard S. Ewell, "General, he who does not see the hand of God in this is blind, Sir, blind!" After Second Manassas, he again hoped that God will "make our arms entirely successful" and bring the war to an end. In all this Jackson saw himself as the Almighty's humble instrument, writing to his wife in the fall of 1862:

> Don't trouble yourself about representations that are made of your husband. These things are earthly and transitory. There are real and glorious blessings, I trust in reserve for us beyond this life. It is best for us to keep our eyes fixed upon the throne of God and the realities of a more glorious existence beyond the verge of time. It is gratifying to be beloved and to have our conduct approved by our fellow-men, but this is not worthy to be compared with the glory that is in reservation for us in the presence of our glorious Redeemer.[14]

It must have been difficult to keep all this in perspective when newspapers, many soldiers, and his superiors heaped so much praise on Jackson, and indeed his repeated advice to credit the Lord for all victories perhaps testified to that difficulty.

"If we fail to trust in God, and to give Him the glory," Stonewall Jackson told his pastor, "our cause is ruined." The good general prayed with special fervor on the eve of battle because he fully believed in the absolute sovereignty of God, a conviction that governed both his military career and private life. "Acknowledge God in all thy ways," he had once advised his sister Laura, quoting from Proverbs, "and He shall direct thy paths." To put too much faith in any human means would only court disaster, not only for one's country but also for one's family. After the birth of a daughter in 1862, Jackson solemnly warned his wife, "Do not set your affections upon her, except as a gift from God. If she absorbs too much of our hearts, God may remove her from us." A pious Virginia woman expressed similar fears about Old Jack himself: "I believe that *God* leads Jackson and Jackson his men, just where it is best they should go. My only fear is that people are in danger of worshiping Gen. Jackson instead of God, who rules over all. If we idolize him, he will be taken from us."[15]

There was great danger of the former if not the latter. "My only hope is that our Heavenly Father will accompany Stonewall Jackson to Washington and give him a decisive victory," wrote one exuberant and hopeful Georgian. All the more reason then to remember that it was God who ultimately controlled the course of human history. During the famous 1862 Shenandoah Valley Campaign, Jackson had urged the troops to recognize the "hand of protecting providence" in their success, and he hoped that such acknowledgments would spread from the army into every Southern home. Devout civilians reciprocated such sentiments, a Georgia minister urging everyone to praise the Lord for his "servant General Stonewall Jackson." Shortly before his men advanced toward Richmond to join Lee in repelling General George B. McClellan's massive army, Jackson ordered a day of rest for the troops during which chaplains would hold worship services crediting God with what surely seemed to many a miraculous string of victories. At the same time, he hoped that people at home understood the proper response. "It cheers my heart to think that many of God's people are praying to our very kind Heavenly Father for the success of the army to which I belong," he wrote in his customary vein to another devout Presbyterian. "Without God's blessing I look for no success, and for every success my prayer is, that all the glory may be given unto Him to whom it is properly due. If people would but give all the glory to God, and regard his creatures as but unworthy instruments, my heart would rejoice." On a more personal note, he observed to his wife how "God has again thrown His shield over me in the various apparent dangers to which I have been exposed." Shortly before and at times during the Seven Days' Battles with the encouragement of pious officers, chaplains held religious meetings not only to thank the Lord for recent victories but to bring converts into the fold.[16]

Praying generals were triumphant generals, it was just that simple to Jackson's many Confederate admirers. Well publicized acts of piety, along with requests that the churches remember the army in their prayers, reinforced images of a righteous God leading the Southern nation toward ultimate victory. Surely the Lord would hear and respond to the prayers of such a devoted servant and soldier of the cross, an example that would long survive Jackson's own death. Hoping the nation would follow this noble hero and humble themselves before the Lord at a dark time, a Georgia woman in the fall of 1863 fervently (though inaccurately) proclaimed, "Praying Jackson never lost a battle."[17]

In late August 1862, the Army of Northern Virginia whipped Major General John Pope's ill-starred and short-lived Army of Virginia at the Battle of Second Manassas—a deeply dispiriting loss for the Federals and a victory that reaffirmed Confederate confidence in both the Lord and in Robert E.

Lee. "God gave us the victory," Stonewall Jackson remarked in his usual fashion, though many Northerners were coming to see Jackson himself as nearly invincible. Old Jack's entirely predictable response along with the prayer meeting held in the Stonewall Brigade right after the battle reflected a broader tendency to assume (and more rarely examine) the providential meaning of each major engagement, and so Confederates reveled in their recent victories as indisputable evidence of divine favor. The press widely reported religious meetings in the army, all under the influence of Christian generals such as Jackson, and the Lexington, Virginia, Presbytery duly noted how the Almighty had enabled their local hero to protect the Valley.[18]

By this time, however, the Confederacy's spiritual resources appeared stretched almost as thin as its physical ones. So many ministers had enrolled as officers and enlisted men that there was an early and as it turned out persistent shortage of chaplains. Jackson implored the Presbyterian General Assembly to address the vast need for "ministers of such acknowledged superiority and zeal" to serve as chaplains. As in his teaching at VMI and, indeed, in military life in general, Jackson believed that what was most lacking here was "system" to bring more soldiers to Christ, and he especially deplored chaplains who sought leaves of absence for "trivial objects." Yet by the spring of 1863, even in Stonewall Jackson's corps, no more than half the regiments had chaplains. Despite the general's dismay that even young and fit ministers refused to serve, and efforts by the chaplains themselves to swell their ranks, the shortage remained acute. Early in 1863, Jackson tapped Reverend B. Tucker Lacy—an old Lexington friend and pastor—to supervise the regimental chaplains and more generally promote a religious awakening in the army.[19]

"Does he preach the Gospel?" was the most important question for any would-be chaplain as far as Jackson was concerned. Regardless of his own Presbyterian convictions, the general discouraged sectarianism in the army and even convinced some Baptists to participate in "open communion" services, a practice that would have seemed shockingly heretical back home. But war and especially the rough democracy of the camp promoted more ecumenical attitudes. As a low-church Episcopalian, Lee warmly approved of evangelism, and along with Jackson attended meetings in camp. By joining the officers and enlisted men for worship, they quietly set an example that was noted and followed. Both generals readily acknowledged the Almighty's hand in the success of Confederate arms and so must have seen the winter revivalism of 1862–63 as yet another sign of divine favor. Remarking on the "season of refreshment from the presence of the Lord" in the Army of Northern Virginia and noting a connection between the generals' piety and their recent victories, Chaplain Robert Franklin Bunting of the famous Terry's

Texas Rangers could only hope that such a religious outpouring would soon occur in the western armies.[20]

During the spring of 1863, revivals in the Confederate camps along the Rappahannock River continued and if anything intensified as men steeled themselves for bloody work ahead. Soon the Army of Northern Virginia and the Army of the Potomac would fight a great battle around an obscure country crossroads at Chancellorsville, Virginia. Major General Joseph E. Hooker thought he had a surefire plan to outflank the Rebels and force them to fight for their supply lines. By April 30, the Federals had crossed the Rappahannock, but the following day Hooker seemed to lose his nerve, and Lee approved the audacious flank attack that would win a battle he should have lost. As news of Stonewall Jackson's wounding from friendly fire spread through the army, the ways of providence became for a time ever more mysterious. An early report that Jackson was "doing well" after the amputation of his left arm led a confident Georgia editor to rejoice that this "favorite of heaven" would live to fight another day. Brigadier General William Nelson Pendleton prayed for Jackson's recovery yet noted that if God chose to remove him from the earth, this would be the Confederacy's loss, not Jackson's—an evangelical message that skimmed over the general's importance to the Confederate cause. When told that Jackson would likely not survive, General Lee exclaimed, "He must not die. Surely God will not visit us with such a calamity. If I have ever prayed in my life I have pleaded with the Lord that Jackson might be spared to us."[21]

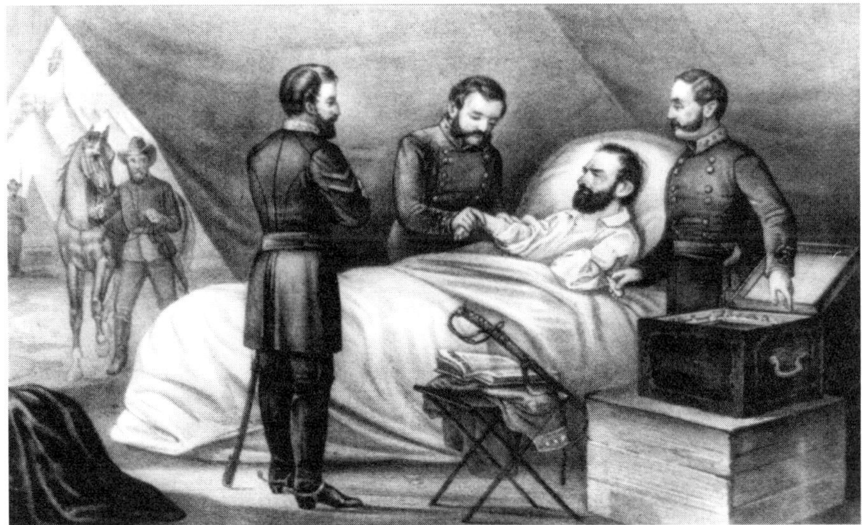

Sketch of Jackson just before he died, mistakenly showing him being cared for in a tent. Library of Congress.

Taken to a small plantation office at Guinea Station, Jackson himself had appeared ready to die. "You find me severely wounded, not unhappy or depressed," he told one minister. "I believe it has been done according to the will of God, and I acquiesce entirely in His holy will. It may seem strange, but you never saw me more perfectly contented than I am today, for I am sure that my Heavenly Father designs this affliction for my good." This was certainly in character, yet at one point he told his wife that he thought he would not die because God had more work for him to do; he appeared to be wrestling with providence. But he quietly said, "If it is the will of my Heavenly Father, I am perfectly satisfied." After Anna gently informed him, "Do you know the doctors say you must very soon be in heaven?" Jackson at first had trouble understanding her but then finally managed to say, "I prefer it." Drifting in and out consciousness, when told it was Sunday, the general rallied enough to reply, "It is the Lord's day. My wish is fulfilled. I have always desired to die on Sunday."[22] And so he did on May 10, 1863—the very day that Lee had proclaimed as a day of thanksgiving for the victory at Chancellorsville.

One Baptist minister immediately commented that Jackson "died with the peace which his Christian life had promised," but to countless Confederates the news seemed overwhelming, the loss unbelievable and unexplainable. "A grievous blow," wrote Kate Mason Rowland in Richmond. One of the great Confederate heroes (an "Elijah to his people—'the chariot of Israel and the horsemen thereof,'" according to one newspaper editor) gone just when he was most needed, but the orthodox knew how to respond. By October 1863, Virginia Presbyterians had concluded that Jackson's "untimely" death was "further chastisement for sins, especially for our ingratitude, pride, and dependence on an arm of flesh." In an even more Calvinistic vein, though one often forgotten when Confederate confidence soared, Kate Cumming mused about the Lord's "dark and mysterious" ways.[23]

Jackson's military reputation and accomplishments had long appalled, frightened, and impressed his foes.[24] Jackson seemed to be one of those "men of narrow minds, but strong passions and tremendous will," Washington journalist John W. Forney remarked. "Religious enthusiasts of all religions and creeds have often devoted themselves with conscientious and determined energy to a wicked cause." Abraham Lincoln himself praised Forney's "excellent and manly article" on this fallen enemy. So too many Northerners could not help but admire Jackson's religious zeal. Henry Ward Beecher termed him a "rare and eminent Christian" and duly praised his devotion to the Presbyterian Church, to temperance, and to prayer, all in contrast, he added, to many Union generals. Beecher seemed almost reluctant to add that Jackson had fought for the slave power and therefore would not be spared the judgment of history—or presumably of God. Of course, any acknowledgment of Jackson's virtues went much too far for abolitionists. "In the cause of Satan, 'Stonewall' Jackson lost his life," William Lloyd Garrison Jr. pointedly observed. Praise for Jackson by Beecher and others would only serve to "discredit Christianity, and make a mockery of religion." Jackson rigorously adhered to various theological tenets highly valued by churches, abolitionist Gerrit Smith sneered, but he had ignored the requirements of justice toward God and men—the essence of true Christianity.[25]

But then the abolitionists had never been all that orthodox anyway, and more typically, Northern editorial comment on Jackson's passing was restrained, respectful, and even reverent. The always conservative *National Intelligencer* of Washington, D.C., praised Jackson as "a noble Christian and a pure man" and prayed that the Almighty would "throw these virtues against the sins of the secessionist." The *New York Herald* offered an almost appreciative assessment of Jackson's personal qualities and military abilities. Even editors who labeled Jackson a "traitor" praised his religious virtues, including an unbending belief in providence and prayer. Comments about Old Jack's religious "fanaticism" and service in a terrible cause were often couched in oddly generous tones. "No man rejoices at his [Jackson's] death," a Massachusetts chaplain wrote to a church newspaper. The general had been "a man of prayer and Christian experience, a brave, gallant and chivalric soldier." The good chaplain added, "May God pardon his one fault! I wish *we* had more generals like him."[26]

"His very enemies reverenced him," North Carolinian Kate Edmondston observed with a kind of awe that only added to the Jackson mystique. Sermons and eulogies quickly completed the process—already well advanced while the general was still alive—of turning Jackson into the model Christian Confederate. One newspaper editor talked of Jackson's grave, "watered by the rains of heaven." Virginia chaplain William Edward Wiatt captured several themes in a few short phrases: "A great general, a noble patriot, brave hero and a pious Christian has fallen." School children learned that Jackson had been both brave and pious, and certainly the eulogies and sermons and even some biographical sketches dwelt more on his religious virtues than his military abilities. Humility, holiness, and an unbending sense of duty to both God and country summed up the qualities most praised by preachers and other religious commentators.[27]

Emphasizing Jackson the devoted Christian over Jackson the relentless fighter turned the general's life into an evangelical object lesson. The pious Mary Jones contrasted Jackson's sanctification to the recent death of Major General Earl Van Dorn, shot by a cuckolded husband and "shrouded in a pall of infamy." To many people, Jackson's exalted spiritual character somehow made his loss to the Confederacy more bearable or at least gave it a larger purpose. No longer would the mighty Stonewall accomplish great deeds on the battlefield, but his example of pious patriotism could still point the way to others seeking salvation for themselves and their country. Young men beset by temptations need look no further than Jackson for inspiration, "a man of prayer and a spotless life," exulted one Georgia editor. One who always "walked in the fear of God with a perfect heart, keeping all his commandments and ordinances, blameless," claimed his staff officer and later biographer Robert Lewis Dabney. Again and again eulogists cited religious faith as the key to Jackson's greatness. Ministers acknowledged that the general had driven his men hard but tried to soften the image of the relentless warrior indifferent to human needs and weaknesses. And in the end Jackson's greatest virtue remained his utter reliance upon God rather than man, a belief the general himself would have used to comfort Lee and other Confederates who could not imagine the Army of Northern Virginia without him.[28]

Struggling to understand why the Lord had taken away their great hero, pious Confederates settled on a thoroughly orthodox answer: The Southern people had relied too much on "an arm of flesh."[29] "They made an idol of him, and God has rebuked them," the general's sister-in-law Margaret Junkin Preston wrote only days after his death. Many other Confederate Christians made almost identical statements, though some thought Southerners had been guilty of idolizing other generals, which might have raised a troubling question about excessive veneration for Lee. The Lord was a "jealous god," as the Old Testament said repeatedly. "God will be honored," Tennessean Eliza Fain warned, "and if we in any way rob him of the honor and glory due to him alone he will bring us to see the evil of our ways." Many men in Jackson's own command, according to the deeply religious artillery officer Willie Pegram, had "lost sight of God's mercies." Therefore the general's death proved the folly of placing too much faith in even the most upright human being.[30]

Devout Confederates made subtle but in their minds important points on this score. Many people had not realized how closely Jackson's deep piety had been linked to his military successes, and they would now have to learn anew the lesson that Jackson himself so well understood: the need to rely upon God absolutely and unconditionally. Now all the people could do, one Virginia woman suggested, was to "bow in meek submission to the great Ruler of events." But this was no mere fatalism. If politicians, generals, and the Southern people had only embodied the "spirit of Jackson," one minister suggested, the war might have already ended in a Confederate triumph.[31] However unlikely that might be, his statement implied that both reformation and victory were still possible.

Nor was Jackson's death the end of the story. The same God who had raised up one Jackson could raise up another, a fond hope that arose even as

Confederates mourned their loss. "He will provide another whose arm he will strengthen to drive the invaders from our soil," a Kentucky staff officer predicted. Governor Joseph E. Brown of Georgia agreed that God had simply reminded his sinful people who ultimately controlled the course of history, adding the usual references to an "idol" or an "arm of flesh" but then urging a convention of Georgia Baptists to humbly pray that the "Head of the church . . . will give us another leader able to stand in the place of the departed." Whether the wily Brown was playing to his audience or whether his comments showed how even politicians at times embraced a providential interpretation of wartime events, many Confederates would surely have echoed his words. The Lord had given, the Lord had taken away, and the Lord would give again—that seemed the most reassuring if not the most logical way to assess the meaning and consequences of Jackson's death. All the people had to do was trust in God, and a new Jackson would deliver them. One North Carolina editor even maintained that there were "many Stonewall Jacksons" who "have not yet had opportunity to exhibit their dormant qualities."[32] Such confidence in the workings of divine providence greatly simplified the understanding of everything from bloody battles to individual deaths. It offered comfort and reassurance but also laid the groundwork for disappointment, disillusionment, and even the loss of faith. A belief in God's sovereignty did not prevent humans from claiming to understand the unfolding of the providential design, an understanding deeply imbued with their own hopes.

In addition to the loss of Jackson, Chancellorsville had been another bloody and costly victory. "I fear we cannot stand many more such," North Carolinian Carrie Fries wrote to a soldier friend. How the Confederates would fare in the next big battle without Stonewall caused great unease, but she suggested simply trusting in the Lord. Although one Virginia private feared Jackson's death would make the Yankees fight harder, the more common assumption was that his noble example would inspire Confederates to enter future battles with greater spirit, élan, and even ferocity. As a chaplain in the Army of Tennessee observed as he searched for spiritual and military meaning in Jackson's death, "God can remove the chief of workmen, and still carry on the cause of liberty."[33]

Certainly the legend, if not always the spirit, of Stonewall Jackson endured and long outlived the Confederacy. Lee's soldiers remained sure that "God is on their side," a Maine private observed early in 1864. "This idea is especially prevalent in Stonewall Jackson's old command, for they are just as superstitious as when old Jack was alive, and their leaders take excellent care to foster the belief, for it spurs men on to fight like demons." A wry story quickly circulated about two angels descending from heaven to carry the general to his eternal home only to discover that Jackson had outflanked them and already entered the pearly gates.[34] After the war, Jackson remained a model Christian held up to the rising generation even as he became a Lost Cause icon—most notably on October 26, 1875, when the Jackson statue on Monument Avenue in Richmond was dedicated.[35] Yet had Jackson been alive, he might well have deprecated all this as little better than idolatry.

Such thinking resonated in the North as well. On the Sunday after Abraham Lincoln's assassination, a rural New York preacher concluded his sermon with two verses from Psalm 118: "It is better to trust in the Lord than to put confidence in man. It is better to trust in the Lord than to put confidence in princes." And as the war came to an end, Jackson's death, especially the public adulation heaped on both his military skill and religious faith, could ironically help explain the downfall of his beloved Confederacy. Theologically exploring the causes and course of the war also shed light on its consequences. Believers north and south had interpreted the war, including its battles and carnage, as divine punishment for a long list of sins. On hearing of Lee's surrender, a Georgian who had seen some of the worst fighting and had lost an eye at Chancellorsville, thought that perhaps Southerners had come to "idolize" the Confederacy "as we did Stonewall Jackson, and God suffered it to fall into the power of the enemy to humble us and teach us to look to Him instead of relying upon an arm of flesh." There was that familiar image that had so often been invoked after Jackson's death and now could account for what had once seemed inconceivable. Perhaps the Lord had finally decreed the defeat of the Confederacy, a possibility that made the divine will appear more inscrutable than ever.[36]

But there was one final irony. Writing privately for his own family after the war, the Confederate artillerist Edward Porter Alexander scorned religious interpretations of the contest. "Providence did not care a row of pins about it," he commented sharply. "If it did it was a very unintelligent Providence not to bring the business to a close—the close it wanted—in less than four years of most terrible and bloody war." Yet he acknowledged that countless fellow Confederates—and he no doubt included Stonewall Jackson—would have disagreed: "Our president and many of our generals really and actually believed that there *was* this mysterious Providence always hovering over the field and ready to interfere on one side or the other, and that prayers and piety might win its favor from day to day." Alexander considered this a "serious incubus" and thought it a "weakness to imagine that the victory could ever come in even the slightest degree from anything except our own exertions." More specifically, Alexander cited Jackson's religious beliefs as the "one defect" in the man's character: "He believed with absolute faith, in a personal God, watching all human events with a jealous eye to His own glory—ready to reward those people who made it their chief care, and to punish those who forgot about it." Pointing to Jackson's lackluster performance during the Seven Days' Battles, Alexander criticized him for trusting too much in God to lead the Confederates to victory.[37] Jackson would have heatedly denied that any human could place *too much* trust in the Lord of Hosts. But he might well have seen his own life and death as a kind of Confederate parable that could make sense of Appomattox and the entire war. A faith that God stood with the Confederacy—a view held by Jackson and many others—had prolonged the war and added to its bloody toll; but then, too, divine providence offered an explanation for Confederate defeat.

Notes

1. James I. Robertson Jr., *General A. P. Hill: The Story of a Confederate Warrior* (New York, 1987), 157.
2. James I. Robertson Jr., *Stonewall Jackson: The Man, the Soldier, the Legend* (New York, 1997), 18–19; Frank E. Vandiver, *Mighty Stonewall* (New York, 1957), 10. Joseph A. J. Lightburn would later become a Union general and Baptist minister.
3. Mary Anna Jackson, *Life and Letters of General Thomas J. Jackson* (Harrisonburg, VA, 1995), 60. In analyzing the religious significance of Jackson's life and death, I have greatly benefited from the arguments and evidence presented in Daniel W. Stowell's superb essay, "Stonewall Jackson and the Providence of God," in *Religion and the American Civil War*, ed. Randall M. Miller, Harry S. Stout, and Charles Reagan Wilson (New York, 1998), 187–207.
4. Robertson, *Stonewall Jackson*, 73–74; Jackson, *Life and Letters*, 48–49; Robert Lewis Dabney, *Life and Campaigns of Lieut.-Gen. Thomas J. Jackson* (Harrisonburg, VA, 1983), 55–57.
5. Robertson, *Stonewall Jackson*, 88–89; Dabney, *Life and Campaigns*, 59–60; Vandiver, *Mighty Stonewall*, 52; Thomas Jackson Arnold, *Early Life and Letters of General Thomas J. Jackson* (New York, 1916), 148–49. See the still valuable and insightful analysis on the relationship between the precariousness of life, the anticipation of heaven, the nature of Christ's kingdom, and millennial hope in H. Richard Niebuhr, *The Kingdom of God in America* (New York, 1937), 126–63.
6. Dabney, *Life and Campaigns*, 83–107; Vandiver, *Mighty Stonewall*, 86–88; Henry Kyd Douglas, "Stonewall Jackson in Maryland," in *Battles and Leaders of the Civil War: Being for the most part contributions by Union and Confederate officers based upon "The Century War Series" edited by Robert Underwood Johnson and Clarence Clough Buel, of the editorial staff of The Century Magazine*, 4 vols.,

ed. Robert U. Johnson and Clarence C. Buel (New York, 1884–88), 2:623; Arnold, *Early Life and Letters,* 159.

7. Arnold, *Early Life and Letters,* 168–69, 180–81, 197–98; Robertson, *Stonewall Jackson,* 133–38; Dabney, *Life and Campaigns,* 83–93; Vandiver, *Mighty Stonewall,* 86–88. Chronic dyspepsia may have contributed to Jackson's drowsiness in church. Elizabeth Preston Allan, *Life and Letters of Margaret Junkin Preston* (Boston, 1903), 82. Jackson appeared equally stiff—if not asleep—during wartime camp services. Joseph T. Glatthaar, *General Lee's Army: From Victory to Collapse* (New York, 2008), 235.

8. Allan, *Life and Letters,* 61–64, 72–73; Robertson, *Stonewall Jackson,* 158; Vandiver, *Mighty Stonewall,* 105–7; Arnold, *Early Life and Letters,* 219–20.

9. Dabney, *Life and Campaigns,* 93–96; Jackson, *Life and Letters,* 60, 142–43 and appendix, 1–6; Thomas J. Jackson to John Lyle Campbell, June 7, 1858, Thomas J. Jackson Papers, Virginia Military Institute Archives, Lexington (hereafter cited as Jackson Papers); Robertson, *Stonewall Jackson,* 167–69; Vandiver, *Mighty Stonewall,* 109–10; "Stonewall Jackson in Lexington, Va.," *Southern Historical Society Papers* 9 (1881): 43–46.

10. Arnold, *Early Life and Letters,* 291, 293–94; James Beverlin Ramsey, *True Eminence Founded on Holiness* (Lynchburg, VA, 1863), 16.

11. Jackson, *Life and Letters,* 177.

12. Dabney, *Life and Campaigns,* 540–41; D. H. Hill to Robert L. Dabney, June 7, 1863, Robert L. Dabney Papers, Union Theological Seminary, Richmond, VA (hereafter cited as Dabney Papers); William S. White, *Sketches of the Life of Captain Hugh A. White of the Stonewall Brigade* (Columbia, SC, 1864), 124–25; W. C. Corsan, *Two Months in the Confederate States: An Englishman's Travels Through the South,* ed. Benjamin H. Trask (Baton Rouge, 1996), 100–101; Robert Lewis Dabney, *True Courage* (Richmond, VA, 1863), 12–21; Josiah Gorgas, *The Journals of Josiah Gorgas, 1857–1878,* ed. Sarah Woolfolk Wiggins (Tuscaloosa, 1995), 50; Richard Taylor, *Destruction and Reconstruction: Personal Experiences of the Late Civil War,* ed. Richard B. Harwell (New York, 1955), 89–91; James A. Garfield, *The Wild Life of the Army: Civil War Letters of James A. Garfield,* ed. Frederick D. Williams (East Lansing, MI, 1964), 173. Confederates themselves could not quite agree whether the term "fanatic" applied to Jackson. *Raleigh (NC) Semi-Weekly Register,* May 23, 1863; Allan, *Life and Letters,* 79.

13. Dabney, *Life and Campaigns,* 103–5, 643; Allan, *Life and Letters,* 123; Vandiver, *Mighty Stonewall,* 333; J. William Jones, *Christ in the Camp or Religion in the Confederate Army* (Atlanta, 1904), 82–83; Robertson, *Stonewall Jackson,* 274–75; Charles Royster, *The Destructive War: William Tecumseh*

Sherman, Stonewall Jackson, and the Americans (New York, 1991), 69. Like any good theological hairsplitter, however, Jackson could rationalize fighting and even attacking the enemy on the Sabbath. Jackson, *Life and Letters,* 249.

14. Henry Kyd Douglas, *I Rode with Stonewall* (Chapel Hill, 1940), 91; Jackson, *Life and Letters,* 363–64; Allan, *Life and Letters,* 153; Dabney, *Life and Campaigns,* 540–41.
15. Dabney, *Life and Campaigns,* 107; Jones, *Christ in the Camp,* 88–93; Arnold, *Early Life and Letters,* 195; Jackson, *Life and Letters,* 377, 419; Martha White Read to Thomas Griffin Read, June 19–21, 1862, Read Family Correspondence, Department of Special Collections, Hesburgh Libraries, University of Notre Dame Archives, Notre Dame, IN.
16. Mary Eliza Callaway to Morgan Callaway, June 11, 1862, Callaway Papers, Morgan Callaway Papers, Special Collections Department, Robert W. Woodruff Library, Emory University, Atlanta; U.S. War Department, *The War of the Rebellion: A Compilation of the Official Records of the Union and Confederate Armies,* 128 vols. (Washington, DC, 1880–1901), series 1, vol. 51, pt. 2:563–64; Robert Manson Myers, ed., *The Children of Pride: A True Story of Georgia and the Civil War* (New Haven, 1972), 901; Robertson, *Stonewall Jackson,* 451; Thomas J. Jackson to Francis McFarland, July 31, 1862, Jackson Papers; George Braxton Taylor, *Life and Letters of George Boardman Taylor, D.D.* (Lynchburg, VA, 1908), 71–72; William W. Bennett, *A Narrative of the Great Revival Which Prevailed in the Southern Armies* (Harrisonburg, VA, 1989), 172–73, 176.
17. Allan, *Life and Letters,* 145; entry for Jan. 1, 1863, Nancy Emerson Diary, Special Collections, University of Virginia, Charlottesville; George Richard Browder, *The Heavens Are Weeping: The Diaries of George Richard Browder, 1852–1886* (Grand Rapids, MI, 1987), 124–25; Susan M. Kollock, ed., "Letters of the Kollock and Allied Families, 1826–1884," *Georgia Historical Quarterly* 34 (Dec. 1950): 313.
18. Jackson, *Life and Letters,* 341; *Religious Herald* (Richmond), Aug. 21, 1862; Sept. 6, 1862, Lexington Presbytery Minutes, Union Theological Seminary, Richmond, VA.
19. Bennett, *Narrative of the Great Revival,* 52–53; Jones, *Christ in the Camp,* 230–41, 515; D. H. Hill to Robert L. Dabney, June 7, 1863, Dabney Papers; Frank L. Hieronymus, "For Now and Forever: The Chaplains of the Confederate States Army" (Ph.D. dissertation, Univ. of California, Los Angeles, 1964), 58–74; Robertson, *Stonewall Jackson,* 683–85.
20. Robertson, *Stonewall Jackson,* 685; Sidney J. Romero, *Religion in the Rebel Ranks* (Lanham, MD, 1983), 70–71; Dabney, *Life and Campaigns,* 647,

649–55; Robert Campbell, *Lone Star Confederate: A Gallant and Good Soldier of the 5th Texas Infantry,* ed. George Skoch and Mark W. Perkins (College Station, TX, 2003), 31–32; William R. Stillwell, *The Stillwell Letters: A Georgian in Longstreet's Corps, Army of Northern Virginia,* ed. Ronald H. Moseley (Macon, GA, 2002), 147; Robert Franklin Bunting, *Our Trust Is in the God of Battles: The Civil War Letters of Robert Franklin Bunting, Chaplain, Terry's Texas Rangers, C.S.A.,* ed. Thomas W. Cutrer (Knoxville, 2006), 93.

21. *Macon* (GA) *Telegraph,* May 6, 1863; William H. Routt to "Dear Bettie," May 10, 1863, Routt Papers, Museum of the Confederacy, Richmond, VA; Jones, *Christ in the Camp,* 75–76, 484. See also *Jackson Daily Mississippian,* May 7, 1863.

22. Dabney, *Life and Campaigns,* 706–10, 713–15, 719, 721–23; Robertson, *Stonewall Jackson,* 740, 748–52.

23. Entry for May 10, 1863, William F. Broaddus Diary, Library of Virginia, Richmond; Katharine M. Jones, ed. *Ladies of Richmond, Confederate Capital* (Indianapolis, 1962), 167; Edward L. Ayers, *In the Presence of Mine Enemies: War in the Heart of America, 1859–1863* (New York, 2003), 384; entry for May 17, 1863, Annie G. Baker Diary, Presbyterian Historical Society, Montreat, NC; Presbyterian Church, Synod of Virginia, *Minutes 1863* [Richmond, 1863?], 332–33; *Milledgeville* (GA) *Southern Recorder,* May 19, 1863; Kate Cumming, *Kate: The Journal of a Confederate Nurse,* ed. Richard Barksdale (Baton Rouge, 1959), 103. A Catholic chaplain serving in a Louisiana regiment described Jackson as an "austere Presbyterian" but no religious bigot and believed there was a possibility that he would receive the Lord's mercy. Père Louis-Hippolyte Gache, *A Frenchman, a Chaplain, a Rebel: The War Letters of Pere Louis-Hippolyte Gache, S.J.,* trans. Cornelius M. Buckley (Chicago, 1981), 176–80.

24. There was some reluctance to believe that this almost superhuman enemy was finally dead. *Wisconsin State Register* (Portage), May 16, 1863; *New Haven* (CT) *Daily Palladium,* May 16, 1863.

25. Mark E. Neely Jr., Harold Holzer, and Gabor Boritt, *The Confederate Image: Prints of the Lost Cause* (Chapel Hill, 1987), 109; Abraham Lincoln, *The Collected Works of Abraham Lincoln,* ed. Roy P. Basler, 8 vols. (New Brunswick, NJ, 1953), 6:214; *Independent* (New York, NY), May 14, 1863; *Liberator* (Boston), May 29, June 19, 1863. Abolitionists had earlier ridiculed Jackson for convincing Baptists in his camp to practice "open communion" while ignoring scriptures about "adulterers and murderers"—here meaning slaveholders—not entering the "kingdom of heaven." *Liberator* (Boston), Nov. 7, 1862.

26. Harry S. Stout, *Upon the Altar of the Nation: A Moral History of the Civil War* (New York, 2006), 229; *Washington Daily National Intelligencer,* May 16, 1863; *New York Herald,* May 14, 1863; *New Haven* (CT) *Daily Palladium,*

May 16, 1863; *New Hampshire Statesman* (Concord), May 22, 1863; *New York Observer and Chronicle*, May 21, 1863; *Lowell* (MA) *Daily Citizen and News*, May 15, 1863; *New York Times*, May 14, 1863; Alonzo Quint, *The Potomac and the Rapidan: Army Notes from the Failure at Winchester to the Reinforcement of Rosecrans, 1861–3* (Boston, 1864), 305.

27. Catherine Ann Devereux Edmondston, *"Journal of a Secesh Lady": The Diary of Catherine Ann Devereux Edmondston, 1860–1866*, ed. Beth G. Crabtree and James W. Patton (Raleigh, NC, 1979), 392; Protestant Episcopal Church, Diocese of Virginia, *Journal of the Sixty-Eighth Annual Council* (Richmond, 1863), 88; *Milledgeville* (GA) *Southern Recorder*, May 19, 1863; William Edward Wiatt, *Confederate Chaplain William Edward Wiatt: An Annotated Diary*, ed. Alex L. Wiatt (Lynchburg, VA, 1994), 52; *The New Texas Primary Reader. Designed for the Use of Schools in Texas* (Houston, 1863), 169–72; [Charles Hallock,] *A Complete Biographical Sketch of "Stonewall" Jackson* (Augusta, GA, 1863), 9–28.

28. Myers, *Children of Pride*, 1063; Presbyterian Church, General Assembly, *Minutes 1863*, 126; *Milledgeville* (GA) *Confederate Union*, May 19, 1863; Francis H. Smith, *Discourse on the Life and Character of Lt. Gen . Thos. J. Jackson, (C.S.A.), Late Professor of Natural and Experimental Philosophy in the Virginia Military Institute* (Richmond, 1863), 3–14; *Milledgeville* (GA) *Southern Recorder*, May 19, 1863; Dabney, *True Courage*, 8; *Christian Observer* (Richmond), May 21, 1863; George William White, "On the Death of Stonewall Jackson," White Collection, Presbyterian Historical Society, Montreat, NC. Confederate Quartermaster General Alexander Lawton suggested that Jackson preferred fighting to praying, but if things were quiet, a good long Calvinistic sermon suited his tastes. "He had no sympathy with human infirmity," Lawton tartly commented. Mary Chesnut, *Mary Chesnut's Civil War*, ed. C. Vann Woodward (New Haven, 1981), 499–500.

29. The scripture reference is to 2 Chronicles 32:8.

30. Allan, *Life and Letters*, 165; *Milledgeville* (GA) *Confederate Union*, May 19, 1863; Eliza Rhea Anderson Fain, *Sanctified Trial: The Diary of Eliza Rhea Anderson Fain, a Confederate Woman in East Tennessee*, ed. John N. Fain (Knoxville, 2004), 70–71; William J. Pegram to Mary Evan Pegram, May 11, 1863, Pegram-Johnson-McIntosh Papers, Virginia Historical Society, Richmond; Dabney, *True Courage*, 22–24; George William White, "On the Death of Stonewall Jackson," White Collection, Presbyterian Historical Society, Montreat, North Carolina. One poet suggested that Jackson had been a Confederate Moses, and like the biblical Moses not permitted to enter the Promised Land. H. M. Wharton, *War Songs and Poems of the Southern Confederacy, 1861–1865* (Edison, NJ, 2000), 302–3.

31. *Religious Herald* (Richmond), July 9, 1863; *Southern Churchman* (Richmond), May 15, 1863; Judith W. McGuire, *Diary of A Southern Refugee during the War, by a Lady of Virginia* (New York, 1867), 211–12; Ramsey, *True Eminence Founded on Holiness,* 18–21.

32. *Weekly Raleigh (NC) Register,* May 13, 1863; Ada Harris to her parents, May 16, 1863, Henry St. George Harris Papers, Special Collections Department, William R. Perkins Library Duke University, Durham, NC; Edward O. Guerrant, *Bluegrass Confederate: The Headquarters Diary of Edward O. Guerrant,* ed. William C. Davis and Meredith L. Swentor (Baton Rouge, 1999), 276; *Milledgeville* (GA) *Confederate Union,* June 16, 1863; John Samuel Apperson, *Repairing the "March of Mars": The Civil War Diaries of John Samuel Apperson, Hospital Steward in the Stonewall Brigade, 1861–1865,* ed. John D. Roper (Macon, GA, 2001), 439; Anne S. Frobel, *The Civil War Diary of Anne S. Frobel,* ed. Mary H. and Dallas M. Lancaster (McLean, VA, 1992), 183; *Fayetteville* (NC) *Observer,* May 18, 1863. One slight variation on this theme held that Jackson's "fiery and unquailing spirit survives in his men." *Charleston Mercury,* May 13, 1863.

33. Carrie Fries to J. F. Shaffner, May 12, 1863, Fries and Shaffner Family Papers, Southern Historical Collection, University of North Carolina at Chapel Hill; William Burch Short to Barbara Burch Short, May 15, 1863, William Burch Short Letters, Museum of the Confederacy, Richmond, VA; Thomas W. Cutrer and T. Michael Parrish, eds., *Brothers in Gray: The Civil War Letters of the Pierson Family* (Baton Rouge, 1997), 198; Bunting, *Our Trust Is in the God of Battles,* 162.

34. John Haley, *The Rebel Yell and the Yankee Hurrah: The Civil War Journal of Maine Volunteer,* ed Ruth L. Silliker (Camden, ME, 1985), 138; *Milledgeville* (GA) *Confederate Union,* Dec. 8, 1863.

35. Beth Barton Schweiger, *The Gospel Working Up: Progress and the Pulpit in Nineteenth-Century Virginia* (New York, 2000), 116–18; Charles Reagan Wilson, *Baptized in Blood: The Religion of the Lost Cause, 1865–1920* (Athens, GA, 1980), 18–57.

36. O. E. Daggett, *A Sermon on the Death of Abraham Lincoln* (Canandaigua, NY, 1865), 16; Samuel A. Burney, *A Southern Soldier's Letters Home: The Civil War Letters of Samuel A. Burney, Cobb's Georgia Legion, Army of Northern Virginia,* ed. Nat S. Turner III (Macon, GA, 2002), 293.

37. Edward Porter Alexander, *Fighting for the Confederacy: The Personal Recollections of the General Edward Porter Alexander,* ed. Gary W. Gallagher (Chapel Hill, 1989), 58–59, 96–97. For a skeptical assessment of how many soldiers actually embraced a providential view of the conflict, see Basil W. Duke, *Reminiscences of General Basil W. Duke, C.S.A.* (Garden City, NY, 1911), 416–18.

Lieutenant General James Longstreet. Courtesy of the U.S. Army Military History Institute, Carlisle, Pennsylvania.

"The Road to Hell Is Paved with Good Intentions": James Longstreet in War and Peace

William L. Richter

St. Bernard of Clairvaux, a medieval French cleric, sponsor of the Crusades, and confessor to the Knights Templar, is credited with the aphorism that aptly describes those of good purpose whose best efforts fall short of expectations.[1] The Civil War is full of officers on both sides who suffered from such frustration. But few of the war's generals felt the sting of disappointment and failure more during their lifetime of high hopes and aspirations than General Robert E. Lee's "old warhorse," his ever-stalwart corps commander, Lieutenant General James "Old Pete" Longstreet.[2]

The man who would become arguably the Confederacy's preeminent corps commander was born into a middle-class farm family in Edgefield District, South Carolina, on January 8, 1821.[3] "Pete," as the young Longstreet was called, applied to the national military academy, entering as a member of the class of 1842, where he graduated fifty-four out of sixty-two students.[4] By the time of the war with Mexico, Longstreet was an infantry company commander. He fought under Major General Zachary Taylor in the battles across southern Texas and northern Mexico.[5] Then Longstreet was transferred to Major General Winfield Scott's army for Scott's campaign against Mexico City, where he was seriously wounded in the hip at Chapultepec. After his wound had healed, Longstreet served a decade on the Texas frontier.[6]

Upon secession of the South, like many officers who transferred to the South (including Robert E. Lee),[7] Longstreet received his Confederate commission as lieutenant colonel of infantry before he resigned from the U.S. Army and then a promotion to brigadier general. Described as "slightly below middle height, broad shouldered and somewhat heavy," Longstreet was considered "essentially a combat officer."[8]

Longstreet's assignment was as brigade commander for three Virginia regiments stationed at Manassas Junction under the overall command of Brigadier General P. G. T. Beauregard. As the Yankees heeded the Northern public's demand, "On to Richmond," Longstreet and the rest of the Confederate army in northern Virginia began to station themselves at the various crossings along Bull Run, north of Manassas. Longstreet's Brigade guarded Blackburn's Ford.

Here, on July 18, 1861, three days before the Battle of First Manassas, in his first independent combat command, Longstreet beat off a Union reconnaissance in force and became the first hero of the impending Confederate victory. Blackburn's Ford was a defensive battle; Longstreet's attempt to counterattack using reinforcements of Jubal Early's supporting brigade was stopped by difficulty fording the creek and the Union withdrawal. He took no further part in the real fight, which raged to his left a few days later.

Although Longstreet missed the big battle, he received plaudits from General Beauregard for turning back the Yankee probe at Blackburn's Ford. Beauregard considered Longstreet's able defense as the key to making Union Brigadier General Irwin McDowell more cautious and hesitant in pushing his initial advantage at First Manassas. This allowed Confederates under General Joseph E. Johnston to arrive from the Shenandoah Valley in time to win the battle. The result was that Johnston, who outranked Beauregard, recommended Longstreet's promotion from brigadier to major general, citing his "promptness of thought and action."[9]

As winter approached, quarrels over rank and honors sprang up between President Jefferson Davis and both Beauregard and Johnston. Eventually Beauregard was sent west, while Davis and Johnston sniped at each other by letter in Virginia. Longstreet, meanwhile, took over a division and drilled his troops incessantly. He was the only division commander who drilled his whole division at once, giving himself and his men the feel for what it took to operate on future battlefields.

Longstreet's active command attitude, assisted by one of the best staffs on either side, prompted Johnston to ignore Major General G. W. Smith, his senior division officer, and assign the more difficult administrative tasks to Longstreet. Old Pete in effect became Johnston's second in command. The close relationship between Longstreet and Johnston may have had other benefits, too. Johnston was an expert at defensive tactics (indeed, he really only fought two purely offensive battles in the war, Seven Pines [1862] and Bentonville [1865]), and Longstreet seems to have absorbed much of Johnston's tactical preferences. But whereas Johnston favored retreat after his defense line was flanked or breached, Longstreet would come to prefer to counterattack and defeat the enemy on the field.[10]

In the spring of 1862, Longstreet and the rest of Johnston's army moved from Manassas Junction to the Virginia Peninsula east of Richmond to face a new Union attack orchestrated by the Yankee general in chief, Major General George B. McClellan. The concentration of forces to defend the Confederate capital brought together numerous Confederate units under Johnston's command which had never operated together before. Some of their top officers outranked Longstreet by date of appointment but had little of his experience on the field of battle.

True to his military philosophy, Johnston met McClellan at Yorktown and proceeded to retreat when McClellan ponderously readied the Union army for attack. To gain time, Johnston ordered Longstreet to fight a rearguard action at Williamsburg. Using favorable terrain and previously constructed earthen fortifications, Longstreet wore out the attacking Union pursuers. Then he launched a counterattack, again led by Brigadier General Jubal Early's Brigade. Early was stopped by the vigorous riposte of Union Brigadier General Winfield Scott Hancock, who earned the sobriquet "the Superb" for his action.[11]

By the end of May, Johnston was in the defenses of Richmond with no place to retreat to. McClellan's army lay astride the Chickahominy River, with two-fifths of his force south of the stream. Johnston decided to attack this weaker part and chose Longstreet to command the southern half of the army against the Union forces at Seven Pines. Major General G. W. Smith would lead the other part of the army against Union positions on Longstreet's left flank at Fair Oaks Station.

This was Longstreet's first opportunity to command an attacking force of considerable size, and he botched the opportunity. His own division took the wrong road, blocking two other divisions. Longstreet got into an argument with Major General Benjamin Huger, who outranked him and refused to recognize his authority as wing commander. Although Union positions were breached and the Yankees forced to retreat, the attack was made at a fraction of its designed strength. The other wing of the Confederate attack achieved similar results. However, the army's commander, Joe Johnston, was seriously wounded and had to be replaced by the next-ranking general, G. W. Smith.

Unfortunately, Smith buckled under the responsibility of full command and suffered a partial mental breakdown. At this point President Davis ordered his chief military advisor, General Robert E. Lee, to take over the recently named Army of Northern Virginia. Lee's first and obvious objective was to repel McClellan's invading army and destroy it if possible.[12]

Longstreet quickly discovered that Lee was a far cry from Johnston as army commander. Lee believed in taking the war to the enemy through fixing him in place, followed by maneuver and attack. His outflanking units were Major General Thomas J. "Stonewall" Jackson's men from the Shenandoah Valley. The fixing force would be the rest of the army, primarily the divisions of Longstreet and Major General A. Powell Hill.

In the interim, as Lee reorganized his forces, McClellan had reversed the strength of his army to bring more to bear on Richmond. Now the majority of it was south of the Chickahominy River and only a small part, under Brigadier General Fitz John Porter, was left north of the river to guard McClellan's supply line to the Pamunkey River. So Lee reversed his forces, too, secretly moving most of his army, including Longstreet's Division, north of the river with a small holding force left entrenched before McClellan's strength at Richmond.

A. P. Hill led off what would be called in later histories the Seven Days' Battles by attacking Porter's contingent at Beaver Dam Creek to hold him in place. The maneuver element was to be Jackson's divisions, but Stonewall's troops never showed up on the field. Hill's Division got butchered. As Longstreet and others moved in too late to assist Hill, night fell and Porter retreated to a new defensive line at Gaines' Mill behind Boatswain's Swamp.

Lee renewed the assault the next day, primarily employing Hill and Longstreet. Both divisions suffered heavy casualties, and again, Jackson's maneuver element failed to show. Late in the day, Longstreet's men broke through Porter's lines, capturing nearly a full division of Pennsylvania troops. Porter managed to get the rest of his command south of White Oak Swamp, where he set up a new defensive line. By now Lee realized that McClellan was transferring his supply line to the James River. There was one road junction through which everyone would have to pass to get there. Lee sent Longstreet and Hill to intercept the Yankees. Jackson's assignment was to force White Oak Swamp and appear on the Union flank.

Once more, Jackson failed in his task. Longstreet and Hill, supported by other Confederate units, attacked the road junction in a bloody battle that raged all day (usually referred to as the Battle of Glendale or Frayser's Farm). This time, Longstreet and Hill got into an argument as to who was to provide support to the other. Hill became so heated that he challenged Longstreet to a duel. Lee would later transfer him to Jackson's command, where the hapless Hill also quarreled incessantly with the equally acerbic Jackson, who placed him under more or less perpetual arrest when not in battle.

Meanwhile, the decimated divisions of Longstreet and Hill lay in reserve as Jackson finally came up and saw his own units butchered at Malvern Hill. From a distance, Longstreet witnessed the slaughter, too. Lee's offensive had saved Richmond, but he had lost twenty thousand men to McClellan's fifteen thousand. Worse yet, almost all of Lee's losses came from gunshot wounds as killed or wounded. McClellan losses in killed and wounded were less than half of Lee's. The rest were prisoners of war, soon to be exchanged to fight on other battlefields another day.[13]

Of all the division commanders in the Army of Northern Virginia, Lee singled out Longstreet for special praise, calling him "the staff in my right hand." But Lee was not happy with most of the others. He got rid of Theophilus Holmes, Benjamin Huger, John Magruder, and G. W. Smith, all of whom ranked above Longstreet. This left Old Pete as senior major general and second in command to Lee, as he had been for all practical purposes to Beauregard and Johnston. Along with Longstreet, Lee kept Jackson (whose lackadaisical movements caused one dismayed officer to comment, "Jackson ought to have been shot"), Richard S. Ewell, Daniel H. Hill, and A. P. Hill, and he secured promotions for Richard H. Anderson and James E. B. Stuart.[14]

As commander of one of Lee's most beat-up divisions (forty-four hundred casualties), the headlong assaults of the Seven Days' Battles had taught Longstreet a bitter lesson in Civil War tactics: attack and die.[15] Lee's predilection for constant offense would bleed the Confederacy dry, whereas Johnston's defensive tactics, by failing to engage the enemy, would have led to the fall of Richmond in 1862 and did lead to the loss of Vicksburg in 1863 and Atlanta in 1864. There had to be a middle way. In the upcoming Second Manassas Campaign, Longstreet worked to perfect a synthesis between the two extremes.[16]

Immediately after the Seven Days, Lee reorganized his army into two corps or wings. Longstreet took over five divisions of what became the First Corps, and Stonewall Jackson received the command of three divisions of the Second Corps. Although Longstreet on the surface looked to have the bigger force, they were actually almost equal in numbers and brigades.[17]

Evidently Lee saw something in Jackson that was not revealed in the Seven Days. He quickly sent Jackson north to oppose a new Federal army under Major General John Pope. A Radical Republican sycophant (Congress disliked McClellan, who was a Democrat and thus "soft" on the war), Pope proceeded to employ harsher measures of warfare to central Virginia: property seizures, managed arson, and confiscation of slaves. Lee determined to "suppress" him.

Jackson swept up to Pope's main supply depot at Manassas Junction, scene of the first big battle in the East the year before, which he methodically looted and burned. Pope followed in several confused marches. Longstreet remained near Richmond, keeping an eye on McClellan's army at Harrison's Landing on the James River. When President Lincoln began to transfer troops from McClellan to augment Pope's army, Lee and Longstreet proceeded after Jackson, placing Pope between two Confederate forces.

Jackson meanwhile took shelter behind the hills and ridges in back of Manassas, causing Pope to lose track of him. While Pope searched for his enemy near Manassas, Longstreet's column made some of the fastest marches of the war, making Stonewall Jackson's "foot cavalry" look slow by comparison. As Lee and Longstreet approached Jackson's position, he attacked Pope. Having found Jackson, Pope now lost track of Longstreet's approach. As Pope wasted his forces by attacking the entrenched Jackson, Longstreet came up on the Union left rear. This was a perfect chance to show how the tactical defense could wear down the enemy leading to a masterful counterattack. Three times Longstreet refused Lee's order to advance. There was to be no repeat of Seven Pines here. Longstreet spent a full thirty-six hours in preparation before launching a devastating attack, which drove Pope from the field back into Washington, D.C.[18]

Lee's next two battles did not give Longstreet any opportunities for a counterstroke as did Second Manassas. But they were defensive classics. After Pope withdrew into Washington, the Rebels invaded Maryland. Lee, dividing his army into six parts, three of which were to take Harper's Ferry, stayed near Boonesboro with Longstreet, collecting supplies and looking in vain for recruits in this Union-leaning part of Maryland.

Having fortuitously obtained a set of Lee's orders, McClellan, who had once again been placed in charge of the Federal Army of the Potomac, advanced and caught Lee at the town of Sharpsburg on Antietam Creek. Here the outnumbered Confederates fought McClellan to a standstill. Longstreet was in the central part of Lee's line. By the afternoon, so many Rebel soldiers had been killed or wounded that Longstreet and his staff manned two guns of the Washington Artillery of New Orleans. His foot swollen from a nonbattle injury, Longstreet fought in carpet slippers.[19]

When Longstreet was detained on his way to a staff meeting that evening, Lee became concerned. When Longstreet appeared, Lee complimented him: "Ah! here is Longstreet; here's my old *war-horse!* Let us hear what he has to say."[20] Lee's confidence in Longstreet, however, was not fully reciprocated. Longstreet wrote to General Joseph Johnston that if he were to return to the Army of Northern Virginia in any capacity, Johnston would soon become its commanding general to the army's benefit.

Longstreet thought Lee too bold for his own good. He cost the Confederacy too many casualties by offering battle at Sharpsburg with the Potomac at his back. Longstreet believed that refusing battle until a more favorable position in Virginia could be found was the better strategy. Lee compounded the problem by audaciously staying at Sharpsburg and daring McClellan to make a final attack and win the war, then and there.[21]

But Johnston remained in the Western Theater, and Longstreet's fortunes in Virginia depended on Lee. Disappointed in McClellan's unwillingness to make the last attack needed to destroy Lee, Lincoln replaced him with Major General Ambrose Burnside. In mid-November, the new Union general stole a march on Lee and moved to Fredericksburg where he hoped to cross the Rappahannock River and force Lee to attack him on favorable ground south of the town. But Union bureaucracy managed to delay the transport of the necessary pontoons to cross the river. This allowed Longstreet time to come up and entrench his corps on the hills behind the town. Jackson soon joined him and extended the Confederate line to the south with no entrenchments. Longstreet used traverse trenches to section off his main line and not allow exploding shells or enfilade fire to sweep down his whole line.

Determined to give his superiors the victory they so desperately wanted, Burnside crossed and attacked Longstreet's entrenchments and Jackson's open line. In one of the more lopsided victories of the war, the Confederates inflicted twelve thousand casualties on the Union army. Longstreet lost fewer than two thousand, while the unfortified position held by Jackson suffered thirty-five hundred killed and wounded.[22]

After the battle, Jackson sent his engineers over to Longstreet for lessons in building traverse trenches in field fortifications. Longstreet felt vindicated in his tactical military philosophy by heavier Union casualties and Jackson's sudden interest in finer aspects of defensive warfare.[23]

Although Burnside tried to outflank Lee's army by trudging up the Rappahannock, in an operation derisively named the "Mud Match," operations in Virginia would have to await the arrival of spring. Because the Fredericksburg area had been occupied and fought over for a year by both armies, neither side could adequately feed their armies off the land.

The Yankees relied on rations brought down the Potomac. Lee had no such luxury as the single-track Richmond, Fredericksburg & Potomac Railroad proved inadequate to the task. Forced to disperse his forces, he decided to send Longstreet and two divisions into southeastern Virginia. Longstreet's mission was to scour the countryside for supplies and forward them to Lee at Fredericksburg. In addition, Longstreet was to coordinate Confederate attacks against Union forces occupying Suffolk, Virginia, and New Bern, North Carolina. Longstreet was quite successful in North Carolina, but at Suffolk he failed, losing three times the casualties as the Yankees after a long siege, confirming once more his lack of faith in attack against field fortifications.[24]

The following spring, before Lee could recall Longstreet, Major General Joseph Hooker, the new Union commander, led the Federals in a quick moving attack on the Fredericksburg position. Hooker used the same plan as had Burnside in the Mud March, crossing the Rapidan and Rappahannock upstream April 27–28 and coming in on Lee's rear through a second-growth forest called the Wilderness. Encountering feeble Confederate resistance on April 30 caused Hooker to stop and concentrate his forces around the small crossroads of Chancellorsville. This pause allowed Lee to fix him in place with a portion of his army and send Stonewall Jackson around Hooker's position and hit him on his open right flank.

The result was Lee's greatest victory and a bloodletting on both sides. By the time Longstreet rejoined Lee, the Union army had retreated, leaving seventeen thousand men on the field or in the hospital, and Lee had lost thirteen thousand, nearly a quarter of his infantry. Once again Longstreet saw a pyrrhic victory. His solution lay in the usual strategic offensive and tactical defensive.[25]

It was during his stint as department commander in southeastern Virginia, away from Lee, that Longstreet began to develop his concept of wining the war in the Western Theater, between the Mississippi River and the Appalachians. As department commander, he consulted many times with advocates of the western strategic campaign, such as Secretary of War James A. Seddon, Senator Louis T. Wigfall of Texas, and his old commanders, Generals Johnston and Beauregard. Unlike President Davis, who stuck behind his old military friends well past their usefulness to the cause in the field, Longstreet adjudged western generals Braxton Bragg and John C. Pemberton as impediments to victory. The unimaginative Pemberton, especially, was slow moving and had allowed himself to be maneuvered into the defenses at Vicksburg, where he was besieged by Union Major General U. S. Grant.

But when queried about sending some of his men west, Lee said he could better aid Vicksburg by advancing deep into Pennsylvania. The Union forces would have to follow and Lee could garner much food and materiel, beat them on favorable ground, save Vicksburg, and gain possible European recognition for the Confederate government. Besides, such a campaign in the North would give Virginia a much needed break from the war.

Lee's presentation to President Davis was convincing and won out over a western strategy. After all, Lee was the only general who had consistently delivered victory in the past year. Even Sharpsburg was but a temporary setback. When he and his divisions returned to the Rappahannock, Longstreet and Lee discussed the Pennsylvania Campaign. In the end, Longstreet seemed to think that Lee favored a strategic offensive, and a tactical defensive and counterattack after the enemy was spent attacking on unfavorable ground held by a clever Confederate defense, much like Second Manassas.[26]

In broad, general outline, Longstreet and Lee shared similar beliefs: direct attacks cost too many casualties, the South cannot win a war of attrition, the North must be outgeneraled on its own ground. Lee was still operating under Longstreet's idea when he concentrated Rebel forces at Gettysburg. He held true to the concept when he ordered his generals not to bring on a full battle until the army was brought together.[27]

But by the time Longstreet and Lee arrived on the battlefield at Gettysburg during the afternoon of July 1, Stonewall Jackson's replacement, Lieutenant General Richard Ewell, had driven Union forces across the plain, through the town, and onto Cemetery Hill. Much to the dismay of Jackson's old staff, Ewell dithered. They knew that Ewell ought to push his fresh division under Early up the slope and send the Federals off in full retreat. Jackson would have done it. But Lee had warned against bringing on a battle before the whole army was up. The golden opportunity of the war was lost to indecision.[28]

Then suddenly, Lee took a look at the ragged Union defenses on Cemetery Hill and smelled blood. Sometime late on July 1 and early July 2, he junked the idea of a tactical defensive for all-out attack. And to his horror, Longstreet and his corps received the assignment. Longstreet took the change personally. He recalled Lee's earlier promise. Move across the Union front, argued Longstreet. Impose the Confederate army between Washington and force the Yankees to attack. Lee refused.

The grumpy Longstreet, normally a slow and methodical planner and organizer of attack, moved even more slowly in carrying out his assignments, or so it seemed to many observers. Longstreet saw victory in Second Manassas, Antietam, Fredericksburg, and other defensive battles. Lee saw victory in the Seven Days and Chancellorsville—attacking.

On July 2, Longstreet, after awaiting arrival of his Alabama brigade with Lee's approval, lined up two divisions and attacked the Union left flank up the Emmitsburg Road near the Round Tops at the southern end of the Union line. The result was a bloody victory, kept from being complete when support troops from A. P. Hill's Third Corps failed to become completely engaged.[29]

But Lee was not finished yet. On July 3, with Longstreet's final fresh division under Pickett, supported by a division and a half of Hill's corps from the first day's battle, Lee ordered an attack at the center of the Union position. Longstreet protested prophetically: "No 15,000 men can take that hill." Lee insisted, and Pickett's Charge marched into history. It was another Malvern Hill or a Fredericksburg in reverse. Pickett's men were slaughtered. The Battle of Gettysburg was over. Lee, Longstreet, and their army retreated into Virginia.[30]

The day after Pickett's Charge, Vicksburg fell. This left only one small Confederate army under Johnston in Mississippi and another larger force under Bragg in Tennessee to defend the Western Theater. Having failed in Pennsylvania, Lee could no longer effectively oppose sending part of his army to the West. President Davis acted immediately and ordered Longstreet and two divisions (under Major Generals Lafayette McLaws and John Bell Hood, the same two who had attacked at Gettysburg on July 2) to join Bragg's force.[31]

Because a Union force had taken Knoxville, Longstreet's men traveled by train in a roundabout route through the Carolinas to Atlanta and then north, to where Bragg had already engaged Union Major General William S. Rosecrans along Chickamauga Creek just below Chattanooga. Longstreet arrived after the first day's fighting. Bragg put him in control of the army's left wing. Longstreet took over numerous commands he had never worked with before and inserted his First Corps troops into the battle line. It was a marvelous piece of work that showed him at his best as a wing or corps commander.

When Longstreet's men moved forward the next day, it was a frontal attack much like Pickett's at Gettysburg. But there were significant differences. Longstreet never protested the arrangement to Bragg as he had done to Lee. But then, Longstreet considered himself to be Lee's military conscience, something he never thought of with Bragg. The field at Chickamauga was wooded and could not be seen in its entirety as that at Gettysburg. Moreover, Longstreet never understood the Army of Tennessee or the Union Army of the Cumberland as he had the Army of Northern Virginia and the Army of the Potomac. Finally, there was no time.[32]

Longstreet's attack at Chickamauga was one of the most devastating of the war. He organized his First Corps in brigade column for strength. Just as his men stepped off, a foul-up on the Union side caused an entire division to be pulled out of line in the exact same spot Longstreet was headed for. The jubilant Confederate infantry penetrated and got behind the Union position before a defense could be organized. Rosecrans's army fled the field, leaving it to the Confederates.[33]

Once the Confederates had bottled up the Federals in Chattanooga, Longstreet got mixed up in the numerous officers' intrigues against Bragg, a common facet of life in the Army of Tennessee. Longstreet did not do well at Chattanooga. His own First Corps failed to keep the siege from being lifted, and Bragg sent him away into eastern Tennessee to take Knoxville. Longstreet's attack against Fort Sanders was a mess—his men were shot to pieces by Federal troops who had suffered before his lines at Fredericksburg, led again by none other than General Burnside.

After failing to capture Knoxville, Longstreet's men withdrew toward the Virginia line, where they spent the winter, Longstreet quarreling with some of his oldest comrades in a style that would have honored Bragg at his worst. Longstreet also planned at least two offenses into Kentucky that were rejected by the War Department.[34] Spring saw Longstreet and his corps recalled to Lee's army, still along the Rappahannock, awaiting attack by the new Union head general, Ulysses S. Grant. This came in May at the Wilderness, the same place that saw the disastrous Yankee defeat at Chancellorsville.

Acting as Lee's reserve force, Longstreet and his First Corps stopped Grant's attack cold and launched a counterattack that threatened to drive the Federals back across the river. At the critical moment, not far from where Stonewall Jackson received the wounds that cost him his life, Longstreet went down with a nasty wound that penetrated his neck and funneled through his upper shoulder. It was also fired by his own men, like Jackson's, and caused a successful attack to lose its strength.[35]

The injury kept Longstreet out of the war until October 1864. Then he rejoined Lee at Petersburg with his arm in a sling, still paralyzed, and was given command of the left of the defenses, those near Richmond, which included his old First Corps. In the spring of 1865, Lee's army was forced to leave the siege lines and flee westward, with Grant in hot pursuit.

On April 8, various officers asked Longstreet to intercede with Lee and demand a surrender. Longstreet refused. That night, however, the two senior generals met and discussed the situation. Lee wanted to attack the next day. Longstreet volunteered to lead the assault. But the opposing Federal cavalry was joined by infantry during the night. Assured that Grant was an honorable man, Lee went forth to Appomattox to end the war for the Army of Northern Virginia. Longstreet and Lee parted on April 12, never to see each other again.[36]

This was the Longstreet who has been called the most modern general of the Southern war effort. But that view would take 140 years to establish. What happened in the interim to change Longstreet's stellar military reputation? The one-word answer is Reconstruction. By the time Longstreet's Reconstruction opponents had finished with him, he would be marked as the one man who had lost the military side of the war for the Confederacy.

After the war, Longstreet drifted southward from his wife's family home in Lynchburg, Virginia, to his sister's home in Canton, Mississippi, then to New Orleans. The Crescent City had been occupied by Federal troops early in 1862 and had escaped the wartime destruction evident throughout urban areas of the South. As the largest and richest of Southern cities, it drew half a dozen ex-Confederate generals like Longstreet, all looking for civilian careers to sustain themselves and their families.

Longstreet fell in with Edward and William Owen, former officers from the Washington Artillery who had served with distinction in Longstreet's

First Corps during the war. The Owens brothers were in the process of setting up a cotton factorage business and invited Old Pete to join in. Longstreet could hardly refuse—after all, he was so close to the officers and men of the Washington Artillery, often camping near or with them on many campaigns, that it was known as "Longstreet's Bodyguard."[37]

The former general also became president of an insurance company (a very common position for ex-Confederate officers) and president of the Southern Hospital Association. He tried to enter the railroad business but failed. Nonetheless, by 1867, Longstreet was doing well as an established businessman, much bolstered by his wartime military reputation. He applied for individual pardon and the restoration of his political rights, only to have President Andrew Johnson refuse, saying, "There are three persons of the South who cannot receive amnesty: Mr. Davis, General Lee, and yourself."[38]

In 1867, the Radical Republicans in the U.S. Congress scrapped the Reconstruction plan ordained by President Johnson and substituted one of its own. Johnson had defied the Radical majority of the party by vetoing key Reconstruction measures it had passed—the Freedmen's Bureau bill and the Civil Rights Act. Congress passed a rigorous set of Reconstruction acts to be enforced in the former Confederate states by the army.[39]

In mid-March 1867, the *New Orleans Times* asked for eighteen prominent citizens by name, including Longstreet, to present their views as to what ought to be done. The general answered immediately. The Southerners were a conquered people, said Longstreet, and the only way to reestablish constitutional government in the former Confederacy was to accede to the congressional plan. Two weeks later, Longstreet wrote the *Times* again, this time on his own volition. He said that the Appomattox surrender marked three developments: the end of secession, the end of the Confederacy, and the end of slavery. Longstreet decried the loss of his individual political rights, but that was one of the hazards of a failed revolution. He asked those who had received amnesty to vote and speed the return of his own political rights.

So far, Longstreet had not crossed that elusive yet invisible line of loyalty to the South. Many others agreed that Southern whites ought to register and vote and send representatives to cancel the "foul conspiracy" of the congressionally mandated Military Reconstruction. But at the same time, there was a strong undercurrent against any cooperation with the Yankees, especially in the area of political and civil rights for the freed slaves.

Longstreet should have been more cognizant of this anti-Reconstruction hostility and listened to wise advice. When he showed a preliminary draft of his next letter to his business partners, they cautioned him not to let it be published. John Bell Hood warned, "They will crucify you." His uncle,

Augustus Baldwin Longstreet, also demurred, saying, "It will ruin you, son, if you publish it."[40]

As predicted, Longstreet's letter of June 3, 1867, to John M. G. Parker, a noted local Republican and brother-in-law of the despised Union Major General Benjamin Butler (better known as "Spoons" for his penchant of having his occupation troops steal everything and anything, especially silverware, causing his likeness to be painted in the bottom of chamber pots throughout the city), was a political disaster. With the general's tacit permission, Parker "leaked" Longstreet's letter to the *New Orleans Republican*, which printed it and an editorial. The result was such a demand for newspapers that the paper had to be reprinted the next day. The headline blared that Longstreet had united with the Republican Party and declared Democratic Party principles had died at Appomattox.

In his letter, Longstreet expressed his willingness to work "in any harness" to bring peace and unity to the nation. He said that Military Reconstruction was a Radical Republican peace offering to the South and ought to be accepted as such. Further, the general spoke out on behalf of the Negro vote. It ought to be tried North and South, said Longstreet. If it proved unwise, or uncontrollable, it could be rescinded later.[41]

James Longstreet after the Civil War. Longstreet posed for this image seated in Abraham Lincoln's chair, which did not sit well with his former Confederate comrades. Library of Congress.

The *Republican* praised Longstreet for his "manly" stance. It editorialized that Longstreet ought to be pardoned and his full political rights restored immediately. But a deafening scream of protest that went up from southern Maryland to western Texas. No one read what his letter really said except the editors of New Orleans' only black newspaper, the *Tribune*. Longstreet's support of the black vote was merely conditional, the *Tribune* pointed out. His "object is not in the least to help the Republican cause, but to continue to work earnestly and faithfully for the cause in whose behalf he drew the sword." The *Tribune* concluded, "A Rebel seeking relief of his comrades is just another friend of the oligarchy, trying to save the oligarchy from its doom."[42]

It is just possible that white Republicans also recognized the inherent threat that Longstreet posed to their programs. So they had the letter published and permitted the Democrats to perform a hatchet-job on their own would-be leader. If he could be saved for the Republicans later, well and good. If not, he had already been compromised as an opposition leader.

Longstreet never quite understood what had happened to him. He tried to explain himself to the ex-Confederates of New Orleans in another letter to the *Republican*. But it was three days too late. Already favors came from the National Republican Party without the general's solicitation. Congress pardoned him and restored all of his political rights. His old friend, General Grant, soon to be President Grant, soon made him surveyor of customs for the port of New Orleans. As all of his business endeavors had failed from lack of public support, Longstreet needed the appointment just to survive economically.[43]

Over the years, the general made his living from Republican patronage in numerous government jobs, beginning in Louisiana. In 1870, Longstreet became adjutant general of the state Black and Tan militia as a supporter of Governor H. C. Warmoth and served as president of the New Orleans & Northeastern Railroad. By 1872, Longstreet was major general of state militia, police, and commander of all civil forces of Louisiana inside the city of New Orleans.

During the presidential election of 1872, the general supported the Liberal Republicans, but when they fused in Louisiana with Democrats under John McEnry, he went over with Custom House Republicans to P. B. S. Pinchback and then the winning gubernatorial candidate, William P. Kellogg (who carefully donned gloves before shaking hands with his black constituents). Longstreet also served on the Republican Returning Board, which validated Kellogg's election ballots.

The state election of 1872 saw a marked increase in violence and intimidation against black voters and their white carpetbag and scalawag supporters, a process known as "bulldozing." Since Longstreet commanded the state militia and the mostly black Metropolitan Police, he was involved in the defeat of McEnry's backers as they unsuccessfully assaulted the Reconstruction government at the Battle of the Cabildo in downtown New Orleans.

The following year, Longstreet received the lucrative appointment as president of the State Levee Board. But he had little time to enjoy it. In 1874, he fought with the Metropolitan Police to repel another McEnry-inspired attack in the Third Battle of New Orleans. Hit by a spent bullet, Longstreet was dragged to safety by McEnry's White League supporters, ex-Confederate soldiers determined that an old Rebel general was not to die in a public street.[44]

Fed up with the violence in Louisiana and realizing that the Republicans were on the losing side, in 1875 Longstreet went back to the old family homestead near Gainesville, Georgia. Supporting the Republican national ticket the following year, the general sought the post of U.S. marshal for Georgia but failed to get it when President Rutherford B. Hayes gave it to a Democrat as part of the electoral Compromise of 1876, which sent him to the White House. In 1877, Longstreet converted to Roman Catholicism on one of several trips back to Louisiana, where he was part of the Orleans Parish school board and an ex officio administrator for the University of Louisiana (now Tulane). He then served in rapid succession as deputy collector of internal revenue, postmaster of Gainesville (another lucrative post), and U.S. minister to Turkey. Finally, in the last year of Hayes's term, Longstreet received the long-sought post of U.S. marshal of Georgia. Because he suffered from rheumatism and his old war wound, which left him paralyzed in his right arm, it is suspected that Longstreet's son Garland exercised the duties of office in a corrupt manner typical of the Gilded Age (as had his Democrat predecessor).

Plagued by charges of managerial and fiscal irresponsibility, Longstreet soon retired from politics and went to work farming and writing his memoirs. It was about time. Longstreet's path from beloved general to detested scalawag had been remarkably swift. He played a big role in his own destruction, stubbornly blundering from political crisis to crisis like the amateur he was.[45]

His descent to the personification of Confederate defeat took place concurrently with his Reconstruction activities and sadly had the same faults. It revolved around two people, Robert E. Lee and Jubal A. Early. Lee and Longstreet had parted April 12, 1865, never to see each other again. Longstreet made his way to New Orleans, still Lee's "warhorse." Histories written in the South after the war lauded his ability as a corps commander, labeling him as "a real bulldog fighter." Lee supposedly considered him to be one of the best generals "in the world," a martyr to the Rebel cause.[46]

Then came Longstreet's controversial advice to his fellow Southerners and transformation into a "scalawag," a Southerner who forsook his white brethren for the "Black Republicans." When Longstreet sought to explain his letters and course of action to Lee, the general wrote back that while he believed in conformity to existing circumstances and abiding in the law, he also believed that "the course pursued by the dominant party [was not] the best for the country." He told others, "General Longstreet has made a great mistake."[47]

But no one dared to attack Longstreet openly, yet. Lee still expressed unlimited confidence in Longstreet's generalship. With Lee's death in 1870, no holds were barred. Lee immediately passed on to sainthood without benefit of clergy. So good a man, so full of character, representing the best that Southern chivalry could offer, such a skillful general, he could not be responsible for losing the war of all wars.

Initial Southern response to who lost the war had placed all blame on President Davis. But his brave stint in Yankee prison and the refusal of the Federal courts to try him for treason left the field open to others. Where was the war lost? Was there one battle, one incident that decided the fate of the Confederacy? Of course! It was Gettysburg, the "high-water mark" of the Confederate war effort. If Lee was too good a commander to lose Gettysburg, who did? No one fit the bill as well as Old Pete, Lee's favored subordinate.

Enter Jubal A. Early, once one of Longstreet's fellow generals at First Manassas and Williamsburg. Early wound up in Stonewall Jackson's Second Corps and later became the corps commander. But his utter defeat in the Shenandoah Valley in late 1864 had eventually led to General Lee's removing him from command in disgrace. Fearing arrest because units under his command burned Chambersburg, Pennsylvania, during the war, Early had fled into Canadian exile before returning to the United States in 1869.[48]

Now Early and others, anxious to apotheosize Lee, turned on Longstreet. It was not hard to do. Early was a vociferous opponent of Republican Reconstruction of the South. Longstreet had gone over to the enemy after the war. But Early took his time. It was to be a carefully planned campaign. Longstreet, still a military hero, was a potentially risky target.[49]

In 1872, Early fired the opening salvo. In a speech, he claimed that Lee told him, his corps commander, Richard Ewell, and fellow division commander, Robert Rodes, that Longstreet was to attack the defeated Federals on the hills south of Gettysburg at dawn on July 2. Such an attack would have won the battle and gained the Confederacy its independence.

Early's motives were not exactly pure. Indeed, if one were to pick a point at which Gettysburg was lost and the South let independence slip through its hands, it might better be the evening of July 1, when Ewell, Rodes, and Early failed to press their day's advantage and sweep over Cemetery Hill and the nearby hummocks, driving the retreating Yankees toward Hanover.

But Early could not command his uncommitted brigade under Brigadier General "Extra Billy" Smith, who went on his own merry course, unaffected by the actual battle. No one saw this clearer than Ewell's staff officer, Major Henry Kyd Douglas, and an unattached major general, Isaac R. Trimble. "Give me a Brigade and I will engage to take that hill," roared Trimble. Ewell stewed. Trimble asked for a regiment. Ewell refused; Early backed him up. "Oh, for the presence and inspiration of 'Old Jack' for just one hour," Douglas heard fellow aide Sandie Pendleton pray quietly in vain.[50]

So Early had a lot to cover up. At first, Lee's staff officers refused to credit Early's story. They had never heard anything like it from Lee. Then Longstreet came to Early's rescue. Longstreet published some letters of his own, asserting that Lee never criticized him but admitted that the Confederates would have won Gettysburg if Lee had adopted Longstreet's plan to attack around the Union right on July 3, rather than Pickett's charge up the middle.[51]

Lee's staff officers were angered at this defense. They believed that it made Longstreet look like the brains behind Lee. The officers went over en masse to Early. It was either Lee or Longstreet—one of them had screwed up at Gettysburg. It certainly was not going to be Robert E. Lee, vowed Early.[52]

And so it went for the rest of the nineteenth century, Lee's advocates versus Longstreet, Longstreet versus Lee's advocates. The latter came to include, besides Early, William N. Pendleton, J. William Jones, Fitzhugh Lee, Richard Taylor, Braxton Bragg, William Preston Johnston, Cadmus M. Wilcox, Wade Hampton, President Davis, and Lee's staff (C. S. Venable, Walter Taylor, A. L. Long, and Charles Marshall). James Longstreet's often bitter invective and willingness to see himself as the brains behind Lee's successes, ignored only to Lee's detriment, helped them cover a multitude of their own sins. Again, Longstreet's analysis after the battle of Gettysburg is instructive: "Had we interposed between [Major General George G.] Meade and Washington, . . . Meade would have been obliged to attack us wherever we might be pleased to have him. He would have been badly beaten." Longstreet's pat on his own back would become the thesis of a modern-day best seller written by William Fortschen and Newt Gingrich.[53]

Lee's advocates soon realized that the alleged attack Longstreet was supposed to make on July 2 was at best a lie. So they picked up a new theme: Longstreet cost the Confederates the war because he was grumpy, balky, and slow. This was invalid for the defensive battles at First Manassas, Williamsburg, Antietam, and Fredericksburg. It probably was a pretty far stretch for the offensive battles at Seven Pines, Gaines Mill, and Frayser's Farm, the campaigns in the West, or the Wilderness.

This brought the crux of the argument against Longstreet down to two key offensive battles: Second Manassas (August 29 and 30, 1862) and Gettysburg (July 2 and 3, 1863). Despite the fact that Longstreet's Corps outmarched Jackson's so-called Foot Cavalry to arrive on the battlefield of Second Manassas by August 29, the accusation was that he refused to attack three times under Lee's specific orders and that he also dragged his feet on the following day, allowing Jackson to bear the brunt of the Federal assault. Lee's advocates charged that Longstreet was in fact so dilatory that Lee relied on Jackson to make the principal moves during the campaign and that, further, Longstreet failed to give Jackson and his men credit for their roles.

The first two of these accusations are only true in part. The third (failing to give Jackson credit) is unfortunately completely true. As to Longstreet's refusing to attack under direct orders, Lee seemed unaware that an entire Federal army corps was off his right flank. Longstreet was correct to hold off attacking until this federal unit moved to his front, which it did on August 30. Longstreet used his artillery, although many commentators credit Colonel Stephen D. Lee's independent reserve artillery battalion with breaking up the Union attack on Jackson. Once his men were ready, Longstreet's attack drove the enemy from the field in a retreat that ended in the fortifications around Washington.

It was Lee's nephew, Fitzhugh Lee, who brought up the Longstreet-as-slowpoke notion in 1878. He allegedly got it secondhand from another officer, who supposedly heard General Lee say it. Early soon joined in, saying he had heard the same. Hence, it followed that Jackson had to do all the hard matching and Lee constantly camped near Longstreet to hurry him up. The truth was that Lee preferred Longstreet's relaxed camp to Stonewall's strict quasi-religious regimen. And if Jackson were superior to Longstreet as a corps commander, why was Longstreet given second-in-command status by date of rank? And why did Lee feel compelled to justify Jackson's promotion and not Longstreet's?

Finally, Longstreet *was* jealous of Jackson's historical position as second only to Lee, and he did belittle Jackson's contributions to the cause in his postwar writings. When Fitzhugh Lee criticized Longstreet's actions at Gettysburg, stating that General Lee said he would have won the battle if he had had Jackson with him, Longstreet fired back, "He had Jackson in the Sharpsburg Campaign, which was more blundering than that of Gettysburg." He then snidely mentioned that Major General D. H. Hill's division fought all day while Jackson's command had to "leave the field for refreshments," something a non-Virginian would never do. Longstreet was his own worst enemy and struck back at the anti-Longstreet faction any way he could, even belittling their hero Jackson. He just could not help it, nor could his very supportive second wife.[54]

But in the words of the noted biographer of Lee and his generals, Douglas Southall Freeman, everything paled in the light of Longstreet's refusal to attack on August 29 and early August 30. "The seeds of much of the disaster at Gettysburg were sown at [Second Manassas]," the premier anti-Longstreet historian wrote, "when Lee yielded to Longstreet and Longstreet discovered that he would."[55]

Events at Gettysburg, however, challenged Freeman's assertion. Once the myth that Longstreet was to attack at dawn on July 2 was dismissed, there is little evidence that Longstreet delayed any movement without Lee's assent. Both men were admittedly out of sorts. The morning had been taken up with scouting the Union line near the Round Tops. Longstreet preferred to swing Hood's Division, Lee's last unit on his right, to the rear of Big Round Top. Hood agreed. But Lee insisted that the attack be made perpendicular to the Emmitsburg Road toward Cemetery Ridge by brigades successively in echelon.

A series of delays preceded Longstreet's attack. First, Brigadier General Evander M. Law's brigade came up late. Longstreet waited on Law with Lee's approval. Next, the movement of Longstreet's Corps directly into attack position could be seen by Union signalmen on the Round Tops. Longstreet countermarched to a more secluded route. Lee approved again. He also supervised the starting alignment of Longstreet's brigades in line of battle.

Anti-Longstreet writers made much of Longstreet's supposed slow march onto the field. But in the 1930s, retired army officer Donald B. Sanger did an awfully commonsense sort of thing: He walked the route taken by Longstreet's men. Lo and behold, Sanger found that they had actually made good time, not delaying in the least. No one could deny that Longstreet's men delivered a devastating attack once they arrived. Any lack of success was due to the failure of Lieutenant General A. P. Hill's Third Corps to support the attack as planned.[56]

Despite Longstreet's smashing parts of three enemy army corps, the Union troops were still on the ridges and hills south of Gettysburg on July 3. Lee moved to attack the center of the Federal line with Longstreet's recently arrived division of Virginians under Pickett. Supporting him would be a division and a half from Hill's Third Corps, bloodied on July 1, because Longstreet thought his right flank vulnerable to a Union counterstroke.

There is little doubt that Longstreet was aghast at Lee's plan. He proposed a flank attack from the Confederate right. Lee refused. He saw victory. Longstreet saw Malvern Hill. But he went ahead with the attack, anyway.[57] His artilleryman in charge of the preliminary bombardment of the Union position, Colonel E. Porter Alexander, believed that Longstreet was so opposed to the attack that he half-expected the colonel to order it. Alexander refused. Pickett asked for clarification. Longstreet dropped his head to his chest. Pickett's disastrous charge went forward into military history as the high point of the Confederacy.[58]

After the Rebel defeat at Gettysburg, Longstreet threw himself into the strategic move of a part of Lee's army to the West. Longstreet always denied self-interest in moving west, maintaining that he preferred to serve in a subordinate position under Beauregard or Johnston. But here it is possible that anti-Longstreet writers had it more correct than not—he hungered for an independent command, first Suffolk, then East Tennessee. Longstreet proved to be less than an imaginary, autonomous commander. In the end, he became as quarrelsome with his subordinates, unfairly blaming them for his errors, as had Bragg before him.[59]

This, then, was Lieutenant General James Longstreet: a lower-South officer in an army commanded by Virginians,[60] arguably the best corps commander in the armies of either side,[61] careful and almost modern in the attack, exacting in defense,[62] a man of ambition until the Peter Principle caught up with him,[63] and a visionary of the New South on the Southern white man's terms.[64]

Tragically, Longstreet, like many disparate thinkers in a time of societal revolution, had his good intentions and his civil and military reputation swept away by the suspicions, confusions, and deceptions endemic to so much of the dark and bloody ground of the American Iliad. Without trying to sanctify Longstreet, his life's work seems right out of the New Testament: "A prophet is not without honor, but in his own country, and among his own kin, and in his own house."[65]

Not only was that honor which Longstreet believed was his by rights taken from him, but undeserved evil was spoken of him and his words were misrepresented. Perhaps it is as modern revisionist writers say, James Longstreet made three mistakes that have denied him his deserved place in Southern history: He argued with Lee tactically and strategically, he was right, and he became a Republican.[66] His was truly a road to hell paved with good intentions.

Notes

I wish to thank Ephraim Williams Professor of American History Charles B. Dew at Williams College, Williamstown, Massachusetts. When I was a student in his seminar at Louisiana State University, he encouraged me to research James Longstreet and to publish my findings.

1. "Bernard of Clairvaux, St.," *Catholic Encyclopedia,* http://www.newadvent.org/cathen/02498d.htm/ (accessed May 11, 2012).
2. The "big three" in Longstreet biographies are Jeffry Wert, *General James Longstreet: The Confederacy's Most Controversial General* (New York, 1993); Donald B. Sanger and Thomas R. Hay, *James Longstreet: I. Soldier; II. Politician, Office Holder, and Writer* (Baton Rouge, 1952); and H. J. Eckenrode and Bryan Conrad, *James Longstreet: Lee's War Horse* (Chapel Hill, 1936). Also of interest is Wilbur Thomas, *General James "Pete" Longstreet, Lee's "Old Warhorse": Scapegoat for Gettysburg* (Parson, WV, 1979). Longstreet's own account is *From Manassas to Appomattox* (Philadelphia,1896; reprint, Bloomington, IN, 1960). His second wife's always favorable story is Helen D. Longstreet, *Lee and Longstreet at High Tide* (Gainesville, GA, 1904).
3. Wert, *Longstreet,* 17–26.
4. Ibid., 26–32; Mark M. Boatner III, *The Civil War Dictionary* (New York, 1959), 490.
5. Wert, *Longstreet,* 33–45.
6. William Garrett Piston, "Petticoats, Promotions, and Military Assignments: Favoritism and the Antebellum Career of James Longstreet," in *James Longstreet: The Man, the Soldier, the Controversy,* ed. R. L. DiNardo and Albert Nofi (New York, 1998), 53–78.
7. Alan T. Nolan, *Lee Considered: General Robert E. Lee and Civil War History* (Chapel Hill, 1991), 30–58, especially 41.
8. Douglas Southall Freeman, *Dictionary of American Biography,* quoted in Boatner, *Civil War Dictionary,* 491.
9. John Hennessey, *The First Battle of Manassas: An End to Innocence, July 18–21, 1861* (Lynchburg, VA, 1989); Wert, *Longstreet,* 62–78; William Garrett Piston, *Lee's Tarnished Lieutenant: James Longstreet and His Place in Southern History* (Athens, GA, 1987), 12–14. The Confederate side of Civil War battles in the East is detailed in Douglas Southall Freeman, *Lee's Lieutenants: A Study in Command,* 3 vols. (New York, 1943–44).
10. Wert, *Longstreet,* 94–95, 108–9, 205–6, 247.
11. Ibid., 96–109; Stephen W. Sears, *To the Gates of Richmond: The Peninsula Campaign* (New York, 1992); William Miller, ed., *The Peninsula Campaign of 1862: Yorktown to the Seven Days* (Campbell, CA, 1993).
12. Steven H. Newton, *The Battle of Seven Pines* (Lynchburg, VA, 1993); Wert, *Longstreet,* 110–26.
13. Wert, *Longstreet,* 127–53; Clifford Dowdey, *The Seven Days: The Emergence of Robert E. Lee* (Boston, 1964).

14. Wert, *Longstreet,* 152; Edward Porter Alexander to Frederick Colston, Apr. 7, 1898, Campbell-Colston Family Papers, Southern Historical Collection, University of North Carolina, Chapel Hill.

15. Grady McWhiney and Perry D. Jamieson, *Attack and Die: Civil War Tactics and Southern Heritage* (University, AL, 1982). A different view is in Richard E. Beringer, Herman Hattaway, Archer Jones, and William N. Still Jr., *Why the South Lost the Civil War* (Athens, GA, 1986), 458–81.

16. Piston, *Lee's Tarnished Lieutenant,* 28, 35; Wert, *Longstreet,* 108–9, 179. Confirming Longstreet's suspicions, J. F. C. Fuller, *Grant and Lee: A Study in Personality and Generalship* (London, 1933), was the first to point out that Lee was one of the most costly of generals when it came to losses per thousand in battle, exceeding even U. S. Grant, heretofore the "butcher."

17. Freeman, *Lee's Lieutenants,* 1:655–75; Wert, *Longstreet,* 150–55.

18. John Hennessey, *Return to Bull Run: The Campaign and Battle of Second Manassas* (New York, 1993); Wert, *Longstreet,* 153–79.

19. Stephen W. Sears, *Landscape Turned Red: The Battle of Antietam* (New York, 1983); Gary W. Gallagher, ed., *Antietam: Essays on the 1862 Maryland Campaign* (Kent, OH, 1989); Wert, *Longstreet,* 180–203.

20. William Miller Owen, *In Camp and Battle with the Washington Artillery of New Orleans* (1885; reprint, Baton Rouge, 1999), 157.

21. Piston, *Lee's Tarnished Lieutenant,* 27.

22. George C. Rable, *Fredericksburg! Fredericksburg!* (Chapel Hill, 2002); Gary W. Gallagher, ed., *The Fredericksburg Campaign: Decision on the Rappahannock* (Chapel Hill, 1995); Wert, *Longstreet,* 203–24.

23. Piston, *Lee's Tarnished Lieutenant,* 34–35.

24. Steven A. Cormier, *The Siege of Suffolk: The Forgotten Campaign, April 11–May 4, 1863* (Lynchburg, VA, 1989); Wert, *Longstreet,* 224–42.

25. John Bigelow Jr., *The Campaign of Chancellorsville: A Strategic and Tactical Study* (New Haven, 1910); Freeman, *Lee's Lieutenants,* 2:524–602.

26. Longstreet's strategic offensive/tactical defensive is the thesis used by Newt Gingrich and William R. Forstchen in *Gettysburg: A Novel of the Civil War* (New York, 2003).

27. Wert, *Longstreet,* 242–47.

28. Edwin B. Coddington, *The Gettysburg Campaign: A Study in Command* (New York, 1968); Gary W. Gallagher, ed., *The First Day at Gettysburg: Essays on Confederate and Union Leadership* (Kent, OH, 1992).

29. Gary W. Gallagher, ed., *The Second Day at Gettysburg: Essays on Confederate and Union Leadership* (Kent, OH, 1993); Harry W. Pfanz, *Gettysburg: The Second Day* (Chapel Hill, 1987).

30. Gary W. Gallagher, ed., *The Third Day at Gettysburg and Beyond* (Chapel Hill, 1994); Kathleen R. Georg and John W. Busey, *Nothing but Glory: Pickett's Division at Gettysburg* (Hightstown, NJ, 1987).

31. Wert, *Longstreet,* 298–303.

32. Piston, *Lee's Tarnished Lieutenant,* 70.

33. Peter Cozzens, *This Terrible Sound: The Battle of Chickamauga* (Urbana, IL, 1992).

34. Judith Lee Hallock, *General James Longstreet in the West: A Monumental Failure* (Ft. Worth, TX, 1998).

35. Gordon C. Rhea, *The Battle of the Wilderness, May 5–6, 1864* (Baton Rouge, 1994); Wert, *Longstreet,* 378–88.

36. Wert, *Longstreet,* 392–404.

37. The sobriquet was Stonewall Jackson's. Piston, *Lee's Tarnished Lieutenant,* 26.

38. Wert, *Longstreet,* 407–10, quote on 409.

39. For the Military Reconstruction acts, see William L. Richter, *The ABC-CLIO Companion to American Reconstruction, 1862–1877* (Santa Barbara, CA, 1996), 269–70.

40. Quoted in Wert, *Longstreet,* 412.

41. That the *Tribune* was correct in its analysis of the general's motives is proven in Longstreet's letter to R. H. Taliaferro, July 4, 1867, reprinted in Piston, *Lee's Tarnished Lieutenant,* 106.

42. *New Orleans Tribune,* June 9, 1867.

43. Unless noted otherwise, Longstreet's change in politics and all quotes are from William L. Richter, "James Longstreet: From Rebel to Scalawag," *Louisiana History* 11 (1970): 215–30.

44. On Reconstruction in Louisiana, see George C. Rable, *But There Was No Peace: The Role of Violence in the Politics of Reconstruction* (Athens, GA, 1984), 122–43; Joseph G. Dawson III, *Army Generals and Reconstruction: Louisiana, 1862–1877* (Baton Rouge, 1982), 140ff., passim; and Francis J. Wetta, "The Louisiana Scalawags" (Ph.D. diss., Louisiana State Univ., 1977), 331–34. Sadly, only a portion of Wetta's fine dissertation is in print as "Bulldozing the Scalawags," *Louisiana History* 21 (1980): 43–58.

45. Wert, *Longstreet,* 417–25.

46. Piston, *Lee's Tarnished Lieutenant,* 95–103, quotes on 97.

47. Quotes from Richter, "James Longstreet," 226.

48. Boatner, *Civil War Dictionary,* 254–55; Piston, *Lee's Tarnished Lieutenant,* 118–19.

49. Most of this attack on Longstreet follows Piston, *Lee's Tarnished Lieutenant,* 96–138.

50. Freeman, *Lee's Lieutenants,* 3:93, 95.

51. This flanking maneuver idea is what got President Dwight D. Eisenhower and Field Marshal Sir Bernard Montgomery in so much trouble when they publicly approved of it after the fact in 1957. See *Time,* May 20, 27, 1957.

52. *Southern Historical Society Papers;* the relevant articles are listed in Piston, *Lee's Tarnished Lieutenant,* 229–32, passim.

53. The list of anti-Longstreet men is compiled from Gary W. Gallagher, "Scapegoat in Victory: James Longstreet and the Battle of Second Manassas," *Civil War History* 34 (1988): 294; Piston, *Lee's Tarnished Lieutenant,* 129. Longstreet's analysis is his article, "Lee's Right Wing at Gettysburg," in *Battles and Leaders of the Civil War: Being for the most part contributions by Union and Confederate officers based upon "The Century War Series" edited by Robert Underwood Johnson and Clarence Clough Buel, of the editorial staff of The Century Magazine,* 4 vols., ed. Robert U. Johnson and Clarence C. Buel (New York, 1884–88), 3:354. The best seller is Newt Gingrich and William R. Fortschen, *Gettysburg: A Novel of the Civil War* (New York, 2003).

54. For a full account, see Gallagher, "Scapegoat in Victory," 293–307. Longstreet's quotes in *From Manassas to Appomattox,* 401.

55. Douglas Southall Freeman, *R. E. Lee,* 4 vols. (New York, 1934–35), 2:325.

56. Donald B. Sanger, "Was Longstreet a Scapegoat?" *Infantry Journal* 43 (Jan./Feb. 1936): 39–46; Sanger, *General James Longstreet and the Civil War* (Chicago, 1936); Sanger and Hay, *Longstreet,* 173–89.

57. In defense of Lee, Pickett's Charge was actually a pincer attack, the second arm of the attack being Stuart's cavalry coming down Cress Ridge and the Old Dutch Road east of the main battlefield into the Union rear on the Baltimore Pike. But Federal cavalry stymied this effort as Pickett approached the Union lines on Cemetery Ridge. See William L. Richter, "The Federal Cavalry during the Gettysburg Campaign: The Development of the Mobile Arm of the Army of the Potomac" (master's thesis, Arizona State Univ., 1965), 86–87, 104–6. See also Edward G. Longacre, *The Cavalry at Gettysburg: A Tactical Study Of Mounted Operations During The Civil War's Pivotal Campaign, 9 June–14 July 1863* (Rutherford, NJ, 1986), 220–45, 238–39.

58. Glenn Tucker, "Longstreet: Culprit or Scapegoat?" *Civil War Times Illustrated* 1 (Apr. 1962): 4–7; Tucker, *High Tide at Gettysburg: The Campaign in Pennsylvania* (Indianapolis, 1958); Tucker, *Lee and Longstreet at Gettysburg* (Indianapolis, 1968).

59. Hallock, *Longstreet in the West.*

60. Wert, *Longstreet,* 207, 249; Piston, *Lee's Tarnished Lieutenant,* 40.

61. Wert, *Longstreet,* 405–6; Piston, *Lee's Tarnished Lieutenant,* 36; R. L. DiNardo, "James Longstreet, the Modern Soldier: A Broad Assessment," in *James Longstreet: The Man, the Soldier, the Controversy,* ed. R. L. DiNardo and Albert Nofi (New York, 1998), 42–44.

62. Piston, *Lee's Tarnished Lieutenant,* 31–51; Harold M. Knudson, *General James Longstreet: The Confederacy's Most Modern General* (Tarentum, PA, 2007), 16–17, 93–100.

63. Laurence J. Peter and Raymond Hull, *The Peter Principle: Why Things Always Go Wrong* (New York, 1969). Wert gives the most balanced view of Longstreet as an independent commander in *Longstreet,* 229–35, 359, 365–66. See also Knudson, *General James Longstreet,* 60–73.

64. Wert, *Longstreet,* 411–12; Richter, "James Longstreet," 228–29.

65. Mark 6:4; Matthew 13:57 (KJV).

66. Thomas L. Connelly and Barbara L. Bellows, *God and General Longstreet: The Lost Cause and the Southern Mind* (Baton Rouge, 1982), 31–38.

Jubal Anderson Early after the Civil War. Library of Congress.

Jubal Early: Confederate in the Attic

Thomas E. Schott

Ever since the 1870s, when an utterly unreconstructed Jubal A. Early was rendering far better service to the Confederate States than he ever did in a major general's uniform, his grizzled, bearded countenance has been the face of the Lost Cause. An interconnected bundle of partisan interpretations of the American Civil War that virtually exonerated the Southern states from any part in its origins and the Confederate army from any part in losing it, the Lost Cause survives today largely as an echo of its earlier days. And Early? He is but a barely visible shadow of what he once was.

He was not an easy man to like. "Hail, fellow, well met" hardly describes Jubal Anderson Early. He himself admitted, "I was never what is called a popular man." It's not difficult to understand why. Of all the Confederacy's high-ranking generals, Early was one of the most disliked. He is habitually described as being dogmatic and opinionated about everything, constantly carping in a "a piping treble" voice, and as having a sour, irritable disposition. And a biting, sarcastic tongue, which he used to lash both his troops and his enemies, of which he had many. One of his staff officers described him as having a "grim" air and with subordinates, "abrupt, rough, peremptory, and formidable." As General John B. Gordon delicately put it, Early had "a pungent style of commenting on things he did not like," which for one of the most profane officers in the Confederate high command is almost complimentary. Old age did not soften him; four years before his death at age seventy-seven, U.S. Army Major General George Crook described the feeble old man as still "bitter and violent as an adder."[1]

To these lovable traits, Early added an arresting physical appearance and pronounced eccentricity. Rheumatism he contracted as a young man in Mexico messed up his back; he walked severely stooped the rest of his life. Prematurely gray, he always looked older than he was. His utter indifference to his appearance produced gems of description from witnesses. "His face with the whiskers he always wore," wrote a Confederate soldier, "looked like a malignant and very hairy spider. . . . On his head he wore the queerest imaginable old gray felt hat, almost like one of the hats a clown wears in a circus, with a single feather, like the tail feather of a rooster stuck in it." (After the war, Early wore nothing but Confederate gray suits—"I never go back on my colors," he said—and gold cuff buttons with the Confederate flag enameled on them.) In a country saturated with religion, Early was decidedly irreligious. In the midst of Victorian sexual mores, Early never married but lived openly for almost twenty years with a woman in his hometown of Lynchburg, Virginia, and had four children by her.[2]

But for all this, the general was not without compensating virtues. No one doubted his physical courage—he was "one of the coolest and most imperturbable of men under fire," said Gordon—or his loyalty. Self-reliant and intelligent, he had amazing energy and a prodigious capacity for work. He was also doggedly motivated. During the war, Lee, who called Early "my bad old man," had great confidence in him and relied on him heavily in difficult and critical positions. People who knew Early well testified to his great generosity to innumerable individuals and organizations, even churches, as well as to his wit and finely developed sense of humor.[3]

One searches in vain for some traumatic event in Early's childhood or youth to illuminate his "exclusive and repellent" characteristics in maturity. His biographer sees them as products of "his extreme vulnerability . . . his overdeveloped regard for what other people thought of him," a trait he inwardly and fiercely denied. The emotional energy it required to do this obscured his softer side and produced a "profound pessimism" that "robbed his life of any substantial enjoyment other than his love for his family."[4]

Certainly there was nothing in his childhood or youth that could have predicted this. He was born into privilege, the second son of ten children, on November 3, 1816, in Franklin County, Virginia. Not only was his father a successful large planter, but Early was closely related to some of the biggest, most prosperous slaveholders in the state. So his youthful years were blessed with all the gentility and advantages such an exalted social and economic station bestowed. When he was sixteen years old, his father secured him an appointment to West Point. After an indifferent, rather lackluster stint as a cadet, Early graduated (eighteenth in a class of fifty) and was commissioned in June 1837. The young lieutenant chose artillery as his branch.

Early's ensuing military career would be, to say the least, brief, barely over a year. After a training stint at Fortress Monroe, in October he was posted to Florida for service in the Seminole War. He participated in a skirmish there, and by spring he had decided to submit his resignation from the army to pursue a legal career. After a short period of study, he set up practice in the little town of Rocky Mount in Franklin County, Virginia, and began a profession that would occupy him, except for a short period of service in the Mexican War, for almost the next two decades.

In 1841, Early won election as a Whig to the Virginia House of Delegates but was voted out of office the following year. Fortuitously, when the winner of the election vacated his position as commonwealth attorney for the county, Early assumed that post. Doubtless eager for a break in the quotidian life of a country lawyer, in 1846, with the onset of the Mexican War, Early procured an appointment as a major in the 1st Virginia Volunteers. By the time the regiment actually reached Mexico near the mouth of the Rio Grande, far to the south General Winfield Scott was driving on Mexico City, which fell on September 14. So Early's role in the war consisted of a few weeks of garrison duty, including a short time as military governor of Monterrey. What he took away from his short service was some experience at training and leading troops and his lifelong disability, the arthritic spine. The young Virginian, looking decades older than he was, and his troops were discharged from the army in August 1848. He spent the next dozen years in quiet practice of his profession. Oddly, though he passionately defended the institution of slavery, and would for the rest of his life, Early himself never owned more than one slave. But he worried constantly about attacks from the North on the sanctity of private property in slaves, not to mention the security of his family's vast slave holdings.[5]

Like many Southern Whigs, Early vehemently opposed the idea of secession when the storm burst after the election of Lincoln in 1860. He and another Unionist candidate were elected to represent Franklin County in Virginia's secession convention in mid-February 1861. Early addressed the convention several times, most memorably in fulsome praise of the virtues of the Union and in defense of Lincoln after his inaugural address. The firing on Fort Sumter and Lincoln's call for seventy-five thousand volunteers propelled the convention to approve secession on April 17; Early voted no. Ten days later, Virginia joined the Confederacy. "The adoption of that ordinance," he said, "wrung from me bitter tears of grief," but much like his idol Robert E. Lee, he felt duty-bound to support his state and protect it against invasion.[6]

In the space of two weeks, Early was transformed from dedicated lover of the Union to its lifelong enemy. He damned the assault on Fort Sumter as a violation of the contract between Virginia and the United States for the protection of property and civil order. In early May he offered his services as a soldier to the governor of Virginia. He was appointed general in the state's militia, and when Virginia joined the Confederacy, he became a colonel and the first commander of the 24th Virginia Infantry. His troops, struck by their commander's grizzled stoop, dubbed him "Old Jube" or "Old Jubilee," a moniker that would endure.[7]

If Old Jube Early were not remembered for his role with the Lost Cause, he would be almost as renowned as one of the finest upper echelon commanders in the Army of Northern Virginia. Arguably, of Lee's subordinates, only Jackson and Longstreet surpassed him in ability. Early participated in every major campaign of that army. Commanding a brigade at the first battle at Manassas, he performed well enough to be promoted to brigadier general. He grew steadily as a soldier over the next two years, earning promotion to major general and division command after the Battle of Fredericksburg. After Jackson's death at Chancellorsville and subsequent reorganization of the army, Early's division formed part of Richard Ewell's 2nd Corps. His division was not overly engaged at Gettysburg, a battle destined to become pivotal in the general's life. After assuming temporary corps command twice in the following months, in late May 1864, he was promoted to lieutenant general and assumed command of Ewell's Corps when that general retired. Following Cold Harbor, Early's command was detached from the army, and he undertook his famed Valley Campaign. Initially successful, he suffered a series of devastating defeats at the hands of General Phil Sheridan in the fall of 1864. After the pitiful remnant of Early's command was obliterated at Waynesboro in March 1865, public outcry against Early forced a reluctant Lee to relieve him of command.[8]

Even after Appomattox, Early did not believe the cause lost. Determined to join General Kirby Smith in the Trans-Mississippi, he and a young kinsman rode southwest. Upon hearing that Smith had surrendered in June, Old Jube, even more resolute to "get out from the rule of the infernal Yankees," decided to flee to Mexico. Months passed before he got there, via Galveston, Bimini, and Havana, and but for the kindness of new friends and the generosity of Texans who raised two hundred dollars in gold for him, he might never have fled the country. He intended his exile to be permanent—he would never return to the states but under a Confederate flag, he wrote—but Mexico, which he hoped would be at war with the United States, he adjudged "an infernal humbug" and struck out once again, this time to Canada. After a roundabout route through the Caribbean and Halifax, Early settled in Toronto in the fall of 1866.[9]

Early started documenting the Lost Cause almost immediately. And from the first, he staked out ground he would occupy the rest of his life. In a lengthy letter to the *New York News,* he denied having applied for a pardon or being paroled. He held no allegiance to the United States and remained an exile unwilling "to submit the foreign yoke" laid on his country. Moreover, he determined that a properly Southern viewpoint on the war be preserved for the world, urging that it reject the "history of this struggle from the mouths and pens of our enemies" and wait for a time when "a true history" could be produced. While still in Texas, he began requesting copies of reports about the Valley Campaign from former officers in his command. "My memory is very retentive," he told one of them—as well as inventive and selective, he might have added.[10]

Part of the reason Early left Mexico was to find better facilities for publishing his own history of the late war. Although he probably would have published quickly anyway, a pair of letters from Robert E. Lee in November 1865 and March 1866 spurred him on. Lee, who desired materials about the war in 1864–65 for his own book, reinforced Early's bedrock convictions. "Truth" should be transmitted to posterity out of "justice to our brave Soldiers," he wrote. Part of his goal was to demonstrate "the discrepancy in strength between the two armies." Only with difficulty would the world come to "understand the odds against which we fought."[11]

One scholar has speculated that Lee's requests prompted Early's celerity in publishing his work on the Valley Campaign and notes that the outline of the work covered precisely the period Lee defined in his letter. Early's memoir of the war's last year, published as a pamphlet in 1866 and in book form the following year, was the first account by a high-ranking officer on either side. It emphasized the Northern numerical advantage and the depredations of Sheridan's troops in the Valley. Likely Lee's letters had spurred Early on, for he idolized Lee, from even before the war. After it he openly avowed his "profound love and veneration" for him. For his part, Lee reposed a good deal of confidence in Old Jube. Only Jackson did he give tougher assignments. And when the clamor for Early's head became too vociferous to ignore in the waning days of the war, the general in chief had let him down easy, with solicitude. Early would repay this confidence and kindness many times over, for he soon became the driving force in the virtual canonization of Lee across the South.[12]

Early's years in Canada were the worst of his life. At one point in 1867, he briefly considered then discarded the idea of moving to Venezuela. Nonetheless, he mused that "it might be better to go and be killed off by the climate so that there may be an end to my troubles in this world at last." Living mostly on borrowed money, away from friends and family, his conscience pricking him about his absence from home, he could do little but work on his writing and vast correspondence and nurture his hatred for the Yankees.[13]

And he hated every last one: Lincoln, Grant, the "miserable, cowardly renegade" Andrew Johnson. Gladly would he lead twenty to thirty thousand Comanches and Apaches through the North, he said, and "leave a trail behind that would not be erased in this century." He scoffed at the idea being floated by some in Virginia that he run for governor. He would "have the whole state in another war in less than a week," he said. He dreamed almost nightly of doing battle with the Yankees, and, he said, "I wish it were not a dream." As Radical Reconstruction settled on the South, he wrote that he had gotten into such a state "I think I could scalp a Yankee woman and child without winking my eyes." So diabolical did he believe the Radicals that Early for a time entertained the bizarre notion—wishful thinking, actually—that the union of Northern Republicans and Southern blacks would cause such revulsion in the rest of the country that the war would be reignited. He relished this prospect.[14]

Like many another expatriate Confederate, Early was bound eventually to return home. He chose to interpret Andrew Johnson's Christmas Day amnesty in 1868 as acknowledging the government's "inability to hold [the South] responsible under the laws and Constitution" for its resistance. This construction, most certainly not a pardon, Early averred, allowed him to return to Virginia "without compromise of principle." After several months visiting relatives in Missouri, Early returned to Virginia in May 1869 and settled in Lynchburg two months later. His brother Sam lived there, and it offered better prospects of making a living than war-ravaged and dirt-poor Franklin County. Here he would spend the rest of his life.[15]

A man of simple tastes, few debts, and few wants, Early wasn't interested in riches, but at the least the penury of the immediate postwar years had to be avoided. His prominence afforded him access to some local government jobs and a few select legal clients, which provided a tolerable living. But in just a few years, his money problems disappeared. In 1877, at the urging of General P. G. T. Beauregard, Early became a fellow commissioner for the Louisiana State Lottery Company at an annual base salary of five thousand dollars. Old Jube's rectitude required that Beauregard provide assurances that the company's management harbored no carpetbaggers, and that it was an honest enterprise. Although the latter proposition was certainly arguable, Early took the job, stipulating that he could withdraw from the company if he smelled trouble. That the lottery considered it necessary that he and his fellow Confederate general serve as visible guarantors of the company's uprightness seems to have escaped his notice. Within a year, Old Jube was stoutly defending the company against several charges of shady practices. He remained in their employ until the company lost its charter in 1890.[16]

By the time Early had settled in Lynchburg in July 1869, Virginia's reconstruction was almost complete; it had proceeded comparatively swiftly. This was largely due to a split in the state's Republican Party in the previous year and the rise of a coalition of moderate Republicans and conservatives under the leadership of former Confederate General William Mahone. This group came to power the same month Early settled in Lynchburg. The coalition had engineered a deal with Congress for separate votes on a new state constitution and some of the clauses in it that disfranchised and excluded former Confederates from public office. In the July election, the voters approved the constitution, rejected the restrictions on ex-Confederates, and swept the so-called True Republicans into office in the state. The following January Congress readmitted Virginia to the Union, thus, unlike most of the Southern states, sparing it the experience of Military Reconstruction.[17]

It made no difference to Jubal Early. He opposed it all: the "negro constitution" and the state government, with a special dollop of hatred for that scalawag "Little Billy" Mahone, who had committed the most heinous of sins. He had joined the enemy and become a Republican, a traitor to his country and, at a more visceral level, a traitor to his race. Indeed, Early contended, the abolition of slavery had been a mistake. In fact, almost the entire world had maltreated the South over the issue. Few nations, he wrote in 1867, were innocent of inflicting wrongs on the Southern people: "I want to see all the nations punished for their folly & wicked intermeddling [with] slavery, about the propriety, advantages, and justice of which my opinion grows daily stronger."[18]

Like some prehistoric insect preserved in amber, Early never modified his antebellum racist presumptions, never recognized the abolition of slavery as a positive event, never abandoned a single tenet of the proslavery argument. Blacks were an inferior race, designed so by God. Therefore, common sense, "true humanity" to them, as well as "safety to the white race," dictated their subordination. Slavery had not only improved blacks morally and physically but also produced "a class of laborers as happy and contented as any in the world" as well as prosperity for the entire country.[19]

But Early went beyond these standard Southern rationalizations in his fear and loathing for freed blacks, especially in anything connected to the war. For example, in 1875 he refused to march in a procession in Richmond connected with dedication of a bronze statue to Stonewall Jackson because two black militia units would be marching at the rear. In a letter to the governor, James L. Kemper, Early pronounced himself "inexpressibly shocked" at this "indignity" to him personally and to the memory of Jackson; it was an "insult" to all Confederates. He feared the presence of twenty to thirty thousand blacks swarming the square and the prospect of whites being forced to "struggle for place with buck negroes . . . anxious to show their consequence." Kemper with some heat told Early to mind his own business. Despite his vows not to, the general attended the parade but otherwise washed his hands of it.[20]

In the preface to his *Memoir of the Last Year of the War of Independence in the Confederate States of America* (1867), Early sounded one of the foundational themes in what became known as the Lost Cause myth: the notion that the South had not fought to preserve the institution of slavery. The institution "was the mere occasion of the development of the antagonism between the . . . sections." The second foundational theme he could only allude to. (Other Confederates, Jefferson Davis and Alexander H. Stephens among them, spilled more than enough ink on the subject.) This was the firm conviction of the legality and constitutionality of secession. Six years and a bloody war later, Early now characterized his opposition to secession as "scruples" about the doctrine. And these had been swiftly dispelled by Washington's "mad, wicked, and unconstitutional measures" and the lust of the North for war.[21]

There has been extraordinary interest among historians of the last couple of generations in the Lost Cause myth. A consistent problem, however, is that "myth" is often used and understood in two distinct ways. First, in the popular sense, and the most common understanding, myth is regarded as something that's untrue, as a falsehood that has drifted down the corridors of history and taken on a life of its own. This is the way the majority of historians treat the term—"myths and realities," after all is almost a required phrase in the profession. Even when they issue disclaimers that myths are not falsehoods, as did William C. Davis, it's difficult to regard something described as containing only "some tendril of truth or fact or *perceived* fact" as much more than a falsehood. Especially when this little tendril of fact is "magnified and elaborated" to meet various needs and aspirations of the myth makers.[22]

Indeed, most historians today approach the Lost Cause Myth as essentially an elaborate fabrication consciously constructed by high-ranking ex-Confederates with only an attenuated connection to the truth. But extremely convincing fabrications nonetheless. Several have observed that the Confederate myth makers effectively succeeded in convincing a couple of generations of historians to their view of the war. According to Alan T. Nolan, a "vast mythology" surrounds the Civil War. The Lost Cause, he contends, is a "codified" Southern interpretation of the war that first migrated north and then went national. It's become the "national memory" of the conflict, an "American legend" that has been substituted for the *history* of the war. Here it appears that "myth" is being used in both the first sense of the word and in a second, much broader, sense—that is, an ostensibly true narrative or collection of narratives that reside in the consciousness of a people and which serves to define them.[23]

The recent Lost Cause studies have been fruitful. The efforts of scholars such as Nolan, Gary W. Gallagher, Thomas L. Connelly, William Garrett Piston, and others in untangling, identifying, and analyzing the various threads comprising the myth; tracing their development over time; and, not least, examining the lives and motivations of the Lost Cause myth's founding fathers—Jubal Early foremost among them—as well as their friends and enemies have deepened our understanding of how this particular American myth originated, took root, and blossomed.[24]

Other scholars have discussed the Lost Cause in the context of the larger complex of ideas about myth in general. Rolin G. Osterweis sees the Lost Cause as primarily a literary expression of a defeated, bitter people and a restoration of antebellum Southern romanticism along with a new and more virulent racism. For Charles Reagan Wilson, the Lost Cause is essentially a religious movement, a civil religion, the actual "basis for a Southern religious-moral identity . . . as a chosen people." Perhaps frustrated with these interesting but fuzzy concepts as well as the plethora of definitions for myth itself, Gaines M. Foster characterizes the Lost Cause as "tradition," which he defines as "a cultural belief held over time." For what it may lack in sexiness, this definition boasts two distinct virtues: brevity and clarity. And it emphasizes a crucial component of myth (or tradition), its continuance over time.[25]

No one writing about the Lost Cause can escape Jubal Early. He looms over the endeavor like some spectral enforcer of correct interpretation, pretty much the same role he fulfilled in his postwar life. But writers differ on what ultimately motivated him and exactly how to weigh his significance. All agree that Early had a pivotal role in establishing the foundations of the Lost Cause. As early as 1866, when his piece about the Shenandoah Campaign came out, people recognized him as some sort of prophet for the "true history" of what happened. Modern appraisals follow a similar track. He understood right away about the struggle to control the public memory of the war, and in the process of shaping that memory became "perhaps the most influential figure in nineteenth-century Civil War writing, North or South."[26]

Leaving aside the question of influence upon whom and for how long, this is doubtless a defensible proposition. But only if aperture of focus is narrow and the shutter speed quick. From any longer, wider viewpoint, Jubal Early's significance diminishes, and from the vantage point of the early twenty-first century, he appears far less formidable than the fierce, familiar portraits painted by some of the Lost Cause scholars. The oft-quoted remark Confederate veteran Robert Stiles made about the general—"As long as the 'old hero' lived, no man ever took up his pen to write a line about the great conflict without the fear of Jubal Early in his eyes"—offers strong evidence of his clout in what was then a hugely popular genre of American letters: first-person accounts of Civil War military history. As Gary Gallagher has observed, Early and other Lost Cause writers created an interpretive framework of the war that elevated its military aspects high above all other subjects.

Which was immensely useful to a defeated people seeking justification because it removed the Confederacy's "messy" political and social history, not to mention slavery.[27]

And justification was profoundly required after the catastrophe of death, destruction, and suffering—the unequivocal failure—the South had brought upon itself. Of course, no red-blooded Southerner could ever make that admission. So among the immediate planks established in the Lost Cause platform were the related assertions that the war had not been about slavery, and that secession was a constitutional expression of state rights. Thoughtful Southerners recognized that this element was sine qua non. "If we cannot justify the South in the act of Secession," wrote Clement A. Evans, former Confederate general and prolific postwar chronicler, "we will go down in History solely as a brave, impulsive but rash people who attempted in an illegal manner to overthrow the Union of our Country."[28]

The entire Lost Cause canon sprouted from these two fundamental assertions. The Confederates were the true heirs of the Revolutionary generation, ran the argument, who had been defeated only by the Union's huge reservoir of men and materiel by an army that waged brutal war against Confederate civilians as well as its army, both of which endured horrific sacrifices. But the undefeated, overwhelmed Robert E. Lee and his splendid Army of Northern Virginia stood as the shining martial example of all the myriad Southern virtues: courage, honor, chivalry, and valor.[29]

The theme of superior Southern morality permeates the Lost Cause rationale. The political justification: Had not the South been true to the virtues of the Founders and to the Constitution they bequeathed? Chivalric conduct: One had to look no further than the exploits of General J. E. B. Stuart. And Lee's military prowess: He had "set a standard of valor and accomplishment equal to anything in the military history of the western world," Early wrote. All were grounded in the simple truth that the defeated Confederates were simply the better men, morally superior to their enemies.[30]

So for many of the Lost Cause adherents a seething rage accompanied the psychological trauma of dealing with defeat. The impossible had happened. A morally superior people had been brought low by inferiors, unscrupulous minions of the devil himself in the eyes of many. And for a cold, cruel, impersonal reason that overrode all their virtue, all the excellence of their culture and society: the weight of numbers. From a solely secular viewpoint, the explanation worked for Southerners. But for questions arising from their evangelical Christian souls, explanations were far more tentative. God smote sinners, the righteous he blessed. How then if the South's cause had been just, could it have suffered this disaster? Though nobody ever satisfactorily answered the question, the South managed to retain its belief in its own righteousness by asserting its unsullied motives in taking up arms—for independence and in defense of constitutional liberty, not to preserve slavery—and ultimately ascribing crushing defeat on the battlefield to God's inscrutable design.[31]

Early agreed that the correctness of the South's course had no connection to war's outcome. Like many other ex-Confederates, he could not reconcile himself to the South's defeat on the battlefield. The logic of theological disquisition explained nothing for him. He needed no God to discern the self-evident. Given the courage, pluck, and ability of the Confederate soldier and the superiority of his leaders, especially the transcendent skills of Robert E. Lee, on any level playing field the South would have unquestionably won. In fact, had it not been for the perfidy of James A. Longstreet at Gettysburg, the South even then would have overcome the crushing odds against it. Early never deviated from this position, even long past the end of Reconstruction, when he and his fellow Lost Cause Virginians had already begun fading into the mists of time.[32]

There's little question "the principal driving force behind the entire Lost Cause mentality came from Virginia," a state long accustomed to a leadership role in the South. Virginia spawned the Ladies Memorial Association immediately after the war ended. Disputes over the proper memorials for Lee, fund raising for Confederate monuments, formation and revitalization of organizations dedicated to the Lost Cause, such as the Southern Historical Society (SHS) and the Association of the Army of Northern Virginia (AANVA), as well as leaders in those organizations all emerged from Virginia. The Old Dominion was the birthplace and spiritual center of the cult of Robert E. Lee and the site of monumental shrines to him.[33]

Nor is there much question that the principal driving force in the constellation of Lost Cause activities and organizations in Virginia came from Jubal Early. A little over two years after he returned to Virginia, in November 1870, Lee died in Lexington, an event that galvanized Virginians to erect some imposing and suitable memorial to the great man. The ensuing controversy over the location of Lee's grave and memorial—in Lexington, the place where he died and served as president of Washington College, or Richmond, the capital of the Confederacy, Early's preference—first brought Old Jube to prominence. For the next year or so an intense struggle ensued between rival Lee memorial associations until a compromise was reached: Lee's grave in Lexington and a massive equestrian monument of him in the capital. The rift between the rival memorial efforts could not have lasted long in any event. Lee occupied too hallowed a place in Southern memory to have been the object of protracted unseemly squabbling. Early's attitude about the Lexington location underwent visible softening after his having been invited to deliver a speech there at the annual Lee birthday celebration. By spring the following year, the controversy had essentially disappeared. In the meantime, Early donated many hours of his time and a goodly sum of money to the drive for funding the statue. Many years later, in 1889, Early presided over its unveiling in Richmond before a crowd of well over one hundred thousand people.[34]

Early's speech at Washington and Lee on January 19, 1872, virtually established the cult of Robert E. Lee and anointed Early its grand shaman. The address dealt at length with Lee's Confederate career, from his first assignment in West Virginia to Appomattox. Old Jube spent a good bit of time discussing the Battle of Gettysburg, from any objective perspective the one indisputable blotch on the sainted Lee's military record. But explaining away this blotch posed no problem for Early. He simply fabricated a story, assigned a villain to the piece, and bequeathed to history a grand falsehood not yet totally eradicated. Early reported that on the evening of July 1, after Union forces had been defeated and driven through the town of Gettysburg to the heights south of town, General Lee had informed Generals Richard S. Ewell, Robert Rodes, and himself of his intention to attack the Union left "at daylight" with his own right using troops from Longstreet's Corps. Then, according to Early, Lee left the conference to pass his orders to Longstreet "in time to begin the attack at dawn next morning." Thus was the placard "Villain" hung around the neck of Pete Longstreet, who, as is well known, did not begin his attack on July 2 until 4:00 P.M. According to Old Jube, Longstreet doubted Lee's plans and followed them only reluctantly, lacking the "confidence and faith necessary to succeed." Naturally, said Early, had the attack been carried out as Lee directed, it would have resulted in a brilliant, decisive victory.[35]

Lee remained unconquered to the end. The army he surrendered at Appomattox was but a "mere ghost . . . gradually worn down by the combined agencies of numbers, steam power, railroads, mechanism, and all the resources of physical science." Moreover, the fall of Richmond and the surrender of the Army of Northern Virginia was attributable to events in the West and Southwest and "not directly the operations in Virginia." So where could be found a peer to Lee "our great and pure soldier and hero?" cried Early. The answer, in short, was nowhere. Not among the Greek heroes or great Roman generals, not in Alexander the Great, Hannibal, Gustavus Adolphus, Napoleon, or Wellington. Not even in Washington, Sidney Johnston, or Stonewall Jackson. As for Ulysses S. Grant, why "as well compare the great pyramid which rears its majestic proportions in the valley of the Nile to a pygmy perched on Mount Atlas."[36]

With Robert E. Lee triumphantly ensconced on Mount Olympus, Early concluded with a snarling warning to traitors to the Cause: "If there be any, in all the land, who have proved renegade to their comrades and our holy cause, let them go out from among us with the brand of Cain upon them!" Obviously, the notorious scalawag Pete Longstreet above all others bore Cain's brand. He had failed Lee at Gettysburg, had the temerity to criticize his generalship, and, worse, had committed the unspeakable crime of joining the Republican Party and accepting a placeman's job from the Grant administration. Longstreet paid dearly for his sins, forfeiting the respect previously accorded him as a Confederate hero and donning the raiment of a virtual traitor to the Confederacy.[37]

Early's seminal address at Lexington had hammered virtually every remaining plank in the Lost Cause platform into place. But while "true history" had been established for the present generation, even more vital to Early and his like-minded compatriots was its preservation and transmission to the future. At the hands of the Yankees, Early complained, "it has been sought to make our cause and our conduct in the struggle . . . odious, and to present a one-sided view" of its entire history. The same impulse to correct the "unjust and unreasonable" account of the war by Northerners impelled Dabney H. Maury, a Virginian living in New Orleans, to organize the Southern Historical Society in May 1869. For several years the society foundered, until a reorganization meeting in White Sulfur Springs, Virginia, on August 14, 1873, which Early stacked with Virginia supporters, moved the headquarters to Richmond and elected the general its president. The Virginia clique now had effective control of a pair of monument associations, the primary Confederate veterans organization and a historical society. And Jubal Early, at the pinnacle of his influence, controlled them all. The embittered old warrior wielded his power like a hammer. "Believe me dear Genl, the fear of your rebuke has held many a weak-kneed Confederate to his duty," wrote an admirer in 1875.[38]

The "history of our war has not been written and it devolves upon the survivors of those who participated in that war, to furnish the authentic materials for that history," Early had declaimed at the 1873 convention. The SHS began immediately to furnish those materials beginning in the pages of Baltimore's *Southern Magazine* and, in 1876, with the initial issue of what would become the primary repository of the Lost Cause myths, the *Southern Historical Society Papers* (*SHSP*). By that time, Early had established himself as the supreme arbiter of what constituted the "true history" of the war, and he was a frequent contributor to the early volumes of the *SHSP*.[39]

According to most accounts, the *SHSP* formed the capstone of a deliberate campaign by Early and his Virginian coterie to forge an enduring pro-Confederate interpretation of the Civil War. That the founders of the SHS meant to preserve this interpretation in writing there is no doubt. There is also no doubt that Early and his allies used the *SHSP* to glorify Robert E. Lee by exaggeration and damn James Longstreet by lies and innuendo, and to concoct an account of the Battle of Gettysburg that exonerated Lee from any hint of error in leadership and laid the blame for the Confederate defeat in this crucial battle squarely on Longstreet. It was, in the words of one historian, "one of the most highly orchestrated grassroots partisan histories ever conceived." Hyperbole aside, the statement captures the essence of our modern understanding of the Lost Cause, that it was deliberately fashioned history by people with no pretensions to objectivity. Understandably, then, Alan Nolan points out the limited utility of the *SHSP* as evidence and attenuated value as history for just this reason: The *Papers* were "written after the fact during creation of the Lost Cause tradition."[40]

Although the intentions of Confederate diehards of Jubal Early's ilk are clear and their distortions now evident—one historian describes the campaign in the *SHSP* to smear James Longstreet's Gettysburg performance as "one of the cleverest orchestrations of innuendo and unsubstantiated accusations in American historiography"—whether the Lost Cause myth maintains anything more than an interest to historians and a rally point for small bands of neo-Confederates is a logical question. Indeed, at this remove, nearly a century and a quarter from Reconstruction and the early New South, it's logical not only to situate the Lost Cause in historical context but also to evaluate the continued viability of the myth. Certainly David W. Blight is correct when he observes, "Like all great mythologies, the Lost Cause changed with succeeding generations and shifting political circumstances." The question is whether the Lost Cause qualifies as a great mythology (or even as mythology at all, except in the sense of a body of falsehoods transmitted through time).[41]

A great mythology? Certainly not by any commonly understood concept of the term. Great mythology is Homer; great mythology is recounted in the pages of Edith Hamilton, Joseph Campbell, and Thomas Bullfinch, and in the Bhagavad Gita and the Bible. Great mythology, if the term means anything, is sustained over centuries; it shapes entire cultures; it seeps into the marrow and DNA of peoples. It is not transitory and ultimately ephemeral, which the Lost Cause of Jubal Early arguably is.[42]

Ironically, perceptible decline of that Cause began almost at the very moment of its greatest consolidation. Signs of a softening of attitude among Southerners, even veterans, against the once-hated foe appeared immediately with the end of Reconstruction, which had been a palpable period of continuing "war" against the Northern enemy for the vast majority of Southerners. A door to reconciliation had been thrown open, and many former Rebels were quite willing to walk through it. John T. Morgan, addressing the SHS at its annual meeting in 1877, signaled as much: "If we have now met in peace and reconciliation upon the broad concessions, mutually accepted, that the war was not a crime . . . we need not inquire who was right or who was wrong."[43]

Besides enduring such statements of public heresy, the diehards also witnessed a diminishing interest in the affairs of the SHS. In July 1877, only a year after the *SHSP* began publication, it lost over eleven hundred subscribers and had difficulty paying the printer. Efforts at fund raising and a few short-lived local chapters did nothing to alleviate the problems. Beset by financial difficulties, the SHS declined for the next fifteen years. It became increasingly difficult to recruit leaders for the organization. Early despaired at its decreased importance. "The work of the Society has been very much neglected," he lamented.[44]

The emergence of another veterans association, the Robert E. Lee Camp, in Richmond in the early 1880s, challenged the domination of the AANVA and at least indirectly lessened the influence of Early and his Virginia cohorts. The Lee Camp embraced sectional reconciliation and wanted to avoid the animosities of the war. Further, this organization cooperated directly with Grand Army of the Republic groups in the North and even appealed to them and other Northerners for financial contributions toward construction of a veterans' home. Early, of course, fulminated at the very idea of using Yankee dollars for a Confederate home.[45]

But at this point, what Early thought meant little. Although he would not die until early March 1894, he had become an anachronism long before then. The kind of anger and bitterness that stoked diehard Confederates such as Jubal Early and others like him could hardly be sustained over time, so even before the passing of the Confederate generation, their rendition of the war that had forever seared their souls, its origins and purposes, its heroes and villains, the Lost Cause that they articulated and espoused, was fading away.[46]

Historians have documented how the Lost Cause myth, transformed and reshaped, survived into the twentieth century. Those of the more literary frame of mind have proven the most inventive in teasing vestiges of the Lost Cause out of elements as diverse as the Southern good ol' boy, country music, Elvis Presley, evangelical Christianity, the Southern Agrarians, George Wallace, *Gone with the Wind,* and William Faulkner. Other writers, who terminated their studies of the transformation of the Lost Cause phenomenon nearer to the close of the nineteenth century, connect more securely with Early and the other Southern diehards, showing how what Gaines Foster calls the "Confederate celebration" grew out of the Lost Cause while shaping its tenets to fit the growing New South.[47]

Gary W. Gallagher is the most cogent proponent for the view that major elements of the Lost Cause myth have survived to the present, specifically the ideas of Jubal Early, which, he writes, have had "long term impact on the ways which Americans have understood the Civil War." He points out the overwhelming popularity of Robert E. Lee—on a par with that of Lincoln—the seminal impact of Douglas Southall Freeman's multivolume studies of Lee and the Army of Northern Virginia, and the hostility that greeted revisionist studies of Lee. He cites recent pro-Lee books that echo Early's arguments, as well as the widespread availability of reprinted works that do the same—books by Clifford Dowdey, for example, and a goodly number of titles for young people, such as Hodding Carter's *Robert E. Lee and the Road of Honor*. He notes the preponderance of pro-Lee sentiment in writings by British historians, as well as the triumph of Lee over Grant in the fiction and art of the late twentieth century.[48]

It's difficult to argue with any of these facts. Undoubtedly, many history books and articles echo ideas Old Jube and his allies propagated. Mass-market media, movies such as *Gone with the Wind*, and popular art has done the same thing. Gallagher has shown that many printed sources, especially history books, perpetuate Early's adoration of Robert E. Lee and the hyper-glorification of his military achievements. But does this demonstrate the current survival of the Lost Cause myth? Or does it prove its survival only in the pages of books read by relatively few people beyond historians and other small, specialized groups which have no discernable effect on American society?

Indeed, in this postmodern society, increasingly characterized by frenetic fragmentation and dispersal of information into numerous media channels, especially cyberspace, does the Lost Cause myth have salience in the South, much less the rest of the country? Conversely, does the concept resonate in a twenty-first-century South homogenized like all other parts of the country by transnational communications, corporations, and mass media? In a Sunbelt South flooded by immigrants from the North and Latin America? Further, the ignorance and indifference of American people to their history, a well-documented and growing phenomenon, argues not only against the mass of the people knowing anything about the Civil War, much less caring about the Lost Cause.[49]

Most important, at this time, some 135 years beyond the period of Jubal Early at the height of his influence and almost 50 years from the culmination of the civil rights struggle, a substantial segment of the American population, which may or may not know anything about Civil War history, is actively hostile to symbols of the Confederacy such as the battle flag and state flags that incorporate it, the song "Dixie," and other reminders that something called the Confederate States of America ever existed. Confederate symbols have become inextricably linked in the minds of many with the defense of slavery, resistance to the extension of civil rights, and the KKK and other white supremacist organizations that adopted the battle flag as their own symbol of defiance. Consequently, there's been an unrelenting and largely successful campaign to erase any public reminders of these things. When tennis champion Arthur Ashe occupies a place of honor with Jefferson Davis, Lee, Stonewall Jackson, and J. E. B. Stuart on Monument Avenue in the capital of the old Confederacy, when the Ole Miss Rebels become the Black Bears—these are incontrovertible signs that the Lost Cause has basically faded away.[50]

But not completely. It's still cherished by small cadre of modern-day diehards, the dedicated neo-Confederate contingent which understands the Civil War, its origins and outcomes, pretty much the same way Jubal Early did. The grizzled old Rebel would be right at home in their company—and just as irrelevant.[51]

Notes

I am grateful to my friend John Mooney of the University of Oklahoma Department of History for his several cogent readings of this essay and for his excellent insights and suggestions.

1. Thomas L. Connelly, *The Marble Man: Robert E. Lee and His Image in American Society* (Baton Rouge, 1977), 52; Gaines M. Foster, *Ghosts of the Confederacy: Defeat, the Lost Cause, and the Emergence of the New South* (New York, 1987), 55; G. Moxley Sorrel, *Recollections of a Confederate Staff Officer* (New York, 1905), 56; William M. Thornton, "John Warwick Daniel," *Southern Historical Society Papers* 51 (1916): 94 (hereafter cited as *SHSP*); John Brown Gordon, *Reminiscences of the Civil War* (New York,1903), 318; Charles C. Osborne, *Jubal: The Life and Times of General Jubal A. Early, CSA, Defender of the Lost Cause* (Baton Rouge, 1992), 469. The "snarling and stooped" old man terrified young Douglas Southall Freeman, Robert E. Lee's famous biographer, who grew up a few doors down from him in Lynchburg, Virginia. See David Johnson, "Douglas Southall Freeman (1886–1953)," *Encyclopedia Virginia,* http://www.EncyclopediaVirginia.org/Freeman_Douglas_Southall_1886–1953/ (accessed Sept. 20, 2010).
2. [Anonymous], "Recollections of Jubal Early by One Who Followed Him," *Century Magazine* 70 (May 1905): 311; Martin F. Schmitt, "An Interview with General Jubal A. Early in 1889," *Journal of Southern History* 115 (1945): 50; Osborne, *Jubal,* 31–32.
3. Gordon, *Reminiscences of the Civil War,* 317; Gary W. Gallagher, introduction to Jubal Early, *A Memoir of the Last Year of the War of Independence in the*

Confederate States of America, by (Columbia, SC, 2001), x; Sorrel, *Recollections,* 55–56; John W. Daniel, "Memorial Address by Hon. John W. Daniel, before the Association of the Army of Northern Virginia, at the Annual Meeting held at Richmond, Va., December 13, 1894," *SHSP* 22 (1894): 327, 329; William Conway, "Talks with General Early," *SHSP* 30 (1902): 251. For instances of Early's wit, see Millard K. Bushong, *Old Jube: A Biography of General Jubal A. Early* (Shippensburg PA, 1955), 304; and Schmitt, "Interview with General Jubal A. Early," 56.

4. Osborne, *Jubal,* 475.

5. The above paragraphs are based upon Bushong, *Old Jube,* 1–25, and Osborne, *Jubal,* 3–33; Gary W. Gallagher, "From Antebellum Unionist to Lost Cause Warrior: The Personal Journey of Jubal A. Early," in *New Perspectives on the Civil War: Myths and Realities of the National Conflict,* ed. John Y. Simon and Michael E. Stevens (Lanham, MD, 1998), 103.

6. Osborne, *Jubal,* 34–52, passim; Ruth Hairston Early, *Lieutenant General Jubal A. Early: Autobiographical Sketch and Narrative of the War Between the States* (Philadelphia, PA, 1912), vii.

7. Gallagher, "Personal Journey of Jubal Early," 105.

8. Osborne, *Jubal,* 55–398, passim; Bushong, *Old Jube,* 38–282, passim. For a short account of Early's Civil War career, see Thomas E. Schott, "Early, Jubal Anderson," in *Dictionary of American Military History,* ed. Roger J. Spiller, 3 vols. (Westport, CT, 1984), 1:295–98.

9. Jubal A. Early to T. L. Rosser, May 10, 1866, in William D. Hoyt, "New Light on General Jubal A. Early after Appomattox," *Journal of Southern History* 9 (1943): 115–16.

10. Osborne, *Jubal,* 403; Jubal A. Early to Editor of *New York News,* Dec. 18, 1865, *SHSP* 24 (1894): 176, 182; Hoyt, "New Light on General," 115. The bulk of Early's letter to the *News* disputed in minute detail Secretary of War Edwin M. Stanton's report of the Valley Campaign, especially the disparity in numbers between the two sides. This kind of microscopic poring over numbers also became characteristic of Early's writing about the war.

11. Robert E. Lee to Jubal A. Early, Nov. 22, 1865, in Early, *Autobiographical Sketch,* 473.

12. Gary W. Gallagher, "Jubal Early, the Lost Cause, and Civil War History: A Persistent Legacy," in *The Myth of the Lost Cause and Civil War History,* ed. Gary W. Gallagher and Alan T. Nolan (Bloomington, IN, 2000), 37–38; Jubal A. Early, *A Memoir of the Last Year of the War of Independence in the Confederate States of America* (New Orleans, LA, 1867), xiii; Osborne, *Jubal,* 440.

13. Osborne, *Jubal,* 405, 407; Foster, *Ghosts of the Confederacy,* 37.

14. Bushong, *Old Jube,* 289, 290, 293; Gallagher, "Jubal Early, the Lost Cause, and Civil War History," 37.

15. Osborne, *Jubal,* 412–13; Bushong, *Old Jube,* 491.

16. Bushong, *Old Jube,* 293; Osborne, *Jubal,* 420–28. On the Louisiana State Lottery, see T. Harry Williams, *P. G. T. Beauregard: Napoleon in Gray* (Baton Rouge, 1955), 291–303.

17. Osborne, *Jubal,* 405–14. The so-called Underwood constitution "called for ratification of the 14th and 15th Amendments, making blacks citizens with full civil rights . . . enfranchised all adult males, established free public schools, and called for increased taxes on landed property" (408).

18. Gary G. Gallagher, *Jubal Early, the Lost Cause, and Civil War History: A Persistent Legacy* (Detroit, MI, 1995), 7–8. A public feud between Mahone and Early entertained Virginians for years. See Osborne, *Jubal,* 462–67.

19. Early, *Memoir of the Last Year,* ix.

20. David W. Blight, *Race and Reunion: The Civil War in American Memory* (Cambridge, MA, 2001), 81, 83. Early's overt racism could be extremely ugly. Just one example of many: Referring to a speech the general delivered in Lynchburg in August 1881, a reporter opined, "His address . . . was so undignified and insulting that it is hard to see how a man who was half sober at least could have made it. Snuffing his nose about the stage he said, 'I hope some one [*sic*] has fumigated this place since that nigger convention was held here.' [What] he referred to was the Republican State Convention which met in this building last Wednesday." *New York Times,* Aug. 22, 1881.

21. Early, *Memoir of the Last Year,* vi, ix.

22. William C. Davis, "Myths and Realities of the Confederacy," chap. 11, *The Cause Lost: Myths and Realities of the Confederacy* (Lawrence, KS, 1996), 175.

23. Jeffrey D. Wert, "James Longstreet and the Lost Cause," in *The Myth of the Lost Cause and Civil War History,* ed. Gary W. Gallagher and Alan T. Nolan (Bloomington, IN, 2000), 133; Alan T. Nolan, "The Anatomy of the Myth," in Gallagher and Nolan, *The Myth of the Lost Cause,* 12.

24. Among the more prominent volumes that deal heavily with aspects of the Lost Cause are Rolin G. Osterweis, *The Myth of the Lost Cause, 1865–1900* (Hamden, CT, 1973); Foster, *Ghosts of the Confederacy;* Charles Reagan Wilson, *Baptized in Blood: The Religion of the Lost Cause, 1865–1920* (1980; with new preface, Athens, GA, 2009); Alan T. Nolan, *Lee Considered: General Robert E. Lee and Civil War History* (Chapel Hill, 1991); William Garrett Piston, *Lee's Tarnished Lieutenant: James Longstreet and His Place in Southern History* (Athens, GA,

1987); Gary W. Gallagher, *Lee and His Army in Confederate History* (Chapel Hill, 2001); Gary W. Gallagher, *Lee and His Generals in War and Memory* (Baton Rouge, 1998); Caroline E. Janney, *Burying the Dead but Not the Past :Ladies Memorial Associations and the Lost Cause* (Chapel Hill, 2008); Connelly, *Marble Man;* Thomas L Connelly and Barbara L. Bellows, *God and General Longstreet: The Lost Cause and the Southern Mind* (Baton Rouge, 1982); plus Gallagher and Nolan, *Myth of the Lost Cause;* and Blight, *Race and Reunion.*

25. Blight, *Race and Reunion,* 452n7.

26. Gallagher, *Lee and His Army,* 259; Gallagher, *Jubal Early, the Lost Cause, and Civil War History,* 6; Connelly, *Marble Man,* 51.

27. Early, *Memoir of the Last Year,* xvii; Gallagher, *Lee and His Army,* 261.

28. Osborne, *Jubal,* 430; Gallagher and Nolan, *Myth of the Lost Cause,* 13. General Clement A. Evans of Georgia, who served in Gordon's division, survived five wounds during the war and went on to write and edit the twelve-volume *Confederate Military History* series as well as coedit a three-volume history of Georgia. See Thomas Spaulding, "Clement A. Evans," in *Dictionary of American Biography,* ed. Allen Johnson and Dumas Malone (New York, 1931), 6:196–97.

29. Early, *Memoir of the Last Year,* xvi.

30. Connelly and Bellows, *God and General Longstreet,* 21–27; Gallagher, *Jubal Early, the Lost Cause, and Civil War History,* 5.

31. Osborne, *Jubal,* 430–31; Wilson, *Baptized in Blood,* 58–78.

32. Osborne, *Jubal,* 429; Foster, *Ghosts of the Confederacy,* 60.

33. Connelly and Bellows, *God and General Longstreet,* 42; Connelly, *Marble Man,* 42–47; Janney, *Burying the Dead,* 3–4; Osborne, *Jubal,* 447–52; Bushong, *Old Jube,* 298–99. Among the Virginia leaders of the Lost Cause besides Early are Generals Bradley T. Johnson, a transplanted Marylander; Fitzhugh Lee, Robert E. Lee's nephew and a future governor; Dabney H. Maury, the originator of the SHS; and William N. Pendleton. Also Colonel William Preston Johnston, son of General Albert Sidney Johnston, and J. William Jones, a Lexington minister and former chaplain of the Army of Northern Virginia.

34. Osborne, *Jubal,* 231, 438–39, 451–52; Foster, *Ghosts of the Confederacy,* 53; Connelly, *Marble Man,* 43–45. The day after the formation of the Lee Monument Association in Richmond on November 3, 1870, a second gathering of Confederate veterans there, including many of the same people, established the Association of the Army of Northern Virginia, again electing Early as president. The AANVA would remain the foremost organization for these men until formation of the United Confederate Veterans in 1889. On the prominence of Virginians in the Lost Cause movement, see Foster, *Ghosts of the Confederacy,* 55–56, 60–61.

35. Connelly, *Marble Man,* 55–56; [Jubal A. Early], *The Campaigns of Robert E. Lee. An Address by Lt. Gen. Jubal A. Early before Washington and Lee University, January 19th, 1872* (Baltimore, MD, 1872), 33–34.

36. [Early], *Campaigns of Robert E. Lee,* 45, 46, 47–49, 50.

37. Ibid., 53; Osborne, *Jubal,* 454; Connelly and Bellows, *God and General Longstreet,* 37. On Longstreet's controversial postwar career and Jubal Early's skillful prosecution of him, see Piston, *Lee's Tarnished Lieutenant,* 95–136.

38. Osborne, *Jubal,* 433–34; Foster, *Ghosts of the Confederacy,* 50–51, 54; Piston, *Lee's Tarnished Lieutenant,* 131. See also account of SHS founding in New Orleans in "The Southern Historical Society," *SHSP* 1 (1876): 40–43.

39. Gallagher, *Jubal Early, the Lost Cause, and Civil War History,* 23; Osborne, *Jubal,* 439.

40. Blight, *Race and Reunion,* 259; Alan T. Nolan, "Robert E. Lee and July 1 at Gettysburg," in *The First Day at Gettysburg: Essays on Confederate and Union Leadership,* ed. Gary W. Gallagher (Kent, OH, 1992), 25.

41. Piston, *Lee's Tarnished Lieutenant,* 135; Blight, *Race and Reunion,* 258.

42. Edith Hamilton, *Mythology* (Boston, 1942); Joseph Campbell, *The Masks of God,* 4 vols. (New York, 1955–68); Thomas Bulfinch, *The Age of Fable or Beauties of Mythology* (Boston, 1855).

43. Blight, *Race and Reunion,* 264.

44. Foster, *Ghosts of the Confederacy,* 91–92.

45. Ibid., 93–94.

46. Connelly and Bellows, *God and General Longstreet,* 85.

47. Ibid., 142–48; Osterweis, *Myth of the Lost Cause,* 145–48; Blight, *Race and Reunion,* 264–99; Foster, *Ghosts of the Confederacy,* 115–59, 194–98. On the historical distortions in the two most prominent and influential films about the Civil War, *The Birth of a Nation* and *Gone with the Wind,* see Bruce Chadwick, *The Reel Civil War: Mythmaking in American Film* (New York, 2001), 96–150, 183–211.

48. Gallagher, "Jubal A. Early, the Lost Cause, and Civil War History," 35–59. In a later article, Gallagher laments the influence of several of Early's Lost Cause ideas in documentary filmmaker Ken Burns's widely popular TV series *The Civil War.* See Gary W. Gallagher, "How Familiarity Bred Success: Military Campaigns and Leaders in Ken Burns's *The Civil War,*" in Gallagher, *Lee and His Generals,* 249, 251.

49. On the homogenization of American culture, see Katharine Washburn and John Thornton, eds., *Dumbing Down: Essays on the Strip Mining of American Culture,* (New York, 1996); Sam Dillon, "History Survey Stumps U.S. Teens,"

New York Times, Feb. 26, 2008, http://www.nytimes.com/2008/02/26/education/27history.html; George Archibald, "Ignorance of American History Called Threat to Security," *Washington Times,* Apr. 11, 2003, http://www.informationclearinghouse.info/article2862.htm; Andrew Romano, "How Dumb Are We?" *Newsweek,* Mar. 20, 2011, http://www.newsweek.com/2011/03/20/how-dumb-are-we.html (all websites accessed July 4, 2011).

50. "Arthur Ashe—A Monumental Man?" American Studies at the University of Virginia website, http://xroads.virginia.edu/~UG97/monument/ashe.html/ (accessed Oct. 25, 2010); UPI.com, "Black Bear Becomes Ole Miss Mascot," http://www.upi.com/Sports_News/2010/10/14/Black-bear-becomes-Ole-Miss-mascot/UPI-37641287084775/ (accessed Oct 14, 2010).

51. Tony Horowitz, *Confederates in the Attic: Dispatches from the Unfinished Civil War* (New York, 1998), passim.

John Brown Gordon after the Civil War. Library of Congress.

John B. Gordon and the "Gospel of Reconciliation"

Ralph L. Eckert

John B. Gordon of Georgia became one of the most popular and important Southerners in the decades following the American Civil War. The reputation he earned while "wearing the gray" not only endeared him to former Confederates and eventually won him the respect of his opponents in blue but also influenced almost every aspect of his life over the next forty years. Although only twenty-eight years old at the war's outset and lacking any formal military training, Gordon nevertheless proved himself a natural soldier on all of his battlefields. The courage, instincts, and audaciously offensive spirit he displayed in the Eastern Theater made him a superb combat officer. Gordon's speeches before battle, his martial bearing, and his coolness under fire inspired men and allowed him to draw greatness from them. His spectacular rise from untrained captain to trusted corps commander was unmatched in the Army of Northern Virginia, an army overwhelmingly commanded by professionals. As a contemporary proclaimed shortly after Gordon's death, his fame and military record rest "upon his natural, untrained, military genius, supported by courage to which fear was a stranger."[1] Few, if any, soldiers emerged from the war with a record more stunning than Gordon's, and he ranked probably second only to Robert E. Lee in the adoration of his countrymen.

Although Gordon's military participation in the Confederacy's attempt to tear asunder the United States served as the central event in his life, ironically it would be his steadfast commitment to healing the emotional wounds of the Civil War, during the last third of the nineteenth century, that provided his most significant and enduring contribution to American history. Make no mistake, he promoted Southern interests and fiercely defended his section and its residents whenever he sensed a threat or an insult, but Gordon also devoted much of the postbellum period to national pacification and forging a new sense of nationalism that almost all Americans could champion. He sought to supplant still-festering sectional antagonisms and replace them with a shared devotion to building a stronger, more united nation which would cement fraternal bonds between the former warring sections. Gordon demonstrated his commitment to national reconciliation throughout the forty years following the war, but it was during the last decade of his life that his efforts were most spectacular. Indeed, in the late 1800s and early 1900s, Gordon became the most prominent, the most outspoken, and the most widely traveled proponent of national reconciliation. He employed several different means to reach the American people, yet he always brought the same message when he enthusiastically preached his "Gospel of Reconciliation."[2]

Gordon seemingly began his propitiatory efforts almost immediately after he led the surrender procession of Lee's army at Appomattox Court House on April 12, 1865. Following the furling of Confederate flags and the stacking of arms, he spoke poignantly to his defeated and dispirited troops of their bravery and heroic service to the Southern cause. Perhaps more important, he offered words of "hope and encouragement" in the face of "the countless and stupendous barriers across the paths they were to tread."[3] He urged them to return home, to obey the laws, to help rebuild the South, and to give "the same loyal support to the general Government [the reunited United States] which they had yielded to the Confederacy."[4] So began John B. Gordon's nearly four decade commitment to reuniting the former foes of the Civil War.

Despite Gordon's acceptance of defeat almost from the moment of his surrender, and his realization that the Southern way of life would be inevitably altered, he dedicated himself to vigilantly protecting Southern interests and vigorously defending Southerners' motives and actions in fighting the Civil War. As the future would manifestly demonstrate, whether in the business, political, social, cultural, or historical arenas, Gordon would proudly act as a Southerner. He "never allowed an opportunity to pass," stressed a close friend, "in which he might reiterate his belief that the South was right in its position. [Yet at] the same time, he urged the people to cherish no malice or bitterness, but to accept without a word the true arbitrament of arms and proceed with all diligence to the upbringing of their depleted fortunes and to the prospering of their own section."[5] However—unlike many unrepentant, hard-line former Confederates who refused ready association with Northerners—Gordon would also move forward as an American, working to bring together all of his countrymen.

Thrust into prominence by his military service, Gordon assumed a myriad of responsibilities that befell him after the war. He wedded the necessity of earning a livelihood with a commitment to helping the defeated South recover from the devastation of the war. In the immediate postwar period, he frequently worked with Northern businessmen and capitalists in a variety of economic forays, including sawmills and timber-related enterprises, plus insurance and publishing ventures. In the insurance field, he sought to slow the flow of capital out of the South, believing that the more money that remained at home, the more that would be available for developing Southern business and industry. Similarly, he worked to provide Southern children with a series of school books that the publishers claimed were "divested of the injurious reflections upon the Southern people and Southern history, which were usually found in Northern elementary works."[6] Gordon, by supplying an alternative to textbooks which maligned Southerners' role in American history, wanted to preserve the South's heritage and justify the oft-disparaged motives which prompted Southerners to go to war in 1861. This maintenance of Southern pride and honor was a critical part of his vision of the future wherein Southerners could endorse and embrace a new, broader postwar nationalism.

Beyond his energetic promotion of Southern business and educational interests, the Georgian lent his support to efforts by Southern whites to maintain their social order. Specifically, when whites in the South felt threatened by the Republican-led movement to provide blacks with all forms of equality, Gordon endorsed restrictions of the freedmen in order to preserve white-dominated society. Although his precise involvement with the Ku Klux Klan remains shrouded in the veil of secrecy surrounding this often terroristic organization, he was recognized as at least titular head of the Klan in Georgia. He may not have condoned many of the violent excesses by the society's members, but he did not question them when the South's white-controlled social order was in jeopardy. In the nineteenth-century South, white supremacy was to remain inviolate.

Given the respect accorded Gordon in Georgia and the turbulence of Reconstruction, it was natural that he gravitated to politics. In 1873, he won his first triumph on the political field of battle when he was selected as one of the state's U.S. senators. Gordon ably and eloquently defended the honor and integrity of Southern whites on the national stage when they were often assailed by Radical Republicans in Congress. However, he stubbornly refused to be drawn into bitter, heated partisan debates with the Radicals; rather, when he responded with passion, he did so in a relatively moderate manner, without resorting to all of the vindictiveness and acerbity which characterized much of the political discourse of the decade. As a result of his moderation and rhetorical skill, Gordon was soon recognized as a premier Southern spokesman and became a favorite of Northern Democrats. To this end, he undertook frequent, often lengthy speaking tours in and through Northern states on behalf of Democratic causes in the 1870s as well as in the two decades that followed. Therefore, long before Gordon had fully developed and finely honed his Gospel of Reconciliation, his name and reputation were well known and widely respected by many Northerners.

As a senator, Gordon labored doggedly to remove Federal military troops from the South and to restore home rule there. Clearly he wanted to end Reconstruction and formally reunite the former enemies, but in this case, it most assuredly had to be accomplished on terms favorable to white Southerners. His devotion to the task at hand was amply demonstrated by his intimate involvement in the secret negotiations with close advisors of Rutherford B. Hayes following the disputed presidential election of 1876. Gordon played an important part in the informal, behind-the-scenes talks which resulted in the Compromise of 1877 and the subsequent withdrawal of military forces and the support for the last Republican governments in South Carolina and Louisiana. He regarded his role in the Compromise as one of his proudest accomplishments because, in part, he was convinced that meaningful national reconciliation could be achieved only with restoration of home rule throughout the entire South. In little more than a decade after the Civil War, Gordon had become a Southern man with whom Northerners—Democrats and Republicans—could confidently deal. In 1880, however, citing financial embarrassment, Gordon to almost everyone's surprise resigned his Senate seat to enter the wild business world of the New South.

The first half of the 1880s resembled a roller-coaster ride of frenetic entrepreneurial activity on Gordon's part. "In the business world," observed a friend, "his mind ran on large schemes," and while often "on the verge of making a great fortune," Gordon would die "leaving only a modest sum."[7] His most spectacular success involved his establishment of the Georgia Pacific Railroad, which quickly netted him a fortune when he sold it to a large railroading syndicate. He also invested in a myriad of other businesses, but what he hoped would be his crowning economic glory revolved around the ill-fated International Railroad and Steamship Company of Florida. This grandiose vision entailed not only building a railroad all the way through Florida down to Key West but also creating steamship and telegraphic lines throughout the Caribbean which would effectively link the Sunshine State with Central and South America. Despite Gordon's almost total commitment to this project, his dreams failed to materialize and he soon lost almost all his money in the process. Having been financially bloodied and virtually bankrupted in the whirl of New South economics, Gordon in 1886 moved into the calmer, more familiar waters of Georgia politics. He served two rather nondescript terms as the state's governor before returning to the U.S. Senate in 1890.

Rather than being a major player on the national political scene in the last decade of the nineteenth century, Gordon assumed a role for which he was especially qualified, both by temperament and desire. He would focus his energies on closing the as-yet-unhealed emotional wounds of the American Civil War. In particular, he endeavored to create a common vantage point from which Northerners and Southerners alike could view the Civil War and take pride in their participation while yet recognizing the sincerity of their opponents' motivations. As noted earlier, Gordon had lent his efforts throughout the postwar period to helping the North and the South reunite, but beginning in 1893, he elevated his cause to a much higher level when he took his show on the road.

In part out of economic necessity, Gordon at some point in the early 1890s decided to develop a public lecture based upon his experiences in the Civil War. He titled his speech the "Last Days of the Confederacy" and debuted it in New York City in November 1893. Gordon did not concentrate on battles or political controversies; rather, he spoke "of those less grave but scarcely less important phases or incidents of the war which illustrate the spirit and character of the American soldier and people."[8] Although he naturally spoke from a Southern perspective, Gordon presented a talk devoid of sectional bias, as he professed to be "as true as any man to this Republic's flag and to all that it truly represents."[9] A St. Louis reporter later characterized Gordon's highly entertaining lecture as focused on the "heroic bravery of Union soldiers, the undaunted courage of the Southern men, the self-sacrifice of noble Southern women, the patriotism of Northern womanhood, interspersed with lively anecdotes and abundant incidents illustrating the grim humor of the camp and the deep pathos and the suffering on the field and in the home as phases of the great civil war."[10] Gordon presented a romanticized portrait of the war in which soldiers both North and South were brave, honorable, and patriotic and each side was right in the cause for which it fought. "Every element of Gordon's lecture," wrote rhetorician Howard Dorgan," was designed to make audiences feel good about themselves, about their respective section, and about the nation as a whole."[11]

Gordon spent much of the last decade of his life delivering this lecture before hundreds of generally sold-out audiences as he engaged in long, exhausting national tours organized by professional booking agencies. The core of this two- to two-and-a-half- hour presentation remained basically the same, but Gordon constantly tailored his talk to the specific locales in which he spoke. His aptitude for ad-libbing, his forte at striking resonant connections with the particular audiences, and his constant polishing of the lecture resulted in slightly different talks each night and helped make him "one of the greatest attractions on the lecture list of the country."[12] He would in the late 1890s develop a second, companion lecture, "First Days of the Confederacy," but it was his emotional treatment of the final stages of the war and the death of the Southern bid for independence that was styled "a masterpiece," "a gem of oratory" which captivated listeners all over the country.[13]

Newspaper reviews unstintingly paid tribute to both Gordon's presentation and to his message. His intrepid, chivalrous, soldierly bearing, "his fine presence on the platform," his stentorian voice, and his "magnetic eloquence" rarely escaped mention.[14] A Minneapolis listener felt that "there was something so much deeper in the man than even in what he uttered that his very presence lent a solemn and sacred grandeur to the occasion."[15] Three New Orleans newspapers marveled at Gordon's "spell of hypnotism," his "mastery over the human heart," and his ability to cast "a spell [over his listeners] which enchanted and enchained them through every word of his resounding eloquence."[16] Northerners and Southerners alike attributed Gordon's talent at mesmerism to his skill at eloquently mingling humor, pathos, and patriotism, which allowed him to move his listeners from laughter, to tears, to spontaneous outbursts of wild enthusiasm and back again. Still, it was the message that Gordon brought with him each night that warmed even the coldest hearts in his audiences. So successful was Gordon at avoiding sectional animus that reporters called his lecture "a mission . . . of peace," "a matchless sermon from the gospel of peace," and "a superb outburst of patriotism" in which "every syllable was emotional, each shade of accent an inspiration to higher patriotism."[17] A Missourian found that "every sentence of his lecture was wreathed in an olive branch of peace. His every thought was sweetly tempered with magnanimity."[18] And after attending the lecture in Kansas City, another reviewer proclaimed, "General Gordon is performing a patriotic service. He is keeping green the memories of the war and its heroes on both sides, but he is obliterating the asperities of the strife."[19] Even though numerous Northern newspapers praised the general for the nonpartisan, nationalistic, patriotic tone of his speech, it was a Georgia editorial that best expressed most Americans' opinion of Gordon's efforts: "General Gordon can not in the halls of Congress [during his 1890s service in the Senate] do his country more valuable service, than he is doing, in instilling into the hearts of thousands of people, North and South, a higher appreciation of the gallant men who fought under Grant and Lee; a deeper veneration for American valor and unswerving fidelity, and a warmer love and a loftier pride in this great and reunited country."[20]

Perhaps the most dramatic episode illustrating Gordon's success in dowsing the smoldering embers of sectional hatred came in Vermont after one of his lectures. An elderly man who had lost his son in the Civil War fighting for the North came face to face with the Southerner. The tearful Yankee announced, "General Gordon, I have hated you for more than thirty years; I have hated everything South. . . . [But] when I had listened to you and heard you tell the history of your hardships, how the [Southern] soldier marched barefooted, how he lived without a bite some days, how he suffered, I can see that he was fighting for the cause which he esteemed more dear than life."[21] Whereupon the previously embittered and still bereaved father offered an extended hand to Gordon and ardently announced, "I will never hate you anymore. . . . My hatred for the South is gone forever."[22] This encounter provides poignant evidence of Gordon's ability to help assuage even the deepest of sorrows; his lecture acted as "a healing balm for sectional ill will."[23] As a result of his tireless touring and presentation of "Last Days of the Confederacy," John B. Gordon became one of the most effective and widely admired proponents of national reconciliation.

Even before Gordon began crisscrossing the country on his lecture tours after 1893, he was already working in other forums to mend the still-rankling wounds carrying over from the war three decades earlier. In addition to his longtime role as the most prominent dedicator of monuments to Confederate civilian and military leaders, Gordon participated alongside former Union soldiers in the dedications of numerous national military parks. He frequently attended the funerals of Northern generals and had earlier delivered a stirring eulogy for Ulysses Grant when his old adversary died in 1885. He spearheaded or lent his support to movements to aid—medically and financially—not only disabled veterans in both sections but also their widows and orphans. In so many ways, Gordon drew upon his business, political, and personal associations with Northerners as he worked to directly connect Union and Confederate veterans. However, it was his leadership of the most prominent Confederate veterans' organization that afforded him his best opportunity to at once defend their wartime actions and push forward his mission of completely reconciling the North and the South.

When Confederate veterans met in New Orleans in 1889 and organized the United Confederate Veterans (UCV), they overwhelmingly selected Major General John B. Gordon as their commander in chief. He took immense pride in once again leading the now-aged soldiers of the South and became more than the symbolic head of the organization by playing an active role in its supervision. Gordon would remain as the UCV's leader until his death a decade and a half later. At numerous annual reunions—recognized by Gaines Foster as the "central ritual of the Confederate celebration"—Gordon would proffer his resignation in order to permit another veteran the high honor of leading the UCV; however, his efforts would invariably set off wild, almost uncontrollable displays of affection and protest by the rank and file, who would not even consider his offer.[24] As the "primary ceremonial figure in the Confederate celebration," Gordon, if not in fact even earlier, became the most widely recognized "living symbol of the Confederacy" and the veritable "embodiment of the Lost Cause."[25] And as head of the UCV, he endorsed and participated in many of the joint blue-gray reunions which were organized in the latter years of the nineteenth century.

Gordon saw these joint meetings as doing more than bringing soldiers of the North and the South together; they were another useful means to reunify the two sections. At a UCV convention shortly after the United States went to war with Spain in 1898, Gordon predicted that the current war would completely and forever obliterate the sectional antagonisms still lingering. His prediction proved a bit premature, as a July 1900 blue-gray reunion in Atlanta demonstrated. Gordon as the UCV's leader and his Northern counterpart with the Grand Army of the Republic, Albert D. Shaw, attended and spoke at the meeting. Following Gordon's speech, Shaw delivered what Gordon called an "eloquent tribute to American manhood . . . [and] our fathers' flag."[26] Overall, it was a patriotic, conciliatory address until its very end, when Shaw urged Southerners to stop teaching their children that their reasons for going to war were just and right. He labeled such teachings as "all out of order, unwise, unjust, and utterly opposed to the bond" established at the war's end by Robert E. Lee.[27] Gordon, immediately sensing the incendiary impact Shaw's closing remarks might have on former Confederate attendees, and no doubt apprehending a direct threat to his thoroughgoing commitment to defending Southerners' motives for fighting, leaped to his feet to protest. Although he concurred "with almost every word and sentiment" in Shaw's speech, Gordon calmly but earnestly challenged the Northerner's last suggestion.[28] With flashing eyes and tensely compressed lips, Gordon asserted he could not ever teach Southern children that the cause for which he fought was wrong. Instead, he encouraged all of the war's participants to cherish their memories because "history will yet record and heaven reveal . . . that both sides were right because both were fighting for the constitution of the fathers as they had been taught to interpret it."[29] Then, to Shaw's credit, either recognizing how his words may have been misinterpreted or seeing the deleterious effect they were having on the assemblage, he immediately responded and attempted to clarify his comments. He heartily endorsed what Gordon had just said and claimed that had he been a Confederate soldier and faced demands that he repudiate his cause as unjust or wrong, he would have responded even more forcefully than Gordon had. With that, "Shaw undid much of the impression made by his first speech"; the two leaders enthusiastically shook hands, "harmony reigned once more," and this potentially disruptive incident was diffused.[30]

Still, this episode provided fuel for a number of former Confederates who were not nearly as ready to embrace their wartime foes as were Gordon and the majority of Southern soldiers. Irreconcilables' criticism of Gordon for misusing his position as head of the UCV in such joint reunions revealed that emotions remained very raw for some Southerners. Gordon answered both their attacks upon him personally and upon his reconciliatory efforts in an open letter (meant for national publication) in the *New York Times* the month after the Atlanta reunion. Beyond refusing to apologize for his reconciliatory actions, Gordon forcefully asserted that he would "continue the efforts which I have made for thirty years in the interest of sectional harmony and unity."[31] He insisted on resolutely doing everything possible "for the truth of history, for justice to the South, and to all sections for fostering our cherished memories and for the obliteration of all sectional bitterness and for the settlement of all sectional controversies on a basis consistent with the honor and the manhood and the self-respect of all."[32] Gordon once again expressed his unshakeable commitment to national reconciliation while also ensuring that Southerners' reasons for going to war not be denigrated.

Even as he struggled in the late nineteenth and early twentieth century to extinguish sectional brushfires like these, Gordon was at work on his final, most complete contribution to burying forever the divisive passions of the Civil War. He had begun negotiations with the publishing house of Charles Scribner's Sons in the mid-1890s over his reminiscences of the Civil War. Given the phenomenal popularity of "Last Days of the Confederacy" and claiming that friends had been urging him to pen such a book for years, he began to write. He enunciated his vision and purpose in the book's introduction. Rather than "attempt a comprehensive description of that great struggle . . . [or] an elaborate analysis of the momentous interests and issues involved," he proposed "to make a brief but dispassionate and judicially fair analysis of the divergent opinions and ceaseless controversies" which eventually plunged the nation into civil war.[33] More pointedly, as in his famous public lecture, he would focus primarily on "the distinguished magnanimity and lofty manhood of the American soldier"—the men who fought on both sides, as he endeavored to preserve "a unique and hitherto unwritten phase of the war, the story of which should not be lost."[34] In the process, he hoped that his account would "lift to a higher plane the estimate placed by victors and vanquished upon their countrymen of the opposing section, and thus strengthen the sentiment of intersectional fraternity which is essential to complete national unity."[35] In other words, he would do what he had so often done before in different ways and in different arenas, to preach the Gospel of Reconciliation.

He acknowledged slavery as "undoubtedly the immediate fomenting cause of the woful [*sic*] American conflict" and stated "it is fair to say that had there been no slavery there would have been no war."[36] However, reflecting one of the central themes of the Lost Cause mythology, he immediately clarified his point that "slavery was far from being the sole cause of the prolonged conflict" because "neither its destruction on the one hand, nor its defense on the other, was the energizing force that held the contending armies to four years of bloody work."[37] Looking beyond slavery as the principal cause, Gordon maintained that conflicting constitutional interpretations over the relative powers of the state and national governments lay at the heart of sectional difficulties. In his opinion, opposing points of view in the years after the writing of the Philadelphia Constitution increasingly clashed and led inexorably to civil war. Southerners, fearing a dangerously powerful central government and perceiving efforts by the free states to restrict slavery's westward expansion as infringements upon their constitutionally guaranteed rights, finally employed what they considered to be their lawful prerogative to secede when they withdrew from the Union in 1860 and 1861. For Gordon, given this fundamental constitutional disagreement, Southerners were just as justified in breaking away from the Union as Northerners were in their efforts to preserve it. He saw nothing to be gained from an extended debate over slavery or rehashing constitutional questions, because, for him, both sides fought honorably for core beliefs and principles. "Truth, justice, and patriotism unite in proclaiming that both sides fought and suffered for liberty as bequeathed by the Fathers, the one for liberty in the union of the States, the other for liberty in the independence of the States," he wrote.[38] And in the end, Gordon —unlike unrepentant Lost Cause advocates—readily accepted the fact that the North's victory in the Civil War forever ended human bondage in America and finally answered the most basic questions about the nature of the Union and the Constitution.

Having briefly and in a nonjudgmental way addressed the causes of the war, Gordon then explained his primary reason in recording his reminiscences. He wanted "to perpetuate incidents illustrative of the character of the American soldier, whether he fought on the one side or the other."[39] But he had "a still higher aim," an overarching goal which was to establish "the common ground on which all may stand; where justification of one section does not require or imply condemnation of the other."[40] As he had earlier done in "Last Days," Gordon throughout his memoir had nothing but praise for the men of the North and the South who waged war against one another for four bloody years. This lively, almost five-hundred-page recollection of the Civil War chronologically discusses the battles, primarily in the Eastern Theater, and lightly touches upon some of the controversies of the war. Although

Gordon deals with what happened on the battlefields, he also includes numerous anecdotes and incidents of what went on behind the lines. He recounts stories of camp life and the fraternization and verbal jockeying between the combatants; he praises the courage and strength of women on both sides; but, most of all, he stresses the devotion to duty and the chivalrous, honorable service of the soldiers of the North and the South. Indeed, Gordon positively gushes in his glorification of the Civil War's soldiery. He lauds the conduct and commitment of the common soldiers, but also that of their leaders, particularly Robert E. Lee and Ulysses S. Grant.[41] So universal is his celebration of American bravery, honor, and patriotism, that it is impossible to ascertain any distinction at all between the character of those who wore the gray or those who were clad in blue. His veneration of "Johnny Reb" and "Billy Yank" was specifically intended to provide that "common ground" he had so long sought—a place where all Americans could meet and stand, where Southerners and Northerners alike could take pride in their participation in the war as well as that of their former foes. Written in the flowery, romantic style of the time, *Reminiscences of the Civil War* presents a heartwarming tale which most readers found altogether charming and fascinating.

In the last paragraph of *Reminiscences,* Gordon beautifully expressed what he had been working to accomplish since the war's end and what he hoped his book might finalize: "The unseemly things which occurred in the great conflict between the States should be forgotten, or at least forgiven, and no longer permitted to disturb complete harmony between North and South."[42] He firmly believed that all young Americans "should be taught to hold in perpetual remembrance all that was great and good on both sides; to comprehend the inherited convictions for which saintly women suffered and patriotic men died; to recognize the unparalleled carnage as proof of unrivaled courage; to appreciate the singular absence of personal animosity and the frequent manifestation between those brave antagonists of a good-fellowship such as had never before been witnessed between hostile armies."[43] Looking ahead, he envisioned

> a glorious day for our country when all the children within its borders shall learn that the four years of fratricidal war between the North and the South was waged by neither with criminal or unworthy intent, but by both to protect what they conceived to be threatened rights and imperilled [*sic*] liberty; that the issues which divided the sections were born when the Republic was born, and were forever buried in an ocean of fraternal blood.[44]

For him, the Civil War was the nation's trial by fire, and having survived it, "the Republic, rising from its baptism of blood with a national life more robust, a national union more complete, and a national influence ever widening, shall go forever forward in its benign mission to humanity."[45]

Reviews of *Reminiscences* following its October 1903 publication clearly showed that most of Gordon's countrymen embraced his patriotic, nationalistic exposition. The public praise can in part be attributed to the fact that Gordon died less than three months after the book's release, and as a consequence, reviews of the memoir were often intermingled with—and in some cases overwhelmed by—personal tributes to the gallant Gordon. Nevertheless, reviewers from all over the country lauded the book's "charming simplicity," "its judicial and generous spirit," and its "unaffected, luminous, and often eloquent" style.[46] It was characterized as "simply and modestly told," "genial, magnanimous, and tolerant," "a modest tale filled with vitality," and "a model of modesty and charity" brimming with "the liveliest and most amusing anecdotes."[47] "There is not a page in the book," declared a Minnesota newspaper, "which bears the stamp of prejudice, not a sentiment which can offend any honest man;" two New Yorkers likewise found "not a trace of prejudice much less rancor" and "no bitterness of feeling, no pent-up animosity toward the North."[48] One journal even claimed that *Reminiscences* was "not only one of the most important contributions yet made to the literature of a great period, but one of the most fascinating and charming books that has come from the hand of an American man of action."[49] The same reviewer believed Gordon's *Reminiscences* would serve as "a monument to his memory more beautiful than any that will be built by those who loved and honored him, a tribute more eloquent than any that can ever be paid by those who knew him best."[50]

Although *Reminiscences* proved to be a popular and financial success and is still recognized as one of the most engaging of Civil War recollections, historians have been increasingly unkind in their evaluation of Gordon's memoir. They criticize its style and florid language, its bland neutrality, and what they believe was the author's claiming of undeserved credit for himself. Moreover, some readers have targeted his tendency to place his particular spin on several Civil War controversies, and as additional evidence comes to light, they accuse him of altogether fabricating stories or specifics in *Reminiscences.* The most notable questions and criticisms include the famous Gordon-Barlow encounter at Gettysburg, Gordon's fault finding of James Longstreet at the same battle, his accounts of some of the details at the Battles of the Wilderness and Cedar Creek, and his dramatic recounting of the surrender ceremony at Appomattox, which mirrored the now-challenged version presented by Joshua Lawrence Chamberlain. Even one of Gordon's greatest admirers, Douglas Southall Freeman, delicately danced around the possibility that the Georgian shaded the truth when he admitted that he was "perplexed . . . to know where General Gordon's memory ended and where his imagination began."[51] Lee's biographer also later cautioned readers to subject *Reminiscences* to a careful "critique that always must be applied to oft-told tales committed to print late in life."[52]

While critics may be correct in pointing out that Gordon's book contains inaccuracies, they are wrong to imply that Gordon's espousal of national pacification and his commitment to national reconciliation was self-serving, deviously calculated, or anything less than wholehearted. His embrace of national reunification was genuine and sincere. Even if he at times embellished his role in the war (which was absolutely unnecessary) or invented tales to make his lectures or book more appealing and heartwarming, such actions do not in any way detract from the purposes for which Gordon had long labored. He sincerely sought to heal the emotional wounds inflicted by the war largely by venerating the honor and courage of the soldiers of both sides who fought for what they held dear. This tactic provided a common interpretation of the war that contributed mightily to helping reunite the North and the South. He also could not permit Southern motives or conduct to be disparaged, for protecting Southerners' heritage and history was a vital part of his vision for national reconciliation. It allowed them to take hold of their Northern opponents as countrymen again, just as his glorification of the soldiers in blue permitted them to accept and return that embrace.

As "a quintessential narrative of reconciliation," *Reminiscences of the Civil War* serves as the capstone, the crowning achievement of Gordon's nearly four-decade career as a national reconciler.[53] Its publication and popularity represents, in a sense, his triumphant summit of the mountain of national pacification that he had been climbing since Appomattox. Certainly, it is the most complete explication of the message he had been expounding for so long. For Gordon, the Civil War was America's flaming crucible, in which the national character was tested, tempered, and strengthened in the fire of battle; what emerged was a stronger, reunited nation, now at the turn of the century poised to assume its position as a world power. In the aftermath of the Spanish-American War and amid steadily increasing expressions of national unity, Gordon must have experienced a deep-felt sense of accomplishment in his final days. Shortly before his last illness, he confided to a friend, "I feel in my heart there is not much left for me to do."[54] He expressed how gratified he was to have lived long enough to see the goals for which he had worked so earnestly finally being realized. He died one month shy of his seventy-second birthday on January 9, 1904, at his winter home near Miami, Florida.

The effusiveness of the eulogies and encomiums that greeted Gordon's passing vividly reflects what the South and the nation thought of the Hero of Appomattox. Called an "evangel of fraternity" and "an apostle of peace and good will," and recognized as "among the first to lead in the great work of the reconciliation of the sections," Gordon, according to a Connecticut newspaper, did not waste "time in lamentations and cherishing resentments" but "accepted the situation and advised his fellow citizens . . . of the south to do the same."[55] The same editor exhorted all Americans to pay "due tribute to the memory of one than whom no stauncher patriot and lover of his country and institutions now lives."[56] Another common theme emphasized his preeminence in the reconciliatory process, his desire "without sacrificing principle, to create brotherly love all around."[57] A New Yorker felt Gordon "did more by word and pen and deed than any other southern man to assuage the feeling of animosity and restore real harmony and fraternal good will between the north and south."[58] Almost exactly the same sentiments were expressed by a South Carolinian: Gordon, "in his lectures and his public speeches and by his commanding influence . . . has done as much as any one man to wipe out sectional feeling and to restore fraternity and brotherhood between the north and the south—between the blue and the gray."[59] Similarly, "No man did more to heal the scars of war and unify the sections," asserted a Florida eulogist, or "paid a more just tribute to the valor displayed by both armies in that heroic struggle" than the general.[60] His successor as commander in chief of the UCV believed that "while as loyal to the tender memories of the Confederate cause as the most loyal," Gordon "set an example of loyalty" to the reunited United States by becoming "the great apostle of reconciliation and obliteration of sectional feeling between the north and south."[61]

Both Northerners and Southerners recognized his "noble generosity of spirit and catholicity of mind" which made him "eminently fitted to take a leading part in that great work of binding together forever the north and the south."[62] While a Georgia paper observed that Gordon "charmed even the north" and another tribute described Northerners' "kindly admiration" of him, the *Chicago Tribune* confirmed that few former Confederates were "more highly respected or warmly received in the north" than the gallant Gordon.[63] A Tennessee editor declared that Gordon "was largely instrumental . . . in impressing the north with a fairer and truer idea of the south and southern character and sentiment, and his influence in the south was salutary in promoting a more tolerant view of the aspects of the sectional differences."[64] Although "true to his section and the traditions of his beloved south, insistent upon the world recognition of the honesty and nobility of the motives and contentions of the southern people," observed the *Nashville Banner*, Gordon "sought to allay the rancorous feelings engendered by strife without imputing unworthy motives to the union cause."[65] And the *Outlook*, in its tribute titled "Soldier and Gentleman," perhaps put it best when it averred, "He loved the South and was loyal to its interests and its spirit, but he rose completely above the plane of sectional feeling. He was one of the most eloquent and persuasive advocates of reconciliation between the sections."[66]

And so Gordon died as he had lived—a Southerner loyal to his native section but also a proud American. Only days before his death, he announced, "Now I see peace in every heart, the bitterness of civil strife forgotten, and a promise of universal brotherhood under a reunited flag which is today just as dear to my heart as the stars and bars under which on a former occasion I risked my life."[67] It seems certain that John B. Gordon went to his grave knowing that he had done as much as anyone in the forty years following the Civil War to help reunite the former adversaries of that fratricidal struggle. His passing served as an emphatic amen to his Gospel of Reconciliation.

Notes

1. John S. Wise, "Two Great Confederates. General John B. Gordon and General James Longstreet: Characterizations by a Friend of Both," *American Monthly Review of Reviews* 29 (Feb. 1904): 204.
2. For a full treatment of Gordon's life, see Ralph Lowell Eckert, *John Brown Gordon: Soldier, Southerner, American* (Baton Rouge, 1989). In this essay, focusing primarily on the last decade of Gordon's life, only direct quotations will be cited.
3. John B. Gordon, *Reminiscences of the Civil War* (New York, 1904), 449.
4. Ibid., 449–50.
5. Clement A. Evans, "General Gordon and General Longstreet," *Independent* 56 (1904): 312.
6. Eckert, *John Brown Gordon,* 137.
7. Evans, "General Gordon and General Longstreet," 313.
8. John B. Gordon, "Last Days of the Confederacy," in *Modern Eloquence,* 15 vols., ed. Thomas B. Reed (Philadelphia,1900–1903), 5:471–72.
9. Ibid., 471.
10. *St. Louis Republic,* quoted in Southern Lyceum Bureau Program for Gordon lecture, 1897–98 season, John B. Gordon Folder, Atlanta Historical Society, Atlanta (hereafter cited as Southern Lyceum Program).
11. Howard Dorgan, "A Case Study in Reconciliation: General John B. Gordon and 'The Last Days of the Confederacy,'" *Quarterly Journal of Speech* 60 (Feb. 1974): 90.
12. *Atlanta Journal,* Jan. 10, 1904.

13. *Philadelphia Ledger,* quoted in Slayton Lyceum Bureau Program for Gordon lecture, n.d., John Brown Gordon Family Papers, Hargrett Rare Book and Manuscript Library, University of Georgia Libraries, Athens (hereafter cited as Slayton Lyceum Program); *Louisville Courier-Journal,* quoted in Southern Lyceum Program.

14. *Boston Daily Globe,* quoted in Southern Lyceum Program; *New York Daily Tribune,* quoted in Southern Lyceum Program.

15. *Minneapolis Sunday Times,* quoted in Southern Lyceum Program.

16. *New Orleans Daily States,* quoted in Extracts from Press Comments on Gen. Gordon's Lecture (Sept. 1894), John B. Gordon Papers, Letters, Manuscript, Archives, and Rare Book Library, Emory University, Atlanta (hereafter cited as Extracts from Press Comments); *New Orleans Times-Democrat,* quoted in Slayton Lyceum Program; *New Orleans Daily Picayune,* quoted in Southern Lyceum Program.

17. *New York Times,* Nov. 26, 1893; *Augusta* (GA) *Chronicle,* quoted in Slayton Lyceum Program; *Louisville Courier-Journal,* quoted in Southern Lyceum Program; *Chicago Daily Inter Ocean,* quoted in Southern Lyceum Program.

18. *St. Louis Republic,* quoted in Southern Lyceum Program.

19. *Kansas City* (MO) *Times,* quoted in Southern Lyceum Program.

20. *Augusta* (GA) *Chronicle,* quoted in Extracts from Press Comments.

21. *Atlanta Journal,* Jan. 9, 1904.

22. Ibid.

23. Dorgan, "Case Study in Reconciliation," 86.

24. Gaines M. Foster, *Ghosts of the Confederacy: Defeat, the Lost Cause, and the Emergence of the New South* (New York, 1987), 133.

25. Ibid., 112; Eckert, *John Brown Gordon,* 328.

26. *Atlanta Constitution,* July 21, 1900.

27. Ibid.

28. Ibid.

29. Ibid.

30. Ibid.

31. *New York Times,* Aug. 21, 1900.

32. Ibid.

33. Gordon, *Reminiscences,* xxv–xxvi.

34. Ibid., xxvi–xxvii.

35. Ibid., xxvii.

36. Ibid., 18–19.

37. Ibid., 19.

38. Ibid., 25.

39. Ibid.

40. Ibid.

41. There are a few exceptions to Gordon's overflowing praise. He attempted to shift much of the blame for the Confederate loss at Gettysburg away from Lee and toward James Longstreet; however, his criticism of Longstreet is mild when compared to his opinions of Jubal A. Early and Philip H. Sheridan. Early was frequently Gordon's commander, and the two men often clashed during the war and their quarrels carried over into the postwar period. Gordon always considered Sheridan atypical of Union generals in that he acted particularly ungraciously in the Shenandoah Valley and at Appomattox.

42. Gordon, *Reminiscences,* 464.

43. Ibid.

44. Ibid.

45. Ibid., 465.

46. Wise, "Two Great Confederates," 204; *New York Sun,* Nov. 1, 1903, clipping in John Brown Gordon Collection, 1832–1904, Hargrett Rare Book and Manuscript Library, University of Georgia Libraries, Athens (hereafter cited as Gordon Collection); *New York Evening Sun,* ad in *Dial,* Nov. 16, 1903.

47. *New York Times,* Nov. 21, 1903; *New York Evening Sun,* ad in *Dial,* Nov. 16, 1903; *Nation* 78 (May 1904): 375; Wise, "Two Great Confederates," 204; review in *Dial,* Nov. 1, 1903.

48. *St. Paul Dispatch,* ad in *Dial,* Dec. 16, 1903; *New York Sun,* Nov. 1, 1903, clipping in Gordon Collection; *New York Times,* Nov. 21, 1903.

49. "Soldier and Gentleman," *Outlook: A Weekly Newspaper* 76 (Jan.1904): 152.

50. Ibid.

51. Douglas Southall Freemen, *Robert E. Lee: A Biography,* 4 vols. (New York, 1934–35), 3:302n.

52. Douglas Southall Freeman, *Lee's Lieutenants: A Study in Command,* 3 vols. (New York, 1942–44), 3:813.

53. Craig A. Warren, *Scars to Prove It: The Civil War Soldier and American Fiction* (Kent, OH, 2009), 146.

54. *Atlanta Journal,* Jan. 8, 1904.

55. John Temple Graves's eulogy, quoted in the *Atlanta Journal,* Jan. 14, 1904; *Nashville Banner,* quoted in *Atlanta Journal,* Jan. 13, 1904; editorial in

Atlanta Constitution, Jan. 11, 1904; *Bridgeport* (CT) *Morning Telegram,* quoted in *Atlanta Journal,* Jan. 14, 1904.

56. *Bridgeport* (CT) *Morning Telegram,* quoted in *Atlanta Journal,* Jan. 14, 1904.
57. *Augusta* (GA) *Chronicle,* quoted in *Atlanta Journal,* Jan. 11, 1904.
58. Horatio King in the *Brooklyn Eagle,* quoted in *Atlanta Constitution,* Jan. 14, 1904.
59. *Anderson* (SC) *Daily Mail,* quoted in *Atlanta Journal,* Jan. 16, 1904.
60. *Ocala* (FL) *Banner,* quoted in *Atlanta Journal,* Jan. 16, 1904.
61. Stephen D. Lee's eulogy, quoted in *Atlanta Journal,* Jan. 14, 1904.
62. *Memphis Courier-Journal,* quoted in the *Atlanta Journal,* Jan. 12, 1904; editorial in *Atlanta Journal,* Jan. 10, 1904.
63. *Augusta* (GA) *Chronicle,* quoted in *Atlanta Journal,* Jan. 11, 1904; Wise, "Two Great Confederates," 208; *Chicago Tribune,* quoted in *Atlanta Journal,* Jan. 14, 1904.
64. *Nashville Banner,* quoted in *Atlanta Constitution,* Jan. 13, 1904.
65. Ibid.
66. *Outlook* 76 (Jan. 1904): 152.
67. *Atlanta Journal,* Jan. 8, 1904.

T. Harry Williams giving his final lecture at Louisiana State University in Baton Rouge. George C. Rable, a contributor to this volume, can be seen in the background working the projector. Courtesy LSU University Relations.

Williams among the Rebels: Southern Generalship in the Civil War

Roger Spiller

T. Harry Williams was a Union man, through and through. Although he spent the greater part of his career in the deepest South and had great understanding and sympathy for his adopted home, he never went native. In his sensibilities and in his values he remained the resolute Midwesterner. That was the vantage point from which he taught and wrote about the Civil War, and he did a great deal of both.[1]

The sport of sitting in judgment on generals is one of the oldest in literature, and Williams was temperamentally and intellectually well suited to play the game. The inherent drama of war as well as its far-reaching consequences ensure that those who direct war will stand before the court of history. Writers protect or attack the defendants' reputation, assess their successes and failures, and assign them a place on a cosmic scale from incompetence to greatness—at least until the jury meets again. Then the general's record will be argued over once more, his ranking reassessed, and, depending on the fashions of time and place, perhaps even be rehabilitated and advanced in rank. Keeping track of the ups and downs of generals' reputations is a lesser sort of sport, diverting at least, enlightening at best.

Far less often are the judges themselves called to account. They hand down their rulings with near impunity. Critics may question their arguments on the facts of the case or the logic and skill with which they advance them, but seldom are the judges' own understanding of the subject examined. Yet if an injustice to the defendant is to be avoided, it seems only fair to ask what are the sources of verdicts so confidently delivered? What standards guide their deliberations? Are their judgments applied evenhandedly or tendentiously? What are the origins of their standards, and how do they evolve, if indeed they evolve at all?

For the longest time, generals were judged only by the victories they won. How and why they won their victories were rarely addressed until the eighteenth century. During the Enlightenment, generalship was thought of as an art, one that like any art revealed techniques and skills that, properly studied, might guide future practitioners. At the same time, the persistence with which certain patterns of technique could be gleaned from historical accounts of wars suggested to some military writers that war, far from being an art, was in reality a science, one that could be conducted according to fixed, timeless principles. These two views clashed at the end of the eighteenth century and persisted throughout the nineteenth and, some say, even the twentieth century, and were best represented in the classic studies of Henri Jomini and Carl von Clausewitz.

Many of those who produced these works on military science were professional soldiers who knew war firsthand; few of them were classically trained and drew on the historical record to justify their prejudices. Not until the last half of the nineteenth century did professional historians, inspired by the works of Leopold von Ranke, address the complexities of war with the intellectual rigor the subject demanded. Of these historians, the Prussian Hans Delbrück led the way in applying the "scientific method" to the study of the military past, the object of which was "clearing away the underbrush of legend which obscured historical truth."[2]

American scholars did not take up the formal study of military history as the Europeans had until after World War I, leaving the field instead to talented writers, memoirists, and soldiers. From Appomattox until World War II, the most vigorous—and widely read—works of military history took the Civil War as their subject. Few of these books addressed the nation's military past with the rigor that would have satisfied Delbrück, however. When Williams was doing his graduate work in the 1930s, the few academics interested in the critical, systematic analysis of war came from the emerging social sciences. The political scientists Quincy Wright of the University of Chicago, Alfred Vagts of Harvard, and Edward Mead Earle of Princeton were the most prominent of a small band who aimed to advance knowledge about the nature and conduct of war in general. For them, however, history served only as a starting point, a resource from which they hoped to deduce theoretical propositions and general principles that might be applied to future conflicts.

Should novice scholars wish to broaden their knowledge of military history and the theory of war, they could turn to the best-known British military writers of the day, J. F. C. Fuller, B. H. Liddell Hart, G. F. R. Henderson, and Sir Frederick Maurice—none of whom, it must be said, quite fit the mold of the disinterested academic.[3] Whatever their shortcomings, all these writers were experienced soldiers. They were well schooled in the general history of war and the military thought that had proliferated in the nineteenth century.[4] They were knowledgeable about war's technical details and they were especially expert in the reconstruction and analysis of military operations from the strategic to the tactical level. Williams would draw from the works of all these men over the course of his career.

Even though the Americans trailed the Europeans in studying the general history of war and military thought, the pace of Civil War scholarship quickened after World War II. A new generation of scholars, having come of age during the Great Depression, and some of them having experienced war themselves, seemed more contentious than their forebears. Of this period, Williams's lifelong friend David Herbert Donald would write, "There must be more historians of the Civil War than there were generals fighting it, and of the two groups, the historians are the more belligerent."[5]

Williams entered the fray gradually. He did his graduate work at the University of Wisconsin in the late 1930s, first under the tutelage of Carl Russell Fish, and when Fish died Williams joined the stable of talented graduate students then working under the Southern historian William Best Hesseltine.[6] By all accounts, Hesseltine was eccentric, contentious, and brilliant, and his seminars were said to have been marked by a certain intellectual ruthlessness. His common reply to students who asked him to direct their dissertations was, "I don't direct dissertations. Can you write a book?"[7]

Williams's own natural contentiousness fit well in the intellectual climate that Hesseltine created in his seminars, and Williams was one of his favorites.[8] A slight man, nervous and ferret-like in his movements, constantly fiddling with his pipe, self-assured to a point just short of arrogance, Williams liked nothing better than to engage in cut-and-thrust arguments. Behind all the contentiousness, however, a real and lifelong affection grew up between Williams and his mentor. Toward the end of Hesseltine's life, Williams let down his armor for a moment, writing Hesseltine a fulsome note. Hesseltine wrote back: "Its [*sic*] embarrassing to have the odd, occasional, and highly unusual displays of affection from you. I know you love me: I love you, too. But lets [*sic*] keep this on the comic level—neither of us is really suited for sentiment, and we'd look like hell being maudlin."[9]

The dissertation Williams wrote under Hesseltine did indeed become a book. Although "drastically different" than his dissertation, *Lincoln and the Radicals,* a study of the Committee on the Conduct of the War, marked Williams's coming out as a skillful young historian with a literary flair. Looking back on his work from the mid-1960s, Williams saw it "displayed some qualities often found in a dissertation—and also in a first book. It did not hesitate to hand down judgments on people and events, and it did not boggle to state cases." Williams saw some of these judgments as "extreme" and "overstated"; he would "soften or qualify" some of these were he rewriting the book.[10]

If Williams's treatment of Union political leaders was unforgiving, his opinion of Union generals was temperate at first. But over time his criticisms became sharper, more defined, and in his treatment of Major General George B. McClellan we can see the evolution of a standard of judgment that he would later apply to all Civil War generals, Union and Confederate alike.

When Williams's sketch of McClellan in this first book is laid alongside the McClellan that appears in Williams's later works, the earlier version—though critical enough—is more sympathetic. The McClellan who appears in *Lincoln and the Radicals* is as much a victim of his own vanity as the Jacobins' machinations:

> He was one of the most widely read military scientists of his generation: indeed, his detailed knowledge of military history was his greatest handicap. . . . He knew what Napoleon would have done in every situation, but Napoleon had never seen Virginia mud. . . . He knew what had been done in the past, but he was not always sure what George B. McClellan would do in the future. And yet he might—if the politicians had let him alone—he might have won the Civil War.[11]

In 1942, a year after *Lincoln and the Radicals* came out, Williams reviewed an admiring biography of McClellan by H. J. Eckenrode and Bryan Conrad for the *Journal of Southern History*. There, Williams pronounced McClellan "a master of the art of war and the ablest of the Union generals." To this surprising judgment, Williams added that "had [McClellan] been given the command in 1864 . . . there is every reason to believe that he would have achieved victory and would have emerged as the laureled [*sic*] hero of the great struggle."[12] Yet at this early date in Williams's career, the reader can see a foreshadowing of his later, far more critical view of the general: "The authors do not see how intensely the General himself played the political game. He favored Democratic generals; he angled for the support of papers . . . and he hobnobbed with the Democratic politicos. . . . The whole conduct of the war was shot through with politicos, and McClellan was far from being the exception."[13]

Given Williams's upbringing in the small farming communities of the Midwest under a father who was an avowed LaFollette progressive, McClellan and his world were never likely to win many concessions from Williams. His perspective had been shaped by reading of Lincoln's life and writings at an early age. Remembering his early education on the president whose reputation he would play a role in restoring, he wrote to a friend, "To me, [Lincoln] expresses some pretty great ideals—controlled, pragmatic reform, a sense of both man's capacities and his limitations, and a broad and compassinate [*sic*] wisdom. My study of Lincoln has had a tremendous influence on my interpretation of the meaning of American history."[14]

Williams's early perspective could only have been reinforced during his time at Wisconsin, when the elite classes of the East that McClellan represented so well were seen not only as obstacles to political and social progress but also as the authors of the Great Depression Williams and everyone else were living through at the moment.[15] And Williams's outlook persisted; well into his career, he happily confessed a lifelong affinity with "Midwestern left wing agrarian democracy."[16]

Williams took these values with him into the Deep South in 1941, when he joined the faculty at Louisiana State University. He was among the Rebels now, and he would spend the rest of his life in their company. For the first few years, Williams taught American history and American military history. The Civil War course at LSU was the preserve of Bell I. Wiley, who already had a considerable reputation in the field. That did not deter Williams from pursuing his interests, however, and when Wiley told him that P. G. T. Beauregard's papers were in the LSU archives, Williams set to work on the general's biography.[17] Although he managed to edit a collection of Lincoln's speeches and write a few reviews, Williams spent World War II in Beauregard's company and establishing his reputation as a teacher.

These years were important, formative ones for Williams. America's entry in World War II did not prompt any stirrings of patriotism or dreams of martial glory in him. He wanted nothing to do with real war, or real armies. He did not offer himself up to government work as did many of his colleagues, and he assiduously avoided active military service. Thirty-two years old at the time of Pearl Harbor and with a checkered medical history, Williams was nonetheless classified 1A in April 1943, ready for induction. "I'd be a poor physical specimen for the Army but that won't stop them from taking me," he told Hesseltine, who himself had registered as a conscientious objector. "Pray for me," Williams wrote as he appealed for deferment. Finally, in early 1944, he was given another medical examination, which he failed. "Halleluya [*sic*]," he exclaimed to his old prof, and when later that year Hesseltine asked if he would be interested in joining him on an official junket to Europe, he replied, "I don't want to be connected with the army in any way, shape or form."[18]

Apparently keeping these views to himself, throughout the war Williams lectured to classrooms full of young men who expected to go to war. And after the war, his classes were crowded by what seemed to one student as "an infantry division of older veterans."[19] One of those was Charles P. Roland, who began his graduate work in 1947 under Wiley and later worked as Williams's graduate assistant. Roland had been a front-line infantry officer in the hard campaigns in northwestern Europe, taking part in the famous defense of Elsenborn Ridge during the Battle of the Bulge and fighting his way across the Rhine as part of the Allied breakout at Remagen Bridge. His war had ended as one of the occupation forces guarding Nazi war criminals during the Nuremberg trials. Roland had seen the worst war had to offer.[20] One might wonder what Williams or anyone else could tell Roland and his fellow veterans about war?

Historians who write and teach about war must sooner or later confront a question that does not much trouble their colleagues in other fields: Have you, so confident in your judgments, ever seen war yourself? Behind this question lies the belief that one cannot understand war without personal experience of it. Although this belief can be challenged easily, it is nevertheless fervently held by those who have seen the hard face of war. Walt Whitman, after helping treat the human wreckage from the battlefields of the Civil War, gave voice to this belief, laying down an uncompromising dictum. "The real war will never get into the books," he wrote in *Specimen Days*.[21] Roland was very much of Whitman's mind. In his memoirs, Roland considered what his own experience had taught him about war. It "gave me an insight into the nature of my fellow human beings, and particularly that of war and soldiers, an understanding that cannot be gained from books."[22]

How likely was it that Williams could spend his days with the veterans without reflecting on his own lack of military experience? Even though he avoided taking part in the war, only a complete lack of introspection would have spared him from imagining how he would have met the tests his students had survived. Yet Roland remembers only one occasion in which he and Williams talked about the war. Williams "said he could understand clearly how large bodies of troops—divisions and regiments—were moved into a battle position, but he could not understand just how small units—companies or platoons were moved into battle position. I explained to him how this was done." Apart from this one exchange, Roland remembers, Williams "did not take instruction from me."[23]

The veterans Williams encountered then and later could not have added much to his understanding of the politics, grand strategy, and operational campaigning that most interested him at the time. Although his work on Beauregard in the late 1940s did require him to reconstruct Shiloh and other battles in some tactical detail, little of what he was studying took him below the regimental level of action. But there was one veteran within Williams's easy reach who could have given him an extended tutorial on the art of generalship and indeed military leadership at every echelon: the president of Louisiana State University, Troy Middleton.

Middleton enlisted as a private in the U.S. Army in 1910 and won a commission as an infantry officer in 1913. Deployed to Europe in 1918, Middleton's performance as a combat commander propelled him from the rank of captain to colonel in four months. When he took command of the 39th Infantry Regiment, he was twenty-nine years old, the youngest regimental commander in the American Expeditionary Forces.

Middleton's connection with LSU began in the 1930s, when he was assigned to command LSU's corps of cadets. Although an officer normally served only three years on this assignment, the university convinced the army to leave Middleton in place for an unprecedented six years. In 1937, Middleton retired from the army to join the university as dean of administration.

In 1941, only a few months before Williams arrived to take up his new appointment at LSU, and seeing America's involvement in the war on the horizon, Middleton returned to active duty. Promoted rapidly to major general, he was given command of the 45th Infantry Division for the invasions of Sicily and Italy. In early 1944, he was promoted to lieutenant general at Eisenhower's insistence and given command of the U.S. VIII Corps for the cross-channel invasion of Normandy. Later that year, Middleton led his corps into the Battle of the Bulge. Many echelons below Middleton, Captain Charles P. Roland and his men in the 394th Infantry Regiment held the line against the I SS Panzer Corps.[24]

Contemporaries and historians alike never failed to mention the general's "common touch" with troops under his care, and his practical, commonsense approach to command. He never stood on ceremony or the dignity of his rank, and he made it a point to visit his front line troops daily. He was not a prima donna like his friend Patton and so many other general officers. When George Marshall asked Middleton how many staff officers he wanted to take with him when he assumed command of his corps, Middleton's answer was "None." Middleton was a regular army officer, but he was not a graduate of West Point. All these attributes would have met with Williams's approval; in his eyes, they were what made an effective, genuinely American general.

Judging from their few exchanges of correspondence, the professor and the general enjoyed a warm, mutual regard. But there seems to be no documentary evidence that Williams ever availed himself of the general's professional military knowledge and experience commanding American soldiers from squad to corps—a lapse all the more surprising in a scholar who would become a pioneer in the field of oral history. Perhaps Williams's view of military professionals, historical and modern, always ambivalent, prevented him from getting too close to a living primary source.[25]

Williams was not convinced that military professionals, especially those who had learned their trade at West Point, were particularly well suited to lead

America's common man into battle during the Civil War. In one of his earliest essays, drawn from his dissertation and published three years before *Lincoln and the Radicals* came out, Williams described the Radicals' attacks on the academy during the first years of the war, attacks that ran out of steam after the Union victories of 1863.[26] Of course the Radicals were alarmed by the lackluster performance of Union generals; their criticism of West Point did not take into account that the South had its own West Pointers who were winning. For the historian, the question was how to assess the academy's influence on the conduct of both sides of the entire war. Williams would return to this question time and again. How he dealt with it is a clue to understanding the standards by which he judged the performance of every Civil War leader.

Poorly prepared as they were, generals on all sides misunderstood the nature of the war, which, Williams argued, was not the last of the old wars but the first of the modern ones, and "one that missed totality by a narrow margin." It was above all a democratic war between citizens who could find no common ground between their antithetical ideas, and this ensured it would be "ruthless, lethal, no-holds barred."[27] The conception of war and the military system that both sides drew from were antiquated, owing more to the age of limited war, far from equal to the demands about to be made of them. From its outset, this war escaped the bounds of military orthodoxy as it had been handed down to America's nascent class of military professionals at West Point.

Without the West Pointers, the war could not, would not have taken the shape it did. More than fifty years old by the outbreak of the war, the academy had produced an officer corps in sufficient numbers and seniority to assume leading commands on both sides. Jefferson Davis, himself a graduate and steadfast defender of the academy, assiduously built his new army around a cadre of West Pointers. All of the South's full generals and not a few lesser field commanders were graduates. West Pointers commanded both sides in fifty-five of the war's sixty largest battles, and in the remaining five a West Pointer was in command on one side or the other.[28] Yet "as a preparatory seminary for future generals," Williams wrote, West Point "had glaring deficiencies. . . . There was little instruction in the higher nature of war—policy, strategy, and military history. . . .West Point turned out good tacticians and narrow specialists; it did not produce men who knew very much about the art of war."[29]

Williams's views on West Point took on a sharper edge in *Lincoln and the Radicals* than in his earlier essay, views that took the form of a character sketch of "the problem child of the Civil War," George B. McClellan. For Williams, McClellan was the exemplar of West Point's deficiencies. He was of the eastern elite whose sons dominated the corps of cadets, well born and educated, technically adept, expert in building an army for battle. He was seemingly as well prepared as any general on either side. But he was neurotic and self-possessed, and when the war departed from the stylized tactical minuet he imagined it would be, he came undone. He expected the war to conform to the neat rules of war the academy had drilled into him; when it would not, he was seized by uncertainty and self-doubt, and full of recrimination against his many traducers. He became one of the best complainers in a war filled with them.

The criticisms Williams aimed then and later at McClellan applied equally well to Confederate leaders, whom West Point had prepared no better than McClellan. Like McClellan, they seemed unable to break free of their professional upbringing to see the war realistically. But they were burdened in a way the North was not. They were under the effective command of Jefferson Davis, the true field marshal of the Confederacy.

Any bookmaker would have laid odds in favor of Davis's success as a war leader. With some reason, Davis "fancied himself a military expert," but in Williams's view, Davis's own military history hung like a millstone around his neck, constricting rather than aiding his imagination. He was a mediocre war leader because, like the generals under his command, "he could not grasp the vital fact that the Confederacy was not a going, recognized government but a revolution." If he could not be a general himself, he meant to run his war according to his own lights, and he did not take kindly to criticism or contrary opinions from any quarter, especially from his field commanders. "Nothing pleased him more," Williams wrote, "than to write a long, lecturing letter to a general who had questioned the wisdom of a Davis decision."[30]

But the military knowledge on which Davis so prided himself was obsolete, and it revealed itself soon enough in the defensive strategy that Davis largely devised and presided over. Davis understood very well the military principle of concentration, and he understood just as well that military strategy could not take precedence over his grand strategy. Military concentration meant stripping the rebellious states of their own defensive forces, the consequence of which he believed would lead to "dissatisfaction, distress, desertion of soldiers, and opposition of State Govt."[31] From Davis's perspective, a grand offensive was politically untenable, and the Confederates' three major offensives—Bragg's in 1862 and Lee's in 1862 and 1863—were simply not powerful enough to withstand the Union's reaction. The reason for their failure, Williams believed, could be found in the Confederates' strategic conception—a conception that changed only by degrees during the war. "The Confederacy was founded on state rights," Williams argued, "localism was imbedded in every segment of its system—and it fought a state-rights war and, on the strategic level, a traditional, eighteenth-century type of war."[32]

Yet Davis, who was notorious for occupying himself with the pettifogging details of office and used up so many secretaries of war by interfering in their business, took pains not to intrude on his generals' operational work. Indeed, he tolerated outrageous behavior and near insubordination from generals whose conduct would have gotten them fired had they been fighting for the other side.[33] "If he had to make use of a general he detested, he would do it," Williams wrote.[34] And few generals tested Davis's forbearance more than P. G. T. Beauregard. The two men were "born to clash," Williams thought.[35]

By 1949, Williams had finished research on the Beauregard biography when an offer from the Knopf publishing house arrived. Would he consider writing a study of Lincoln as a war leader? The Beauregard book was laid aside while Williams wrote what became *Lincoln and His Generals.* But he did not abandon Beauregard. Less than two months after *Lincoln and His Generals* hit the best-seller lists, Williams was back at work on Beauregard's biography.[36]

Despite all the work Williams had put in on Beauregard, he might well have left the general behind after *Lincoln and His Generals* was published in 1952. The years following this book were crowded with articles, reviews, public and academic addresses, and still more books. Williams's longtime friend Frank Vandiver thought the Beauregard book was "almost a reluctant one—Williams found it hard to think well of a rebel." In some way, Vandiver thought, Williams "felt some urge to get right with his surroundings," which "reeked of Moonlight, Magnolias, and the Lost Cause."[37]

Williams could hardly have chosen a better representative of the lush, exotic place he had chosen to settle. His subject's paradoxical, atypical character appealed to him: Beauregard was "an ardent Southerner, and yet, as a Creole, he was in many ways an alien in the Anglo-Saxon Confederacy."[38] How Beauregard's exuberant, foreign character intersected with his experience, not how he rated in the pantheon of Southern generals, most interested Williams. He did not think Beauregard belonged in the first rank of Civil War generals anyway; at best, he thought Beauregard was a first-rate second-class commander. Had he been given time and opportunity, he might have improved, but his character and personality as much as his battlefield performance, barred his way.

The rigidity of mind that so many of his fellow officers had acquired at West Point, and that Williams so deplored, was especially powerful in Beauregard. Among his classmates, and indeed among all antebellum regular officers, Beauregard was one of the few who could read the works of Henri Jomini in the original French instead of the potted English renderings then available. Jomini's version of Napoleon was the lens through which Beauregard's understanding of the art of war was refracted.[39] Nothing in Beauregard's pre–Civil War experience caused him to amend the way he saw war. Rather than expanding his thinking, Jominian theory held him in thrall; perhaps more than any other top-ranked general on either side during the Civil War, his approach to larger military problems occurred in what Williams called "a sort of Napoleonic dreamworld."[40]

Beauregard's Jominian tendencies were on display as early as the Mexican War, when, as a very junior officer, he presumed to lecture Winfield Scott, who knew his Jomini as well as Beauregard, and his principal commanders on the proper approach to the assault on Mexico City—and convinced them.[41] If his confidence in the Jominian way of war wanted any reinforcement, this episode certainly made its contribution, and to Williams its effects were wholly negative. "Beauregard entered the [Civil War] with certain rigid ideas about the art of warfare . . . and a rigid belief that certain rules of war must always be followed. . . . Here was Beauregard's greatest weakness as a soldier. He tended to think of war as something that was in books and that was fought in conformity to a fixed pattern. He could not easily adjust his thinking to an actual situation or improvise new ways of war."[42]

Professionally and intellectually, Beauregard felt himself fully equipped when the Civil War began. As with his other talents, Beauregard overvalued his strategic sense. Like so many generals on both sides, he "wrote better than he fought." He would have been sorely wounded by Williams's verdict on his success at Sumter and First Manassas, which "had come without his having done much to bring it about and even despite grave errors on his part that might have brought disaster." He did not understand that a proper staff could amplify his efforts and "his sense of logistics was weak."[43] For Beauregard to have recognized these shortcomings in himself would have been a masterpiece of introspection, and introspection was not in his nature.

On the contrary, Williams believed, Beauregard began spinning military strategies for the Confederacy at the beginning of the war and thereafter his fertile mind seemingly never paused. But the plans he concocted were hastily done, suited only for an imaginary army in an imaginary war. He expected too much from the resources at his command, assumed the enemy would do exactly as he expected, and framed courses of action with little attention to detail.

Moreover, Beauregard's faux-Napoleonic tendencies were infectious, extending even to the drafting of march and battle orders. On the eve of Shiloh, Beauregard's chief of staff Thomas Jordan found the general in bed, scribbling instructions for the movement toward Pittsburg Landing. Jordan dutifully took these notes back to his quarters, where he put them in proper form. For his model, he had before him Napoleon's orders for Waterloo.[44]

Beauregard's extravagant, dramatic personality made him the easiest mark among the Southern generals for Williams. He was the only Southern general Williams would write about at any length. In his other books and articles, Williams's interests ran toward the Union's war and its leaders, and his views on Beauregard's colleagues appeared incidentally as highly compressed character sketches, asides, or digressions. That is not to say, however, that he left the subject of Confederate war leadership behind. Far from it.

In 1953, one year after *Lincoln and His Generals* came out, Williams delivered a paper at a joint meeting of the Mississippi Valley Historical Association and the American Historical Association. The paper was bold, even for Williams: He presumed to criticize the recently deceased dean of American Civil War historians, Douglas Southall Freeman, and his treatment of the South's god of war, Robert E. Lee.[45] The fullest expression of Williams's judgment on Lee or any other Southern general can be found here, and although he would elaborate on Lee's generalship—and, by extension, the whole of Southern military leadership—in later years he did not appreciably change his mind.

Williams believed Freeman overidentified with his subject.[46] What the reader saw in *R. E. Lee* and *Lee's Lieutenants* was "a Virginia gentleman writing about another Virginia gentleman." Like Lee, Freeman did not "criticize the skill of Lee's opponents or . . . compare Lee with other generals," an approach Freeman believed was "beyond the function of a biographer." With this, Williams certainly did not agree. "Why should he not have done so?" Williams asked. "Such comparisons would seem necessary in order to understand Lee and his war."[47]

Nor did Williams approve of Freeman's "fog of war" approach, by which Freeman meant to describe the war only as Lee himself saw it at the time, without benefit of historical perspective. This literary device, Williams believed, had the effect of insulating Lee from the historical and operational contexts that were vital for a reader's understanding of events, which made no sense to Williams.[48] A year after his essay was published, Williams told a Civil War Round Table audience, "I don't know who Freeman wrote for."[49]

Williams did not profess to understand Lee, either. To him, "Lee was a strange, almost baffling creature. . . . He went into the war and waged war in almost an unthinking way." The longer Williams thought about Lee, the more paradoxical the general seemed. Toward the end of his career, Williams thought of Lee as somehow detached from the very environment that had shaped him. In 1975, Williams enlarged on his interpretation of Lee in a letter to an old friend:

> He is certainly not the hell-for-leather cavalier type, does not fit into the Southern stereotype. He could endure stress, work under routine, did not fold up under strain. In this he is unlike other leaders, products of planta-

tion culture, haughty men who would give orders but could not take them or even work with others. Edmund Wilson has something to say on this in *Patriotic Gore*. His discipline gave him a strength that many others did not have. . . . You may want to think about . . . the curious fact that the South erected as its hero a man who was so atypical.[50]

Freeman's narrow perspective mirrored Lee's own shortcomings as a Confederate war leader as well, the most damning of which was that Lee was "unmodern-minded." Lee "did not realize that the Civil War was the first of the modern wars," an "all-out for keeps, ruthless, total war of modern times."[51] To Williams, failing to see the war as it was rather than the war they wished it to be was a cardinal sin, the single most serious charge Williams could lay against any military leader, North or South.

Lee's "un-modern" sensibilities were most prominently on display in his flawed understanding of the strategic requirements that the South faced. The localism that plagued the South's efforts throughout the war acted as a powerful counterweight against the development of a comprehensive national strategy. "Lee persisted always in viewing the war as primarily an affair of Virginia. Operations in other theaters were almost a kind of side show," and Freeman's interpretation suffered the same problem, Williams wrote.[52]

To this "tragic limitation," Williams added another serious charge against Lee: The war seemed to teach him nothing, strategically or tactically, or even as a military professional. Lee did not appear to understand the workings of a "modern army"; he did not appreciate the strategic significance of railroads; his notion of a staff's functions was antiquated, as was his use of artillery and cavalry; and his map work, which was so important to the movements of enormous formations, was deficient, "almost primitive," Williams said later.[53] Nor did Lee appreciate the revolutionary tactical changes wrought by technological advances in the power of small arms, which made frontal assaults against entrenched positions virtually suicidal. Williams was happy to acknowledge Lee's tactical brilliance and inspirational leadership then and later, but he was far less willing to make allowances for Lee's mistakes than the general's biographer, who "came close to arguing that whatever Lee did was right because he was Lee."[54] Had Freeman been alive, he might well have taken Williams's verdict on Lee's tactics as an act of lèse majesté.

Inevitably, Williams's verdict on Lee would be contested. Critics charged that Williams had misconstrued Jominian theory and its influence on Confederate strategy, and that he had unfairly indicted Confederate leadership by subjecting it to a Clausewitzian analysis.[55] Lee was defended as having a far more comprehensive strategic view of the war than Williams was willing to credit.[56]

Williams showed little sign of softening his judgments on Lee or any other Confederate general, although he was more generous in his published work than in his public addresses. Just before an appearance at the Houston Civil War Round Table, a friend reminded him of the audience's reaction to his last speech there, when in the views of some he handled Lee too roughly: "When you criticized General Lee for losing touch with the Yanks on the James River for 3 hours and forty minutes in June of '64, there was some talk among the brothers about getting up a lynching party for you, but that has all passed over and has been, more or less, forgotten. So come along and talk about what you want to."[57]

Privately, Williams admitted that defending his criticisms was becoming tiresome, writing to a friend, "This is beginning to look like open season on Williams among the younger historians" and adding somewhat ironically, "Well, the big men can always expect attacks—look at Freeman."[58] To another friend, a former student who had sent him an essay on Lee to critique, Williams wrote,

> You almost say that all the criticism of Lee is light, personal, and unworthy of notice. I seriously advise that you do something to remove this impression before the essay is published. I can speak with some knowledge because I have criticized Lee. But however wrong I may have been, I certainly intended what I said to be scholarly and thoughtful and I had no intention to topple the man or downgrade him out of dislike or anything else.[59]

In 1960, Williams was invited to deliver the second Harmon Memorial Lecture on Military History at the United States Air Force Academy, choosing as his subject "The Military Leadership of the North and the South." This address would be published later that year as one of the essays collected by David Donald under the title *Why the North Won the Civil War*. The speech stands as Williams's most comprehensive appraisal of the Confederate generals.[60] Williams elaborated on many of the themes that already had appeared in his speeches and written work: the stultifying influence of West Point on professional thought and practice; the limitations of the Jominian interpretation of Napoleonic warfare as a model for the conduct of this modern, democratic war; and, not least, the role of individual personality as it expressed itself in the waging of the war.

Although Williams was adept in his handling of larger, impersonal historical questions, he considered himself a narrative historian, and he had long since decided that narrative was best told through the personalities whose makeup in some way informed the course of events.[61] Williams did not think that a general's performance could be wholly explained merely by reference to his professional upbringing, experience, or even his intelligence. These attributes, however "meritorious and desirable, are not sufficient in themselves to produce greatness," he argued. Instead, he pronounced himself in agreement with Napoleon's view: "Anyone who knows the Civil War can easily tick off a number of generals who fit exactly the pattern described . . . by Napoleon: 'There are certain men, who, on account of their moral and physical constitution, paint mental pictures out of everything: however exalted their reason, their will, their courage, and whatever good qualities they may possess, nature has not fitted them to command armies, nor to direct great operations of war.'"[62]

For Williams, it was the ineffable quality of character, which he defined as "mental strength and moral power," through which any historical figure's behavior and performance could best be explained. This meant above all that a general should not carry preconceived notions or the prejudices of tradition with him into battle, and that he should have a psychological balance that protected him from being "dazzled, or intoxicated, by good or bad news."[63]

Judging Confederate generals by these standards, Williams found them—as well as many of their Union counterparts—sorely wanting. Whereas ten pages earlier, Williams admitted Lee onto the short list of Civil War "greats," in the ensuing discussion he had been found guilty of a flawed character and demoted. Of the entire corps of generals on both sides, Williams believed only two—Grant and Sherman—possessed the force of character sufficient to transcend their past and to understand the war they were waging and thus warranted admission to the ranks of martial greatness.[64]

By contrast, he argued, "the most distinguishing feature of Southern generalship is that it did not grow. Lee and the other Confederate commanders were pretty much the same men in 1865 that they had been in 1861."[65] And if Lee could not escape criticism, the lesser lights of the Confederacy stood little chance. Of the other Confederates who commanded armies—Beauregard, A. S. Johnston, Bragg, Joe Johnston, and Kirby Smith—Williams thought they were either not up to command in the first place or "were no better than average soldiers." As corps commanders, he rated Longstreet and Jackson as outstanding, "probably the best in the war," but even these two he thought had reached their limits at that echelon. Jackson in particular he believed did not possess the requisite administrative skills to go any higher, and in any case he had not been "fairly tested against first-rate opposition." In three paragraphs, Williams set the stage for a generation of arguments between Civil War historians and enthusiasts.[66] Their only consolation was that Williams was every bit as critical—perhaps even more—of Union generals.

Williams saw himself as a tough-minded, evenhanded scholar, yet he clearly identified with the Union cause and the citizens who fought for it. His reading of the war's history seemed to bear out his sympathies, sympathies that were most prominent in his innovative collective biography of a Civil War regiment, *Hayes of the Twenty-third*.[67] To him the war was no more or less than a struggle for the nation's future. The North stood on the side of history's progressive march forward. The South represented the reactionary skein in the nation's past; it was atavistic, mired in an imagined, romantic world that existed for only a few, if even them. For Williams, the South and its leaders failed the ultimate test of looking reality straight in the face, of failing to understand they could not turn back American history itself. From Jefferson Davis to the lowliest soldier, the Confederacy was the victim of its own illusions. These precepts guided Williams through his long academic and public career. As much a creature of his own upbringing and sensibilities as any of the generals on whose performance he sat in judgment, Williams saw no need to rise above his origins. After all, with no bullets flying, the guidance of his own past seemed more than sufficient.

Notes

I am indebted to Joseph Dawson, Joseph Glatthaar, Peter Maslowski, Brian Holden Reid, Richard Swain, and Frank Wetta for their assistance in the preparation of this essay. Long-suffering friends all.

1. The most extensive accounting of Williams's written work is in Roger D. Launius, "A Bibliography of the Works of T. Harry Williams," *Louisiana History: The Journal of the Louisiana Historical Association* 25, no. 1 (Winter 1984): 5–28. See also "Publications of T. Harry Williams" in this volume, pages 295–300.
2. Gordon Craig, "Delbruck: The Military Historian," in *The Makers of Modern Strategy from Machiavelli to the Nuclear Age*, ed. Peter Paret (Princeton, 1986), 261. See also Arden Bucholtz, *Hans Delbrück and the German Military Establishment* (Iowa City, 1985). In the preface to the fourth volume of Delbrück's classic work, *Geschichte der Kriegskunst im Rahmen der politischen Geschichte*, he wrote, "This work has been written not for the sake of the art of war, but for the sake of world history. If military men read it and are stimulated by it, I am pleased and regard that as an honor; but it was written for friends of history by a historian."
3. Fuller and Liddell Hart especially promoted agendas of their own, and military history and commentary were the media through which they advanced them. Both aimed to reform the British army and were men of affairs as well as of ideas. Their studies of the Civil War, especially their biographies of Sherman and Grant, occupied an important place in Civil War historiography from the 1930s onward.

4. The evolution of European military thought in the nineteenth and early twentieth centuries is expertly surveyed in Azar Gat, *A History of Military Thought from the Enlightenment to the Cold War* (Oxford, 2001).

5. David Herbert Donald, *Lincoln Reconsidered: Essays on the Civil War Era* (New York, 1961), 82.

6. His classmates included Richard Current, Kenneth Stamp, and Frank Freidel.

7. Charles Joyner, "A Legacy of Distinction: Introducing Past Presidents of the Southern Historical Association," Southern Historical Association 75th annual meeting, http://www.uga.edu/sha/meeting/presidents/ (accessed Aug. 27, 2010).

8. So remembers Richard Current in "Wisconsin's Civil War Historians," *Wisconsin Magazine of History* 70, no. 1 (Autumn 1986): 28.

9. William Best Hesseltine to T. Harry Williams, Oct. 29, 1961, T. Harry Williams Papers, Louisiana and Lower Mississippi Valley Collections, Special Collections, Hill Memorial Library, Louisiana State University Libraries, Baton Rouge (hereafter cited as THW Papers).

10. T. Harry Williams, *Lincoln and the Radicals* (1941; Madison, WI, 1965), vii–viii.

11. Ibid., 35.

12. T. Harry Williams, review of *George B. McClellan: The Man Who Saved the Union,* by H. J. Eckenrode and Bryan Conrad, *Journal of Southern History* 8, no. 2 (May 1942): 278.

13. Ibid., 279.

14. THW to Fred Benton III, Jan.11, 1964, THW Papers.

15. An excellent picture of the insurgent, combative currents sweeping through the American historical profession at this time is drawn by Peter Novick, *That Noble Dream: The "Objectivity Question" and the American Historical Profession* (Cambridge, 1988), 225–39.

16. Frank Wetta, "T. Harry Williams, 1909–1979," unpublished manuscript in the author's possession.

17. Bell I. Wiley, "T. Harry Williams as I Knew Him," in *Military Affairs* 44, no. 1 (Feb. 1980): 33–34. A faded clipping from LSU's student newspaper, the *Daily Revillie,* dated sometime in February 1942, mentions Williams's research on Beauregard.

18. THW to William Best Hesseltine, Mar. 8, 1943; Apr. 6, 1943; Apr. 12, 1943; Feb. 25, 1944; and [May?] 1945, William Best Hesseltine Papers, Wisconsin Historical Society, Madison (hereafter cited as Hesseltine Papers). In March 1944, Williams signed one of his letters to Hesseltine "T. H. W. D. D. (draft dodger)."

19. Harold B. McSween, "T. Harry Williams: A Remembrance," *Virginia Historical Quarterly* 76, no. 4 (Autumn 2000): 702. At midwar, Williams wrote to Hesseltine that he was "teaching 400 Army students." These students were part of the Army Specialized Training Program, in which certain recruits were sent to colleges instead of military training so as to provide for a cadre of future officers. THW to William Best Hesseltine, July 1, 1943, Hesseltine Papers.

20. Charles P. Roland, *My Odyssey through History: Memoirs of War and Academe* (Baton Rouge, 2004). Otis Singletary and Joe Gray Taylor, both veterans who would go on to successful careers as Civil War historians, were among Roland's classmates at LSU.

21. Walt Whitman, *Prose Works* (Philadelphia, 1892).

22. Roland, *My Odyssey,* 126.

23. Charles P. Roland to the author, e-mail, Feb. 13, 2010. This exchange probably took place in the mid-1950s, when Williams was doing research for his *Hayes of the Twenty-third: The Civil War Volunteer Officer* (New York, 1965). His correspondence includes two long letters on the subject of Civil War small unit command and control from William Kaye, who was then with the National Park Service at the Shiloh National Military Park. See Bill [William Kaye] to THW, Dec. 5 and Dec. 28, 1956, THW Papers.

24. Frank James Price, *Troy H. Middleton: A Biography* (Baton Rouge, 1974), 33, 38, 50–51, 58–59, 63–67, 76, 86–91, 122–23, 134–35, 141, 159, 171, 306. Middleton lost no time retiring from the army once the war in Europe ended. He returned to LSU in August 1945 as university comptroller. Five years later he was appointed president of LSU, a post he held until he retired for good in 1962. See also Roland, *My Odyssey,* 49.

25. The absence of documentary evidence should not be taken as the final word on the relations between the two men. Williams dedicated his *Americans at War* (Baton Rouge, 1960) to "Troy Middleton: A Soldier of the Republic." See also Williams's essay, "The Macs and the Ikes: America's Two Military Traditions," *American Mercury* 75 (Oct. 1952): 32–39. Williams evidently showed Middleton a draft of this essay, or perhaps the published version. Middleton replied, "I only wish that all young officers who aspire to reach the grade of general and those who must serve under those who will see their dream come true would read what you have written." Troy Middleton to THW, Oct. 8, 1952, THW Papers.

26. T. Harry Williams, "The Attack upon West Point during the Civil War," *Mississippi Valley Historical Review* 25, no. 1 (Mar. 1939): 491–504.

27. Williams, *Americans at War,* 47–48.

28. On the eve of the war, the regular army carried 440 West Point graduates on its active rolls. Another 508 had left the army before the war, and of these, 115 re-

turned to the regulars while 338 more volunteered for service with their states. Williams, *Hayes of the Twenty-third,* 21–22.

29. T. Harry Williams, *Beauregard: Napoleon in Gray* (Baton Rouge, 1955), 6–7. The military historian Jay Luvaas was fond of pointing out that West Point did not produce generals at all, but second lieutenants. I am grateful to Joseph Glatthaar for reminding me of Luvaas's remark.

30. Williams, *Beauregard,* 66–67.

31. See William J. Cooper Jr.'s analysis of Davis's war leadership in *Jefferson Davis and the Civil War Era* (Baton Rouge, 2008), 81–89.

32. T. Harry Williams, "The Military Systems of the North and South," in *The Selected Essays of T. Harry Williams,* ed. and with a biographical introduction by Estelle Williams, (Baton Rouge, 1983), 154–57. This essay originally appeared in *Why the North Won the Civil War,* ed. David Donald (Baton Rouge, 1960).

33. Cooper, *Jefferson Davis,* 88–89.

34. Williams, *Beauregard,* 240.

35. Ibid., 67.

36. Wiley, "T. Harry Williams," 33–34; THW to Henry Shaw, Dec. 14, 1951, THW Papers.

37. Frank Vandiver, "Williams and the Generals," in *The Confederate High Command and Related Topics: The 1988 Deep Delta Civil War Symposium: Themes in Honor of T. Harry Williams,* ed. Roman J. Heleniak and Lawrence L. Hewitt (Shippensburg, PA, 1990), 3–4. This is not to say that Williams ever went over to the other side. He seemed to enjoy being a stranger in a strange land, fluent in its language and mores but never to be confused with the indigenes.

38. Williams, *Beauregard,* vii.

39. The version of Jomini's military theory most likely available to Beauregard while he was at West Point was Antoine-Henri Jomini, *Traité des grandes opérations militaires, contenant l'histoire des campagnes de Frédéric II, comparées à celle de l'empereur Napoléon; avec un recueil des principes généraux de l'art de la guerre,* 2d ed., 4 vols. (Paris, 1811). Jomini's *Précis de l'art de la guerre* was not published until 1838, the year Beauregard graduated from the academy. The standard interpretation in English of Jomini's life and thought is by John W. Shy, "Jomini," in *The Makers of Modern Strategy: From Machiavelli to the Nuclear Age,* ed. Peter Paret (Princeton, 1986), 143–85.

40. Williams, *Beauregard,* 93.

41. Ibid., 29.

42. Ibid., 33.

43. Ibid., 93.

44. Ibid., 126–27.

45. Williams's paper was delivered at the AHA's annual meeting on December 28, 1953; Freeman had died six months earlier. The paper was published over a year later as "Freeman, Historian of the Civil War: An Appraisal," *Journal of Southern History* 21, no. 1 (Feb. 1955): 91–100 (hereafter cited as Williams, "Freeman's Lee").

46. Avery Cravens leveled much the same charge against Williams's treatment of Lincoln in a critical review; see his review of *Lincoln and His Generals* in the *Mississippi Valley Historical Review* 39, no. 2 (Sept. 1952): 337–39.

47. Of Freeman himself, Williams was respectful and admiring, praising his literary style, his "sense of fairness and honesty," his scholarship, and his mastery of detail. Striving to be generous, Williams wrote that Freeman "tried to be objective and usually was." That "usually" was an important caveat in an essay that would go on to lodge substantive criticism of both the historian and the general whose life had preoccupied him. Williams, "Freeman's Lee," 92–93.

48. Ibid., 94–96.

49. T. Harry Williams, "A Pattern of a Historian: A Critical Discussion of D. S. Freeman and his Biography of R. E. Lee," Chicago Civil War Round Table, 131st annual meeting, Mar. 18, 1954, on CD-ROM, in possession of the author. I am indebted to Lawrence Hewitt for bringing this recording to my attention.

50. THW to Tom [Thomas Connelly?], June 11, 1975, THW Papers.

51. Williams, "Freeman's Lee," 97.

52. Ibid., 89.

53. Williams had already addressed in some detail his criticism of Lee's staff work in *Lincoln and His Generals,* 312–13. See also T. Harry Williams, *The Military Leadership of the North and the South,* Harmon Memorial Lecture Number Two (Colorado Springs, 1960), 15, available online at http://www.usafa.edu/df/dfh/harmonmemorial.cfm/ (hereafter cited as Harmon Lecture).

54. Williams, "Freeman's Lee," 97–98.

55. The most elaborate, sustained criticisms of Williams's interpretation, which propound the remarkable assertion that Jominian and Clausewitzian theories of war are consistent with one another, came in the form of two works: Herman Hattaway and Archer Jones, *How the North Won: A Military History of the Civil War* (Urbana, IL, 1983); and Richard Beringer, Herman Hattaway, Archer Jones, and William Still Jr., *Why the South Lost the Civil War* (Athens, GA, 1986), see especially 4–34. Also see Frank Wetta's discussion in this volume on the historiographical issues raised by Williams's interpretation.

56. A recent addition to this criticism comes from Brian Holden Reid, *The American Civil War: The Operational Battlefield, 1861–1863* (London, 2008).

57. Palmer Bradley to THW, Mar. 3, 1959, THW Papers.

58. THW to Frank Vandiver, Oct. 5, 1960, THW Papers.

59. THW to Charles Roland, Oct. 11, 1961, THW Papers.

60. Harmon Lecture.

61. Williams, "Biographical Introduction," 4–5.

62. Harmon Lecture, 3.

63. Ibid. This phrase is Napoleon's.

64. Ibid., 6, 16.

65. Ibid., 16.

66. Ibid, 9–10.

67. Williams, *Hayes of the Twenty-third;* see esp. x–xi and 19–38.

Publications of T. Harry Williams

Books

Lincoln and the Radicals. Madison: University of Wisconsin Press, 1941.

Editor. *Selected Writings and Speeches of Abraham Lincoln*. Chicago: Packard, 1943.

Lincoln and His Generals. New York: Alfred A. Knopf, 1952.

P. G. T. Beauregard: Napoleon in Gray. Baton Rouge: Louisiana State University Press, 1955.

Editor. *With Beauregard in Mexico: The Mexican War Reminiscences of P. G. T. Beauregard*. Baton Rouge: Louisiana State University Press, 1956.

Abraham Lincoln: Selected Speeches, Messages, and Letters. New York: Rinehart and Winston, 1957.

With Richard N. Current and Frank Freidel. *A History of the United States*. 2 vols. 1959. Rev. eds., New York: Alfred A. Knopf, 1964, 1969.

Americans at War: The Development of the American Military System. Baton Rouge: Louisiana State University Press, 1960.

With Richard N. Current and Frank Freidel. *American History: A Survey*. 1961. Rev. eds., New York: Alfred A. Knopf, 1966, 1971, 1975, 1979, 1983.

Romance and Realism in Southern Politics. Athens: University of Georgia Press, 1961.

McClellan, Sherman, and Grant. New Brunswick, NJ: Rutgers University Press, 1962.

Editor. *Military Memoirs of a Confederate, by General E. P. Alexander*. Bloomington: Indiana University Press, 1962.

The Union Sundered, 1849–1865. New York: Time, 1963. Vol. 5 of *The* Life *History of the United States*.

The Union Restored, 1861–1876. New York: Time, 1963. Vol. 6 of *The* Life *History of the United States*.

Editor. *Every Man a King: The Autobiography of Huey P. Long*. Chicago: Quadrangle Books, 1964.

Editor. *Hayes: The Diary of a President, 1875–1881*. New York: David McKay, 1964.

Hayes of the Twenty-third: The Civil War Volunteer Officer. New York: Alfred A. Knopf, 1965.

With Hazel Catherine Wolf. *Our American Nation*. Columbus, OH: C. E. Merrill, 1966.

Huey Long. New York: Alfred A. Knopf, 1969. Winner of Pulitzer Prize for Biography and the National Book Award.

One American Nation: Teachers' Annotated Edition. Columbus, OH: C. E. Merrill, 1969.

With Richard N. Current and Frank Freidel. *The Essentials of American History*. 1972. Rev. ed., New York: Alfred A. Knopf, 1976.

Coedited with Thomas C. Cochran and Charles B. Dew. *The Meanings of American History: Interpretations of Events, Ideas, and Institutions, Civil War to the Present*. Vol. 2. Glenview, IL: Scott Foresman, 1972.

The History of American Wars: From Colonial Times to World War I. New York: Alfred A. Knopf, 1981. Reprinted as *The History of American Wars: From 1745 to 1918*.

The Selected Essays of T. Harry Williams. Edited by and with a biographical introduction by Estelle Williams. Baton Rouge: Louisiana State University Press, 1983.

Essays in Professional Publications

"Frémont and the Politicians." *Journal of the American Military History Institute* 2 (Winter 1938): 178–91. Reprinted in *Military Analysis of the Civil War: An Anthology by the Editors of Military Affairs*. Millwood, NY: KTO Press, 1977.

"Benjamin F. Wade and the Atrocity Propaganda of the Civil War." *Ohio State Archaeological and Historical Quarterly* 48 (Jan. 1939): 33–43.

"The Attack Upon West Point During the Civil War." *Mississippi Valley Historical Review* 25 (Mar. 1939): 491–504.

"General Banks and the Radical Republicans in the Civil War." *New England Quarterly* 12 (June 1939): 268–80.

"The Committee on the Conduct of the War." *Journal of the American Military History Institute* 3 (Fall 1939): 139–56.

With Helen J. Williams. "Wisconsin Republicans and Reconstruction, 1865–1870." *Wisconsin Magazine of History* 23 (Sept. 1939): 17–39.

"The Navy and the Committee on the Conduct of the War." *United States Naval Institute Proceedings* 65 (Dec. 1939): 1751–55.

"Andrew Johnson as a Member of the Committee on the Conduct of the War." *East Tennessee Historical Society Publications* 12 (1940): 70–83. Designated best article to appear in *ETHSP* 12.

Coedited with James S. Ferguson. "'The Life of Jefferson Davis,' by M'Arone." *Journal of Mississippi History* 5 (Oct. 1943): 197–203.

"Free State Government for Louisiana." *Illinois State Historical Society Journal* 37 (Mar. 1944): 85–86.

"Voters in Blue: The Citizen Soldiers of the Civil War." *Mississippi Valley Historical Review* 31 (Sept. 1944): 187–204.

"The Louisiana Unification Movement of 1874." *Journal of Southern History* 9 (Aug. 1945): 349–69.

"General Ewell to the High Private in the Rear." *Virginia Magazine of History and Biography* 54 (Apr. 1946): 157–60.

"An Analysis of Some Reconstruction Attitudes." *Journal of Southern History* 12 (Nov. 1946): 469–86. Reprinted in Donald Sheehan, ed., *The Making of American History*. Vol. 2, *Democracy in an Industrial World*. New York: Drydan Press, 1954; and in Frank Freidel and Norman Pollack, eds., *Builders of American Institutions: Readings in United States History*. Chicago: Rand McNally, 1963.

"Abraham Lincoln—Principle and Pragmatism in Politics: A Review Article." *Mississippi Valley Historical Review* 40 (June 1953): 89–106.

"Investigation: 1862." *American Heritage* 6 (Dec. 1954): 16–21.

"Freeman: Historian of the Civil War, an Appraisal." *Journal of Southern History* 21 (Feb. 1955): 91–100.

"Beauregard at Shiloh." *Civil War History* 1 (Mar. 1955): 17–34. Reprinted in *Confederate Generals in the Western Theater*. Vol. 1, *Classic Essays on America's Civil War*, edited by Lawrence Lee Hewitt and Arthur W. Bergeron Jr. Knoxville: University of Tennessee Press, 2010.

Editor. "The Civil War Letters of William L. Cage." *Louisiana Historical Quarterly* 39 (Jan. 1956): 113–30.

"Introduction." In *Rebel Brass: The Confederate Command System*, by Frank E. Vandiver. Baton Rouge: Louisiana State University Press, 1956.

Editor. "The Reluctant Warrior: The Diary of N. K. Nichols." *Civil War History* 3 (Mar. 1957): 17–39.

"Abraham Lincoln: The Military Strategist." *Civil War Times* 1 (Oct. 1959): 1, 3.

"Abraham Lincoln: Pragmatic Democrat." In *The Enduring Lincoln*, edited by Norman A. Graebner. Urbana: University of Illinois Press, 1959.

"Introduction." In *Louisiana State University: A Pictorial Record of the First Hundred Years*, by V. L. Bledsole and Oscar Richard. Baton Rouge: Louisiana State University Press, 1959.

"Lincoln, the Military Strategist." In *Abraham Lincoln: A New Portrait*, edited by Henry B. Kranz. New York: G. P. Putnam, 1959.

"The Gentleman from Louisiana: Demagogue or Democrat." *Journal of Southern History* (Feb. 1960): 3–21. Presidential address delivered to the Southern Historical Association. Reprinted in George B. Tindall, ed., *The Pursuit of Southern History: Presidential Addresses of the Southern Historical Association, 1935–1963.* Baton Rouge: Louisiana State University Press, 1964. In Henry C. Dethloff, ed., *Huey P. Long: Southern Demagogue or American Democrat?* Boston: Houghton Mifflin, 1967; and in Glenn R. Conrad, gen. ed., *Readings in Louisiana History.* New Orleans: Louisiana Historical Association, 1977.

"A Yankee Soldier on Louisiana's Rainy Season." *Louisiana History* 1 (Fall 1960): 344–45.

"The American Civil War." In *The Zenith of European Power, 1830–1870.* Vol. 10, *The New Cambridge Modern History,* edited by J. P. T. Bury. Cambridge: Cambridge University Press, 1960.

"Lincoln: 1861–1865." In *The Ultimate Decision: The President as Commander-in-Chief,* edited by Ernest R. May. New York: George Braziller, 1960.

"Lincoln and the Causes of the Civil War." In *Lincoln Images: Augustana College Centennial Essays,* edited by O. Fritiof Ander. Rock Island, IL: Augustana College Library, 1960.

"Lincoln and the Committee on the Conduct of the War." In *Lincoln for the Ages,* edited by Ralph G. Newman. Garden City, NY: Doubleday, 1960.

"The Military Leadership of North and South." In *Why the North Won the Civil War,* edited by David Donald. Baton Rouge: Louisiana State University Press, 1960. Reprinted in Raymond G. O'Connor, ed., *American Defense Policy in Perspective.* New York: John Wiley and Sons, 1965.

"P. G. T. Beauregard: The South's First Hero." In *The Unforgettable Americans,* edited by John A. Garraty. Great Neck, NY: Channel Press, 1960.

Editor. "Louisiana Regiments in the Civil War." *Louisiana History* 2 (Spring 1961): 256.

"The Politics of the Longs." *Georgia Review* 15 (Spring 1961): 20–33.

"Impact of Leadership on Planning and Strategy [during the Civil War]." *Official Army Information Digest* [Aug. 1961]: 15–21.

"That Strange Sad War." *Colorado Quarterly* 10 (Winter 1962): 265–76.

Editor. "Disruption of the Union: The Secession Crisis of 1860–1861." In *Major Crises in American History: Documentary Problems,* Leonard W. Levy and Merrill D. Peterson, gen. eds. Vol. 1, *1689–1861.* New York: Harcourt, Brace, and World, 1962.

"Badger Colonels and the Civil War Officer." *Wisconsin Magazine of History* 47 (Autumn 1963): 35–46.

"Hour of Surrender." *Louisiana History* 4 (Winter 1963): 93.

"Foreword." In *The Civil War in Louisiana,* by John D. Winters. Baton Rouge: Louisiana State University Press, 1963.

"Foreword." In *The Port Hudson Campaign, 1862–1863,* by Edward Cunningham. Baton Rouge: Louisiana State University Press, 1963.

With Stephen E. Ambrose. "The 23d Ohio—Regiment of Presidents." *Civil War Times Illustrated* 3 (May 1964): 22–25.

"Foreword." In *Military Record of Louisiana: Including Biographical and Historical Papers Relating to the Military Organizations of the State,* by Napier Bartlett. Baton Rouge: Louisiana State University Press, 1964.

"General Grant." In *Readings in American History,* edited by John S. Ezell, Gilbert C. Fite, and Joe B. Franz, vol 1. Boston: Houghton Mifflin, 1964. Excerpts from Williams, *Lincoln and His Generals.*

"Lincoln and the Radicals: An Essay in Civil War History and Historiography." In *Grant, Lee, Lincoln and the Radicals: Essays on Civil War Leadership,* edited by Grady McWhiney. Evanston, IL: Northwestern University Press, 1964.

"Trends in Southern Politics." In *The Idea of the South: Pursuit of a Central Theme,* edited by Frank E. Vandiver. Chicago: University of Chicago Press for William Marsh Rice University, 1964.

"Louisiana Mystery—An Essay Review." *Louisiana History* 6 (Summer 1965): 287–91.

"Introduction to the Third Printing." In Williams, *Lincoln and the Radicals.* Madison: University of Wisconsin Pres, 1965.

"The Military Systems of North and South." In *Patterns in American History,* edited by Alexander DeConde, Armin Rappaport, and William R. Steckel, vol. 1. Belmont, CA: Wadsworth, 1965. Reprinted from Williams, *Americans at War.*

Editor. "Terms of Surrender for the Army of Northern Virginia, 1865." In *An American Primer,* edited by Daniel J. Boorstin. Chicago: University of Chicago Press, 1966.

"Lincoln Surrenders to the Radicals." In *Lincoln and Civil War Politics,* edited by James A. Rawley. New York: Holt, Rinehart, and Winston, 1969. Reprinted from Williams, *Lincoln and the Radicals.*

"Preface." In *The Papers of Ulysses S. Grant.* Vol. 2, *April–September 1861,* edited by John Y. Simon. Carbondale: Southern Illinois University Press, 1969.

With John Milton Price. "The Huey P. Long Papers at Louisiana State University." *Journal of Southern History* 36 (May 1970): 256–61.

"The Civil War." In *Interpreting American History: Conversations with Historians,* edited by John A. Garraty, vol. 1. New York: Macmillan, 1970.

"Foreword." In *The Earl of Louisiana,* by A. J. Liebling. Baton Rouge: Louisiana State University Press, 1970.

"A Great Natural Strategist." In *The Leadership of Abraham Lincoln,* edited by Don E. Fehrenbacher. New York: John Wiley and Sons, 1970. From "Lincoln the Military Strategist," in *Abraham Lincoln: A New Portrait,* edited by Henry B. Kranz. New York: G. P. Putnam, 1959.

"Huey Long and the Politics of Realism." In *Essays on Recent Southern Politics: The Walter Prescott Webb Memorial Lectures,* edited by Harold M. Hollingsworth. Austin: University of Texas Press, 1970.

"The Issue that Could Not Be Put Off." In *The Leadership of Abraham Lincoln,* edited by Don E. Fehrenbacher. New York: John Wiley and Sons, 1970. From "The Causes of the Civil War." In *Lincoln Images: Augustana College Centennial Essays,* edited by O. Fritiof Ander. Rock Island, IL: Augustana College Library, 1960.

"The Politics of the Longs." In *Huey Long,* edited by Hugh Davis Graham. Englewood Cliffs, NJ: Prentice-Hall, 1970. Excerpt from Williams, *Romance and Realism in Southern Politics.*

"Shall We Keep the Radicals?" In *The Leadership of Abraham Lincoln,* edited by Don E. Fehrenbacher. New York: John Wiley and Sons, 1970. From Williams, "Lincoln and the Radicals."

"Oral History and the Writing of Biography." In *Selections from the Fifth and Sixth National Colloquia on Oral History, 1970, 1971,* edited by Peter D. Olch and Forrest C. Pogue. New York: Oral History Association, 1972.

"Huey, Lyndon, and Southern Radicalism." *Journal of American History* 60 (Sept. 1973): 267–93. Presidential address given at 1973 annual meeting of the Organization of American Historians.

"On the Couch at Monticello." *Reviews in American History* 2 (Dec. 1974): 523–29.

"The Return of Jomini—Some Thoughts on Recent Civil War Writing." *Military Affairs* 39 (Fall 1975): 204–6.

"Lincoln and the Radicalism." In *Lincoln's Decision for Emancipation,* edited by Hans L. Trefousse, 103–5. Philadelphia: J. P. Lippincott, 1975. Excerpt from Williams, *Lincoln and the Radicals.*

"Introduction." In *Military Analysis of the Civil War: An Anthology by the Editors of Military Affairs.* Millwood, NY: KTO Press, 1977.

"The Fight Is Just Beginning." In *Readings in Louisiana History,* Glenn R. Conrad, gen. ed. New Orleans: Louisiana Historical Association, 1978. Excerpt from Williams, *Huey Long.*

"The Coming of the War." In *Shadows of the Storm,* vol. 1, edited by William C. Davis. Garden City, NY: Doubleday, 1981.

"The Military Systems of North and South." In *The Sweep of American History.* 2 vols., edited by Robert R. Jones and Gustave L. Seligmann Jr. New York: John Wiley and Sons, 1981. Excerpt from Williams, *Americans at War.*

Bibliography

Manuscripts

Anderson, Brig. Gen./Maj. Gen. Richard H. File. Compiled Service Records of Confederate General and Staff Officers, and Nonregimental Enlisted Men. National Archives and Records Administration, Washington, DC.

Anderson, Col. R. H. File. 1st (Butler's) South Carolina Regulars. Compiled Service Records of Confederate Soldiers Who Served in Organizations from the State of South Carolina. National Archives and Records Administration, Washington, DC.

Baker, Annie G. Diary. Presbyterian Historical Society, Montreat, NC.

Beauregard, P. G. T. Papers. Manuscripts Division. Library of Congress, Washington, DC.

Broaddus, William F. Diary. Library of Virginia, Richmond.

Callaway, Morgan. Papers. Special Collections Department. Robert W. Woodruff Library, Emory University, Atlanta.

Campbell-Colston Family Papers. Southern Historical Collection. University of North Carolina at Chapel Hill.

Dabney, Robert L. Papers. Union Theological Seminary, Richmond, VA.

Emerson, Nancy. Diary. Special Collections. University of Virginia, Charlottesville.

Fries and Shaffner. Family Papers. Southern Historical Collection. University of North Carolina at Chapel Hill.

Gordon, John B. Collection, 1832–1904. Hargrett Rare Book and Manuscript Library. University of Georgia Libraries, Athens.

Gordon, John B. Folder. Atlanta Historical Society, Atlanta, GA.

Gordon, John Brown. Family Papers. Hargrett Rare Book and Manuscript Library. University of Georgia Libraries, Athens.

Gordon, John Brown. Papers. Manuscript, Archives, and Rare Book Library. Emory University, Atlanta, GA.

Harris, Henry St. George. Papers. Special Collections Department. William R. Perkins Library. Duke University, Durham, NC.

Hesseltine, William Best. Papers. Wisconsin Historical Society, Madison.

Hoke, Robert F. Papers. North Carolina Department of Archives and History, Raleigh.

Jackson, Thomas J. Papers. Virginia Military Institute Archives, Lexington.

Johnston, Albert Sidney and William Preston. Papers. Mrs. Mason Barret Collection. Manuscripts Davison. Howard-Tilton Memorial Library, Tulane University, New Orleans.

Lexington Presbytery Minutes. Union Theological Seminary, Richmond, VA.

Mahone, William. "The Battle of the Crater." Virginia Historical Society, Richmond.

Pegram-Johnson-McIntosh. Papers. Virginia Historical Society, Richmond.

Read Family Correspondence. Department of Special Collections. Hesburgh Libraries. University of Notre Dame, Notre Dame, IN.

Routt, William H. Papers. Museum of the Confederacy, Richmond, VA.

Short, William Burch. Letters. Museum of the Confederacy, Richmond, VA.

Wells, Henry Duplessis. Papers. Southern Historical Collection. University of North Carolina at Chapel Hill.

White, George William. "On the Death of Stonewall Jackson." White Collection. Presbyterian Historical Society, Montreat, NC.

Williams, T. Harry. Papers. Louisiana and Lower Mississippi Valley Collections. Special Collections. Hill Memorial Library. Louisiana State University Libraries, Baton Rouge.

Government Documents

Journal of the Congress of the Confederate States of America, 1861–1865. 7 vols. Washington, DC: Government Printing Office, 1904–5.

U.S. War Department. *The War of the Rebellion: A Compilation of the Official Records of the Union and Confederate Armies.* 128 vols. Washington, DC: Government Printing Office, 1880–1901.

Newspapers and Periodicals

Atlanta Constitution

Atlanta Journal

Charleston Mercury

Christian Observer (Richmond, VA)

Daily Revillie (Baton Rouge, LA)

Dial

Fayetteville (NC) *Observer*

Jackson Daily Mississippian
Liberator (Boston)
Lowell (MA) *Daily Citizen and News*
Macon (GA) *Telegraph*
Milledgeville (GA) *Confederate Union*
Milledgeville (GA) *Southern Recorder*
Nation
New Hampshire Statesman (Concord)
New Haven (CT) *Daily Palladium*
New Orleans Tribune
New York Herald
New York Independent
New York Observer and Chronicle
New York Times
Outlook
Raleigh (NC) *Semi-Weekly Register*
Religious Herald (Richmond, VA)
Southern Churchman (Richmond, VA)
Time
Washington Daily National Intelligencer
Weekly Raleigh (NC) *Register*
Wisconsin State Register (Portage)

Printed Primary Sources

Alexander, Edward Porter. *Fighting for the Confederacy: The Personal Recollections of the General Edward Porter Alexander*. Edited by Gary W. Gallagher. Chapel Hill: University of North Carolina Press, 1989.

———. *Military Memoirs of a Confederate*. New York: Charles Scribner's Sons, 1907. Reprint, edited by T. Harry Williams. Bloomington: Indiana University Press, 1962.

———. "Sketch of Longstreet's Division—Yorktown and Williamsburg." *Southern Historical Society Papers* 10 (1882): 32–45.

Anonymous. "Recollections of Jubal Early by One Who Followed Him." *Century Magazine* 70 (May 1905): 311–13.

Apperson, John Samuel. *Repairing the "March of Mars": The Civil War Diaries of John Samuel Apperson, Hospital Steward in the Stonewall Brigade, 1861–1865*. Edited by John D. Roper. Macon, GA: Mercer University Press, 2001.

Beale, G. W. *A Lieutenant of Cavalry in Lee's Army.* 1918. Reprint. Baltimore: Butternut & Blue, 1994.

Beauregard, P. G. T. "The Battle of Petersburg." In *Battles and Leaders of the Civil War,* vol. 6, edited by Peter Cozzens. Urbana: University of Illinois Press, 2004.

———. "Four Days of Battle at Petersburg." In Johnson and Buel, *Battles and Leaders of the Civil War,* vol. 4.

Bennett, William W. *A Narrative of the Great Revival Which Prevailed in the Southern Armies.* Harrisonburg, VA: Sprinkle Publications, 1989.

Blackford, Susan L., comp. *Letters from Lee's Army.* New York: A. S. Barnes, 1947.

Blackford, W. W. *War Years with Jeb Stuart.* New York: Charles Scribner's Sons, 1945.

Bratton, John. "The Battle of Williamsburg." *Southern Historical Society Papers* 7 (1879): 299–302.

Brook-Rawle, William. "Further Remarks on the Cavalry Fight on the Right Flank at Gettysburg." *Journal of the U.S. Cavalry Association* 4 (June 1891): 157–60.

———. "Gregg's Cavalry Fight at Gettysburg." *Journal of the U.S. Cavalry Association* 4 (Sept. 1891): 257–75.

Browder, George Richard. *The Heavens Are Weeping: The Diaries of George Richard Browder, 1852–1886.* Reprint. Grand Rapids, MI: Zondervan, 1987.

Brown, Campbell. *Campbell Brown's Civil War: With Ewell and the Army of Northern Virginia.* Edited by Terry L. Jones. Baton Rouge: Louisiana State University Press, 2001.

Bunting, Robert Franklin. *Our Trust Is in the God of Battles: The Civil War Letters of Robert Franklin Bunting, Chaplain, Terry's Texas Rangers, C.S.A.* Edited by Thomas W. Cutrer. Knoxville: University of Tennessee Press, 2006.

Burney, Samuel A. *A Southern Soldier's Letters Home: The Civil War Letters of Samuel A. Burney, Cobb's Georgia Legion, Army of Northern Virginia.* Edited by Nat S. Turner III. Macon, GA: Mercer University Press, 2002.

Campbell, Robert. *Lone Star Confederate: A Gallant and Good Soldier of the 5th Texas Infantry.* Edited by George Skoch and Mark W. Perkins. College Station: Texas A&M University Press, 2003.

Chesnut, Mary. *Mary Chesnut's Civil War.* Edited by C. Vann Woodward. New Haven, CT: Yale University Press, 1981.

Conway, Wm. B. "Talks with General J. A. Early—Valley Campaign and the Movement on Washington." *Southern Historical Society Papers* 30 (1902): 250–55.

Cooke, John Esten. *Wearing of the Gray.* 1867. Reprint. Bloomington: Indiana University Press, 1959.

Corsan, W. C. *Two Months in the Confederate States: An Englishman's Travels Through the South.* Edited by Benjamin H. Trask. Baton Rouge: Louisiana State University Press, 1996.

Cumming, Kate. *Kate: The Journal of a Confederate Nurse.* Edited by Richard Barksdale. Baton Rouge: Louisiana State University Press, 1959.

Cutrer, Thomas W., and T. Michael Parrish, eds. *Brothers in Gray: The Civil War Letters of the Pierson Family.* Baton Rouge: Louisiana State University Press, 1997.

Dabney, Robert Lewis. *True Courage: A Discourse Commemorative of Lieut. General Thomas J. Jackson.* Richmond, VA: Presbyterian Committee of Publication of the Confederate States, 1863.

Daggett, O. E. *A Sermon on the Death of Abraham Lincoln.* Canandaigua, NY: Milliken, 1865.

Davis, Jefferson. *The Papers of Jefferson Davis.* Vol. 8, *1862.* Edited by Lynda L. Crist, Mary S. Dix, and Kenneth H. Williams. Baton Rouge: Louisiana State University Press, 1995.

———. *The Papers of Jefferson Davis.* Vol. 9, *January–September 1863.* Edited by Lynda L. Crist, Mary S. Dix, and Kenneth H. Williams. Baton Rouge: Louisiana State University Press, 1997.

———. *The Papers of Jefferson Davis.* Vol. 10, *October 1863–August 1864.* Edited by Lynda L. Crist, Kenneth H. Williams, and Peggy L. Dillard. Baton Rouge: Louisiana State University Press, 1999.

Davis, Varina Howell. *Jefferson Davis, Ex-President of the Confederate States of America: A Memoir by His Wife.* 2 vols. Belford, NY: Belford, 1890.

Dawson, Francis W. *Reminiscences of Confederate Service, 1861–1865.* Charleston, SC: News and Courier Book Presses, 1882.

Douglas, Henry Kyd. *I Rode with Stonewall.* Chapel Hill: University of North Carolina Press, 1940.

Duke, Basil W. *Reminiscences of General Basil W. Duke, C.S.A.* Garden City, NY: Doubleday, Page, 1911.

Early, Jubal A. *The Campaigns of Robert E. Lee. An Address by Lt. Gen. Jubal A. Early before Washington and Lee University, January 19th, 1872.* Baltimore: John Murphy, 1872.

———. *Lieutenant General Jubal Anderson Early, C.S.A.: Autobiographical Sketch and Narrative of the War Between the States.* 1912. Reprint with introduction and notes by Gary Gallagher. Wilmington, NC: Broadfoot, 1989; New York: Da Capo, [1991].

———. *A Memoir of the Last Year of the War of Independence in the Confederate States of America.* New Orleans: Blelock, 1867.

Early, Ruth Hairston. *Lieutenant General Jubal A. Early: Autobiographical Sketch and Narrative of the War Between the States.* Philadelphia: J. B. Lippincott, 1912.

Edmondston, Catherine Ann Devereux. *"Journal of a Secesh Lady": The Diary of CatherineAnn Devereux Edmondston, 1860–1866.* Edited by Beth G. Crabtree and James W. Patton. Raleigh, NC: Division of Archives and History, 1979.

Evans, Clement A. "General Gordon and General Longstreet." *Independent* 56 (1904): 311–16.

Fain, Eliza Rhea Anderson. *Sanctified Trial: The Diary of Eliza Rhea Anderson Fain, a Confederate Woman in East Tennessee.* Edited by John N. Fain. Knoxville: University of Tennessee Press, 2004.

Field, C. W. "Campaign of 1864 and 1865." *Southern Historical Society Papers* 14 (1886): 542–63.

Fremantle, Arthur J. L. *Three Months in the Southern States.* New York: John Bradburn, 1864.

Frobel, Anne S. *The Civil War Diary of Anne S. Frobel.* Edited by Mary H. and Dallas M. Lancaster. McLean, VA: EPM, 1992.

Gache, Pere Louis-Hippolyte. *A Frenchman, a Chaplain, a Rebel: The War Letters of Pere Louis-Hippolyte Gache, S.J.* Translated by Cornelius M. Buckley. Chicago: Loyola University Press, 1981.

Garfield, James A. *The Wild Life of the Army: Civil War Letters of James A. Garfield.* Edited by Frederick D. Williams. East Lansing: Michigan State University Press, 1964.

Gordon, John B. "Last Days of the Confederacy." In *Modern Eloquence,* edited by Thomas B. Reed, vol. 5. Philadelphia: John D. Morris, 1900–1903.

———. *Reminiscences of the Civil War.* New York: Charles Scribner's Sons, 1903.

Gorgas, Josiah. *The Journals of Josiah Gorgas, 1857–1878.* Edited by Sarah Woolfolk Wiggins. Tuscaloosa: University of Alabama Press, 1995.

Gregg, David M. *The Second Cavalry Division of the Army of the Potomac in the Gettysburg Campaign.* Philadelphia: Loyal Legion of the United States, Pennsylvania Commandery Memorial Meeting, 1907.

Guerrant, Edward O. *Bluegrass Confederate: The Headquarters Diary of Edward O. Guerrant.* Edited by William C. Davis and Meredith L. Swentor. Baton Rouge: Louisiana State University Press, 1999.

Hagood, Johnson. *Memoirs of the War of Secession.* 1910. Reprint, Germantown, TN: Guild Bindery Press, 1994.

Haley, John. *The Rebel Yell and the Yankee Hurrah: The Civil War Journal of a Maine Volunteer.* Edited by Ruth L. Silliker. Camden, ME: Down East Books, 1985.

Heth, Henry. *Memoirs of Henry Heth.* Edited by James L. Morrison. New York: Greenwood Press, 1974.

Hewett, Janet E. *Supplement to the Official Records of the Union and Confederate Armies.* 100 vols. Wilmington, NC: Broadfoot, 1994–2004.

Jackson, Mary Anna. *Life and Letters of General Thomas J. Jackson.* Harrisonburg, VA: Sprinkle Publications, 1995.

Johnson, Robert U., and Clarence C. Buel, eds. *Battles and Leaders of the Civil War: Being for the most part contributions by Union and Confederate officers based upon "The Century War Series" edited by Robert Underwood Johnson and Clarence Clough Buel, of the editorial staff of The Century Magazine.* 4 vols. New York: Century, 1884–88.

Jones, John B. *A Rebel War Clerk's Diary at the Confederate States Capital.* 2 vols. Philadelphia: J. P. Lippincott, 1866.

Jones, J. William. *Christ in the Camp or Religion in the Confederate Army.* Atlanta: Martin and Hoyt, 1904.

Jones, Katharine M., ed. *Ladies of Richmond, Confederate Capital.* Indianapolis: Bobbs-Merrill, 1962.

Kidd, J. H. *Personal Recollections of a Cavalryman with Custer's Michigan Cavalry Brigade.* Ionia, MI: Sentinel Printing, 1908.

Kollock, Susan M., ed. "Letters of the Kollock and Allied Families, 1826–1884." *Georgia Historical Quarterly* 34 (Dec. 1950): 313–27.

[Lee, G. W. C.] "Report of General G. W. C. Lee, from the 2d to the 6th of April, 1865." *Southern Historical Society Papers* 13 (1885): 258.

Lee, Robert E. *Lee's Dispatches: Unpublished Letters of General Robert E. Lee, C.S.A., to Jefferson Davis and the War Department of The Confederate States of America, 1862–1865.* Edited by Douglas Southall Freeman. 1915. New ed. by Grady McWhiney. New York: G. P. Putnam's Sons, 1957.

———. *The Wartime Papers of R. E. Lee.* Edited by Clifford Dowdey and Louis H. Manarin. Boston: Little Brown, 1961; New York: Bramhall House, 1961.

Lincoln, Abraham. *The Collected Works of Abraham Lincoln.* Edited by Roy P. Basler. 9 vols. New Brunswick, NJ: Rutgers University Press, 1953–55.

Long, A. L. *Memoirs of Robert E. Lee: His Military and Personal History, Embracing a Large Amount of Information Hitherto Unpublished.* New York: J. M. Stoddart, 1886.

Longstreet, James. *From Manassas to Appomattox.* Philadelphia: J. B. Lippincott, 1896. Reprint, Bloomington: Indiana University Press, 1960.

———. "Lee's Right Wing at Gettysburg." In Johnson and Buel, *Battles and Leaders of the Civil War,* vol. 3.

Lyman, Theodore. *Meade's Army: The Private Notebooks of Lt. Col. Theodore Lyman.* Edited by David W. Lowe. Kent, OH: Kent State University Press, 2007.

Mahone, William. "On the Road to Appomattox." Edited by William C. Davis. *Civil War Times Illustrated* 11, no. 9 (Jan. 1971): 4–11, 42–47.

Marshall, Charles. *An Aide-de-Camp of Lee: Being the Papers of Colonel Charles Marshall.* Edited by Frederick Maurice. Boston: Little, Brown, 1927.

McGuire, Alexander K., ed. *Annals of the War Written by Leading Participants.* 1879. Reprint, Dayton, OH: Morningside, 1988.

McGuire, Judith W. *Diary of A Southern Refugee during the War, by a Lady of Virginia.* New York: E. J. Hale, 1867.

McSween, Harold B. "T. Harry Williams: A Remembrance." *Virginia Historical Quarterly* 76, no. 4 (Autumn 2000): 704–12.

Moore, Frank, ed. *Rebellion Record.* 11 vols. plus supplement. New York: G. P. Putnam, 1862–69.

Mosby, John S. *Memoirs of Colonel John S. Mosby.* Bloomington: Indiana University Press, 1959.

Myers, Robert Manson, ed. *The Children of Pride: A True Story of Georgia and the Civil War.* New Haven, CT: Yale University Press, 1972.

The New Texas Primary Reader. Designed for the Use of Schools in Texas. Houston: E. H. Cushing, 1863.

Owen, William Miller. *In Camp and Battle with the Washington Artillery of New Orleans.* 1885. Reprint, Baton Rouge: Louisiana State University Press, 1999.

"Paroles of the Army of Northern Virginia." *Southern Historical Society Papers* 15 (1887).

Patterson, Edmund D. *Yankee Rebel: The Civil War Journal of Edmund DeWitt Patterson.* Edited by John G. Barrett. 1966. Reprint, Knoxville: University of Tennessee Press, 2004.

Presbyterian Church, General Assembly. *Minutes 1863.* Columbia, SC: Southern Guardian Steam-Power Press, 1863.

Presbyterian Church, Synod of Virginia. *Minutes 1863.* [Richmond, VA, 1863?]

Protestant Episcopal Church, Diocese of Virginia. *Journal of the Sixty-Eighth Annual Council.* Richmond: Macfarlane and Fergusson, 1863.

Quint, Alonzo. *The Potomac and the Rapidan: Army Notes from the Failure at Winchester to the Reinforcement of Rosecrans, 1861–3.* Boston: Crosby and Nichols, 1864.

Ramsey, James Beverlin. *True Eminence Founded on Holiness.* Lynchburg, VA: Water-Power Presses Print, 1863.

Royall, William L. *Some Reminiscences.* New York: Neale Publishing, 1909.

Schmitt, Martin F. "An Interview with General Jubal A. Early in 1889." *Journal of Southern History* 115 (1945): 547–63.

Sorrel, G. Moxley. *Recollections of a Confederate Staff Officer.* New York: Neale Publishing, 1905; reprint, edited by Bell I. Wiley, Jackson, TN: McCowat-Mercer Press, 1958.

Southern Historical Society Papers. 52 vols. Richmond, VA: Southern Historical Society, 1876–1919.

Stillwell, William R. *The Stillwell Letters: A Georgian in Longstreet's Corps, Army of Northern Virginia.* Edited by Ronald H. Moseley. Macon, GA: Mercer University Press, 2002.

"Stonewall Jackson in Lexington, Va." *Southern Historical Society Papers* 9 (1881): 41–46.

Stuart, James E. B. *Letters of Major General James E. B. Stuart.* Edited by Adele H. Mitchell. n.p.: Stuart Mosby Historical Society, 1990.

Taylor, Richard. *Destruction and Reconstruction: Personal Experiences of the Late Civil War.* Edited by Richard B. Harwell. New York: Longmans, Green, 1955.

Taylor, Walter H. *Four Years with General Lee.* New York: D. Appleton, 1878; Bloomington: Indiana University Press, 1962; New York: Bonanza Books, 1962.

Thomas, Henry G. "Twenty-two Hours Prisoner of War in Dixie." In *War Papers Read Before the Commandery of the State of Maine, Military Order of the Loyal Legion of the United States.* 4 vols. Portland, ME: Lefavor-Tower, 1898.

Wharton, H. M. *War Songs and Poems of the Southern Confederacy, 1861–1865.* Edison, NJ: Castle Books, 2000.

White, William S. *Sketches of the Life of Captain Hugh A. White of the Stonewall Brigade.* Columbia: South Carolina Steam Press, 1864.

Wiatt, William Edward. *Confederate Chaplain William Edward Wiatt: An Annotated Diary.* Edited by Alex L. Wiatt. Lynchburg, VA: H. E. Howard, 1994.

Wise, Henry A. "The Career of Wise's Brigade, 1861–5." *Southern Historical Society Papers* 25 (1897): 1–22.

Printed Secondary Sources

Abbott, John. *History of the Civil War in America.* 2 vols. New York: Henry Bill, 1866.

Adcock, F. E. *The Greek and Macedonian Art of War.* Berkeley and Los Angeles: University of California Press, 1957.

Allan, Elizabeth Preston. *Life and Letters of Margaret Junkin Preston.* Boston: Houghton Mifflin, 1903.

Angle, Paul. *A Shelf of Lincoln Books: A Critical, Selective Bibliography of Lincolniana.* New Brunswick, NJ: Rutgers University Press, 1946.

Arnold, Thomas Jackson. *Early Life and Letters of General Thomas J. Jackson.* New York: Fleming H. Revell, 1916.

Ayers, Edward L. *In the Presence of Mine Enemies: War in the Heart of America, 1859–1863.* New York: W. W. Norton, 2003.

Becker, Ernest. *The Denial of Death.* 1973. Reprint, New York: Free Press, 1997.

Beringer, Richard E., Herman Hattaway, Archer Jones, and William N. Still Jr. *Why the South Lost the Civil War.* Athens: University of Georgia Press, 1986.

Bigelow, John Jr. *The Campaign of Chancellorsville: A Strategic and Tactical Study.* New Haven, CT: Yale University Press, 1910.

Blair, William A. "Grant's Second World War: The Battle for Historical Memory." In *The Spotsylvania Campaign,* edited by Gary W. Gallagher. Chapel Hill: University of North Carolina Press, 223–54. 1998.

Blight, David W. *Race and Reunion: The Civil War in American Memory.* Cambridge: Harvard University Press, 2001.

Boatner, Mark M., III. *The Civil War Dictionary.* New York: Davis McKay, 1959.

Boritt, Gabor S., ed. *The Gettysburg Nobody Knows.* New York: Oxford University Press, 1997.

Brinkley, Alan. *Voices of Protest: Huey Long, Father Coughlan, and the Great Depression.* New York: Vintage, 1982.

Brogan, D. W. "A Fresh Appraisal of the Civil War." *Harper's Magazine,* Apr. 1960, 121–44.

Bucholtz, Arden. *Hans Delbrück and the German Military Establishment.* Iowa City: University of Iowa Press, 1985.

Bulfinch, Thomas. *The Age of Fable or Beauties of Mythology.* Boston: S. W. Tilton, 1855.

Burne, Alfred H. *Lee, Grant and Sherman: A Study in Leadership in the 1864–65 Campaign.* New York: Charles Scribner's Sons, 1939.

Bushong, Millard K. *Old Jube: A Biography of General Jubal A. Early.* Shippensburg, PA: White Mane, 1955.

Campbell, Joseph. *The Masks of God.* 4 vols. New York: Viking Press, 1955–68.

Carhart, Tom. *Lost Triumph: Lee's Real Plan at Gettysburg—and Why It Failed.* New York: Putnam Adult, 2005.

Carmichael, Peter S., ed. *Audacity Personified: The Generalship of Robert E. Lee.* Baton Rouge: Louisiana State University Press, 2004.

Casdorph, Paul D. *Lee and Jackson: Confederate Chieftains.* New York: Paragon House, 1992.

Castel, Albert. "The Historian and the General: Thomas L. Connelly and Robert E. Lee." *Civil War History* 16, no. 1 (Mar. 1970): 50–63.

Catton, Bruce. *A Stillness at Appomattox.* New York: Pocket Books, 1958.

Cavanaugh, Michael A., and William Marvel. *The Battle of the Crater: "The Horrid Pit."* Lynchburg, VA: H. E. Howard, 1989.

Chadwick, Bruce. *The Reel Civil War: Mythmaking in American Film.* New York: Alfred A. Knopf, 2001.

Chandler, D. G. *The Campaigns of Napoleon.* London: Weidenfeld and Nicolson, 1966.

Churchill, Winston. *A History of the English Speaking People.* 4 vols. New York: Dodd, Mead, 1956–58.

Clausewitz, Carl Von. *On War.* 3 vols. New York: Kegan Paul, Trench, Trubner, 1940.

———. *On War.* Edited and translated by Michael Howard and Peter Paret. Princeton, NJ: Princeton University Press, 1976.

Cleaves, Freeman. *Meade of Gettysburg.* Norman: University of Oklahoma Press, 1960.

Clemons, William. "T. Harry Williams, at Home Down South." *New York Times Book Review,* Nov. 1969, 2.

Coddington, Edwin B. *The Gettysburg Campaign: A Study in Command.* New York: Charles Scribner's Sons, 1968.

Cohen, Eliot A., and John Cooch. *Military Misfortunes: The Anatomy of Failure in War.* New York: Free Press, 1990.

Connelly, Thomas L. *Autumn of Glory: The Army of Tennessee, 1862–1865.* Baton Rouge: Louisiana State University Press, 1971.

———. "The Image and the General: Robert E. Lee in American Historiography. *Civil War History* 19, no. 1 (Mar. 1973): 50–64.

———. *The Marble Man: Robert E. Lee and His Image in American Society.* New York: Alfred A. Knopf, 1977. Reprint, Baton Rouge: Louisiana State University Press, 1978.

———. "Robert E. Lee and the Western Confederacy: A Criticism of Lee's Strategic Ability." In Gallagher, *Lee the Soldier.*

Connelly, Thomas L., and Barbara L. Bellows. *God and General Longstreet: The Lost Cause and the Southern Mind.* Baton Rouge: Louisiana State University Press, 1982.

Connelly, Thomas L., and Archer Jones. *The Politics of Command: Factions and Ideas in Confederate Strategy.* Baton Rouge: Louisiana State University Press, 1973.

Cooper, William J., Jr. *Jefferson Davis, American.* New York: Alfred A. Knopf, 2000.

———. *Jefferson Davis and the Civil War Era.* Baton Rouge: Louisiana State University Press, 2008.

Cormier, Steven A. *The Siege of Suffolk: The Forgotten Campaign, April 11–May 4, 1863.* Lynchburg, VA: H. E. Howard, 1989.

Cozzens, Peter. *This Terrible Sound: The Battle of Chickamauga.* Urbana: University of Illinois Press, 1992.

Craig, Gordon. "Delbruck: The Military Historian." In *The Makers of Modern Strategy from Machiavelli to the Nuclear Age,* edited by Peter Paret. Princeton: Princeton University Press, 1986.

Craven, Avery. Review of *Lincoln and His Generals,* by T. Harry Williams. *Mississippi Valley Historical Review* 39, no. 2 (Sept. 1952): 337–39.

Cullen, Joseph E. *The Peninsula Campaign, 1862: McClellan and Lee Struggle for Richmond.* New York: Bonanza Books, 1973.

Cullum, George W. *Biographical Register of the Officers and Graduates of the U.S. Military Academy at West Point, N.Y., from Its Establishment, in 1802, to 1890, with the Early History of the United States Military Academy.* Vol. 2, 3rd rev. ed. Boston: Houghton Mifflin,1891.

Cunliffe, Marcus. *George Washington: Man and Monument.* Rev. ed., New York: Mentor, 1982.

Current, Richard. "Wisconsin's Civil War Historians." *Wisconsin Magazine of History* 70, no. 1 (Autumn 1986): 21–31.

Dabney, Robert Lewis. *Life and Campaigns of Lieut.-Gen. Thomas J. Jackson*. Harrisonburg, VA: Sprinkle Publications, 1983.

Daniel, John W. "Memorial Address by Hon. John W. Daniel, before the Association of the Army of Northern Virginia, at the Annual Meeting held at Richmond, Va., December 13, 1894." *Southern Historical Society Papers* 22 (1894): 281–85.

Davis, William C., ed. *The Confederate General*. 6 vols. Harrisburg, PA: National Historical Society, 1991.

———. *Jefferson Davis: The Man and the Hour*. New York: HarperCollins, 1991.

———. "Myths and Realities of the Confederacy." Chap. 11 in *The Cause Lost: Myths and Realities of the Confederacy*. Lawrence: University Press of Kansas, 1996.

Dawson, Joseph G., III. *Army Generals and Reconstruction: Louisiana, 1862–1877*. Baton Rouge: Louisiana State University Press, 1982.

———. "The First of the Modern Wars?" In *The American Civil War: Explorations and Reconsiderations*, edited by Susan-Mary Grant and Brian Holden Reid. New York: Longman, 121–41. 2000.

———. "T. Harry Williams." In *Twentieth Century Historians*, edited by Clyde N. Wilson. Vol. 17, Dictionary of American Literary Biography Series. Detroit: Gale Research, 1983.

de Gaulle, Charles. *The Edge of the Sword*. New York: Criterion, 1960.

Dickison, J. J. *Confederate Military History Extended Edition*. Vol. 16, *Florida*. Edited by Clement A. Evans. Wilmington, NC: Broadfoot, 1999.

DiNardo, R. L. "James Longstreet, the Modern Soldier: A Broad Assessment." In *James Longstreet: The Man, the Soldier, the Controversy*, edited by R. L. DiNardo and Albert Nofi. New York: Da Capo Press, 1998.

Donald, David. *Lincoln Reconsidered: Essays on the Civil War Era*. New York: Alfred A. Knopf, 1956; New York: Vintage Books, 1961, 2001.

———, ed. *Why the North Won the Civil War*. Baton Rouge: Louisiana State University Press, 1960.

Dorgan, Howard. "A Case Study in Reconciliation: General John B. Gordon and 'The Last Days of the Confederacy.'" *Quarterly Journal of Speech* 60 (Feb. 1974): 83–91.

Douglas, Henry Kyd. "Stonewall Jackson in Maryland." In Johnson and Buel, *Battles and Leaders of the Civil War*, vol. 2. For full publication details on the Johnson-Buel volumes, see the entry under "Printed Primary Sources."

Dowdey, Clifford. *Lee: A Biography*. Boston: Little Brown, 1965. Reprint, London: Gollancz, 1970.

———. *Lee's Last Campaign: The Story of Lee and His Men against Grant—1864.* Boston: Little, Brown, 1960. Reprint, with introduction by Robert K. Krick. Lincoln: University of Nebraska Press, 1993.

———. *The Seven Days: The Emergence of Robert E. Lee.* Boston: Little, Brown, 1964.

Dubbs, Carol Kettenburg. *Defend This Old Town: Williamsburg during the Civil War.* Baton Rouge: Louisiana State University Press, 2002.

Dupuy, R. Ernest, and Trevor N. Dupuy. *The Compact History of the Civil War.* New York: Hawthorn Books, 1960.

Eaton, Clement. "The Confederacy." In *Interpreting American History,* edited by John A. Garraty. New York: Macmillan, 1970.

Eckenrode, H. J., and Bryan Conrad. *James Longstreet: Lee's War Horse.* Chapel Hill: University of North Carolina Press, 1936.

Eckert, Ralph Lowell. *John Brown Gordon: Soldier, Southerner, American.* Baton Rouge: Louisiana State University Press, 1989.

Elliott, Joseph Cantey. *Lieutenant General Richard Heron Anderson: Lee's Noble Soldier.* Dayton, OH: Morningside, 1985.

Engle, Stephen D. *Struggle for the Heartland: The Campaigns from Fort Henry to Corinth.* Lincoln: University of Nebraska Press, 2001.

Falls, Cyril. *A Hundred Years of War, 1850–1950.* London: Gerald Duckworth, 1953.

Fellman, Michael. *The Making of Robert E. Lee.* New York: Random House, 2000.

Foster, Gaines M. *Ghosts of the Confederacy: Defeat, the Lost Cause, and the Emergence of the New South.* New York: Oxford University Press, 1987.

Freeman, Douglas Southall. *Lee's Lieutenants: A Study in Command.* 3 vols. New York: Scribner's, 1942–44.

———. *R. E. Lee: A Biography.* 4 vols. 1934–35. Reprint, New York: Scribner's, 1949.

Friddell, Guy. "A Tribute to Clifford Shirley Dowdey Jr." *Virginia Record* 101, no. 7 (July 1979): 6.

Fuller, J. F. C. *Grant and Lee: A Study in Personality and Generalship.* London: Eyre and Spottiswoode, 1933; Bloomington: Indiana University Press, 1957.

Gallagher, Gary W. "Another Look at the Generalship of R. E. Lee." In *Lee the Soldier,* edited by Gary W. Gallagher. Lincoln: University of Nebraska Press, 1986. Annotated ed., Lincoln: University of Nebraska Press, 1996.

———. *The Confederate War.* Cambridge: Harvard University Press, 1997.

———, ed. *The First Day at Gettysburg: Essays on Confederate and Union Leadership.* Kent, OH: Kent State University Press, 1992.

———, ed. *The Fredericksburg Campaign: Decision on the Rappahannock.* Chapel Hill: University of North Carolina Press, 1995.

———. "From Antebellum Unionist to Lost Cause Warrior: The Personal Journey of Jubal A. Early." In *New Perspectives on the Civil War: Myths and Realities of the National Conflict,* edited by John Y. Simon and Michael E. Stevens. Lanham, MD: Rowman & Littlefield, 1998.

———. "How Familiarity Bred Success: Military Campaigns and Leaders in Ken Burns's *The Civil War.*" In *Lee and His Generals in War and Memory,* edited by Gary W. Gallagher. Baton Rouge: Louisiana State University Press, 1998.

———. "Introduction." In *A Memoir of the Last Year of the War of Independence in the Confederate States of America,* [by Jubal Early]. Columbia: University of South Carolina Press, 2001.

———. *Jubal Early, the Lost Cause, and Civil War History: A Persistent Legacy.* Detroit: Marquette University Press, 1995.

———. "Jubal Early, the Lost Cause, and Civil War History: A Persistent Legacy." In *The Myth of the Lost Cause and Civil War History,* edited by Gary W. Gallagher and Alan T. Nolan. Bloomington: Indiana University Press, 2000.

———. *Lee and His Army in Confederate History.* Chapel Hill: University of North Carolina Press, 2001.

———. *Lee and His Generals in War and Memory.* Baton Rouge: Louisiana State University Press, 1998.

———. *Lee the Soldier.* Lincoln: University of Nebraska Press, 1996.

———. "Scapegoat in Victory: James Longstreet and the Battle of Second Manassas." *Civil War History* 34 (1988): 293–307.

———, ed. *The Second Day at Gettysburg: Essays on Confederate and Union Leadership.* Kent, OH: Kent State University Press, 1993.

———, ed. *The Third Day at Gettysburg and Beyond.* Chapel Hill: University of North Carolina Press, 1994.

Gat, Azar. *A History of Military Thought from the Enlightenment to the Cold War.* Oxford: Oxford University Press, 2001.

Georg, Kathleen R., and John W. Busey. *Nothing but Glory: Pickett's Division at Gettysburg.* Hightstown, NJ: Longstreet House, 1987.

Gingrich, Newt, and William R. Forstchen. *Gettysburg: A Novel of the Civil War.* New York: St. Martin's Press, 2003.

Glatthaar, Joseph T. *General Lee's Army: From Victory to Collapse.* New York: Free Press, 2008; Chapel Hill: University of North Carolina Press, 2008.

———. *Partners in Command: The Relationship between Leaders in the Civil War.* New York: Free Press, 1994.

Govan, Gilbert E., and James W. Livingood. *A Different Valor: The Story of General Joseph E. Johnston, C.S.A.* New York: Bobbs-Merrill, 1956.

Graham, Hugh Davis. "The Enigma of Huey Long: An Essay Review." *Journal of Southern History* 36 (May 1970): 205–11.

Greene, A. Wilson. *The Final Battles of the Petersburg Campaign: Breaking the Backbone of the Rebellion.* 2nd ed. Knoxville: University of Tennessee Press, 2008.

———. "Morale, Maneuver, and Mud: The Army of the Potomac, December 16, 1862–January 20, 1863." In *The Fredericksburg Campaign: Decision on the Rappahannock,* edited by Gary W. Gallagher. Chapel Hill: University of North Carolina Press, 1995.

Hagerman, Edward. *The American Civil War and the Origins of Modern Warfare.* Bloomington: Indiana University Press, 1988.

[Hallock, Charles.] *A Complete Biographical Sketch of "Stonewall" Jackson.* Augusta, GA: Steam Power Press Chronicle and Sentinel, 1863.

Hallock, Judith Lee. *Braxton Bragg and Confederate Defeat.* Vol. 2. Tuscaloosa: University of Alabama Press, 1991.

———. *General James Longstreet in the West: A Monumental Failure.* Ft. Worth, TX: Ryan Place, 1998.

Hamilton, Edith. *Mythology.* Boston: Little, Brown, 1942.

Harman, Troy D. *Lee's Real Plan at Gettysburg.* Mechanicsburg, PA: Stackpole Books, 2003.

Harrison, Gordon A. *Cross Channel Attack.* Washington, DC: Department of the Army, 1951.

Harsh, Joseph L. *Confederate Tide Rising: Robert E. Lee and the Making of Southern Strategy, 1861–1862.* Kent, OH: Kent State University Press, 1998.

———. *Taken at the Flood: Robert E. Lee and Confederate Strategy in the Maryland Campaign of 1862.* Kent, OH: Kent State University Press, 1999.

Hassler, William W. "'Fighting Dick' Anderson." *Civil War Times Illustrated* 12, no. 10 (Feb. 1974): 4–6, 40–43.

Hattaway, Herman, and Archer Jones. *How the North Won: A Military History of the Civil War.* Urbana: University of Illinois Press, 1983.

Henderson, G. F. R. *The Science of War: A Collection of Essays and Lectures, 1892–1903.* New York: Longmans, Green, 1905.

Hennessey, John. *The First Battle of Manassas: An End to Innocence, July 18–21, 1861.* Lynchburg, VA: H. E. Howard, 1989.

———. *Return to Bull Run: The Campaign and Battle of Second Manassas.* New York: Simon & Schuster, 1993.

———. *Second Manassas Battlefield Map Study.* 2nd ed. Lynchburg, VA: H. E. Howard, n.d.

Hess, Earl J. *In the Trenches at Petersburg: Field Fortifications and Confederate Defeat.* Chapel Hill: University of North Carolina Press, 2009.

———. *Pickett's Charge: The Last Attack at Gettysburg.* Chapel Hill: University of North Carolina Press, 2001.

Holden Reid, Brian. *The American Civil War: The Operational Battlefield, 1861–1863.* London: Prometheus Books, 2008.

———. "British Military Intellectuals and the American Civil War." In *Warfare, Diplomacy and Politics: Essays in Honour of A. J. P. Taylor,* edited by Chris Wrigley. London: Hamish Hamilton, 1986.

———. "The Civil War, 1861–1865." In *A Companion to American Military History,* edited by James C. Bradford. Malden, MA: Wiley-Blackwell, 2010.

———. "The Influence of the Vietnam Syndrome on the Writing of Civil War History." *RUSI Journal* 147, no. 1 (Feb. 2002): 44–46.

———. "Michael Howard and the Evolution of Modern War Studies." *Journal of Military History* 73 (June 2009): 869–904.

———. Review of *Lee Considered: General Robert E. Lee and Civil War History,* by Alan T. Nolan. *Journal of American Studies* 27 (Apr. 1993): 113–14.

———. *Robert E. Lee: Icon for a Nation.* New York: Prometheus Books, 2007.

———. "'A Sign-Post that Was Missed'? Reconsidering British Lessons from the American Civil War." *Journal of Military History* 70 (Apr. 2006): 386–414.

———. "William T. Sherman and the South." *American Nineteenth Century History* 11, no. 1 (Mar. 2010): 1–16.

Horn, John. *The Destruction of the Weldon Railroad.* Lynchburg, VA: H. E. Howard, 1991.

Horowitz, Tony. *Confederates in the Attic: Dispatches from the Unfinished Civil War.* New York: Pantheon Books, 1998.

Howe, Thomas J. *Wasted Valor, June 15–18, 1864.* Lynchburg, VA: H. E. Howard, 1988.

Hoyt, William D. "New Light on General Jubal A. Early after Appomattox." *Journal of Southern History* 9 (1943): 113–17.

Hunter, Steven H. *Joseph E. Johnston and the Defense of Richmond.* Lawrence: University Press of Kansas, 1998.

Janney, Caroline E. *Burying the Dead but Not the Past :Ladies Memorial Associations and the Lost Cause.* Chapel Hill: University of North Carolina Press, 2008.

Johnson, Ludwell H. "Civil War Military History: A Few Revisions in Need of Revising." *Civil War History* 17 (June 1971): 115–30.

Jones, Archer. *Confederate Strategy from Shiloh to Vicksburg.* Baton Rouge: Louisiana State University Press, 1961.

Knudson, Harold M. *General James Longstreet: The Confederacy's Most Modern General.* Tarentum, PA: Word Association Publishers, 2007.

Krick, Robert K. "It Appeared as Though Mutual Extermination Would Put a Stop to the Awful Carnage: Confederates in Sharpsburg's Bloody Lane." In *The Antietam Campaign,* edited by Gary W. Gallagher. Chapel Hill: University of North Carolina Press, 1999.

Launius, Roger D. "A Bibliography of the Works of T. Harry Williams." *Louisiana History: The Journal of the Louisiana Historical Association* 25, no. 1 (Winter 1984): 5–28.

Lee, Fitzhugh. *General Lee.* New York: University Society, 1904.

Longacre, Edward G. *The Cavalry at Gettysburg: A Tactical Study of Mounted Operations During the Civil War's Pivotal Campaign, 9 June–14 July 1863.* Rutherford, NJ: Fairleigh Dickinson University Press, 1986.

Longstreet, Helen D. *Lee and Longstreet at High Tide.* Gainesville, GA: Helen D. Longstreet, 1904.

Machiavelli, Niccolo. *The Art of War.* Albany, NY: H. C. Souithwick, 1815.

Marvel, William. *Burnside.* Chapel Hill: University of North Carolina Press, 1991.

———. *Lee's Last Retreat: The Fight to Appomattox.* Chapel Hill: University of North Carolina Press, 2002.

———. "The Making of a Myth: Ambrose E. Burnside and the Union High Command at Fredericksburg." In *The Fredericksburg Campaign: Decision on the Rappahannock,* edited by Gary W. Gallagher. Chapel Hill: University of North Carolina Press, 1995.

Maurice, Frederic. *Robert E. Lee the Soldier.* Boston: Houghton Mifflin, 1925.

McClellan, H. B. *The Life and Campaigns of Major General J. E. B. Stuart, Commander of the Cavalry of the Army of Northern Virginia.* Boston: Houghton Mifflin, 1885.

McMurry, Richard M. "The Pennsylvania Gambit and the Gettysburg Splash." In Boritt, *The Gettysburg Nobody Knows.*

———. *Two Great Rebel Armies: An Essay in Confederate Military History.* Chapel Hill: University of North Carolina Press, 1989.

McPherson, James M. *Battle Cry of Freedom: The Civil War Era.* New York: Oxford University Press, 1988.

McWhiney, Grady, and Perry D. Jamieson. *Attack and Die: Civil War Military Tactics and the Southern Heritage.* University: University of Alabama Press, 1982.

Melvin, Mungo. *Manstein: Hitler's Greatest General.* London: Weidenfeld and Nicolson, 2010.

Miers, Earl Schenck. *Robert E. Lee.* New York: Alfred A. Knopf, 1956.

Miller, William, ed. *The Peninsula Campaign of 1862: Yorktown to the Seven Days.* Campbell, CA: Savas Woodbury, 1993.

Millis, Walter. *Arms and Men: A Study in American Military History.* New York: Mentor, 1956.

Millsaps, Bill. "Clifford Dowdey and the Sweet Life." *Richmond Times-Dispatch,* June 8, 1969.

Mosby, John S. *Stuart's Cavalry in the Gettysburg Campaign.* New York: Moffat, Yard, 1908.

Neely, Mark E., Jr. "Abraham Lincoln vs. Jefferson Davis: Comparing Presidential Leadership in the Civil War." In *Writing the Civil War: The Quest to Understand,* edited by James M. McPherson and William J. Cooper Jr. Columbia: University of South Carolina Press, 1998.

Neely, Mark E., Jr., Harold Holzer, and Gabor Boritt. *The Confederate Image: Prints of the Lost Cause.* Chapel Hill: University of North Carolina Press, 1987.

Nesbitt, Mark. *Saber and Scapegoat: J. E. B. Stuart and the Gettysburg Controversy.* Mechanicsburg, PA: Stackpole Books, 1994.

Nevins, Allan. *The War for the Union.* 4 vols. New York: Scribner's, 1959–71.

Newton, Steven H. *The Battle of Seven Pines.* Lynchburg, VA: H. E. Howard, 1993.

Niebuhr, H. Richard. *The Kingdom of God in America.* New York: Harper and Brothers, 1937.

Nolan, Alan T. "The Anatomy of the Myth." In The *Myth of the Lost Cause and Civil War History,* edited by Gary W. Gallagher and Alan T. Nolan. Bloomington: Indiana University Press, 2000.

———. *Lee Considered: General Robert E. Lee and Civil War History.* Chapel Hill: University of North Carolina Press, 1991.

———. *"Rally Once Again!" Selected Writings.* Madison, WI: Madison House, 2000.

———. "R. E. Lee and July 1 at Gettysburg." In *The First Day at Gettysburg: Essays on Confederate and Union Leadership,* edited by Gary W. Gallagher. Kent, OH: Kent State University Press, 1992.

Novick, Peter. *That Noble Dream: The "Objectivity Question" and the American Historical Profession.* Cambridge: Cambridge University Press, 1988.

Osborne, Charles C. *Jubal: The Life and Times of General Jubal A. Early, CSA, Defender of the Lost Cause.* Baton Rouge: Louisiana State University Press, 1992.

Osterweis, Rolin G. *The Myth of the Lost Cause, 1865–1900.* Hamden, CT: Shoestring Press, 1973.

Palmer, Michael A. *Lee Moves North: Robert E. Lee on the Offensive.* New York: John Wiley & Sons, 1998.

Patterson, A. *From Blue to Gray: The Life of Confederate General Cadmus M. Wilcox.* Mechanicsburg, PA: Stackpole Books, 2001.

Peck, M. Scott. *The Road Less Travelled and Beyond: Spiritual Growth in an Age of Anxiety.* London: Rider, 1997.

Peter, Laurence J., and Raymond Hull. *The Peter Principle: Why Things Always Go Wrong.* New York: William Morrow, 1969.

Pfanz, Donald C. *Richard S. Ewell: A Soldier's Life.* Chapel Hill: University of North Carolina Press, 1998.

Pfanz, Harry W. *Gettysburg: Culp's Hill and Cemetery Hill.* Chapel Hill: University of North Carolina Press, 1993.

———. *Gettysburg: The Second Day*. Chapel Hill: University of North Carolina Press, 1987.

Piston, William G. "Cross Purposes: Longstreet, Lee, and Confederate Attack Plans for July 3 at Gettysburg." In *The Third Day at Gettysburg and Beyond*, edited by Gary W. Gallagher. Chapel Hill: University of North Carolina Press, 1994.

———. *Lee's Tarnished Lieutenant: James Longstreet and His Place in Southern History*. Athens: University of Georgia Press, 1987.

———. "Petticoats, Promotions, and Military Assignments: Favoritism and the Antebellum Career of James Longstreet." In *James Longstreet: The Man, the Soldier, the Controversy*, edited by R. L. DiNardo and Albert Nofi. New York: Da Capo Press, 1998.

Pogue, Forrest C. *George C. Marshall: Education of a General, 1880–1939*. London: Macgibbon and Key, 1964.

———. *The Supreme Command*. Washington, DC: Department of the Army, 1954.

Price, Frank James. *Troy H. Middleton: A Biography*. Baton Rouge: Louisiana State University Press, 1974.

Prowell, George R. *Encounter at Hanover: Prelude to Gettysburg*. Shippensburg, PA: Burd Street Press, 1962.

Pryor, Elizabeth Brown. *Reading the Man: A Portrait of Robert E. Lee Through His Private Letters*. New York: Viking, 2007.

Rable, George C. *But There Was No Peace: The Role of Violence in the Politics of Reconstruction*. Athens: University of Georgia Press, 1984.

———. *Fredericksburg! Fredericksburg!* Chapel Hill: University of North Carolina Press, 2002.

Rafuse, Ethan S. *Robert E. Lee and the Fall of the Confederacy, 1863–1865*. Lanham, MD: Rowman & Littlefield, 2008.

Reardon, Carol. "'I Think the Union Army Had Something to Do with It': The Pickett's Charge Nobody Knows." In Boritt, *The Gettysburg Nobody Knows*.

Rhea, Gordon C. *The Battle of the Wilderness, May 5–6, 1864*. Baton Rouge: Louisiana State University Press, 1994.

———. *Cold Harbor: Grant and Lee, May 26–June 3, 1864*. Baton Rouge: Louisiana State University Press, 2002.

———. "Lee, Grant, and 'Prescience' in the Overland Campaign." In *Audacity Personified: The Generalship of Robert E. Lee*, edited by Peter S. Carmichael. Baton Rouge: Louisiana State University Press, 2004.

———. *To the North Anna River: Grant and Lee, May 13–25, 1864*. Baton Rouge: Louisiana State University Press, 2000.

Richter, William L. *The ABC-CLIO Companion to American Reconstruction, 1862–1877*. Santa Barbara, CA: ABC-CLIO, 1996.

———. "James Longstreet: From Rebel to Scalawag." *Louisiana History* 11 (1970): 215–30.

Riggs, David F. *East of Gettysburg: Stuart vs. Custer.* Bellevue, NE: Old Army Press, 1970.

Robertson, James I., Jr. *General A. P. Hill: The Story of a Confederate Warrior.* New York: Random House, 1987.

———. *Stonewall Jackson: The Man, the Soldier, the Legend.* New York: Macmillan, 1997.

Robinson, Warren C. *Jeb Stuart and the Confederate Defeat at Gettysburg.* Lincoln: University of Nebraska Press, 2007.

Roland, Charles P. *The Confederacy.* Chicago: University of Chicago Press, 1960.

———. "The Generalship of Robert E. Lee." In *Grant, Lee, Lincoln and the Radicals,* edited by Grady McWhiney. Chicago: Northwestern University Press, 1964.

———. *My Odyssey Through History: Memoirs of War and Academe.* Baton Rouge: Louisiana State University Press, 2004.

———. *Reflections on Lee: A Historian's Assessment.* Mechanicsburg, PA: Stackpole Books, 1995.

Roman, Alfred. *The Military Operations of General Beauregard in the War Between the States, 1861 to 1865: Including a Brief Personal Sketch and a Narrative of His Services in the War with Mexico, 1846–8.* 2 vols. New York: De Capo, 1994.

Romero, Sidney J. *Religion in the Rebel Ranks.* Lanham, MD: University Press of America, 1983.

Ropes, John C. *The Story of the Civil War.* 4 vols. New York: Putnam, 1933.

Royster, Charles. *The Destructive War: William Tecumseh Sherman, Stonewall Jackson, and the Americans.* New York: Alfred A. Knopf, 1991.

Sanger, Donald B. *General James Longstreet and the Civil War.* Chicago: University of Chicago Press, 1936.

———. "Was Longstreet a Scapegoat?" *Infantry Journal* 43 (Jan./Feb. 1936): 39–46.

Sanger, Donald B., and Thomas R. Hay. *James Longstreet: I. Soldier; II. Politician, Office Holder, and Writer.* Baton Rouge: Louisiana State University Press, 1952.

Schmutz, John F. *The Battle of the Crater: A Complete History.* Jefferson, NC: McFarland, 2009.

Schott, Thomas E. "Early, Jubal Anderson." In *Dictionary of American Military History,* edited by Roger J. Spiller. Vol. 1. Westport, CT: Greenwood Press, 1984.

Schweiger, Beth Barton. *The Gospel Working Up: Progress and the Pulpit in Nineteenth-Century Virginia.* New York: Oxford University Press, 2000.

Sears, Stephen W. *Gettysburg.* Boston: Houghton Mifflin, 2003.

———. *Landscape Turned Red: The Battle of Antietam.* New York: Ticknor & Fields, 1983.

———. *To the Gates of Richmond: The Peninsula Campaign*. New York: Ticknor & Fields, 1992.

Sharp, Joseph. *Living Our Dying: A Way to the Sacred in Everyday Life*. New York: Hyperion, 1996.

Shy, John W. "Jomini." In *Makers of Modern Strategy: From Machiavelli to the Nuclear Age*, edited by Peter Paret. Oxford: Oxford University Press, 1986; Princeton, NJ: Princeton University Press, 1986.

Sibley, F. Ray, Jr. *The Confederate Order of Battle*. Vol. 1, *The Army of Northern Virginia*. Shippensburg, PA: White Mane, 1996.

Simpson, Brooks D. "'If Properly Led': Command Relationships at Gettysburg." In *Civil War Generals in Defeat*, edited by Steven E. Woodworth. Lawrence: University Press of Kansas, 1999.

Slotkin, Richard. *No Quarter: The Battle of the Crater, 1864*. New York: Random House, 2009.

Smith, Francis H. *Discourse on the Life and Character of Lt. Gen. Thos. J. Jackson, (C.S.A.), Late Professor of Natural and Experimental Philosophy in the Virginia Military Institute*. Richmond, VA: Ritchie and Dunnavant, 1863.

Snow, William P. *Lee and His Generals*. New York: Richardson, 1867.

"Soldier and Gentleman." *Outlook: A Weekly Newspaper* 76 (Jan. 1904): 152.

Sommers, Richard J. *Richmond Redeemed: The Siege at Petersburg*. New York: Doubleday, 1981.

"The Southern Historical Society." *Southern Historical Society Papers* 1 (1876): 40–43.

Spaulding, Thomas. "Clement A. Evans." In *Dictionary of American Biography*, edited by Allen Johnson and Dumas Malone. New York: Charles Scribner's Sons, 1931.

Spiller, Roger J. *In the School of War*. Lincoln: University of Nebraska Press, 2010.

Starr, Stephen Z. *The Union Cavalry in the Civil War*. 3 vols. Baton Rouge: Louisiana State University Press, 1979–85.

Stoker, Donald. *The Grand Design: Strategy and the U.S. Civil War*. New York: Oxford University Press, 2010.

Stout, Harry S. *Upon the Altar of the Nation: A Moral History of the Civil War*. New York: Viking, 2006.

Stowell, Daniel W. "Stonewall Jackson and the Providence of God." In *Religion and the American Civil War*, edited by Randall M. Miller, Harry S. Stout, and Charles Reagan Wilson. New York: Oxford University Press, 1998.

Taylor, George Braxton. *Life and Letters of George Boardman Taylor, D.D.* Lynchburg, VA: J. P. Bell, 1908.

Taylor, Welford D., gen. ed. *Virginia Authors Past and Present*. Farmville: Virginia Association of Teachers of English, 1972.

Thomas, Emory M. *Bold Dragoon: The Life of J. E. B. Stuart.* New York: Harper & Row, 1986.

———. *The Confederacy as a Revolutionary Experience.* Englewood Cliffs, NJ: Prentice-Hall, 1971.

———. "Eggs, Aldie, Shepherdstown, and J. E. B. Stuart." In Boritt, *The Gettysburg Nobody Knows.*

———. *Robert E. Lee: A Biography.* New York: W. W. Norton, 1995.

Thomas, Wilbur. *General James "Pete" Longstreet, Lee's "Old Warhorse": Scapegoat for Gettysburg.* Parson, WV: McClain, 1979.

Thomason, John W. *Jeb Stuart.* New York: Charles Scribner's Sons, 1930.

Thornton, William M. "John Warwick Daniel." *Southern Historical Society Papers* 51 (1916): 94.

Tucker, Glenn. *High Tide at Gettysburg: The Campaign in Pennsylvania.* Indianapolis: Bobbs-Merrill, 1958.

———. *Lee and Longstreet at Gettysburg.* Indianapolis: Bobbs-Merrill, 1968.

———. "Longstreet: Culprit or Scapegoat?" *Civil War Times Illustrated* 1 (Apr. 1962): 4–7.

Urwin, Gregory J. W. *Custer Victorious: The Civil War Battles of General George Armstrong Custer.* Rutherford, NJ: Fairleigh Dickinson University Press, 1983.

Vandiver, Frank E. *Mighty Stonewall.* New York: McGraw-Hill, 1957.

———. "Williams and the Generals." In *The Confederate High Command and Related Topics: The 1988 Deep Delta Civil War Symposium: Themes in Honor of T. Harry Williams,* edited by Roman J. Heleniak and Lawrence L. Hewitt. Shippensburg, PA: White Mane, 1990.

Walker, C. Irvine. *The Life of Lieutenant General Richard Heron Anderson of the Confederate States Army.* Charleston, SC: n.p., 1917.

Walker, Paul D. *The Cavalry Battle that Saved the Union: Custer vs. Stuart at Gettysburg.* Gretna, LA: Pelican Publishing, 2002.

Washburn, Katharine, and John Thornton, eds. *Dumbing Down: Essays on the Strip Mining of American Culture.* New York, 1996.

Watson, Richard D. "Clifford Dowdey: Contemporary Romance Novelist and Historian." *Richmond Quarterly* 4, no. 3 (Winter 1981): 19, 20, 21.

Weigley, Russell F. *The American War of War: A History of United States Military Strategy and Policy.* 1973. Reprint, Bloomington: Indiana University Press, 1977.

Welsh, Jack D. *Medical Histories of Confederate Generals.* Kent, OH: Kent State University Press, 1995.

Weitz, Mark A. *More Damning than Slaughter: Desertion in the Confederate Army.* Lincoln: University of Nebraska Press, 2005.

Wert, Jeffry D. *Cavalryman of the Lost Cause: A Biography of J. E. B. Stuart.* New York: Simon and Schuster, 2008.

———. *From Winchester to Cedar Creek: The Shenandoah Campaign of 1864.* Carlisle, PA: South Mountain Press, 1987.

———. *General James Longstreet: The Confederacy's Most Controversial General.* New York: Simon & Schuster, 1993.

———. "James Longstreet and the Lost Cause. " In *The Myth of the Lost Cause and Civil War History,* edited by Gary W. Gallagher and Alan T. Nolan. Bloomington: Indiana University Press, 2000.

Wheeler, Richard. *Sword Over Richmond: An Eyewitness History of McClellan's Peninsula Campaign.* New York: Harper & Row, 1986.

Whitman, Walt. *Prose Works.* Philadelphia: David McKay, 1892.

Wiley, Bell I. "T. Harry Williams as I Knew Him." *Military Affairs* 44, no. 1 (Feb. 1980): 33–34.

Williams, Estelle. "A Biographical Introduction by Estelle Williams." In Williams, *Selected Essays of T. Harry Williams.*

Williams, T. Harry. *Americans at War.* Baton Rouge: Louisiana State University Press, 1960.

———. "An Analysis of Some Reconstruction Attitudes." In Williams, *Selected Essays of T. Harry Williams.*

———. "The Attack upon West Point during the Civil War." *Mississippi Valley Historical Review* 25, no. 1 (Mar. 1939): 491–504.

———. "The Civil War." In *Interpreting American History: Conversations with Historians,* edited by John A. Garraty. New York: Macmillan, 1970.

———. "Freeman, Historian of the Civil War: An Appraisal." *Journal of Southern History* 21, no. 1 (Feb. 1955): 91–100.

———. *Hayes of the Twenty-third: The Civil War Volunteer Officer.* New York: Alfred A. Knopf, 1965.

———. *The History of American Wars, from 1745 to 1918.* New York: Alfred A. Knopf, 1981.

———. *Huey Long.* New York: Alfred A. Knopf, 1969.

———. *Lincoln and His Generals.* New York: Alfred A. Knopf, 1952.

———. *Lincoln and the Radicals.* 1941. Reprint. Madison: University of Wisconsin Press, 1965.

———. "Lincoln and the Radicals: An Essay in Civil War History and Historiography." In *Grant, Lee, Lincoln and the Radicals,* edited by Grady McWhiney. New York: Harper Colophon Books, 1964.

———. "The Louisiana Unification Movement." In Williams, *Selected Essays of T. Harry Williams.*

———. "The Macs and the Ikes: America's Two Military Traditions." *American Mercury* 75 (Oct. 1952): 32–39.

———. *McClellan, Sherman, and Grant.* New Brunswick, NJ: Rutgers University Press, 1962.

———. *The Military Leadership of the North and the South.* Harmon Memorial Lecture Number Two. Colorado Springs: U.S. Air Force Academy, 1960.

———. "The Military Leadership of North and South." In *Why the North Won the Civil War,* edited by David Donald. Baton Rouge: Louisiana State University Press, 1960.

———. "A Pattern of a Historian: A Critical Discussion of D. S. Freeman and His Biography of R. E. Lee." Chicago Civil War Round Table 131st annual meeting, Mar. 18, 1954. CD-ROM.

———. *P. G. T. Beauregard: Napoleon in Gray.* Baton Rouge: Louisiana State University Press, 1955.

———. Review of *George B. McClellan: The Man Who Saved the Union,* by H. J. Eckenrode and Bryan Conrad. *Journal of Southern History* 8, no. 2 (May 1942): 278.

———. *Romance and Realism in Southern Politics.* Athens: University of Georgia Press, 1961.

———. *The Selected Essays of T. Harry Williams,* edited by Estelle Williams. Baton Rouge: Louisiana State University Press, 1983.

———. "Trends in Southern Politics." In *The Idea of the South: Pursuit of a Central Theme,* edited by Frank E. Vandiver. Chicago: University of Chicago Press for William Rice University, 1964.

Wilson, Charles Reagan. *Baptized in Blood: The Religion of the Lost Cause, 1865–1920.* 1980. Rev. ed., Athens: University of Georgia Press, 2009.

Wise, John S. "Two Great Confederates. General John B. Gordon and General James Longstreet: Characterizations by a Friend of Both." *American Monthly Review of Reviews* 29 (Feb. 1904): 204.

Wise, Stephen R. *Gate of Hell.* Columbia: University of South Carolina Pres, 1994.

Wittenberg, Eric J., and J. David Petruzzi. *Plenty of Blame to Go Around: Jeb Stuart's Controversial Ride to Gettysburg.* New York: Savas Beatie, 2006.

Wolseley, Garnet J. *General Lee.* Rochester, NY: C. Mann Printing, 1906.

Woodworth, Steven E. *Davis and Lee at War.* Lawrence: University Press of Kansas, 1995.

———, ed. *Leadership and Command in the American Civil War.* Campbell, CA: Savas Woodbury Publishers, 1995.

———, ed. *No Band of Brothers: Problems of the Rebel High Command.* Columbia: University of Missouri Press, 1999.

Wright, Marcus J., comp. *General Officers of the Confederate Army, Officers of the Executive Departments of the Confederate States, Members of the Confederate Congress by States.* New York: Neale Publishing, 1911.

Young, Bennett H. *Confederate Wizards of the Saddle.* Boston: Chapple Publishing, 1914.

Dissertations and Theses

Hieronymus, Frank L. "For Now and Forever: The Chaplains of the Confederate States Army." Ph.D. diss., University of California, Los Angeles, 1964.

Richter, William L. "The Federal Cavalry during the Gettysburg Campaign: The Development of the Mobile Arm of the Army of the Potomac." Master's thesis, Arizona State University, 1965.

Wetta, Francis J. "The Louisiana Scalawags." Ph.D. diss., Louisiana State University, 1977.

Internet Resources

"Alan T. Nolan." *Indianapolis Star,* Aug. 5, 2008. http://www2.indystar.com/cgi-bin/obituaries/index.php?action=show&id=94323/. Accessed Oct. 19, 2010.

Archibald, George. "Ignorance of American History Called Threat to Security." *Washington Times,* Apr. 11, 2003. http://www.informationclearinghouse.info/article2862.htm. Accessed July 4, 2011.

"Arthur Ashe—A Monumental Man?" http://xroads.virginia.edu/~UG97/monument/ashe.html/. Accessed Oct. 25, 2010.

"Bernard of Clairvaux, St." *Catholic Encyclopedia.* http://www.newadvent.org/cathen/02498d.htm/. Accessed May 11, 2012.

"Black Bear Becomes Ole Miss Mascot." http://www.upi.com/Sports_News/2010/10/14/Black-bear-becomes-Ole-Miss-mascot/UPI-37641287084775/. Accessed Oct. 14, 2010.

Civil War Trust. Maps of Gaines' Mill, Virginia (1862). http://www.civilwar.org/battlefields/gainesmill/maps/gainesmillmap.html/. Accessed May 3, 2010.

Dillon, Sam. "History Survey Stumps U.S. Teens." *New York Times,* Feb. 26, 2008. http://www.nytimes.com/2008/02/26/education/27history.html. Accessed July 4, 2011.

Johnson, David. "Douglas Southall Freeman (1886–1953)." *Encyclopedia Virginia.* http://www.EncyclopediaVirginia.org/Freeman_Douglas_Southall_1886–1953/. Accessed Sept. 20, 2010.

Joyner, Charles. "A Legacy of Distinction: Introducing Past Presidents of the Southern Historical Association." http://www.uga.edu/sha/meeting/presidents%20tribute.pdf/. Accessed May 10, 2011.

Lewis, Richard B. Review of *Rally Once Again! Selected Civil War Writings of Alan T. Nolan,* by Alan T. Nolan. Madison, WI: Madison House, 2000. H-Net online, http://www2.h-net.msu.edu/reviews/showrev.php?id=4831/. Accessed Oct. 19, 2010.

McSween, Harold B. "T. Harry Williams: A Remembrance." *Virginia Quarterly Review.* http://www.vqronline.org/articles/2000/autumn/mcsween-t-harry-williams/. Accessed Apr. 16, 2011.

Romano, Andrew. "How Dumb Are We?" *Newsweek,* Mar. 20, 2011. http://www.newsweek.com/2011/03/20/how-dumb-are-we.html. Accessed July 4, 2011.

U.S. National Archives and Records Administration. "Statistical information about casualties of the Vietnam War: Electronic and Special Media Records Services Division Reference Report." http://www.archives.gov/research/military/vietnam-war/casualty-statistics.html/. Accessed Sept. 30, 2010.

Miscellaneous Sources

Hess, Earl J. "Into the Crater: The Mine Attack at Petersburg." Unpublished manuscript. 2010.

Roland, Charles P., to Roger Spiller, e-mail, Feb. 13, 2010.

Wetta, Frank. "T. Harry Williams, 1909–1979." Unpublished manuscript. c. 1980.

Williams, T. Harry, to Frank J. Wetta. Conversation. c. 1967.

Contributors

Note: The institution granting the contributor's highest degree is given in parentheses following his name.

Joseph G. Dawson III (Louisiana State University) is Professor of History at Texas A&M University–College Station. His books include *Army Generals and Reconstruction: Louisiana, 1862–1877* (1982), which won the General Kemper Williams Prize, and *Doniphan's Epic March: The 1st Missouri Volunteers in the Mexican War* (1999), and his articles have appeared in the *Journal of Military History* and *Civil War History,* among other journals. He has contributed several chapters to edited books, including "The First of the Modern Wars?" in *Themes in the American Civil War* (2010), edited by Susan-Mary Grant.

Ralph L. Eckert (Louisiana State University) attended Pennsylvania State University (B.A., 1971; M.A., 1975) before moving to Louisiana to study under T. Harry Williams. Since 1983, he has taught history at Penn State–Erie, Behrend College, specializing in Revolutionary America, the Civil War and Reconstruction, and American military history. He authored *John Brown Gordon: Soldier, Southern, American* (1989) and published widely in the Civil War and military history fields.

A. Wilson Greene (Louisiana State University) is the executive director of Pamplin Historical Park and the National Museum of the Civil War Soldier near Petersburg, Virginia. His books include *Whatever You Resolve to Be: Essays on Stonewall Jackson* (2005), *Civil War Petersburg: Confederate City in the Crucible of War* (2006), and *The Final Battles of the Petersburg Campaign: Breaking the Backbone of the Rebellion* (second edition, 2008). He has been a study leader and tour guide for the Smithsonian travel program since 1989.

Lawrence Lee Hewitt (Louisiana State University) was professor of history at Southeastern Louisiana University. The recipient of SLU's 1991 President's Award for Excellence in Research, the 1991 Charles L. Dufour Award, and the 2011 Dr. Arthur W. Bergeron Jr. Award, he is the author of *Port Hudson, Confederate Bastion on the Mississippi* (1987). His other publications include *The Confederate High Command & Related Topics* (1990) and *Leadership during the Civil War* (1992), with Roman Heleniak; *Kentuckians in Gray: Confederate Generals and Field Officers of the Bluegrass State* (2008), with Bruce Allardice; and, with Art Bergeron, *Louisianans in the Civil War* (2002), *Confederate Generals in the Western Theater*, volume 1 (2010), volume 2 (2010), and volume 3 (2011).

Brian Holden Reid (University of London) is professor of American history and military institutions, King's College London, and since 2010 an academic member of College Council. A former head of the Department of War Studies (2001–7), in 2007 he was awarded the Fellowship of King's College London, the highest honor the college can award its alumni and staff. He is an Honorary Vice President of the Society for Army Historical Research and served as a trustee of the Society for Military History, 2003–11, and, in 2004–10, a member of the Council of the National Army Museum, London. He is a Fellow of the Royal Historical Society, the Royal Geographical Society, the Royal United Services Institute, and the Royal Society for the Encouragement of the Arts, Manufactures and Commerce. In 2004–5 he was the first non-American to serve on the Lincoln Prize Jury Panel, and in 2007 he was the first non-American to deliver the Elizabeth Roller Bottimore Lecture at the University of Richmond, Virginia, during the Lee Bicentenary. His books include *J. F. C. Fuller: Military Thinker* (1987), *The Origins of the American Civil War* (1996), *Studies in British Military Thought* (1998), *Robert E. Lee: Icon for a Nation* (2005), and *America's Civil War: The Operational Battlefield, 1861–1863* (2008).

George C. Rable (Louisiana State University) is the Charles G. Summersell Chair in Southern History at the University of Alabama. A native of Lima, Ohio, he received his B.A. from Bluffton College (1972) before attending graduate school at LSU. His books include *Fredericksburg! Fredericksburg!* (2002), which won the Lincoln Prize, the Society for Military History Distinguished Book Award in American Military History, the Jefferson Davis Award, and the Douglas Southall Freeman History Award; *The Confederate Republic: A Revolution Against Politics* (1994); *Civil Wars: Women and the Crisis of Southern Nationalism* (1989), which won the Julia Cherry Spruill Prize and the Jefferson Davis Award; and *But There Was No Peace: The Role of Violence in the Politics of Reconstruction* (1984). His most recent book, *God's Almost Chosen Peoples: A Religious History of the American Civil War* (2010), also won the Jefferson Davis Award.

WILLIAM L. RICHTER (Louisiana State University) is a retired businessman turned historian. He has written eleven volumes, two dozen articles, and numerous book reviews about the Old South, the Civil War and Reconstruction (particularly in Texas), and the participants in the Lincoln assassination. His book *The Army in Texas during Reconstruction, 1865–1870* won the 1989 Certificate of Commendation from the American Association of State and Local History. His latest work is *Sic Semper Tyrannis: Why John Wilkes Booth Shot Abraham Lincoln* (2009). He currently resides in Tucson, Arizona.

CHARLES P. ROLAND (Louisiana State University), a native of Tennessee, served as a combat infantry captain in Europe in World War II, and received the Bronze Star Medal for meritorious service and the Purple Heart Medal for wounds sustained in action. He served as Assistant to the Chief Historian of the U.S. Army, 1951–52. He was a member of the History Department at Tulane University, 1952–70, and served as the Alumni Professor of History at the University of Kentucky, 1970–88. He served as the Harold Keith Johnson Visiting Professor of Military History at the United States Army Military History Institute and Army War College, 1981–82, and as the Visiting Professor of Military History at the United States Military Academy, 1985–86 and 1991–92. He is the author of many books on the Civil War and the American South, including *The Confederacy* (1960), *Albert Sidney Johnston: Soldier of Three Republics* (1964), *An American Iliad: The Story of the Civil War* (1991), and *History Teaches Us to Hope: Reflections on the Civil War and Southern History* (2007).

THOMAS E. SCHOTT (Louisiana State University) served for many years as a historian for the U.S. Air Force and U.S. Special Operations Command. He is the author of *Alexander H. Stephens of Georgia: A Biography* (1988), which won both the Society of American Historians Award and the Jefferson Davis Award. His other publications include "Lieutenant General William J. Hardee, the Historians, and the Atlanta Campaign" and "William Preston's Civil War" in *Confederate Generals in the Western Theater: Essays on America's Civil War*, vols. 2 (2010) and 3 (2011), respectively, and "Major General Gustavus Woodson Smith" in *Kentuckians in Gray: Confederate Generals and Field Officers of the Bluegrass State* (2008). He is also the author of a collection of poems, *Buried Above Ground: Poems for Here, There, and In-Between* (2009).

ROGER SPILLER (Louisiana State University) was for many years the George C. Marshall Professor of Military History at the United States Army Command and General Staff College, and in 2007–8 he was the Charles Boal Ewing Distinguished Visiting Professor of History at the United States Military Academy, West Point. He is now an affiliated Professor of History at the University of Kansas. His most recent works are *An Instinct for War* (2005), *In the School of War: Selected Essays* (2010), and an essay in *Between War and Peace: How America Ends Its Wars* (2011), edited by Colonel Matthew Moten.

FRANK J. WETTA (Louisiana State University) is Senior Fellow, Center for History, Politics, and Policy, Department of History, at Kean University, New Jersey. Formerly dean and vice president of academic affairs at colleges in Texas, Florida, and New Jersey, he was the 1976 recipient of a Leverhulme Visiting Fellowship in American Studies (University of Keele, England). His works include *The Louisiana Scalawags: Politics, Race, and Terrorism during the Civil War and Reconstruction* (2012); *Celluloid Wars: A Guide to Film and the American Experience of War* (1992); "'Romantic isn't it, Miss Dandridge?' Sources and Meanings of John Ford's Cavalry Trilogy," in *American Nineteenth Century History* (2006), with Martin Novelli; "Battle Histories: Reflections on Civil War Military Studies," in *Civil War History* (2007); "Telling the Truth about War: World War II and Hollywood's Moral Fiction, 1945–1956," in *Why We Fought* (2008), with Martin Novelli; and "Photography and the Military," in *Blackwell Companion to American Military History* (2010).

Index

Page numbers in **boldface** refer to illustrations and maps. THW stands for T. Harry Williams.

Lee and His Generals was designed and typeset on a Macintosh OS 10.4 computer system using InDesign software. The body text is set in 10/13 Galliard and display type is set in Galliard Ultra. This book was designed and typeset by Stephanie Thompson and manufactured by Thomson-Shore, Inc.